The Canadian Rockies
ACCESS GUIDE

◆

REVISED AND EXPANDED

John Dodd
Gail Helgason

LONE
PINE

Copyright © 1987 by Lone Pine Publishing

First Printed 1985 5 4 3 2 1
Revised Edition 1988

Printed in Canada

The Publishers:
Lone Pine Publishing
414, 10357 - 109 Street
Edmonton, Alberta
T5J 1N3

Typesetting by Pièce de Résistance Ltée., Edmonton
Printing by Khai Wah Litho Pte. Limited

Canadian Cataloguing in Publication Data

Dodd, John, 1941-
    The Canadian Rockies access guide

    Authors' names in reverse order in 1st ed.
Includes index.

    ISBN 0-919433-35-9

    1. Trails - Rocky Mountains, Canadian - Guide-books. 2. HIking - Rocky Mountains, Canadian - Guide-books. 3. Rocky Mountains, Canadian - Description and travel - Guide-books. I. Helgalson, Gail, 1950- The Canadian Rockies access guide. II. Title.
FC219.H44 1987   917.123'3   C87-091294-1   F1090.H44 1987

Cover Design: Yuet C. Chan
Front Cover Photos: Travel Alberta, Robin Bovey, Adrian Thysse.
Cartography: Lillian Wonders, Yuet C. Chan, Ewa Pluciennik.
Illustration: Ewa Pluciennik, David Marko.

Publisher's Acknowledgement
The publisher gratefully acknowledges the assistance of the Federal Department of Communication, Alberta Culture, the Canada Council and the Alberta Foundation for the Literary Arts in the production of this book.

Contents

4

How To Use This Book

For an overview of just about everything there is to do in the Rocky Mountain national parks (and Kananaskis), both outdoors and indoors, skim through chapters 1, 2, 3 and 4. You'll find everything from alpine courses to teahouse tripping. Outdoor adventures are followed by indoor activities and a guide for what to do on a rainy day.

Chapter 1 details all these activities in Banff, the most popular national park, plus Kootenay and Yoho. The second chapter is for Jasper, the third for Kananaskis and the fourth for Waterton.

Some items in the first four chapters, such as the alphabetical listings for backpacking, boating, camping, bicycling, skiing, fishing and so forth require more detailed information. Details on some of the major activities in the mountains are found in Chapter 5.

You'll discover the best places to camp, where to launch your canoe, where to go with your family for a bicycling outing — and more.

Chapter 6 looks at wildlife throughout the mountain parks and gives specific suggestions about the best places to spot game. In addition, it examines visitors' fears about bears, and identifies some of the most common trees.

Chapter 7 suggests how best to see and enjoy the national parks without embarking on long hikes or other athletic pursuits. It has specific suggestions for the best way to spend a day or day in Banff, Jasper, Lake Louise, Kananaskis or Waterton without over-exerting yourself — or spending a lot of money.

This chapter also serves as an introduction to the hiking section of the book, containing the authors' personal selections for the best hikes in each park, plus some remarks about footwear, maps, water, park regulations and the hiking season.

The hiking sections begin with Chapter 8 which describes day walks, long and short, in and around Banff townsite.

Chapter 9 looks at walks north of the townsite and those heading off from the Trans-Canada Highway, Bow Valley Parkway and Banff-Windermere Highway.

Chapter 10 describes walks along Lake Louise and Moraine Lake in Banff National Park.

Chapter 11 moves further north and describes all the day walks heading off from the Icefields Parkway in Banff National Park.

Chapter 12 describes all the day walks along the Icefields Parkway in Jasper

National Park. This includes the popular Columbia Icefields area.

Chapter 13 details walks in and around Jasper townsite.

Chapter 14 looks at walks in the Maligne area, including Maligne Canyon and east of Jasper townsite.

Chapter 15 describes walks south and east of Banff in Kananaskis Country, including the lavishly-developed Peter Lougheed Provincial Park.

Chapter 16 describes walks in Waterton Lakes National Park.

At the end, you'll find lists of where to write or telephone for more information, plus a comprehensive index.

Acknowledgements

Many thanks to Parks Canada staff in Banff and Jasper National Parks. Rob Harding, chief park interpreter in Banff and Jim Todgham, chief park interpreter in Jasper, and their staffs kindly reviewed the trail descriptions, offered many helpful suggestions and lent photographs.

Our gratitude as well to Travel Alberta for supplying photographs, to Olive Dodd who helped compile and check Jasper and Waterton material, to Runa Helgason for giving us the idea, to research assistants Stephen and Chris Dodd and to Katherine Dedyna and Grant and Kathie Kennedy for their support.

Introduction

"Where are the washrooms?"
—Most common question asked of park staff
"What's there to do here?"
—Most dreaded question asked of park staff

Mist still hangs thickly over Lake Louise when the first cars begin to cruise into the huge, multi-level parking lot. Doors slam and sleepy-eyed visitors walk briskly down to the famous lake, first sunshine illuminating its aquamarine depths, water reflecting the brilliant glaciers beyond. Here is one of the most photographed sights in North America.

The visitors stand on the shore for a minute, take a photograph and then snap another with themselves in the foreground. The lake is gorgeous. The visitors are impressed. They walk over to the hotel, drift through the souvenir store—and begin to realize there's nothing more to do. They trudge back to the car, feeling vaguely disappointed. That's it?

"What's there to do here?" they ask at park information centres in Banff, Lake Louise, the Columbia Icefield, Jasper, Kananaskis and Waterton Lakes. The best view of the best lake is not enough.

This book tries to answer that question for some of the eight million who annually visit the national and provincial parks in the Rocky Mountains, although the emphasis is on Banff and Jasper where six of the eight million go. It is an attempt to urge visitors of all ages and physical condition out of their cars or tour buses, away from the parking lots, even if only for a few minutes, to experience the mountains, to become participants.

Once away from the road, the parking lot, the viewpoint, the hotel, the feel of everything begins to change. Imagine the vaguely-bored visitor at Lake Louise going for a little hike. It could be the lakeshore trail at Lake Louise or a smaller, less spectacular lake—or almost any mountain trail. The route isn't steep or long but the walker leaves the crowds behind in minutes, falling into an easy rhythm. The air is fresh, a duck takes flight. The morning seems to belong to the walker. The wonder returns.

Walking is the primary focus of this book. All the trails described can be walked in a day, most of them in just an hour or two. This is the trend in mountain travel as the backpacking boom of the 70s appears to have peaked and turned into more enthusiasm for day trips.

The day walker travels light. He or she can wear super-light running shoes or light boots and sleep in a comfortable bed at night. While backpacking remains a rewarding activity—and major trips are described here—day walking allows any visitor to experience the mountains without heavy exertion or extensive planning and on a spare day or weekend. Most routes are excellent for families, even for people who seldom walk far at home.

Many of these walks start from the vicinity of campgrounds and are suitable for evening strolls or anytime. Some walk descriptions simply provide more information about flora, fauna and geology on short, graded strolls to popular viewpoints. Some guide the walker to areas seldom visited.

Walking the trails isn't the only way to appreciate these mountains—and it's not the only direction of the book. Our aim is to get people away from cars, roadside pullouts and townsites, whether by walking, canoeing, bicycling, sailing, boating, fishing, cross-country skiing, river-running, rock scrambling, animal-watching or dozens of other possibilities for safe adventure.

We also realize that not everybody wants to walk trails or do something energetic every day, especially in cold or rainy weather. So we've also included an extensive section describing commercial and rainy-day activities, even indoor pastimes, everything from video games to bus tours, gourmet restaurants, museums, pub crawling and hot pool soaking.

What's there to do here? Here are hundreds of answers.

1 Banff, Kootenay and Yoho National Park

Outdoor Adventures
Rainy Day Guide
Indoor Activities

Banff National Park

Banff National Park, the most famous in Canada, offers everything for the sightseer, walker and outdoors person: glaciers, castellated peaks, deep forests, lakes, rivers, hot springs, wildlife, activities from waterfall ice climbing to downhill skiing, all accessed by 350 km of roads and 1,300 km of hiking trails. If there's a price, it's that Banff is busier and more crowded than the four other Rocky Mountain national parks: Jasper, Kootenay, Yoho and Waterton. About four million people visit Banff annually, compared with two million in Jasper, a larger park. Banff townsite, with a permanent population of about 5,500 and a summer population of thousands and thousands more, has everything from art galleries to fudge shoppes on a teeming, throbbing main drag. Visitors stay an average of 1.5 days.

The park, situated 114 km (70 miles) west of Calgary, encompasses 6,641 square km (2,600 square miles), cut by parts of two mountain ranges, the Front and Main ranges. Hikers ascending a peak may pass through three vegetation zones—montane, subalpine and alpine. There are nearly 250 species of birds and 53 species of mammals, including plenty of elk, moose, black bear, bighorn sheep, deer, plus 80 to 100 grizzly bears.

The oldest of Canada's national parks, Banff really began in 1883 when railway workers discovered a hot sulphur spring near the south bank of the

Bow River. A dispute soon arose over ownership of the potentially-profitable hot spring, resulting in a takeover by the federal government and the creation of a national reserve in 1885. This heralded the creation of Canada's national park system which now contains 29 national parks. The mountain parks are among the finest in the world.

Kootenay National Park

Kootenay National Park, situated across the Continental Divide from Banff in British Columbia, was actually established in 1920 to border the scenic Banff-Windermere Highway. The park, which has its headquarters in Radium, is 96 km long but only about 30 km wide. The federal government wanted another national park but could only persuade British Columbia to cede the land if a highway were built through it. Much of the backcountry is therefore more accessible than in Banff or Jasper on 200 km of hiking trails. Of course, the possibilities for extended trips are fewer. It is a splendid park for the casual hiker, however. Kootenay is usually quieter than most of Banff. Even non-hikers will find plenty to see.

At the south end of the park is Radium Hot Springs where subterranean heat keeps the water between 35 and 47 °C. Above is Sinclair Canyon with its red walls and shattered rock. Marble Canyon features a deep gorge and waterfalls. The Paint Pots were a sacred place where Indians used to obtain the vermilion color used for rock paintings, and decoration of bodies and clothing. Vermilion Pass shows the effects of the devastating forest fire of 1968 when some 6,000 acres were burned in four days.

Yoho National Park

Yoho, the Cree word for *awe*, is an apt name for the second smallest of the Canadian Rocky Mountain parks. It encompasses 1,313 square km and is bounded by Banff to the east and Kootenay to the south.

Many visitors find their most intimate mountain experiences within Yoho, where the Trans-Canada cuts under spectacular peaks and dozens of lacy waterfalls are visible in spring and summer. The park is famous for the Burgess Shale fossils, which preserve marine life from more than five million years ago. Its recent history is also notable — the park contains the most famous stretch of railway track in Canada. The Spiral Tunnels were built to solve the problem of the sharp gradient up to Kicking Horse Pass.

The small town of Field is the service centre for Yoho. The two most outstanding areas for hiking are the Yoho Valley beyond Takakkaw Falls and Lake O'Hara, across the Great Divide from Lake Louise.

While enjoying the many recreational opportunities these parks have to offer, please keep in mind their mandate:

The parks are hereby dedicated to the people of Canada for their benefit, education and enjoyment, and such parks shall be maintained so as to leave them unimpaired for the enjoyment of future generations.

—National Parks Act, 1930

Outdoor Adventures

Alpine Courses and Guided Climbs: You can climb the mountain of your choice with a guide from Banff Alpine Guides. The year-round program includes courses in rock climbing, snow and ice climbing, mountain rescue, backpacking, hiking, ski touring and telemark skiing.

Private guided trips can also be arranged. Call (403) 762-2791 or write Box 1025, Banff, Alta. T0L 0C0. The Canadian School of Mountaineering in Canmore also offers a full range of climbing courses, including waterfall ice schools and a 5 1/2-day ski-touring expedition at the Columbia Icefields from February to May, beginning at $360. Call (403) 678-4134 or 678-5727. Or write the Canadian School of Mountaineering, Box 1552, Banff, Alta. T0L 0C0.

Bush survival, climbing, river kayaking and mountain rescue are taught at Lac Des Arcs Climbing School. Transportation is provided from Calgary if required. Call (403) 289-6795 or 240-6502, or write 1116-19th Ave. N.W., Calgary, Alta. T2M 0Z9. Marion and Al Schaffer of the Nordic Ski Institute offer excellent telemark, ski mountaineering and avalanche courses in winter. Call (403) 678-4102, or write to Box 1050 Canmore, Alta., T0L 0M0. The Yamnuska Mountain School offers a complete package of skiing, mountain leadership skills and survival courses. Write Box 7500, Canmore, Alta. T0L 0M0 or call (403) 678-4164.

Major sporting goods stores in Banff rent climbing equipment.

Backpacking: See Chapter 5 for recommendations on some of the best overnight trips in the backcountry.

Bicycling: See Chapter 5 for bicycle rental locations and a guide to the best bicycle day trips and short trips around Banff park.

Boating and Canoeing: See Chapter 5 for boat and canoe rentals and a guide to travelling lakes and rivers.

Buffalo Paddocks: See Rainy Day Guide—Banff.

Cemetery Creeping: See Rainy Day Guide—Banff.

Columbia Icefield Excursion: Here's a fine day trip from Banff, a must for many visitors. The Columbia Icefield, largest ice cap south of the Arctic circle, covers an area the size of Vancouver. You can see a small portion of it from the highway or take one of two short walks along the lunar-like approach. You can touch the toe of the Athabasca Glacier, the most accessible glacier in North America (Walks 74 and 75). Brewster runs daily 9 1/2-hour round trips from Banff to the Icefield, April 14 to Nov. 1. A "Snocoach" ride on the glacier is optional at an extra charge. Check at the bus depot in Banff townsite or call 762-2241 for times. The "Snocoach" tour which takes you onto the glacier in a big-wheeled, over-snow bus is available from the last week in May until near the end of September, 9 a.m. to 6 p.m. The last tour begins at 5 p.m. Reservations for groups of 10 or more. Call (403) 762-2241. The Icefield Centre contains exhibits, including a scale model of the entire Icefield, and shows films. Parks personnel are available to answer questions. Open May 24 to Thanksgiving.

Cruise Devil's Gap: Daily cruises on Lake Minnewanka to Devil's Gap are popular. Lake Minnewanka, 24 km long, is Banff's largest lake and bear, deer, bighorn sheep may be seen along the shore. Tours in the glass-covered boats take about 1 1/2 hours. They depart from the Minnewanka boat dock 11 km (7 miles) north of Banff townsite. Dinner cruises are available by reservation, for groups only. Drive the scenic Lake Minnewanka Road to the boat dock or take bus transportation to Minnewanka leaving from the downtown bus depot and Banff Springs Hotel. Call the bus depot for times at 762-2286, or Minnewanka Tours at (403) 762-3473 for information or reservations.

Drives: Banff has 350 km (217 miles) of public roads. Most offer excellent views of the mountains, rivers and lakes of the park. Near Banff townsite, drives around the Banff Springs golf course, up to Mt. Norquay for a view of the townsite, or along Vermilion Lakes Drive are recommended. If going to Lake Louise, Highway 1A—the Bow Valley Parkway with its interpretive stops—is the choice scenic route. Be sure to take the side trip from Lake Louise to Moraine Lake and the beautiful Valley of the Ten Peaks.

The Icefields Parkway going up to the Columbia Icefield and Jasper is reputed to be one of the world's most scenic drives. Parks Canada publishes a brochure of suggested auto tours, available free from the Banff Information Centre. Also see Rainy Day Guide—Banff for information on guided autotape tours.

Fishing and Guided Fishing: See Chapter 5 for where to fish, where to find fishing guides, which lakes have which fish—and where to get your fresh fish cooked.

Golfing: The Banff Springs' golf course is often listed as one of the world's 10 most scenic. The beauty of the par-71, 18-hole, 6704-yard velvet lawn under the cliffs of Mt. Rundle, is enough to make even non-golfers consider taking up the sport. Design was by the late Stanley Thompson, one of the world's foremost golf architects. The clear air and the huge scale of the mountains often cause golfers to under-estimate the distance to the green. For non-golfers, trails and a scenic road lead all around the course (Walk 8). Open daily 7 a.m. to 8 p.m. Tee-off reservations required. Lessons and golf equipment rentals available at the pro shop. Call 762-2962 or 762-2211 for reservations.

Banff residents, however, gravitate to the 18-hole Canmore Golf Course, scenic but less expensive. Call 678-4784. For golfers who don't mind an hour's drive, there's the spectacular 36-hole Kananaskis Golf Course. It's complete with imported white sand and 18 water hazards, dazzling testimony to the province's affluent boom years. The course is situated 27 km south of the Trans-Canada on the Kananaskis Trail. Call 1-800- 372-9201.

Sulphur Mountain Gondola

Gondola Sight-Seeing: The visitor who wants peak panorama without pain, has the choice of four gondola lifts in Banff, each with a teahouse at its destination. Short trails radiate from lifts at Sulphur, Norquay and Lake Louise. But the richest opportunities for hiking await at Sunshine, northwest of Banff up the Sunshine Road which turns off the Trans-Canada. Sunshine, a high ski area also open in the summer, has miles of trails over alpine meadows.

The gondola ride up Sulphur Mountain soars 2,285 metres (7,500 feet) above Banff townsite. Two short strolls (Walks 12 and 13), good for spotting wildlife, can be taken along the ridge. A short interpretive tour is conducted daily, June 15-Sept. 15, weather permitting. There's also a trail up—those who walk up may ride down free. The ride takes only eight minutes.

The view stretches for 90 miles and seems almost like an aerial photo. A modern teahouse with a licensed restaurant, coffee shop, gift shop, and observation terraces is situated on top. Adults $6. Taxi service and Brewster bus connections are available from the townsite. The lift is 3.2 km from the townsite on Mountain Ave., next to the Upper Hot Springs. Open April 1-June 17, 9:30 a.m.-5:30 p.m.; June 18 to August 14, 8:30 a.m. to 8 p.m.; Sept. 6-Oct. 16, 9:30 a.m.-5:30 p.m; Oct. 16, 17 to mid-November, 10 a.m. to 4:30 p.m. For information call 762-5438 or 762-2523.

• *Mount Norquay Gondola.* Visitors can enjoy panoramas of Banff townsite and Mt. Rundle, by riding a gondola up to 2,135 metres (7,000 feet) at Cliffhouse Point, high on Mt. Norquay. There's a licensed restaurant on top. Open mid-June to Labor Day, as well as during the skiing season. Call 762-4421.

• *Sunshine Gondola.* The Sunshine Gondola ride takes visitors to flower-covered alpine meadows where they can hike to Rock Isle Lake or across the Continental Divide. An alpine interpretive centre is situated at Sunshine Village. The Sunshine access road starts 11 km (7 miles) west of Banff townsite on the Trans-Canada. From there, an 8-km (5-mile) drive takes you to the Bourgeau parking lot where the gondola ride starts. A restaurant and accommodation are provided at Sunshine Village, open June 29 to Labor Day, as well as the long skiing season. Call (403) 762-3381. In winter months, this is a major resort for downhill and cross-country skiing.

• *Lake Louise Gondola.* Soar to 1,075 metres (6,680 feet) at Whitehorn Lodge on Mt. Whitehorn for views across the Bow Valley to the Lake Louise and the Valley of the Ten Peaks. You can work up an appetite on short strolls through the forests and meadows before dining in the licensed restaurant. Call 522-3555.

Guided Hiking: Enjoyable as it is to strike off into the backcountry on your own, some trips present challenges best tackled in a group with a knowledgeable guide. Novice backpackers may also welcome the opportunity to learn outdoor skills in a group. This is where Banff Alpine Guides may help. They offer glacier hikes, a two-day hike from Lake O'Hara to Moraine Lake via Wenkchemna Pass, and from Lake Louise to Moraine Lake, via Abbott Pass. Strong hikers might enjoy a challenging guided hike to the top of Mt. Temple, highest peak in the Lake Louise area, and 10th highest in the Canadian Rockies. Banff Alpine Guides offers this adventurous outing several weekends in July, for $50 per person. For groups of three or more, trips can be arranged to suit your schedule. Write Box 1025, Banff, Alta., T0L 0C0, or call (403) 762-4277.

Helicopter Skiing: Helicopter skiing in the Cariboos and Monashees in British Columbia is available through Cariboo Helicopter Skiing Ltd., Box 1824, Banff, Alta., T0L 0C0, or call (403) 762-5548.

Horse-Back Riding: Alberta is horse country—one government MLA even wanted to set up a department of horses. Horsepacking trips are a long and established tradition in the Canadian Rockies and a visitor can tailor the ride to his wishes or the condition of his rear. It doesn't matter if you've never ridden a horse before.

In Banff, casual dudes can rent horses by the hour, half-day or full day at Banff Springs Corral at the Banff Springs Hotel, call 762-2348, or at Sundance Stables on Birch Avenue., 762-2832. Hourly and day rides are also available at Lake Louise, from Deer Lodge Corral, and Num-Ti-Jah Corral at Bow Lake on the Icefields Parkway.

If you've always wanted to ride a horse to dinner, you have your chance in Banff. Warner and Mackenzie Outfitting offers evening trailrides with a steak fry, and all-day rides with lunch included. Winter barbecues and hayrides are available as well. The stables are across from the recreation grounds on Birch Avenue, (403) 762-2832. For tickets and information, drop into The Trail Rider Store at 132 Banff Avenue (762-4551). Holiday on Horseback offers six-day rides, including a fall color ride in early September. Write Holiday on Horseback, Box 2280, Banff, Alta. T0L 0C0. (403) 762-4551.

Lake Louise is the starting point for three-to-14 day trail rides from Timberline Tours. Private trips of any length and group size may be arranged. Call (403) 522-3743, or write Box 14, Lake Louise, Alta. T0L 1E0. Numerous other outfitters provide trail rides in Rocky Mountain backcountry outside the parks. Several will provide transportation from Calgary. For more information, see Travel Alberta's Adventure Guide.

As an alternative to commercial outfitters, consider Trail Riders of the Canadian Rockies. This non-profit group, formed more than 60 years ago to encourage riding in the Rockies, organizes six-day rides from Lake Louise in July and August. In 1984, they celebrated 60 years of riding with a two-week, 200-mile wilderness ride between Banff and Jasper. For information, write: Box 6742, Station D, Calgary, Alta., T2P 2E6, or call (403) 287-1746.

Hot Springs Soaking: You have a choice of two natural hot springs to soak in. The Upper Hot Springs and the Cave and Basin offer quite different experiences. We recommend indulging in both, rain or shine. The Upper Hot Springs are more modern and offer a commanding view of surrounding mountains. The Cave and Basin, restored to its former 1914 grandeur for the 1985 national parks centennial, is a step back in time—rental bathing suits are 1914-style! The water at the Upper Hot Springs is warmer—it averages 38°C (100°F), compared with an average of 30°C (85°F) at Cave and Basin. When the weather's good, combine a gondola ride with a walk at Sulphur Mountain summit, then relax with a steaming soak at the end. After your soak, retreat to the Viewpoint Lounge at the Rimrock Inn which has marvellous views over the Spray Valley and Mt. Rundle. The Upper Hot Springs, 3 km from the townsite on Mountain Ave., are open 8:30 a.m. to 11 p.m. in summer and 9 a.m. to 9 p.m. in winter. Lockers are provided and towels and bathing suits can be rented. Call 762-2056. Massages and facials are available Monday to Friday, 1 to 8 p.m., Saturday and Sunday

10 a.m. to 8 p.m. Call 762-2966 for appointments. More historic is the Cave and Basin, an easy walk from Banff Avenue (Walk 14) on the south side of the Bow River. An old Indian legend has it that rheumatic grizzlies used to soothe their aches away at these springs. Several walks, including two interpretive trails, radiate from here (Walks 15 and 20). There's also an exhibit centre. The pool is not open in winter.

Motorcoach Touring: Brewster offers several reasonably-priced bus excursions from Banff townsite. Offerings include:

• A three-hour round trip that stops at the hoodoos, Banff Springs Hotel, the Buffalo Paddocks and the Sulphur Mountain Gondola Lift.

• A four-hour round trip from Banff to Lake Louise goes by Vermilion Lakes, Hole-in-the Wall, Castle Mountain and the Continental Divide. At Lake Louise, time is allotted for walking on the trails or just enjoying the views.

• An extremely popular one-day outing is to the Columbia Icefield. The trip takes about 9 1/2 hours. A "Snocoach" tour on the Athabasca Glacier is optional.

• Guided one-way and round trips are also offered on the scenic parkway to Jasper, one of the most beautiful highways in the world.

Check with Brewster at (403) 762-2241 or write Box 1140, Banff, Alta. T0L 0C0. Points of departure from Banff townsite are the Banff Springs Hotel, the Mount Royal Hotel, Banff Park Lodge, the Banff Bus Depot and the Lux Theatre. Passengers staying at other hotels may call 762-2286 for complimentary pick-up.

Pacific Western Tours, 204 Caribou St., also provides group and charter tours. Call 762-5652. There are a number of car rental agencies in Banff as well.

Mountain Biking and Mopedding: See Bicycling, Chapter 5.

Naturalists' Evening Programs: Excellent evening naturalist programs are conducted at numerous campgrounds by park interpretive staff during summer months. You might see a slide show about grizzly bears, healing herbs or how to pack a touring bicycle. Programs are not held in every campground every night so check at the park information centre and campground kiosks for schedules. Interpreters also conduct informal campfire circle talks at Rampart Creek Campground and Protection Mountain Campground.

River Rafting: Rocky Mountain Raft Tours offer peaceful three-hour trips down the Bow River, almost magically scenic from a raft. As well, there are longer wilderness trips on the Kootenay River. Write Box 1771, Banff or phone (403) 762-3632. Tickets and transportation available from the bus depot or Banff Springs Hotel. Foothills Rafting Adventures offers thrilling day trips on the Kootenay River—complete with barbecued steaks served on the river bank! Call (403) 762-5232 in Banff, in Canmore (403) 678-6359, or write: Box 1647, Canmore, Alta. T0L 0M0.

Rock Scrambling: See Chapter 5 for off-trail exploration.

Sailing and Windsurfing: See Chapter 5 for where to sail and windsurf, where to rent and arrange for lessons.

Edith Lake, Jasper National Park

Skating: Best bet is indoors at the Banff Recreation Centre where skate rentals are available. Phone 762-4454. In early winter, before snow crusts on lake surfaces, you may be able to skate on Lake Minnewanka, Vermilion Lakes or Lac des Arcs. Check at the park information centre for ice conditions.

Skiing (Cross-Country): See Chapter 5 for the best trails for all levels, tips on what to take and warnings about avalanches.

Skiing (Downhill): See Chapter 5.

Banff National Park:
Indoor and Rainy Day Guide

When rain clouds blanket Cascade Mountain and an all-day downpour sets in, resist the urge to move on immediately. Banff National Park is one of the few places in the Rockies where you can follow a day of mountain climbing with an evening at a live performance of the Threepenny Opera or bison-watching with a night out over Les Escargots a la Bourguignonne. Rain can even be a blessing. It slows you down enough to discover what's happening right in the townsite.

A thick wallet is not essential to spending a rainy day in Banff—although visitors who insist on sticking to Banff Avenue may be forgiven for thinking so. Banff townsite has the most spectacular hotel in Western Canada—a best bet for lolling about on a rainy day plus two hot springs, three museums, fine alpine archives and a summer arts festival that has Calgary and Edmonton turning shades of chartreuse.

Before raindrops drive you back into your sleeping bag or RV, first give a thought to continuing with outdoor plans. The Banff area is one of the best places in the Rockies for rainy-day walking. Numerous trails described in this book are fine for a wet day. These routes are wide enough to keep sodden branches from your path, low enough in elevation that the focal point of interest is the walk itself, not the alpine scenery, and short enough that you won't be soaked through.

Although it may sound too obvious to mention, take along an umbrella on short walks. When the rain stops you can use it as a walking stick.

In Banff townsite, the short, interpretive Fenland Trail (Walk 18) is a fine choice for a rainy day. So are the Marsh (Walk 20) and Discovery trails by the Cave and Basin Hot Springs. Amble through the new Centennial Centre with its exhibits and films, then chase the chills away with a blissful soak in the naturally-heated pool (Walk 14). Or stroll through the remains of Bankhead, a coal-mining ghost town near Banff (Walk 21). Further afield, prowl Johnston Canyon (Walk 31), Marble Canyon (Walk 39) or the Paint Pots (Walk 40) where you see much the same thing whether it's rainy or not.

Although people who haven't tried it may cringe at the suggestion, bicycling in the rain can be enjoyable—as long as you have a waterproof poncho or jacket and a warm, dry place at the end. The action of cycling keeps the body warm. A fine and mostly flat cycle from Banff townsite follows the Bow Valley Parkway, Highway 1A. See Chapter 5.

If rainy day outdoor adventuring doesn't appeal, here's a menu of toasty-dry diversions. . .

Archives of the Canadian Rockies: Step back into the past in this comforting place, which seems far from the glitz of Banff Avenue. The public is welcome to browse through an extensive historic photograph collection. Nearby are many fascinating items, including books on mountain teahouses and local flora and fauna. A manuscript collection, oral history collection and research library on the Canadian Rockies are housed here. This is also home to the library and archives of the Alpine Club of Canada—the country's largest source of material on mountaineering. Photocopying and photographic copying available. 111 Bear St., Monday through Saturday from 10 a.m. to 6 p.m. Call 762-2291.

Art Gallery Ambles: The Whyte Museum of the Canadian Rockies displays paintings, drawings, sculptures—a wide range of art. Recent offerings in the main gallery include the photography of W. Hanson Boorne in the Canadian West between 1885-1893, works by contemporary Australian printmakers and posters from Nicaragua. The gallery, in the same building as the archives, is at 111 Bear St. Open 10 a.m. to 6 p.m. daily in summer. In winter, closed Sunday and Monday, open Tuesday and Saturday, 10 a.m. to 6 p.m., Wednesday to Friday 10 a.m. to 9 p.m. Phone 762-2291.

• *Walter J. Phillips Gallery.* Paintings, ceramics, weaving, slides—all kinds of visual art exhibits are on display at this gallery, part of The Banff Centre School of Fine Arts. Includes works by Canadian and international artists, faculty members and students. Combine a browse here with a stroll through some of the 27 acres encompassing Banff Centre (Walk 2). The gallery is located in the Studio Building, Banff Centre. Open daily year-round from noon to 5 p.m. Free admission. Phone 762-6283.

Banff Centre—Culture in the Clouds: All this scenery and Bach besides! One of the perks of a Rocky Mountain summer is the Banff Festival of music, theatre, dance, opera, film and visual arts. The centre, occupying 27 acres on Tunnel Mountain, is one of Canada's most prestigious post-graduate schools for professional artists. You can walk there from Banff Ave.

Each summer from May to nearly the end of August numerous performances are open to the public, ranging through jazz, opera, chamber music, drama, movies and mime. Watch for special events. The internationally-known Banff Television Festival, which offers a sampling of the world's best made-for-television productions, is held yearly in summer, and the Banff Festival of Mountain Films each fall.

Activities too numerous to list are open to the public year-round. Noon lunch concerts, for example, are given Wednesdays from September to the end of March, and movie classics screened in the evenings. Find details in local papers or Banff Life magazine. You could call the centre at (403) 762-6100 for a full program or write Box 1020, Banff, Alta. T0L 0C0.

Banff Heritage Homes Tours: Glimpse what life was like in Banff in the first part of the century. Weekly guided tours are given through two log homes, one belonging to Col. A. and Pearl Brewster Moore, built in 1907, the other the home of Catherine and Peter Whyte, built in 1930-31.

The Moore house displays Indian art, eastern American antiques and equine gadgets. The Whyte home reflects the family's lives as artists, skiers, travellers and collectors. Guided tours are from 1-4 p.m. Saturday afternoons. Winter tours were introduced recently. Register in advance at the Whyte Museum of the Canadian Rockies, 111 Bear St. or call 762-2291.

Banff Springs Hotel for High Tea: Pouring rain? Never mind. While the Scottish baronial exterior of Banff Springs Hotel impresses, its interior warms. This is perhaps the most magnificent hotel in Western Canada and deserves a peek inside, rain or shine.

Styles range from 15th century gothic in the Mount Stephen Hall to Spanish in the Alhambra Room. The panes of glass in the Riverview Room were custom-made in Czechoslovakia, and the CPR commissioned a furniture firm to visit Scotland and northern Europe to duplicate furniture found in castles there. The styles are so diverse that guided tours of the hotel, largest in the world when it was built in 1888, are conducted several times a week in high season, both winter and summer, usually around 3:30 p.m. or 4 p.m. Call 762-2211 for times.

The hotel, nestled between Rundle and Sulphur mountains to the confluence of the Bow and Spray Rivers, looks out on one of the most beautiful scenes in the Rockies. Find a writing desk looking out on all this and write a long letter home, or read a romantic novel. The setting's perfect.

Rain or shine, the best way to approach the hotel is to stroll there (Walk 7). When you reach the golf clubhouse, turn right and go up the stairs beside the clubhouse, over a gorgeous log trestle bridge and inside past the outdoor and indoor swimming pools (open to guests only) and up the stairs to the main lobby.

The hotel contains luxurious stores and lounges. High tea is served daily, 2:30 p.m. to 4:30 p.m. in the Van Horne Room on the mezzanine level, July to September.

Or indulge in wine and cheese or a light meal at Grapes, a new lounge on the mezzanine. There is a Japanese Restaurant, specializing in sushi and shabu-shabu, (a Japanese version of fondue), on the arcade level. Insomniacs, try the friendly 24-hour espresso bar on the same level or check out The Works, a night club. You might like to haunt the Rob Roy Room as well, where a skull is said to be visible in a painting.

Bars and Lounges: No. 1 action spot in Banff townsite is still the bar at the King Eddy's, 137 Banff Ave. An alternative is Silver City offering rock and disco music, at the Cascade. Locals often congregate at the upstairs pub at Melissa's Missteak, 217 Lynx St. For a quiet drink, a favorite is the Viewpoint Lounge at the Rimrock Inn, which has marvellous mountain views. Find it just below the Upper Hot Springs on Mountain Ave. The fancier Rundle Lounge or Grapes wine bar, both on the mezzanine level at the Banff Springs Hotel, also rate high.

Buffalo Paddock Peeping: Buffalo are at their least handsome in summer, when visitors are permitted to drive through their 100-acre enclosure. Seeing a herd of free-ranging plains and wood bison is, nevertheless, an experience. The original bison were a gift of Lord Strathcona in 1903. The paddocks are 1 km west of the Banff-Minnewanka interchange on the Trans-Canada Highway. Open May to October. Free.

Burrow in Books and Newspapers: The Book and Art Den is rainy day heaven for outdoorsy-literary types. This fine bookstore is well-stocked with outdoor adventure, maps, Canadiana, mountain lore, poetry, classics, everything from bears to Baudelaire to Bodington. Goro Canyon Smoke and Gift Shop has perhaps the largest selections of newspapers anywhere in the Rockies, as well as a good book collection. It's in the Mount Royal Hotel. Call (403) 762-4172.

Canmore Excursion: For a change of scene, head for Canmore, a former coal-mining town established in 1883. It's situated beneath the famous Three Sisters Mountains in the Bow Valley, 25 km east of Banff townsite on the Trans-Canada. Many hiking trails begin here.

Although clearly in danger now of "Becoming Trendy", Canmore is home to artists, film-makers and outdoorsmen. Some of the old buildings from coal-mining days are still standing. The Canmore Nordic Centre, host of the nordic skiing events for the 1988 Winter Olympics, is an attraction.

Some may choose to laze away a drizzly afternoon by popping into pottery shops and such, sampling desserts at such local eateries as The Village Green or hanging out in Ziggie's Bistro and Bar on 8th St. and 8th Ave. a mountain saloon with several kinds of draft. The town stages a whoop-up Heritage Day Fair the first weekend in August with ethnic food and crafts.

Cemetery Creeping: While not to everyone's taste, tombstone aficionados will be tickled to find the graves of persons famous in local history—Brewster, Whyte and early Banff guides for starters. A walking tour of the cemetery was even on the agenda for the Parks centennial. From Banff Ave., turn left before the bridge and go up three blocks to the corner of Otter and Buffalo.

Classic Movies, Concerts, Readings and Lectures: The discerning Banff visitor is advised to call The Peter and Catherine Whyte Foundation for information on public programming, which changes too rapidly to be listed here.

Wednesday night film classics and Thursday Night movies, with an emphasis on quality documentaries, were recent popular offerings. Free readings and lectures by Canadian writers and playwrights are occasionally scheduled as well as concerts. At the Whyte Foundation, just off Banff Ave., at 111 Bear St. Call 762-2291.

Cruise Devil's Gap: Depending on how low the cloud cover is, a cruise on Lake Minnewanka is a possibility even in the rain. The boats are covered. See Outdoor Adventures—Banff.

Dining: Drowning rainy day blahs in a flat-out feast in Banff isn't such a bad idea if you can afford it—after all, you can always burn away the calories by striking up Sentinel Pass tomorrow.

The Chamber of Commerce on Banff Avenue distributes a booklet entitled *Dining in Banff,* with menus from local restaurants. But alas, no prices. Be forewarned: Eating in Banff is not cheap.

If you're pursuing a peak dining experience, Le Beaujolais, recommended by *Where to Eat in Canada,* will likely send you to gastronomic heights. Try a rack of lamb. Even New Yorkers wax poetic about a dessert called Le Ballon de Framboise, a variation on the classic ice cream with fresh strawberries and whipped cream. At the corner of Banff Ave., and Buffalo St., call 762-2712.

Try Ticino's for Swiss-Italian food, at 205 Wolf St., 762-3848, or the occasional cheese fondue at The Grizzly House, 207 Banff Ave., 762-4055. Giorgio's, at 219 Banff Ave., is actually two restaurants. The more casual La Pasta, downstairs, gets high marks for homemade pasta. Reservations required upstairs at La Casa. Try Magpie and Stump for Mexican favorites at 203 Caribou St., 762-2014. Or head to the Banff Springs Hotel to the Samurai Restaurant, for sushi, shabu-shabu (a Japanese version of fondue), teriyaki and more.

Something less fancy? Locals recommend Melissa's Missteak for reasonable family fare, which includes home-made muffins for breakfast, tuna fish bagels for lunch, and deep-dish pizza for dinner. In a log building at 217 Lynx St., next to the Homestead Inn, call 762-5511.

For brunch, try The Rimrock Inn on Mountain Ave., just below the Upper Hot Springs. Sunday champagne brunch is served from 11 a.m. to 2 p.m. The historic Post Hotel in Lake Louise is also famous for its Sunday brunches, served between 7 and 10:30 a.m. in a rustic setting.

If you have plain but hearty breakfast fare in mind (we usually do), the Rundle Restaurant at 319 Banff Ave., just across the street from the Park Information Centre, is hard to beat. It provides good service and good plain food any time of day.

Enjoying high tea seems the most civilized way to watch the rain (or even the sun) beat down. Sip away at the Banff Springs Hotel, perhaps combining tea with a hotel tour. Tea served from 2:30 p.m. to 4:30 p.m. daily, from July to September, in the Van Horne Room on the mezzanine level. Or drive to the Post Hotel in Lake Louise for its afternoon tea, home-made custard pie with fresh fruit and cake of the day. Daily from 2 p.m. to 5 p.m. The Chateau Lake Louise also serves afternoon tea in the lobby, with beautiful views over the lake and Victoria Glacier, from 1 p.m. to 3 p.m. in summer.

For an afternoon tea that's easier on the waistline and wallet, hike over to the Swiss Guides' Room at the Whyte Foundation, 111 Bear St. Tea and cookies are served every Friday, Saturday and Sunday from 2:30 to 4:30 p.m., for $1.

Guided Auto Tours: The scenery won't be as great on a rainy day but at least you'll be dry. Parks Canada publishes a brochure on suggested drives in the park. Also see Outdoor Adventures—Banff for recommendations. Add spice by renting an autotape tour with detailed commentary on Banff and the Icefields Parkway, available at local stores. Inquire at the information centre.

Hot Springs: No better time than a rainy day to soak in the soothing, naturally-heated waters of either the Cave and Basin or Upper Hot Springs.

Numerous short walks, fine for a wet day, radiate from the Cave and Basin. Take an umbrella and explore the interpretive Discovery Trail to the source of the hot springs, which appear much as they did when discovered in 1883. The Marsh Trail illustrates how hot springs affect mountain habitat.

Then browse through the Cave and Basin Centennial Centre with historical exhibits, computer games about the past and films of the first 100 years
of the park. End up with a swim in the pool, recently restored to its 1914
splendour. You can even rent 1914-style bathing suits. The water temperature here averages 30° C (85° F). At the time of writing, the Cave pool
was open June 24 to Labor Day. A retractable roof may be built to permit
winter use.

If it's real warmth you're after, head for the Upper Hot Springs, where
the average water temperature is 38° C (100° F), considerably higher than
at Cave and Basin. Then enjoy a massage (reserve ahead). Open year-round.
See Hot Springs Section in Outdoor Adventures-Banff.

Upper Hot Springs

Lake Louise By Romantic Rail: Discard the jet age for a while. You can ride a train equipped with a dome car for 45 minutes to tiny Lake Louise Village. The Post Hotel in the village is known for its Sunday brunches between 7 a.m. and 10:30 a.m. and afternoon teas daily between 2 p.m. and 5 p.m. You can also take a bus from the village to the world-famous lake above. Then catch the train back to Banff townsite. (Note: Train schedules change. Call VIA RAIL at 1-800-665-8630 for schedules.)

If you have a bicycle, you could take it on the train from Banff and cycle 4 km up from Lake Louise station to see the famous lake and Chateau Lake Louise, which serves an afternoon tea. You'll deserve it. The road is steep and busy, recommended only for experienced cyclists. Bikes go without charge on the baggage car; just tell the conductor before you reach Lake Louise that you'll be taking it off at the station.

Laundry: This is how many visitors spend their rainy days, unromantic but practical. The townsite has several self-serve laundromats. The Laundry, at 203 Caribou St., includes dry-cleaning, washing and folding.

Motorcoach Tours: Points of departure from Banff townsite are Banff Springs Hotel, Mount Royal Hotel, Banff Park Lodge, Banff Bus Depot and Lux Theatre. Passengers staying at other hotels may call 762-2286 for complimentary pick-up.

Movies: The Lux Theatre on Banff Ave., screens first-run movies. For less commercial fare, check at the Whyte Foundation, where classic movies are often screened Thursday evenings. At 111 Bear St., call 762-2291. In winter, the Banff Centre also has public screenings. Call (403) 762-6300 for listings. Film buffs should also check public screenings at the international Banff Television Festival, held in the summer, and The Banff Festival of Mountain Films in the fall.

Museums: Perhaps combine a tour of two or three, and if it's a Friday, Saturday or Sunday, end up in the Swiss Guides' Room at the Peter Whyte Gallery, 111 Bear St. between 2:30-4:30 p.m. Tea and cookies for $1. Choose from this museum menu:

• *Luxton Museum.* Banff's most interesting museum? Our vote goes to the Luxton Museum, situated in a log building across Banff Bridge and right on Cave Ave. The museum, part of the prestigious Glenbow-Alberta Institute based in Calgary, contains a good collection of Plains Indian artifacts. Life-size displays show how Indians made pemmican and performed the Sun Dance.

There's even a shrivelled human scalp, and a gift shop with necklaces for $1.50 made by local Indians. Open 10 a.m. to 6 p.m. (or later) in summer, 10 a.m. to 5 p.m. in winter, seven days a week. Call 762-2388.

• *Banff Park Museum.* Western Canada's oldest, it's free. Situated on the north side of the Banff Bridge, the Banff Museum houses stuffed mountain sheep, goats and the like.

But poke about to find little treasures—a piece of bark where Sir George Simpson, the first white man in the Bow Valley, carved his initials in a tree at Simpson Pass, and perhaps the world's largest stuffed beaver, weighing in at 70 pounds. The building was revamped for the Parks centennial and a reading room added.

The most interesting feature may be the building itself—constructed in the architectural style called "railroad pagoda," and recently restored. The structure, built in 1903 by the CPR as a research facility and tourist attraction, features trestle-like internal supports and a lantern skylight. Open 10 a.m.-6 p.m. daily in summer, closed Tuesday and Wednesday in fall and winter. Phone 762-3324.

• *Natural History Museum.* This little museum contains displays, audio-visuals and models to give glimpses into the geological and natural history of the area. There's an exhibit on the Castleguard Cave, one of the largest caves in North America. Children would perhaps enjoy the model of "Bigfoot." Open 10 a.m. to 10 p.m. May-September, noon to 6 p.m., October-April. 112 Banff Avenue, (Clock Tower Village - 2nd floor) Phone 762-4747.

Skating: The Banff Recreation Centre offers public skating from the end of April to August. Skate rentals available. Phone 762-4454 for times.

A number of motels have racquetball and squash facilities available to non-guests. Inquire at the Park Information Centre.

Lake Minnewanka, Banff National Park

Videogames: The august splendour of the Banff Springs Hotel is not a setting naturally associated with Pacman and Donkey Kong. Its selection of video games, however, is popular indeed. Track 'em down in the Games Arcade at pool level. Also in the stand-up bar upstairs at Melissa's Missteak, 217 Lynx St., next to the Homestead Inn, a popular local hangout.

Lake Louise:
Outdoor Adventures and Rainy Day Guide

If you only have an hour or so, walk along the lakeshore (Walk 49), a level and inspiring outing. If more energetic, hike up to Fairview Lookout for an unforgettable view (Walk 51), in about the same time. Those with half a day and lots of energy could take the classic jaunts to the Plain of Six Glaciers (Walk 50) or Lake Agnes (Walk 53). Both lead to rustic tea-houses and rich panoramas.

For those with several days to spend hiking, there are few better places in the Rockies. Sentinel Pass (Walk 47) or Eiffel Lake (Walk 45) are excellent for all-day hikes. Consolation Lake (Walk 44) is a shorter and attractive alternative.

Canoes or rowboats are available at the boathouse to the left of Chateau Lake Louise. Canoes and rowboats may also be rented at Moraine Lake in the neighboring Valley of the Ten Peaks.

Horses can be hired for hourly or day rides from Deer Lodge Corral just before the Chateau. Phone 522-3747. Lake Louise is also the starting point for three-to-14-day trail rides from Timberline Tours. Private trips of any length or group size may be arranged. Call (403) 522-3743 or write Box 14, Lake Louise, Alta. T0L 1E0.

Picnicking? While there are no tables by the lakeshore, a large picnic area is found on Highway 1A above the Moraine Lake turnoff.

The Lake Louise Gondola Lift will take you to a height of 2,036 metres (6,680 feet) up Mt. Whitehorn, where views stretch across to the Bow Valley and the Valley of the Ten Peaks. Open June 8 to Sept. 3, 9 a.m. to 6:30 p.m. Short strolls can be taken from the licensed restaurant. From the Trans-Canada Highway, turn at the signs for the Lake Louise ski area. Phone 522-3555.

Another excursion from Lake Louise is to the Great Divide, the point where all waters flow either to the Atlantic or the Pacific. A stream there flows two ways, the east branch into the Bow River, South Saskatchewan and Hudson Bay, the other into the Columbia and then into the Pacific at Astoria, Wash. There are picnic tables right on the divide. Continue on 1A past the Lake Louise road towards Kicking Horse Pass.

Brewster's runs several bus excursions from Lake Louise:
• A 2 1/2-hour trip takes visitors to the Lake Louise gondola.
• A 3 1/2-hour trip goes across the Continental Divide into Yoho National

Park to Takakkaw Falls, Emerald Lake, Kicking Horse Pass and the Natural Rock Bridge.

- An 8 1/2 hour round trip to the Columbia Icefield.
- An 8-hour one-way trip to Jasper along the Icefields Parkway.

The departure points from Lake Louise are Chateau Lake Louise and Deer Lodge. Call 762-2241.

Rain or shine, the most genteel way to cap a fine afternoon might well be afternoon tea in the lobby of Chateau Lake Louise. (Served from 1 p.m. to 3 p.m. in summer.) For best views without budget-breaking, try the Tom Wilson Rooftop Restaurant. On a sunny day, the open-air Poolside Terrace is a fine place to eat hot dogs and watch the people and peaks. The newly renovated Post Hotel in Lake Louise Village also serves afternoon tea. Home-made custard pie with fresh fruit and cake of the day are featured. Daily from 2 p.m. to 5 p.m., year-round.

Down the road, the village's stores have been concentrated in the new Samson Mall, a better-than-average development of fieldstone and wood. Spend some time browsing in the splendid Woodruff & Blum bookstore which offers an excellent selection of outdoor books, as well as the novels and classics that can get you through a long rainy spell. You can also pick up topographical maps, newspapers, magazines, posters and cards.

The mall also has a Smitty's restaurant, gifts and clothing stores, the post office, a camera store that offers film processing and, not least, an Alberta liquor store — the big time has come to the once-humble village, thanks to a hotly-debated, but ultimately approved redevelopment plan.

Laggan's Deli and Bakery offers fresh muffins, bread, cream puffs, bagels, cinnamon and chelsea buns and brownies. On a hot day, cool off with a frozen yogurt down the mall.

A Parks Canada information office and the warden office are located across the road from the mall, behind the Texaco Station. Here you'll also find heated washrooms. A major visitors' centre with exhibits and a theatre is planned.

1. LAKE LOUISE TOWNSITE

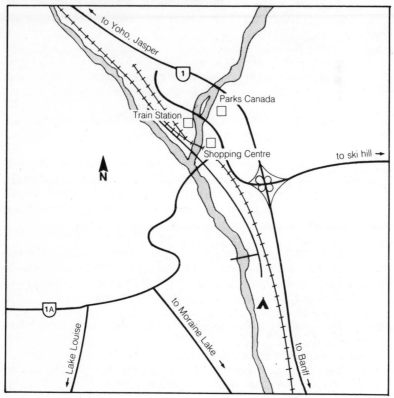

2 Jasper National Park

Outdoor Adventures
Rainy Day Guide
Indoor Activities

Jasper National Park

Jasper National Park is the largest and most northerly of the Canadian Rocky Mountain national parks, a vast wilderness of peaks, glaciers, deep forests, clear lakes and the largest ice cap south of the Arctic Circle.

The park covers more than 10,800 square km (4,170 square miles) and is dominated by two mountain ranges—the Front and the Main ranges. Here are more than 1,000 km (620 miles) of hiking trails, where walkers can observe three vegetation zones—montane, subalpine, and alpine. Mammals ranging from grizzlies and cougars to elk, deer, mountain goats and bighorn sheep inhabit the park, along with more than 250 bird species, from white ptarmigan to the ubiquitous Gray Jay.

The fur traders of the early 19th century were the first to explore much of what now is Jasper National Park. It was named after a local trading post operated by Jasper Hawse and known as Jasper's House. The federal government declared the area a national park in 1907.

Jasper is visited by about two million people annually and retains a more mellow, low-key atmosphere than Banff, its busy southern sister. The two are connected by the famous Icefields Parkway. While less crowded and superb for backpacking, Jasper does not offer the same rich menu of day walks as Banff. Nor does Jasper, with 4,000 permanent residents, offer the same variety of restaurants, cultural activities, nightlife or stores. On the other hand, you may see elk from its main street.

Jasper is situated 362 km (224 miles) west of Edmonton on Highway 16, or 426 km (264 miles) northwest of Calgary on the Icefields Parkway. CNR provides daily service from Vancouver and Edmonton. Bus routes from those cities pass through Jasper. Brewster Transport has daily service between Banff and Jasper.

Outdoor Adventures

Alpine Courses and Guided Climbs: The Jasper Climbing School and Mountaineering Service has two-and five-day climbing schools for beginners and intermediates, June through September. Rates from $60 to $160. In winter, offerings include two-day avalanche and ice climbing schools, five-day alpine ski touring courses, a three-day ski tour of the Columbia Icefield area and a four-day tour over eight passes in the Maligne area.

Strong hikers, especially those with some climbing experience, could consider hiring a professional guide. Swiss guide Hans Schwarz is known for his emphasis on safety and clear teaching techniques. His Jasper Climbing School and Mountaineering Service offers excellent one-day guided climbs to the east ridge of Mt. Edith Cavell (3,363 metres), Mt. Athabasca (3,491 metres) and Mt. Morro, (1,677 metres). The last is an excellent climb for beginners. Prices for one day start at $170 for one person, $85 each for two persons and $60 each for three persons. Longer guided climbs can be taken to the peaks surrounding Fryatt Creek hut, Tonquin Valley, the Columbia Icefield and Maligne Lake. Write Jasper Climbing School and Mountaineering Service, Box 452, Jasper, Alta. T0E IE0, or phone (403) 852-3964.

Backpacking: See Chapter 5 for recommendations on some of the best overnight trips.

Bicycling: See Chapter 5 for bicycle rental locations and a guide to the best bicycle day trips and short trips around Jasper park.

Boating and Canoeing: Tomahawk Canoe trips in Jasper offers adventures ranging from half-day trips to week-long outings. Call (403) 436-9189 or write: 11035-64 Ave., Edmonton, Alta. T6H 1T4.

Boat Cruises—Maligne Lake: The most photographed scene in the Rockies—Spirit Island on Maligne Lake—can be reached comfortably by boat. Indeed, many feel the full grandeur of the lake—surrounded by wide glaciers and ranges reaching more than 3,050 metres (10,000 feet)—is not revealed any other way. That's why a two-hour guided tour down Maligne Lake in a covered power boat is perennially popular. Choose a fine day if possible, as the lake is higher than Jasper townsite and can easily be socked in on rainy days. And be prepared for the hefty price: $15 per adult, $7.50 for children ages 6-12. A family special is available at 10 a.m. only for $40, and a senior citizens' discount of $13.50 at 4 p.m. only. The cruises operate from 10 a.m. to 4 p.m. June 1-24; 10 a.m. to 5 p.m. June 25 to Aug. 25; and

10 a.m. to 4 p.m. Aug. 26-Sept. 30. For reservations or information, write Maligne Tours Ltd., Box 280, Jasper, Alta. T0E 1E0, call (403) 852-3370.

For $29 you can take a five-hour Brewster bus and boat tour from the townsite to Maligne Lake, with stops of interest along the way. Tickets and reservations at Brewster's Transport Office in the train station on Connaught, the main street. Call (403) 852-3332. Otherwise, drive to the end of Maligne Lake Road, 48 km (30 miles) from Jasper townsite.

Carriage Ride: Tour Jasper townsite in a surrey with a fringe on top. Donna and Jerry Cummings offer a one-hour tour of the town in a three-seater, horse-drawn carriage, May 15 to the end of September. Minimum charge $20. A taxi service is also available. For special nights out, they provide a pick-up and drop-off service and will cater to weddings and birthdays. They also offer sleigh and hay rides in winter. Call 852-5111 (Sawridge Hotel) during the day or 852-4770 evenings. Reservations required for special events.

Dog Sledding: Mush into Jasper's backcountry on day or overnight dog sled trips offered by Clarey/Bush Outfitting and Guiding. A one-hour orientation is available, using slides, to introduce visitors to dog sledding. On day trips of about 20 km (12 miles) guests learn to harness their own team of friendly sled dogs. Lunch is provided and eaten at a picnic spot along the way. Overnight trips are from two days to 10 days, with accommodation in rustic cabins or tents with wood heating. Hour-long tours designed to introduce guests to sled dogs are also available. For reservations, write Clarey/Bush Outfitting and Guiding, Box 84, Jasper, Alta. T0E 1E0, (403) 852-4078.

Drives: The most popular drive is up the 48-km (30-mile) road to gorgeous Maligne Lake south of Jasper townsite, passing Maligne Canyon and "disappearing" Medicine Lake along the way. A sparkling route with steep limestone mountains and fast-moving rivers. Another drive is up the dead-end road to Mt. Edith Cavell, a narrow, twisting route with good views over the Astoria Valley and an awesome glacier at the end. Highway 93A south from Jasper Townsite is a slower-lane alternative to the Icefields Parkway. The Fiddle River road to Miette Hot Springs south of Highway 16 has been widened and improved. You can also drive west 83 km (51 miles) to Mt. Robson, highest in the Canadian Rockies, though it is often obscured by cloud. The Drive, of course, is the 226-km (140-mile) tour of awe-inspiring alpine scenery to Lake Louise on the world-famous Icefields Parkway. Auto-tape tours are available. See Rainy Day Guide—Jasper.

Jasper Taxi Ltd., offers mini-sightseeing adventures, including photographic safaris. Call (403) 852-3146.

Fishing and Guided Fishing: See Chapter 5 for where to fish, where to find fishing guides and which lakes have which fish.

Golfing: The 18-hole championship golf course at Jasper Park Lodge was one of Canada's finest when it opened in 1925. Designed by the famous golf architect Stanley Thompson, it took 200 men and 50 teams of horses an entire summer to clear the ground of huge boulders and timber. Equipment rental and professional instruction available. Call the lodge at 852-3301.

Guided Cross-Country Ski Trips: For nature lovers who also ski, interpretive cross-country ski trips are available in winter. Ben Gadd conducts easy half-day trips focussing on such themes as the winter landscape, bird life and animal tracks. For information and reservations, call (403) 852-4012 or 852-5665. Free interpretive ski tours are offered by Parks Canada to view the winter environment in areas such as Pyramid Bench above Jasper townsite. For more information, call (403) 852-6161.

Guided Walks: Ben Gadd, a licensed interpretive guide, offers guided walks to Old Fort Point, or sunset strolls off the beaten track. Call (403) 852-4012 or 852-5665.

Hikers' and Sightseers' Shuttle: Jasper Taxi Ltd., offers a shuttle service to trailheads, lakes, beaches or other attractions within park boundaries. Call 852-3146.

Horse-Back Riding: The horsey set and the inexperienced will be well provided for at Jasper Park Lodge. Horses can be rented by the hour at the lodge's Jasper Park Riding Academy. Guided trail rides, instruction in both English and Western pleasure riding, preliminary jumping as well as private guiding services are available. Those with their own horses will find overnight boarding and free trailer parking available.

City dudes might try the four-hour lunch rides or evening barbecue rides to Maligne Canyon. Call the Equus Centre at 852-3301 or 852-5794 for reservations. Longer trail rides of several days to Tonquin Valley and the Skyline Trail may also be booked. Open daily April 1-Oct. 31. There is hourly scheduled bus service from Jasper townsite to the lodge. Call Brewster Transport at 852-3332.

Another popular equestrian spot is at Pyramid Riding Stables, 4 km up Pyramid Lake Road from Jasper townsite. One, two and three-hour rides are offered, as well as day rides, with special early morning rates, and over-nighters to Elysium Pass. The last ride leaves at 4 p.m. For reservations and information, phone 852-3562 or write Box 767, Jasper, Alta. T0E 1E0.

Numerous outfitters operate in Jasper National Park, offering horseback trips of between three and 12 days. Jasper Wilderness and Tonquin Valley Pack Trips go into the beautiful Tonquin Valley. Write Box 550, Jasper, Alberta, T0E 1E0 or phone (403) 852-3909. Miette Trail Rides concentrate on the scenic Upper Fiddle River or Blue Creek areas. Six-to-10-day trips are available, starting at $530 per person. Write Ed Regnier, summer: Box 2044, Jasper, Alta. T0E 1E0, (403) 866-2202; winter: Box 496, Edson, Alta. T0E 0P0, (403) 693-2157.

A classic trip is the 3-day Skyline Trail, over Shovel Pass and through the Snowbowl. Six, 10 and 12-day trips also offered. Contact Skyline Trail Rides, summer: Box 207, Jasper, Alta. T0E 1E0, (403) 852-4215; winter: Brule, Alta. T0E 0C0, (403) 866-3984.

Hot Springs Soak: The best way to get soaked in Jasper is to soothe your cares and aches away at Miette Hot Springs, high up the Fiddle Valley, with good views along the way and a chance to see Punchbowl Falls. (See Rainy Day Guide—Jasper.) As well, a number of excellent hiking trails radiate from here. See Walks 104 and 105. The original pool was built in 1919 by striking workers from the coal mine at Pocahontas. A new pool was built in 1938, and replaced in 1986. Check at the park information centre for the schedule.

To reach the hot springs, drive 42 km (26 miles) east of Jasper townsite on Hwy 16 and turn south on Miette Road. Punchbowl Falls is 0.5 km up the road. Drive 16.5 km (10 miles) further to reach the pool.

Japanese Language Tours: Enterprising Tokyo Tom, known for cooking up fine seafood, also offers tours of the Jasper area in Japanese. Write Box 1491, Jasper, Alta. T0E 1E0, or call (403) 852-4189.

Jasper Park Lodge: Spend a pleasant afternoon at Jasper Park Lodge, being as energetic or lazy as you want. Those without transportation may enjoy walking to the lodge via Old Fort Point and taking a Brewster bus back to town, or vice versa. (Buses leave every hour between the lodge and townsite. Call Brewster's at 852-3332 or check at the bus depot in the train station.) The exhilarating two-hour stroll starting from the bridge at Old Fort Point (Walk 86) is recommended.

At the lodge, enjoy the short stroll around Lac Beauvert (Walk 87), rent a canoe or paddle boat from Sandy's or ride a horse from the Jasper Park Riding Academy. Or just enjoy the scenic views of Mt. Edith Cavell over the green lake from one of the sun platforms on the edge of the water. In July and August, blow your budget with an outdoor barbecue lunch, held several times during the week on the Belvedere deck. Check at the lodge information centre, 852-3301. See Rainy Day Guide—Jasper for historical background and things to do in the lodge.

Jogging: See Chapter 5 for the best places to run, on both pavement and smooth trails.

Maligne Canyon Crawl: Under-ice prowling is just one of the unusual highlights of the Maligne Canyon Crawl, a safe and popular winter expedition offered Sundays in Jasper National Park.

The crawl features a look into the inky entrance of an ice cave, often encrusted with beautiful "frost feathers" caused by the condensation of warm air from within. Bighorn sheep are frequently seen in their own rocky habitat just across the way. Other attractions include the ice-framed Lace Waterfall which flows all winter. Everywhere, waterfalls are frozen into interesting shapes.

The 2-km crawl takes 2 1/2 to three hours and makes an entertaining finish to a weekend ski trip. It's enjoyable even on extremely cold or stormy days—blizzards can't disturb the calm depths of the canyon.

The crawl, organized by Ben Gadd, a licensed interpretive guide, is offered at a reasonable cost. (The tour is not advised for those aged six and under.)

The crawl is offered every Sunday morning in January, February and March. Meet in front of the Jasper Park Information Centre on Connaught Drive at 9:30 a.m.

Reservations are recommended as groups are limited to 20 participants. Call (403) 852-5665 or 852-4012 in Jasper. There's a direct line from Edmonton: (403) 428-7650. (You can, however, take a chance by simply showing up at 9:30 a.m.) You'll need transportation to the canyon, although rides can usually be arranged if you don't have a car.

Motor Coach Tours: In the outdoor-adventure-through-glass category, Brewster's runs a number of popular excursions from Jasper townsite. They include:
- A 5-hour guided motor coach tour from Jasper to Maligne Lake, with a 1 1/2 hour lake cruise.
- A 9 1/2-hour one-way tour along the Icefields Parkway to Banff townsite, including a stop at the Columbia Icefields.
- A three-day circle tour, starting in Edmonton and including the Icefields, Lake Louise, Banff and Calgary.

Tours start at the Brewster Transport office at the train station, or call (403) 852-3332.

Mountain Biking: See Bicycling, Chapter 5 for where to rent and ride mountain bikes.

Naturalists' Evening Programs: In summer, park naturalists present free interpretive programs every night at the Whistlers Campground Theatre. These excellent programs cover everything from grizzly bears, healing herbs and bicycling down the parkway to how to pack a trail horse. Most are illustrated by slides and films. There's car and bus parking close to the theatre for visitors not staying in the campground. Naturalist talks are also held in a small, cozy theatre at Wapiti Campground. These programs are excellent for children because they end before bedtime. Old-fashioned campfire circle talks are held at Wabasso, Wilcox, Pocahontas and Honeymoon Lake campgrounds.

Parks Canada also offers free indoor interpretive programs in Jasper during the winter. One or two evening slide shows are presented weekly at a local motel. Topics include winter wildlife and avalanche control. Schedules will be posted at the information centre. Twice a week and one evening every weekend, films are shown at the information centre. A naturalist is on hand to field questions.

Raft Tours: See Jasper as the fur traders did, more or less. Try a safe whitewater raft tour down the Athabasca River, where David Thompson travelled in 1810-11 to discover the Athabasca Pass for the North West Company. Half-day (3-hour) trips and full-day (6-hour) trips are available from Jasper Raft Tours. Transportation to and from the river is included, as well as a picnic lunch on day trips. Tickets or reservations for half-day trips, which usually require only one- or two-days advance reservation, are available from the Brewster Bus depot on Connaught Drive (852-3332). Full-day trips must be booked in advance through Jasper Raft Tours, Box 398, Jasper, Alta. T0E IE0. Or phone (403) 852-3613. Charter and tour groups can also be arranged in advance.
Jasper Mountain River Guides also have two-hour and four-hour round trips (includes lunch) on the Athabasca River. Reservations at Marmot Texaco, 702 Connaught Drive, 852-3760 or write Box 362, Jasper, Alta. T0E 1E0.

Rock Scrambling: See Chapter 5 for off-trail, non-climbing exploration.

Sailing and Windsurfing: See Chapter 5 for where to sail and windsurf, where to rent and where to take lessons.

Skating: Head out to the park's frozen ponds and lakes—and lace up your skates. Pyramid Lake offers the skater both solitude and beauty. A small section of the lake is plowed and night lighting is provided. Bring skates or rent them in town as no facilities are provided at the lake. In February and March, the best outdoor skating is east of Jasper townsite where Chinook winds often sweep away the snow. Nearby Talbot Lake and Snaring Ponds are favorites. The park information centre will provide you with maps and directions. You can phone them at 852-6161.

Skiing (Cross-Country): See Chapter 5 for the best trails for all levels, tips on what to take and warnings about avalanches. Licensed guide Ben Gadd conducts easy half-day trips focussing on such themes as the winter landscape, bird life and animal tracks. For information and reservations, call 852-5665 or 852-4012. Free interpretive ski tours are offered by Parks Canada to view the winter environment in areas such as Pyramid Bench above Jasper townsite. For more information, call 852-6161.

Skiing (Downhill): See Chapter 5.

Sleigh Rides and Hay Rides: Donna and Jerry Cummings offer winter sleigh rides and hay rides. Call 852-5111 (Sawridge Hotel) during the day, or 852-4770 evenings, or write Box 692, Jasper, Alta., T0E IE0.

Swimming: Jasper is not a place where visitors usually think of swimming. Those glacial lakes are chilly! Nevertheless, residents swear the water's fine at Pyramid Lake, Lake Annette and Lake Edith, which all have beaches. Beaches are located at the north end of Lake Annette and at two locations on Lake Edith where a number of beautiful cabins are located. Buses run regularly from Brewster's to Jasper Park Lodge.

Pyramid Lake, 7 km up Pyramid Lake Road, has a beach and picnic area on the south side with a fine view of Pyramid Mountain. A swim could be combined with a picnic on Pyramid Lake Island (Walk 94).

Whistlers Skytram: For a panorama of the entire Athabasca Valley, the Jasper tramway whisks visitors up 2,285 metres to the alpine zone below the summit of Whistler's Mountain, just west of Jasper townsite. The tramway takes about seven minutes to reach the top. On clear days, Mount Robson can be seen 100 km to the west. A scenic hiking trail to the barren summit leads from the upper terminal (Walk 85). Some might enjoy taking the tram up and walking down. There's a restaurant at the top. The tramway operates 9 a.m. to 5 p.m. from mid-April to mid-June, and from 8 a.m. to 10 p.m. to mid-August. Then it runs to 9 p.m. until closing at Thanksgiving. The tramway is 8 km (5 miles) south of Jasper townsite. Bus service is available from Jasper townsite and Jasper Park Lodge. Inquire at Brewster's at 852-3332. For more information, write Jasper Tramway, Box 418, Jasper, Alta., T0E 1E0. Or phone 852-3093.

Jasper National Park:
Indoor and Rainy Day Guide

What to do in Jasper National Park when the forecast calls for rain and more rain, your tent is awash, it's so cold you can see your breath and the kids keep whining about playing Pacman?

Of course, you could head 362 km east to West Edmonton Mall, the world's second largest mall, where indoor attractions include a rollercoaster, an aviary and an indoor skating rink where the Oilers' Wayne Gretzky sometimes practices.

Yet many of those those who know Jasper would rather be soaked to their skins in that park any day. Jasper townsite, to be sure, is smaller and more low-key than its counterpart Banff. You won't find the variety of museums and cultural events that make a rainy day almost welcome. Jasper in the rain is a place to relax, gear down, and psyche yourself back to small-town sensibilities. And that can be challenging.

The good news? Many fine walks can be travelled in Jasper National Park despite a little rain. One trick is to use an umbrella, which turns into a fine walking stick when the sun comes out. Some hikers even use umbrellas backpacking, despite supercilious stares from the grin 'n' bear-it types.

Stay off narrow trails where you'll soon be soaked from the wet leaves and grass despite raincoat and boots. Ideal, non-muddy trails to wash away the rainy day blues include the 2.4-km Lake Annette loop (Walk 91), all on asphalt. Or walk part of the 3.5-km Lake Beauvert loop in rubber boots, (Walk 87), then end up with a hot drink in Jasper Park Lodge. The first part of Maligne Canyon (Walk 97) is just as impressive in rain as in sunshine, and you can retreat afterward to the teahouse for tea, chili, brownies and other comforting foods.

You might also enjoy the wide, 9.6-km path to Summit Lake (Walk 99), although the footing can get muddy despite the network of underground drainage systems. Or head south from Jasper townsite to Athabasca Falls (Walk 78) and Sunwapta Falls, a 2.4-km walk on a wide trail mostly through trees (Walk 77). Warm your toes in the friendly, timbered restaurant back on the Parkway at the Sunwapta junction, while munching homemade muffins or chocolate brownies.

If rainy walks don't appeal, there's always rainy day cycling. Not your idea of fun? While it probably has to be tried to be believed, bicycling in the rain can be warm and enjoyable with reliable rain gear and a warm, dry place at the end. Pack some extra dry clothing and socks into a front bag, and head from Jasper townsite to Jasper Park Lodge, Maligne Canyon or Athabasca Falls. See cycling section in Chapter 5. Finish your day with a splurge at Jasper Park Lodge. (Reserve ahead.)

Rainy Day Guide—Indoor Delights

Art Gallery: Jasper Gallery is a co-operative non-profit gallery operated by film-maker Wendy Wacko. Paintings by artists from across Canada. Open Monday to Saturday from 9 a.m. to 5 p.m., upstairs in the Maligne Building on Connaught just east of the Park Information Centre, between Canyon Travel and The Tog Shoppe.

Arts Jasper: In winter, enjoy performances of the Alberta Ballet, Foothills Brass or a variety of other cultural groups through Arts Jasper. This local arts council sponsors performances, mostly musical, between October and March. Performances are usually in the evening, during the week, at the Jasper Activity Centre, 303 Pyramid Ave. Phone (403) 852-3381.

Bars: No. 1 action spot is the bar in the Athabasca Hotel, right in the middle of town. There's a lounge and disco, and you can mix with mountaineers and get burgers and such with beer in what the locals refer to fondly as The Dead Animal Room. The bartender just might be a disillusioned lawyer—like all mountain resorts, Jasper's young labor pool is drawn mostly from university ranks. Who can blame them? It's a great place to opt out, if indeed the mountains are "out."

Billiards and Bowling: Head to Hoppy's Bowling and Billiards at 625 Patricia St., just down from the Alberta Liquor Control Board. Call 852-3988. Mountain Foods at 606 Connaught also has billiards.

Bookstore: The best place for book-browsing has the unlikely name of Jasper Camera and Gifts. You'll find a good selection of Rocky Mountain books, natural history, local history, mountain poetry, as well as classics, and popular novels. Just east of the Park Information Centre at 412 Connaught Dr., the main street. Call 852-3165.

Cemetery Creeping: An interesting time can be had at the Jasper cemetery, for those who enjoy that sort of thing. Early headstones tell of deaths by grizzly maulings and give other evocative hints of what life was like for early settlers. The cemetery is just before the turn into Jasper townsite when travelling west.

Dining: Food is expensive in Jasper. But if you're tired of soggy noodles heated over a Coleman, a rainy day's the time for a change of diet. Chateau Jasper is known for its terrific Sunday brunches—everything from eggs to duck plus salads and desserts. Local residents swear by Tokyo Tom's at Fort Point Lodge for such fresh seafood delicacies as sushi, sashimi, tempura and teriyaki. Call 852-3780. Or splurge at the Tonquin Prime Rib Village on Juniper St. and Connaught Dr., known for juicy ribs and steaks. Call 852-4966. Live entertainment for the dine-and-dance set is often offered at Marmot Motor Lodge.

A budget burger fan? Head straight for Skehill's Burgers in the Athabasca Hotel's licensed Dead Animal Room. Brian Skehill has a reputation for making great burgers, big french fries and an assortment of other occasional delicacies, like egg rolls, chicken burgers or large hot dogs. You can get spanakopita, lasagne, pizza, baklava and such at Something Else at 621 Patricia. The owner is credited with bringing the donair to Jasper, a cultural-culinary advance indeed. Licensed. Phone 852-3850.

A favorite for ice cream fans is Tricia's at 604 Patricia St. Locals rave about her frozen yogurt ice cream, flavored with just about any fruit. Call 852-4945. Owner Shirley Doran, at Scoops and Loops at 504 Patricia St., has a following for her homemade muffins, cookies, ice cream and other great snacks. Ph. 852-4333.

Go Back to Sleep

Drives: Again, the scenery won't look as good as a fine day, but you have to do something! See Outdoor Adventures—Jasper for suggested drives.

Jasper Park Lodge

There are a number of car-rental agencies in town, and it's sometimes possible to arrange a one-way rental to Banff townsite. To add dimension to your drive, consider renting a Rocky Mountain Auto Tape Tour from Keith Allen Photography Inc., 218 Connaught Drive. These tapes are approved by Parks Canada.

Hot Springs: The colder, gloomier and wetter the day, the better for soaking in a natural hot springs! You haven't lived until you've had a steamy bath in a snowstorm! Miette Hot Springs has been recently improved and is well worth the drive. It is situated 61 km from Jasper townsite, off the Miette Road. Open mid-May to Labor Day. Check hours at the Park Information Centre. Drive 42 km (26 miles) east of Jasper townsite on Hwy 16 and turn right on Miette Road. Punchbowl Falls, a mountain creek tumbling over a narrow limestone gorge, is 0.5 km up the road. Drive 16.5 km

(10 miles) further to reach the pool. Check at the Informaton Centre for pool times. The boardwalk path behind the old pool to the source of the hot springs is fine in any weather, although the boards can get slippery (Walk 104).

Jasper Park Lodge: Lounge where the Guggenheims and Princess Margaret have lounged! Fine hotels are always splendid places to wait out the rain. Walk or drive 7 km (4 miles) east of Jasper townsite to the lodge, or take a bus—Brewster buses depart every hour in summer, either on the hour or half-hour. Check at the depot in the train station, or call 852-3332. Jasper Park Lodge is not nearly as grand as its baronial counterpart, the Banff Springs Hotel but it is beautifully set on green Lac Beauvert. There's a fine view of Mt. Edith Cavell over the water and the hotel is holder of the hospitality industry's prestigious and rare Five Diamond award.

Try people-watching in the main lobby. In Joe Clark's brief tenure as prime minister, this seemed on its way to becoming Parliament West. The Pope was scheduled to stay here in 1984, until bad weather forced his cancellation. Watch for bellhops carrying drinks on bicycles—a lodge tradition.

The original lodge of felled logs was built by the CNR in June, 1922. That building burned down in 1952, and most of the original log cabins have been replaced with cedar chalets. Nine are still in use, and they are much sought after by guests. The hotel's lobby features wooden carvings, a bison head and huge fireplaces to warm up by on cool evenings. Several lavish stores are situated on the main floor. Have a cocktail in La Terrasse, which overlooks the lake and surrounding mountains. There are pastries, snacks and light meals available in The Copper Kettle. Five-course international cuisine is available in the more pricey Beauvert Room or The Tonquin Room. Reserve ahead. Check at InfoLodge in the main lobby or call (403) 852-3301. (The lodge is open from mid-April to late October.)

Library Loafing: Occasional author and poetry readings are held, usually in winter, in the Jasper Library at 500 Robson Street, in the old RCMP Building across from the Elementary School and southeast of the hospital. Watch the Jasper Booster for details, or call 852-3652. Hours: Sat. 2-4 p.m., Tues. and Wed. 7-9 p.m., Thurs. 9:30-11:30 a.m., 2-4 p.m., 7-9 p.m., Fri. 2-4 p.m. Closed Mondays.

Lug Laundry to the Laundromat: What else are rainy days for? Find a laundromat at 504 Patricia (downstairs) or 607 Patricia (downstairs). Both have public showers as well.

Motorcoach Tours: While the scenery won't be as fine in the rain, at least you'll be dry. Brewster's runs a number of bus excursions from Jasper townsite. See Outdoor Adventures section. Departure points from Jasper are: Jasper Park Lodge, the Lobstick Lodge, Chateau Jasper and the depot in the train station. Guests at other hotels may call 852-3332 for complimentary pick-up.

Columbia Icefield

Movies—See a Challenging One!: Not long ago, some Jasper residents started to think about what tourists could do in Jasper when they weren't sight-seeing. Why not make a film about the park?

The result was *Challenge of the Canadian Rockies*, produced by Wendy Wacko, wife of the local theatre owner. She'd never made a film before. The film, narrated by Peter Ustinov, was critically acclaimed. She even took the film to the Cannes Film Festival and sold it for showing in dozens of countries.

Watching this film is the next best thing to ice climbing, kayaking over a waterfall or skiing on the edge of destruction. Daily matinees are held at 3 p.m. and 4 p.m. at the Chaba Theatre and at the Marmot Lodge in the evenings. The schedule is subject to change, so call 852-4728 to confirm. Regular Hollywood fare is screened at The Chaba Theatre at 604 Connaught. Call 852-4749.

Museum Musing—Whistlers Wildlife Museum: This tiny and rather crowded museum houses 93 specimens of wildlife, from raccoons and golden eagles to grizzlies and mountain caribou. "Hearphones" tell about the habits of different species. Moderately interesting.

The museum is downstairs in The Whistlers Hotel, 105 Miette Ave., at the corner of Connaught and Miette Drive, just west of the Park Information Centre. Open 10 a.m. to 9 p.m. (Ask at the desk upstairs if no one is downstairs). Call 853-3361.

Racquet Sports, Roller Skating, Indoor Tennis: You can drop in to use the racquetball courts, universal gym, public skating rink, curling rink, sauna and showers for a flat fee at the Jasper Activity Centre, 393 Pyramid Ave. Weekends: 9 a.m. to 11 p.m.; weekdays: 8:30 a.m. to 11 p.m. Call 852-3381 for details, or write in advance to the Jasper Recreation Department, Box 1539, Jasper, Alta. T0E 1E0.

Showers: When it's showering outside, gritty campers might take the opportunity to shower inside. Showers provided downstairs at laundromats at 504 Patricia St. and 607 Patricia St.

Teahouse Tripping: Unfortunately, only two of the Rockies' rustic teahouses built at the turn of the century by the CPR remain. Both are in Banff National Park. But it can still be cozy to idle away part of a rainy day at newer teahouses at Maligne Canyon, Maligne Lake or Pyramid Lake. Just don't expect finery—styrofoam cups are de rigeur at Maligne Lake. At Maligne Canyon, you can get home-baked goodies and see the beginning of the dramatic limestone canyon.

Video Arcades: These ubiquitous machines can be found even in Jasper. Track 'em down at Mountain Foods at 606 Connaught, or the arcade upstairs from Scoops and Loops at 504 Patricia St.

Kananaskis Country

3 Kananaskis Country
Outdoor Adventures
Indoor Activities

Kananaskis Country

The Canadian Rocky Mountain national parks are known and praised around the world — but Kananaskis Country, despite the '88 Winter Olympics, is still mostly the preserve of southern Albertans.

That's a shame, because this splendid land of peaks and foothills, 90 km west of Calgary and 60 km southeast of Banff, has something to offer almost everyone.

This multi-use recreational area, encompassing 4,000 square km, contains: three provincial parks (Peter Lougheed, Bow Valley and Bragg Creek), 41 trout-stocked lakes, hundreds of kilometres of hiking trails, a 36-hole world-class golf course, a network of paved bike paths, downhill skiing at Mt. Allan, site of the '88 Winter Olympic Games, excellent facilities for the disabled, and one of the most luxurious RV campgrounds in North America.

Yet such summations may give the wrong impression. For every RV pad with satellite reception, K-Country offers dozens of rugged out-of-the-way excursions where, even in July, you are unlikely to run into another person.

Wildlife viewing is superb, owing partly to the high elevations at Peter Lougheed Park. You may see moose, mountain goats, even flying squirrels. If auto-touring is your preference, Highway 40 cuts through the lovely Kananaskis Valley and climbs over Highwood Pass, highest paved road in Canada.

The Travel Alberta information centre at Barrier Lake, as you enter K-

Country, is the place to stop to orient yourself. There are no towns in K-Country. Groceries are available at several places, including Mount Kidd, Fortress Junction and the Boulton Trading Post in Peter Lougheed Provincial Park.

Campground, hotel, hostel and guest ranch accommodation is available. Be warned that campground facilities fill up early in summer months.

The following recommendations are meant only as an introduction to what K-Country has to offer. For an excellent overview, from auto-touring to skiing, see *The Complete Guide to Kananaskis Country* by Norma Ramage and Jim Wilson. *The Kananaskis Country Trail Guide*, by Gillean Daffern, is a comprehensive guide to hiking trails in this area.

Outdoor Adventures, Indoor Activities

Bicycling: For those on two wheels, the extra-wide Highway 40 is superb for travel. Families will enjoy a network of asphalt trails which weave between campgrounds in Peter Lougheed Provincial Park; a pleasant path also leads from Ribbon Creek to Wedge Pond. See Chapter 5 for longer tours.

Camp in Luxury: At Mt. Kidd RV Park, amenities include tennis courts, whirlpools, saunas, satellite hookups and an open-air amphitheatre. If the evening is cool, you can retreat to a large lounge with a fireplace. Or play video games! Or just stroll the hiking trails and enjoy the view of Mt. Kidd. Open year-round. Call (403) 591-7700 for reservations.

Canmore Nordic Centre: The Canmore Nordic Centre in K-Country is Alberta's most comprehensive cross-country facility. The site of nordic skiing and biathlon events during the '88 Winter Olympics, it offers more than 27 km of challenging new trails and a cedar-beamed lodge complete with skylights and a fireplace.

The carefully-designed network allows racers to reach speeds of over 80 kph on downhill sections. Recreational skiers can choose their own more comfortable pace. Ten additional kilometres of scenic trails link the nordic centre with the town of Canmore and lead west to the Banff National Park boundary. In summer, you can hike, ride a mountain bike or picnic along these same trails.

For a quick warm-up on a cold day, head to one of eight small team rooms near the day lodge. Just turn on the heating switch. For night skiing, 2.5 km of trails are illuminated.

Après ski or hike, relax in the lodge's lounge, modelled on an alpine chalet. The nordic centre, about 100 km west of Calgary, is 1.8 km south of Canmore on the Smith-Dorrien/Spray Lakes road. Open daily year-round, no admission. For information, call (403) 678-2400.

Facilities for the Disabled: William Watson Lodge in Peter Lougheed Provincial Park offers outstanding facilities for the physically disabled and for seniors. Wheelchair-accessible trails are provided; Mt. Lorette Fishing Ponds are also wheelchair-accessible. Some accommodation is available for the disabled, seniors and their friends or family members. Call (403) 591-7227 for details.

Grab Your Golf Clubs: Head for the Kananaskis Country Golf Course, which offers 36 holes of world-class golf under the towering mass of Mt. Kidd. For easy handicapping, each hole can be played from four different tees. Advance bookings can be made by calling 1-800-372-9201 toll-free. Or call (403) 591-7070 locally.

Horse-Back Riding: Numerous guest ranches in the region offer organized trail rides on 200 km of equestrian trails. Contact Homeplace Ranch and Trail Ride, (403) 931-3245, Kananaskis Guest Ranch (403) 673-3737 or Rafter Six Ranch Resort, (403) 673-3622.

Hot-Tub It: In luxurious Mt. Kidd you can soak in a jacuzzi while looking through the huge windows at mountain scenery. Cost of the hot tub is included in camping fees; if you are not camping you can still soak in the tubs by paying a small fee.

Kananaskis Visitor Centre: The place to go to learn more about the area. You'll find displays about the geological, natural and human history of Kananaskis. Park information staff are on hand to answer questions. There's a pleasant spacious lounge for shelter on a cold day or relaxation after a hike or ski. In Peter Lougheed Park, 4 km from Hwy 40 turnoff.

Nature Programs: Interested in learning how to track an *invisible moose*? Or how Kananaskis got its name? Or why some parts of Peter Lougheed Park receive so much snow? Inquire at Barrier Lake Information Centre on Highway 40 or the Kananaskis Visitor Centre about interpretive programs. Some guided hikes are also available.

Skiing: Downhill and Cross-Country. See Chapter 5.

Kananaskis Village: Billed as a resort for all seasons, Kananaskis Village features three posh lodges, all with full service. The Village is conveniently located by Naskiska, site of the 1988 Winter Olympic downhill skiing events. The lodge at Kananaskis Village has modern alpine architecture, 255 guest suites and luxuries ranging from an aerobics room to saunas and a shabu shabu bar. The 70-room Hotel Kananaskis is a luxurious manor-style hotel. The Kananaskis Inn contains 96 guest suites, many with sleeping lofts and kitchenettes. The central reservation number is 1-800-332-1013 (toll-free in Alberta only). Toll free in Canada: 1-800-661-1064.

Mt. Engadine Lodge: On the Smith Dorrien-Spray Lake Trail (at Mt. Shark turnoff), this lodge is an excellent base for cross-country (403) 678-4080 or call operator, ask for Banff Mobile XJ50437.

4 Waterton Lakes National Park

Outdoor Adventures
Rainy Day Guide
Indoor Activities

Waterton Lakes National Park

Waterton Lakes National Park is the tiny jewel of the Canadian Rockies. Here the mountains rise abruptly from the prairies, creating a stunning landscape of jagged peaks, hanging valleys and glaciers, dramatically set against rolling grasslands.

Situated in the southwest corner of Alberta on the U.S. border, 264 km southwest of Calgary, this park — visited by between 500,000 and 600,000 people a year — is more remote and less well-known than Banff and Jasper.

Waterton Lakes contains some of the oldest exposed bedrock in the Canadian Rockies; eons of geological activity have left a legacy of richly-colored mountains and canyons. Encompassing the transition zone between prairies and mountains, it is home to a rich variety of animal and plant life and offers some of the best wildflower displays in North America.

You'll find more than 175 km of hiking trails, excellent fishing, the opportunity to cruise on a lake between two countries, and much more. Be warned, however, that winds can be cruel in this part of the country — and snow can fly almost any time of year.

The park, which is only about 525 km square, was established in 1895 and in 1932 dedicated as an "International Peace Park" with adjacent Glacier National Park in Montana.

Buses serve Waterton Lakes in summer from Calgary (via Pincher Creek) and from Great Falls and Kalispell in Montana. Waterton townsite is the only residential centre in the park, home to only 50 to 60 permanent residents. Full services are available June to September when the population grows by the thousands.

Outdoor Adventures

Backpacking: See Chapter 5 for recommendations on the best overnight trips.

Bicycling: The townsite provides flat and gentle cycling for all fitness levels. There are also excellent and rewarding longer tours both within the park and into Montana's Glacier National Park. See Chapter 5. You can rent 18-speed mountain bikes (no 10-speeds), tandems and scooters at Pat's Texaco, behind the marina. Call (403) 859-2266.

Boating and Cruises: No one should visit Waterton without viewing the park from the water. Waterton Lake is the deepest in the Canadian Rockies and one of the most beautiful.

Waterton Shoreline Cruises offers scenic cruises up the lake. A stop in Montana, at the end of the lake, is usually included. Along the way, you'll have splendid views of rugged peaks and perhaps even see bighorn sheep or moose. A descriptive commentary is provided. Ask about sunset cruises. Boat service to the trailhead for Crypt Lake is also available. Call (403) 859-2362.

If you have your own boat, you'll find a launch site for Upper Waterton Lake opposite the park administration office.

Note though that strong winds can blow up without warning, creating dangerous conditions for small boats, especially on Upper Waterton Lake.

Climbing: See Chapter 5.

Fishing: See Chapter 5.

Golfing: The 18-hole Waterton Lakes Golf Course is situated about 2 km north of town adjacent to the main entrance road. Club and power cart rentals are available. Call (403) 859-2383.

Guided Hikes: Hike in two countries with the knowledgeable companionship of a park interpreter! The International Peace Park hike is offered every Saturday in summer. Participants hike down the lake to Goat Haunt and take a boat back. The hike is free; there is a small charge for the boat ride. Inquire at the information centre.

Hiker's Shuttle: Mountain Sunset Tours in the Tamarack Mall operates a hiking shuttle service. Call (403) 859-2612. You can also rent tents at Waterton Sports & Leisure in the mall and possibly guide services.

Horses by the Hour: Alpine Stables offers horse rentals and guides from 9 a.m. to 6 p.m. daily. Visitors can also board horses there. Backcountry corrals are provided at Rowe, Alderson, Crypt Landing and Lone Lake. Call (403) 859-2462.

Naturalists' Evening Programs: Lost your hat? Want to find out what makes it so windy in Waterton? Are you interested in learning more about Western Canada's first oil well, drilled in Waterton? Or what kinds of animals live in the park? If so, be sure to attend summer interpretive programs, held summer evenings at the Fall Theatre in the townsite (near Cameron Falls) and at Crandell Theatre at Crandell Campground. Check for programs at the Information Centre.

Scuba-Diving: Emerald Bay in the townsite is considered one of the best places in Alberta to scuba dive. That's because the wrecked hull of a 1920s stern paddle-wheeler lies about 15 metres under the surface.

Skiing (Cross-Country): See Chapter 5.

Surrey-Riding: See Waterton from the vantage of a surrey — with or without a fringe on top! You can rent them from Pat's Texaco, behind the marina. Call (403) 859-2266.

Swimming: The best place to swim in Waterton is in a heated pool. The lakes themselves are frigid. A few brave souls, mostly children, bathe at the beach in front of the campground picnic area. The Waterton Lakes National Park Swimming Pool is on the corner of Windflower Ave., and Cameron Falls Drive. Hot showers and towel rentals. Ask about public fitness classes. Open daily 11 a.m. to 7 p.m. Call (403) 859-2333.

Tennis, Anyone? A public tennis court is situated opposite the swimming pool entrance. Free.

Windsurfing: See Chapter 5.

Waterton Lakes National Park
Indoor and Rainy Day Guide

*Do not leave because it rains. Hang on until the dismal time passes, then
fly to the high places. The mountains will be at their best and appear, even
though far distant, as polished gems. The shining mountains will then be
understood.*

— Morton Elrod, 1924

Elrod's wise advice notwithstanding, even a rainy day needn't be a "dismal
time" in Waterton, although two bad days in a row can get tedious. This
little park has some warm, cozy spots good for waiting out the inclement
weather. Where could one find a friendlier atmosphere than at newly-
refurbished Pearl's Pantry? What could be more relaxing than lounging in
the Prince of Wales Hotel, rumoured to have at least two ghosts?

The people and parks staff of Waterton always seem to have a little more
extra time for visitors than they might in the busier parks to the north.

So make time for the indoor side of Waterton on your travels — and be
ready for a few surprises.

Bars: Looking for action? The younger crowd loves to congregate at The
Thirsty Bear Saloon in the Bayshore Inn, 111 Waterton Ave., (403)
859-2211. Dancing nightly. The more sedate Bayshore Inn Fireside Lounge
is the place for a quiet drink. For a special treat, head up to the Prince
of Wales Hotel Lounge.

Bookstores: Many excellent books are available through the Waterton
Natural History Association, which operates the Waterton Heritage Centre
at 117 Waterton Avenue, near the campground. The association also sells
books at the Park Information Bureau at the entrance to the townsite.

Buffalo Paddocks: You too can roam where the buffalo roam. A 2-km
drive gives visitors the opportunity to see buffalo on their native range.
Turn west upon entering the park (.2 km inside Pincher Creek entrance),
go past viewpoint, then downhill and turn left over the cattle guard.

Check Out the Heritage Centre: Puppet shows on the lawn? Music in
the park? Video programs on Waterton's history? Head for the Waterton
Heritage Centre at 117 Waterton Ave., in the centre of the townsite. This
is the home of the Waterton Natural History Association, which offers everything from information on park highlights to displays from various local artists.
They have excellent outdoor posters for sale. Open daily in summer. The
centre provides a variety of excellent exhibits on the natural and human
history of Waterton. Funds go to help non-profit park ventures. Call the
main office at (403) 859-2624.

Dining, Snacking and Hanging Out: Despite the small size of Waterton townsite, the variety which it offers diners is impressive. Try the Prince
of Wales for lunch or dinner. The dining room, with its high ceilings and

windowed view over the lake, is reminiscent of an earlier, less hurried time. The luncheon specials may include delicious shepherd's pie. The Tea Room is open from 2 p.m. to 5 p.m. A Sunday buffet is featured. Call 859-2231 for times.

Another popular spot in Waterton for sophisticated dining is the Kootenai Brown Dining Room in the Bayshore Inn, where windows on one side of the room overlook the lake. The restaurant is proud of winning the "Silver Spoon Award" in 1984, one of only 355 eating establishments in the U.S. and Canada to be so honored. For lunch you might enjoy strawberry crepes, caesar salad and even burgers; the evening meal is more likely to feature something like baked salmon en croute or Hungarian beef stroganoff. The Bayshore Inn also has a Koffee Shoppe.

Where do the locals eat? Most likely, you'll find them at Pearl's Pantry on Windflower Ave.—and for good reason. The newly-improved Pearl's continues its tradition of tasty home-cooking that is reasonably priced. Its fare has warmed the hearts of many a homesick student! Menu items include corned beef sandwiches, hearty soups, chili, homemade rolls, moist carrot cakes and all kinds of tea. You can't go wrong with the specials, listed daily on the blackboard. Open for lunch and dinner.

Tootsie's Ice Cream, at the corner of Windflower and Cameron Falls Drive (same doorway as theatre) makes a refreshing stop on a hot day. It's known for its tropical shakes and frosts, which include strawberry daiquiri and maitai flavors. At 309 Windflower Ave. The Big Scoop Ice Cream Parlour at 114 Waterton Ave. (part of Caribou Clothes) features old cartwheel tables and a good selection of flavors, including black forest and bubble gum.

Zumburger Haus has eat-in or takeout facilities; you'll find bratwurst and taco salad as well as burgers. Frank's on Waterton Ave., is a family restaurant offering Western and Cantonese cooking. The Tourist Cafe, also on Waterton Ave., advertises home-cooked meals. Look for homemade saskatoon and apple pie.

Guided Tours: Mountain Sunset Tours offers scenic tours to a variety of Waterton's special attractions. Reservations required. A townsite taxi and hiker shuttle service are also provided. Call 859-2612.

Laundry: The Itussistukiopi launderette, on Windflower Ave., is open daily.

Movies: The Waterton Lakes Opera House, corner of Windflower Ave., and Cameron Falls Drive, features movies every night.

Passing the Day at the Prince of Wales: Don't miss having a look at the magnificent wooden hotel, locally known as the POW, which stands as a picturesque sentinel above Waterton Lake. The glassed-in lobby overlooks the lake and has a delicious feel. On a rainy day, this would be a wonderful place to write a few postcards, or read a mystery. If you're hungry, drop in for high tea in the afternoon. Call (403) 859-2231.

2. WATERTON TOWNSITE

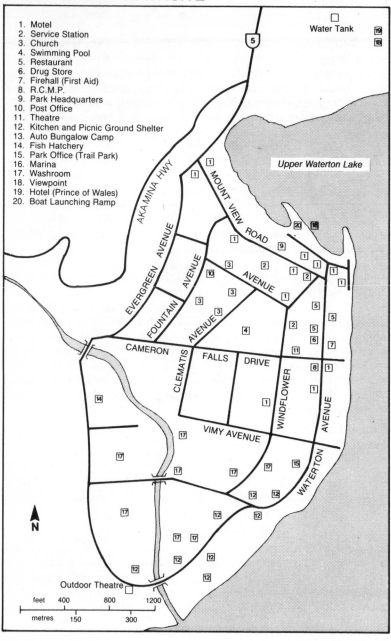

1. Motel
2. Service Station
3. Church
4. Swimming Pool
5. Restaurant
6. Drug Store
7. Firehall (First Aid)
8. R.C.M.P.
9. Park Headquarters
10. Post Office
11. Theatre
12. Kitchen and Picnic Ground Shelter
13. Auto Bungalow Camp
14. Fish Hatchery
15. Park Office (Trail Park)
16. Marina
17. Washroom
18. Viewpoint
19. Hotel (Prince of Wales)
20. Boat Launching Ramp

Water Tank

Upper Waterton Lake

AKAMINA HWY

MOUNT VIEW ROAD

EVERGREEN AVENUE

FOUNTAIN AVENUE

CLEMATIS AVENUE

CAMERON FALLS DRIVE

WINDFLOWER

WATERTON AVENUE

AVENUE

VIMY AVENUE

Outdoor Theatre

N

feet   400   800   1200

metres   150   300

The Prince of Wales: A Prince of a Hotel

The Prince of Wales, the magnificent seven-storied hotel at the north end of Waterton Lake, might have ended up looking quite different than it does today.

Louis Hill, president of the Great Northern Railway, chose the site for the building in 1913. At first he thought the design should be long and low, somewhat like Many Glacier Hotel in Montana. Or, perhaps it should resemble a French or Swiss chalet.

Hill proved to be so indecisive that the building had to be changed four times before he was satisfied. The result is the steep-pitched building which opened the summer of 1927.

Builders had to contend with Waterton's horrendous winds as well as Hill's uncertainties. High winds twice blew the building off its centre during construction; the second time, according to a leaflet published by the hotel, "construction had gone too far for the building to be aligned absolutely."

Today, the building still sways slightly under heavy winds, and guests on upper floors can feel it. No danger exists; the hotel has been constructed to withstand the fiercest gales.

The hotel is named after the Prince of Wales, who later became Edward VIII and abdicated the British throne for the love of a divorced woman. He never visited the hotel, although he was invited to open it.

"Unfortunately, he was unable to accept," states the hotel leaflet. "Legend has it that he did. . . but perhaps legend is better left alone."

One of the peculiarities of the Prince of Wales is the attraction it has for wildlife. Bighorn sheep, deer and coyotes have all been seen quizzically looking at their reflections in the huge glass windows at ground level. Occasionally, an aggressive sheep has even charged!

The hotel's official literature makes no mention of the ghosts rumored to reside there. Staff whisper, however, of "two friendly ghosts" which are occasionally heard locking and slamming doors and taking a shower in the cook's room.

"We're not supposed to tell anyone," confided one young staffer. "We don't want to scare people away."

Prince of Wales Hotel

5 A Detailed Guide to Special Interests

Backpacking
Camping
Cycling
Rock Scrambling
Sailing and Windsurfing
Boating
Cross-Country Skiing
Fishing
Running

Backpacking in the Canadian Rockies

The backpacking boom in the Rockies appears to have diminished since the mid-1970s. Between 70 and 90 per cent of walkers venturing into the backcountry are just out for the day. They travel further than a backpacker between breakfast and dinner; they wear lighter boots or shoes and they sleep in a comfortable bed at night.

Many visitors don't have the funds or time to buy or round up all the lightweight food and dozens of essential items needed for even a weekend backcountry trip. They've discovered too that the mountains can look quite different under a 30-pound load.

Nonetheless, there's a lot of gorgeous country back in the hills that simply can't be reached in one day. And maybe the true wilderness feeling is diminished by returning to a highway campground at night rather than staying in the backcountry alongside a creek.

Here are some of the major backpacking routes in the Rockies, although this isn't the book to explore backpacking in detail. See the excellent *Canadian Rockies Trail Guide* by Brian Patton and Bart Robinson.

You need a park use permit from a park information centre for these overnight trips, although specific camping regulations can vary from park to park, zone to zone. Camping is generally restricted to the primitive backcountry campsites. Reservations are possible in some instances, three weeks in advance, by telephoning or writing the park office. On some popular trails—and the ones mentioned are popular—the backcountry campsites may be filled during peak times in the summer. There are other, less-crowded routes that the park offices can recommend that usually have superb scenery and something just as valuable—a touch of solitude. Fires are allowed only in the metal fireboxes provided by the parks. Many campsites have little firewood left in the vicinity and backpackers usually bring gas-burning stoves which are more efficient for cooking.

Backpacking in Banff

• *Mt. Assiniboine via Citadel Pass (3-5 days).* A classic trip to a classic mountain, along the Continental Divide, over a high pass, culminating in a beautiful subalpine area of lakes, meadows, passes and peaks. Highly popular. Begins at Sunshine Village. Alternate routes from Spray Lakes reservoir south of Canmore.

• *Egypt Lake via Healy Pass (Weekend or longer).* Over a rounded pass into a high valley area under Continental Divide of lakes and meadows. Highly popular. Starts from Bourgeau parking lot below Sunshine ski area.

• *Skoki Valley via Boulder Pass (Weekend).* Across lofty Deception Pass to the Skoki Valley where there are stunning lakes and a network of side trails. Popular. Starts from base of Lake Louise ski area.

Backpacking in Kootenay

• *Floe Lake-Numa Pass-Tumbling Pass (2-3 days).* Trail parallels the crest of steep, glaciated range, crossing several high passes with steep ascents and descents. Route can be tailored to your time and energy. Popular. Starts from Banff Windermere Highway 93 at Marble Canyon, Numa Creek or Floe Creek.

Backpacking in Yoho

• *Yoho Valley circuit (2-3 days).* Loop up valley at one level and return on another. Splendid views, waterfalls, lakes and sidetrip options. Highly popular. Starts from Takakkaw Falls at the end of the Yoho Valley Road which leads off the Trans-Canada above Field.

• *Lake O'Hara (2-4 days).* From a central camp, explore numerous high lakes and alpine areas, one of the most highly developed hiking regions in the parks. Highly popular. Starts at Lake O'Hara fire road off the Trans-Canada on Highway 1A near Kicking Horse Pass. Bus transportation is available to the lake at 8 a.m., 11 a.m. and 4 p.m. With the bus, extended carrying of pack is unnecessary.

Backpacking in Jasper

• *Tonquin Valley (2-3 days).* A visit to a long lake under the towering Ramparts, one of the most stunning valleys in the mountains. Highly popular. Heavy use by horses. Starts from Edith Cavell Road near Cavell Lake or from Marmot Basin Road.

• *Fryatt Creek (2-3 days).* Trail terminates in impressive valley with beautiful lake and an opportunity to scramble higher past cascades to upper valley floor. Popular. Access from Geraldine Lakes fire road near Athabasca Falls.

• *Brazeau River-Poboktan Creek via Nigel Pass (3-4 days).* An extended loop with different campsites every night and a variety of scenery from high passes to remote lakes and long valleys. Popular. Access from Icefields Parkway, 12 km (7.5 miles) south of Icefield Centre and at Poboktan Warden Station on Parkway, 72 km (45 miles) south of Jasper townsite.

• *Skyline Trail (2-3 days).* Follows crest of rounded Maligne Range with exceptional views and several passes. Highly popular. Hikers must plan to hitchhike back to their vehicle or arrange for transportation. Starts at Maligne Lake. Ends at base of old Signal Mountain Fire Road near Maligne Canyon.

Backpacking in Mt. Robson Provincial Park

• *Berg Lake (Weekend).* Easy trail in Mt. Robson Provincial Park leads gently around the base of Robson, highest in the Canadian Rockies, past awesome

rockwalls, waterfalls, cascades and ending at impressive lake at the foot of Berg Glacier. Highly popular. Starts from Robson River parking area, off Highway 16, 58 km (36 miles) west of Yellowhead Pass.

Backpacking in Waterton National Park

• *Tamarack Trail (2-3 days)*. The longest route in Waterton, this 36-km trek follows the Continental Divide, offering everything from windswept ridges to lonely lakes. There are numerous steep ascents and descents. Hikers should make special transportation arrangements because one end of the trail is on the Red Rock Parkway and the other end is on the Akamina Parkway at Rowe Creek. Hikers' transportation available from Waterton Sports and Leisure in the Tamarack Mall (403) 859-2612.

• *Carthew Alderson Trail (1 1/2 days)*. Although strong hikers can do the 20-km route from Cameron Lake to Waterton Townsite in a single-day (see Walk 112), backpackers have the advantage of being able to linger at some of the beautiful lakes, flower-filled meadows and the high pass along the way. The only campsite is at Alderson Lake, a gorgeous place to spend the night.

• *Crypt Lake (1 1/2 days)*. Backpackers who stay at Crypt Lake campground, 7.8 km from the start of the trail at Crypt Landing, have an advantage over day hikers. They have time to explore the fascinating country at the lake above and can even make a sidetrip to Vimy Ridge. The ascent from Waterton Lake is extremely hard slogging with a pack, however.

Boating and Lake Canoeing

Banff National Park: Moraine Lake and Lake Louise are especially splendid from the water, a good way to escape the camera-clicking crowds on the shore. While Lake Minnewanka is beautiful, it can be dangerous because huge waves and high winds build up suddenly. Two Jack Lake just south of Minnewanka is safer.

Canoeists, indeed all boaters, should be especially careful on mountain lakes. The water is usually extremely cold, perhaps only a few degrees above freezing. A capsize can be serious since the unprotected body can't maintain strength for long in water that cold.

In Banff, boats and canoes can be rented at the boathouse docks at Bow Ave., and Wolf St. You can take a boat up into the Vermilion Lakes, probably the best way to observe the abundance of wildlife around the shores. It's not uncommon to come across moose feeding in the shallows.

Boats are also available for rent at Lake Minnewanka, and Two Jack Lake, Moraine Lake and Lake Louise. Life jackets are required at all times.

Jasper National Park: A peaceful paddle on one of Jasper's glacial lakes may be as near to tranquility as is possible.

Rowboats and canoes, including electric motors, are allowed on most ponds and lakes in Jasper National Park. Power boats are permitted only at Medicine and Pyramid Lakes.

There are fine family outings to be had canoeing or boating at Patricia or Pyramid Lake, northwest of Jasper townsite. Lakes Edith, Annette and Beauvert by Jasper Park Lodge also offer tame, scenic paddling. The most magnificent aquatic outing may be at Maligne Lake, largest in the Rockies. Maligne is subject to high winds and waves, however, and the water is extremely cold, even in late summer.

Pyramid Lake

If it floats, you can probably rent it at Pyramid Lake, 7 km (4 miles) from Jasper townsite. Canoes, those silly aqua bikes, kayaks, sailboards, motor boats, fishing tackle, licenses, bait and water-skiing equipment are available from Pyramid Lake Boat Rental. For reservations, call (403) 852-3536.

Lake Beauvert, where Jasper Park Lodge is situated, has boats available from Sandy's in front of the lodge. You can also rent boats at Lake Annette and Lake Edith, the warmest lakes in the park, as well as rowboats on many of the hike-in fishing lakes at lower elevations. Obtain keys beforehand in the townsite from On-Line Sports, 852-3630; Currie's, 618 Connaught Ave., 852-5650; or Jasper Sports Centre, 622 Connaught, 852-3760.

Waterton National Park: Rowboats and canoes can be rented at the Waterton townsite marina. Call Chinook Rentals at (403) 859-2278. Waterton Lake is the deepest in the Canadian Rockies and one of the most beautiful. But the water remains ice-cold, even in late summer, and sudden winds can change the surface from dead calm to high waves in a few minutes. Consequently, those in small boats without motors should probably confine their outings to Emerald Bay and the townsite area. If you must cross the lake in a small boat, it's best to do so at the narrow point near the townsite. Stick to the shoreline thereafter.

A better place for small boats is smaller Cameron Lake at the end of the Akamina Parkway, where rentals are available.

Commercial Canoeing. Adventures range from half-day trips to week-long outings on rivers and lakes in the Rocky Mountains and foothills. Contact: Tomahawk Canoe Trips, 11035-64 Avenue, Edmonton, Alberta. T6H 1T4 (403) 436-9189.

Sailing and Windsurfing

Banff: Lake Minnewanka usually has moderate to strong winds, good-sized waves and cold water, not to mention splendid scenery. It's for the more experienced sailor. Two Jack Lake just below it has smaller waves and is less dangerous when the wind is blowing the sailor away from shore. Sailboarders also use the small Vermilion Lakes just west of Banff.

Calgarians and other residents of south-central Alberta, which is not exactly teeming with lakes, like to head with their sailboards for Lac des Arcs on the Bow River east of the park near the provincial campground. This can be an exceedingly gusty area. There are even signs on the highway warning motorists about the winds.

A mecca for board sailers is Lake Windermere in British Columbia where there are excellent beaches, good facilities and good winds, most of the time.

Be warned that even in mid-summer, the mountain park lakes are notoriously cold. For windsurfing, wear a wet suit, including wet-suit booties or insulated windsurfing shoes.

Jasper: Pyramid Lake north of the townsite is a favorite spot and there are a few sailboards for rent. Winds are often moderate to strong. Patricia

Lake, just below Pyramid, also offers good boating. In the valley, some sailing and sailboarding is done on Lake Annette, one of the warmest lakes around. Annette with its sandy shoreline, has excellent launching places for sailboards.

Waterton Lakes National Park: While windsurfing is a fast-growing sport on Waterton Lake, let the visitor be warned. Windsurfing here is not for beginners. It is, as veteran sailor Steve Kuijt reported in the Mountain Standard Times, for someone ''who wants to crash and burn and go faster than they've ever gone before.''

The winds on the lake, especially in spring, can sometimes whip up to 50 m.p.h., even 75 m.p.h. in gusts. The lake can be almost calm when you set out and you suddenly find yourself overpowered and helpless in a freezing blast from the high peaks.

The second hazard is the cold. Survival is impossible without a good wet suit, including booties. A dry suit is ever better.

Do pick a day when the wind is blowing down the lake towards the townsite. Then you can head back and forth parallel to the shoreline on a good reach and never be too far from shore if you get overpowered.

''Especially in the spring, I get out there and my bloody heart just stops on the first run across,'' Kuijt says.

Camping

At their best, campgrounds bring people closer to the mountains and each other. A campsite is more than a parking stall and picnic table. It must be— people seem to enjoy the mountains as much for the camping as for the scenery: tonic air under the lodgepole pines, campfires, steaks around the picnic table, stars of awesome clarity at night . . .

Of course, you may get noisy neighbors who want to party all night. Trailer owners may want to run their generators for hours. You may get rain, lots of rain, plus mud and creeping cold, even in July and August. You can complain to the wardens who patrol the campsite, though moans about the weather won't get you far. But they understand your need for quiet and will speak to the offending party. For rain, you can rig a large tarp over your picnic table. For cold, you can bundle up and sit closer to the campfire. If you have a heated RV, trailer or sleep-in van, you can just close the door.

First you must find space.

In summer, Tunnel Mountain Campground above Banff townsite, for example, is often filled by noon, the others by 4 p.m. Lake Louise and Kicking Horse campgrounds fill early, as do most others. Overflow sites for late arrivals are just big gravel parking lots.

Space is allocated on a first-come, first-served basis, so come early. No reservations. Some campers spend their first night just outside the park and show up by breakfast time to claim a choice site as the campground begins to clear. Fees, which may change every year, depend on whether you stay at a campground with limited services, such as dry toilets, or one with flush toilets and hot water. You pay more for serviced sites with electrical hook-ups. The highest fees are for sites with electrical, water and sewer hookups.

Everybody who camps a lot has favorite campgrounds and favorite sites in them. Here are some biased selections.

Waterton National Park

• *Waterton Townsite Campground.* In Waterton townsite, 240 sites, 26 acres, flush toilets, showers, complete hookups. A gorgeous location on the edge of the townsite, a grassy open area looking right down Upper Waterton Lake to some of the finest scenery in the Rockies. The townsite is small enough that you can walk everywhere right from your campsite. Exceedingly popular. Visitors often have to spend the night at a large commercial campground just outside the park and line up early in the morning for a place. The effort is worth it. The drawback is that because the campsites are open, there's no privacy and it can be very windy and cold in bad weather. Accessible to the disabled.

Campers who want more privacy and the feel of being in the woods rather than on the edge of a town will prefer Waterton's Crandell Campground, which has 129 wooded sites off Red Rock Parkway. Crandell is also less windy than the townsite campground.

- *Belly River.* 1 km off Chief Mountain Parkway, 24 sites, dry toilets.
- *Crandell Mountain.* 8 km up Red Rock Canyon Road, 129 sites, flush toilets.

Peter Lougheed Provincial Park: All the campgrounds in Peter Lougheed Provincial Park are recommended. They are better designed than in the national parks. There's greater separation between sites, facilities are lavish with heated washrooms and showers everywhere. The only problem is getting in. For reservations at Boulton Creek, Elkwood and Lower Lake campgrounds, call (403) 591-7226. Call far in advance;, the reservation system opens April 1.

Banff National Park

- *Two Jack.* North of Banff townsite on loop right from Lake Minnewanka Road, 381 sites and flush toilets in main campground, 80 sites and flush toilets in Lakeside campground.

For anyone wishing to stay near Banff townsite, these campsites are usually quieter than the Tunnel Mountain metropolis. They are next to Two Jack Lake and handy for boating and hiking in the Minnewanka area.

- *Tunnel Mountain Village 1.* On Tunnel Mountain Drive, 4 km east of Banff, 622 sites and flush toilets.

Not our favorite but not a horror story either. For its size, this campground on the heights above Banff can be surprisingly intimate. Sites are mostly well-spaced on the loops. Try for sites on the outside of loops. The area is well-treed with good facilities, including showers and fine interpretive programs. You can walk to the Hoodoos Viewpoint (Walk 4) or take Walk 3 into Banff, although that's a considerable stroll. This campground tends to become rowdier than some of the less-accessible ones because it's so close to the townsite—and to Calgary. People who are more interested in partying than in mountains tend to end up there.

- *Castle Mountain-Protection Mountain.* Castle Mountain Campground, on Highway 1A, 1 km east of Castle Junction, has 44 sites and flush toilets. Protection Mountain on 1A, 11.5 km west of Castle Junction, has 89 sites and flush toilets.

These small, rather primitive campgrounds in the pines along the Bow Valley Parkway are low-key and usually provide a better outdoor experience than the big, noisy, sometimes unattractive one at hectic Lake Louise. You can often find space there when the big campgrounds are full.

- *Waterfowl Lake.* At km 58 on the Icefields Parkway north of Trans-Canada, 80 sites and flush toilets. Accessible to the disabled.

A medium-sized campground with well-separated sites and facilities, plus a fantastic location right at the end of the beautiful lake where the Mistaya River flows in. The lakeshore is a wonderful place to stroll or sit in the evening. The Chephren and Cirque Lake trails lead from the campground (Walks 65 and 66).

• *Tunnel Mountain Tent Trailer.* Tunnel Mountain Drive, 2.5 km east of Banff with 246 sites, flush toilets, showers.

• *Tunnel Mountain Trailer Camp.* Tunnel Mountain Drive, 4 km east of Banff with 322 sites with sewer, water and electrical connections.

• *Johnston Canyon.* Hwy 1A, 26 km east of Banff with 140 sites, flush toilets.

• *Lake Louise.* Just south of Lake Louise Village, off Trans-Canada with 221 sites, 163 trailer sites, flush toilets.

• *Mosquito Creek.* Km 24, Icefields Parkway north of Trans-Canada with 32 sites, dry toilets. Accessible to the disabled.

• *Rampart Creek.* Km 88, Icefields Parkway north of Trans-Canada with 50 sites, flush and dry toilets. Accessible to the disabled.

• *Cirrus Mountain.* Km 102, Icefields Parkway north of Trans-Canada with 16 sites, dry toilets. Accessible to the disabled.

Kootenay National Park

• *McLeod Meadows.* Situated 26 km north of Radium Hot springs, 100 sites, flush toilets.

Not a beautiful campground, situated in a flat wooded area. However, the sites are exceptionally private and this is one of the best areas in the parks for observing big game such as moose, elk and deer. It doesn't fill up as fast as most of the Banff campgrounds.

• *Redstreak.* 1.6 km southeast of Radium Hot Springs with 241 sites, flush toilets, showers.

• *Marble Canyon.* 86 km north of Radium Hot Springs with 60 sites, flush toilets.

Yoho National Park

• *Chancellor Peak.* Situated 23.8 km west of Field, 64 sites, dry toilets.

This slightly primitive campground is in a gorgeous setting next to the Kicking Horse River. But it's not the place for light sleepers. The main CPR trans-continental route runs right behind the campground and heavy freights roar through at all hours of the night, shaking the ground. Try for a site close to the river and as far away from the tracks as possible.

• *Kicking Horse.* Situated 5 km (3 miles) east of Field, 92 sites, flush toilets, showers.

The main Yoho campground and the busiest. Get there early. It has excellent facilities and a scenic location under Mt. Stephen. Try for sites close to the river.

• *Lake O'Hara.* Situated on km 11, Lake O'Hara fire road (no private vehicle access), 30 walk-in sites, dry toilets.

Reservations are necessary (from Park office in Field) and get you a seat on the bus going several times a day up the fire road which is closed to private vehicles. The campsite is the gateway to a superb hiking area with a network of trails around high lakes.

• *Hoodoo Creek*. Trans-Canada Highway, 23 km west of Field with 106 sites, flush toilets.

• *Takakkaw Falls*. Km 16, Yoho Valley Road off Trans-Canada with 35 walk-in sites, dry toilets.

Jasper National Park

• *Wilcox Creek*. Located 111 km south of Jasper townsite on the Icefields Parkway with 46 sites and dry toilets.

While not quite as scenic as Columbia Icefield Campground only 1 km down the highway, this is the only campground at the Icefields for camper vehicles, trailers, sleep-in vans or RVs. The campground is set on the side of a steep hill and just about every site has a good view looking out over impressive Mt. Athabasca. Sites are nicely separated by this terrace system. Note, however, that this campground is almost as high as Sunwapta Pass, nearly at treeline. The weather can be very cold here. Even in summer, campers have reported finding ice crystals in their dinner.

• *Columbia Icefield*. Situated 109 km south of Jasper townsite with 22 tent sites and dry toilets.

In its unrenovated incarnation, it was small, funky, steep, peopled only with tent campers, often climbers planning an ascent of Mt. Athabasca across the highway or one of the other nearby peaks. Views from the small camp-sites, set on a steep slope, are unsurpassed in any campground and the whole place usually had a low-key, friendly feel. It can be very cold, even in summer.

• *Wabasso*. Situated on Highway 93A, 20 km south of Jasper with 238 sites and flush toilets.

Far enough removed from the Jasper townsite area to escape some of the crowds, Wabasso is beautifully situated along the shore of the fast-moving Athabasca. Try for one of the sites closest to the river. It's handy to Athabasca Falls, Angel Glacier and fishing at Wabasso or Moab lakes.

• *Wapiti*. On the Icefields Parkway, 5 km south of Jasper townsite, 340 sites and flush toilets, showers, power-water hookups.

Smaller than the massive Whistler's Campground across the highway, Wapiti has a more relaxed atmosphere, especially if you can get one of the sites close to the Athabasca River, a good place for a stroll in the evening. See Along the Athabasca (3), Walk 90.

• *Jonas Creek*. Icefields Parkway, 77 km south of Jasper townsite with 13 regular sites, 12 walk-in tent sites, dry toilets.

• *Honeymoon Lake*. Icefields Parkway, 51 km south of Jasper with 30 sites, dry toilets.

• *Mount Kerkeslin*. Icefields Parkway, 36 km south of Jasper townsite with 42 sites, dry toilets.

• *Whistlers*. Icefields Parkway, 3 km south of Jasper townsite with 758 sites, flush toilets, complete hookups.

• *Snaring River*. Hwy 16, 11 km east of Jasper townsite with 50 sites, 10 walk-in tent sites.

• *Pocahontas*. Miette Road, 2 km off Hwy 16, 41 km east of Jasper townsite with 140 sites, flush toilets.

Winter Camping: Winter camping is for the hardy and well-equipped only, although it can be especially satisfying to beat the elements. Camping out in winter teaches survival skills and makes you a complete camper, someone who has really experienced the mountains in all seasons. Backcountry camping might be part of an extended ski tour. Consult the warden service about avalanche hazard and get a permit.

Most winter camping is done by the highway in the few campgrounds that remain open and plowed. Life is easier, of course, in a heated camper. Tunnel Mountain Campground offers electrical hookups for $7.75 or $5.75 for a site without electricity. There are heated washrooms and showers.

Free winter camping is available at the Lake Louise overflow, 5 km east of Lake Louise Village on the Trans-Canada and at Mosquito Creek Campground, 24 km north of Lake Louise on the Icefields Parkway. These areas are unserviced. All you get are (unheated) dry toilets.

In Jasper National Park, winter camping is provided at Wapiti Campground where there are 40 sites with electricity for $7.25. Unserviced sites are $5.25. Washrooms are heated and have showers and hot water, especially welcome after a day's skiing.

Snow camping in the backcountry is definitely not for everyone. Unless the night is exceptionally warm, you'll probably have to climb into bed early and spend more hours in the sack than you did when you were a child. It gets dark early too and there's only so much reading you can do with gloved fingers by the dim light of a candle lantern. Yet those who stay outdoors in the mountains after the others have gone home, do learn to embrace winter — and they certainly avoid the crowds. Cross-country skiing with a heavy pack isn't easy. Yet many of the best routes can only be done with an overnight stopover in the mountains.

There are joys as well as hardships. After a hearty dinner, you can warm yourself by the campfire and perhaps listen to the distant howl of coyotes at sunset. You climb into your sleeping bag, pull the covers close around your chin — and feel the delicious warmth creep up around you.

Getting out of your warm bed in the morning into subzero temperatures requires more mental stamina, although you can soften the transition by having breakfast in bed. The meal can be cooked on a small portable stove in the doorway of your tent.

All you need is a little experience in summer tent camping. It's a good idea to plan your first snow camp for late fall or early spring when the weather isn't too cold. You'll need a tent, closed-cell foam mattress, a good quality winter-weight sleeping bag that can be pulled shut around the neck to keep warmth in (or two summer bags that fit into each other.)

Take a dry change of clothes, including lots of layers so you can adjust for temperature changes, polypropylene underwear which wicks moisture away from the body, warm mitts, toque and a good down or synthetic parka. A great luxury are insulated booties which keep the feet feeling cozy when you finally stop to relax after making camp and change out of your boots.

Canoeing the Easy Rivers

Even hikers get the blues. They begin to have non-walking fantasies which go something like this: You're sitting on a padded seat in a canoe on a warm sunny day, drifting down the Bow or Athabasca river. You're watching the clouds and the mountains, letting the river do most of the work, sipping a cold beer, maybe even dropping a fishing line in a moment of high energy.

This doesn't have to be fantasy. Canoes can be rented. For smaller lakes and some rivers, visitors don't need whitewater or fancy canoeing skills, just the ability to steer. Canoeists with some experience—especially the ability to steer without changing sides with the paddle—could probably handle the easier trips on the Bow or Athabasca Rivers. They should, nonetheless wear life jackets and be reasonably strong swimmers.

The major obstacle may be road transportation. If your party has two vehicles, leave one at your destination and with the other take your canoes to the starting point. Reverse the procedure at the other end.

Otherwise, you might persuade some non-canoeing friend to drop you off and pick you up. Some people hitchhike back to the start, with the canoe hidden in the woods and chained to a tree for good measure. Another method is to leave a bicycle or two at the finishing point, similarly secured, and cycle back. If canoeing from Lake Louise to Banff, take a bus or train back to pick up your car (leaving the canoe behind). The same from Hinton to Jasper or Canmore to Banff. The transportation hassle is only a small obstacle to one of the greatest pleasures in the parks.

Major Canoe Routes: Banff National Park

• *Bow River-Lake Louise to Castle Mountain Junction. (One short day—27 km, 17 miles.)* Don't try to start above Lake Louise townsite. The river can be difficult near the town and is impossible higher up. There is a small set of rapids right beside the Trans-Canada Bridge, just south of Lake Louise. The canoeist can launch just below them. Beyond, there are small waves but no real rapids until after the Castle Mountain junction bridge. A gorgeous trip with sand bars, a winding, glacial-fed river of incredible blue, the mountains and the dry Montane forest.

The river is fast-moving and changes direction frequently. The canoeist must avoid sand and gravel bars, the occasional rock and sweepers (logs jutting into the water). So this is not a route for beginners.

• *Castle Mountain Junction to Trans-Canada Bridge. (One day, 32 km, 20 miles.)* This stretch of the Bow is fascinating with the craggy peaks of the

Sawback Range rising on the left. The one difficulty is the Redearth Rapids, 11 km below the bridge. In June, July and perhaps early August most years, the river is high enough to cover the boulders. But earlier in the spring and later in the summer, many canoeists will want to portage along the right bank, crossing the creek on the Trans-Canada.

Below the rapids, the river starts to slow, becoming braided and ox-bowed. This is an excellent place to see big game such as moose which come to feed in the shallows. The take-out point is on the right side of the river at the picnic grounds just before the double Trans-Canada Bridge that crosses the Bow.

• *Trans-Canada Bridge to Banff Boat House. (Half-day—11 km, 6.8 miles.)* Start at the picnic area just beyond the double Trans-Canada Highway bridges over the Bow, about 7 km (by car) west of Banff. This is a fine trip for inexperienced canoeists because there are no rapids, or fast-moving water. The river has turned into lazy ox-bows and multiple channels. It's more like a long, thin lake than a river. That, however, does mean you have to paddle more to get anywhere. Fortunately, the route is short.

This is an excellent place to observe beaver, waterfowl and other birds, even large game such as moose which frequently come to feed in the marshy shallows. The views ahead to the impressive writing-desk slope of Mt. Rundle and left to the pointed peaks of the Sawback Range are impressive.

The river enters Banff townsite and canoeists take out at the boat house on the left bank where there is a boat rental concession. Heed warning signs. On no account should canoeists go further. Once past the Bow Bridge, the placid river turns to rapids and could sweep a canoeist over the deadly Bow Falls.

• *Banff to Canmore. (One day-21 kilometres.)* Travelling on the Bow River east of Canmore involves portages, a couple of potentially treacherous lakes, a waterfall and four dams. But the short jaunt from Banff to Canmore has none of the difficulties. Although it isn't for the beginner canoeist, it is a lovely, fast-moving trip with small waves and multiple channels but no rapids.

The start is below Bow Falls where there's a parking lot at the falls view-point near the junction with the Spray River beneath Banff Springs Hotel. The river flows swiftly past the golf course with Tunnel Mountain and the hoodoos on the left and the great cliffs of Rundle sweeping up on the right. The Cascade River from Lake Minnewanka enters left and the Bow begins to divide into multiple channels, still fast-moving. Watch for sweepers (logs jutting out into the river) when you take some of the narrower channels.

The river leaves the national park and canoeists are advised to take out at the first bridge leading into Canmore.

Jasper National Park

• *Miette River to Old Fort Point. (Two hours—5 km, 3.1 miles.)* This is a calm, easy stretch along a relatively narrow but deep river winding through lodgepole forest in beautiful country just west of Jasper, an excellent place to see moose and elk, especially in the evening.

Start at the Yellowhead Highway Bridge over the Miette River, just west of Jasper townsite. The Miette winds through level forest, passes under the Icefields Parkway Bridge and eventually under the 93A Bridge, just before entering the broad, faster-moving Athabasca. This is an alternate take-out point. The Athabasca carries you swiftly down to the old bridge at Old Fort Point where there's a convenient, sandy take-out on the right, just past the bridge.

• *Athabasca River. Old Fort Point to Jasper Lake. (One day—25 km, 15.5 miles.)* This is an ideal mountain river trip. While the river is fast-moving, there are no rapids or treacherous areas. The Athabasca flows through a historic valley, once the route of explorers like David Thompson who were followed by the fur traders. Away from the highway, it seems unchanged from those early days. The mountains on both sides of the valley are steep and spectacular. Near the end are sand dunes. On a sunny day, there's no better place to be.

Start at the Old Fort Point Bridge at Jasper. From there, the river flows gently past numerous islands. Take the channels that appear to have the most water. The river passes Maligne Road Bridge and leads out past interesting rock formations. At km 15, canoeists can stop and climb the right bank through a few trees to an open field where John Moberley's old cabin is situated. He was the son of Henry Moberley, factor at Jasper House until 1861.

The river passes the junction with the fast-moving Snaring River and goes under Highway 16. This is an alternative pull-out point.

The gray mountain on the right is Morro, a favorite practice spot for climbers. The river slows and widens into Jasper Lake and the paddler is in for some interesting going. The lake is so clogged with sandbars that only a couple of inches of water may sometimes be left under the keel. While the maps show deeper channels, you probably won't be able to follow one for long. You may even have to get out in places and pull the canoe along through the shallows. While the water is extremely cold, your feet do get used to it and the bottom is pleasantly sandy. This small area along the lake is in the rain shadow of nearby mountains and has a semi-arid climate.

From this point, paddlers could keep to the right close to the highway for the most direct route to a take-out point. Those with more time will find it interesting to keep left for a while and explore the sand dunes which begin to appear on the north bank. From there, you'll have to cut straight across the lake to the pullout point.

Take out along the right bank on Jasper Lake where the highway runs close to the road. Don't go too far down the lake or you'll have to portage to get back to the highway. And beyond the lake, there's only one, easy-to-miss access point close to the highway. After that, it's a long, overnight trip to the bridge near Hinton, a fine trip for those prepared to camp out, a nightmare for those who aren't. Note that camping out along any river requires a park permit and overnighters will be asked to stay in designated areas.

Cycling in the Rockies

The roads and highways of the Canadian Rockies provide some of the most spectacular cycling in the world. Cyclists come from all over Canada and the U.S., even from Europe, to spend a few days on the Icefields Parkway between Jasper and Banff. This route was rated by Outside magazine recently as "one of the 10 best in North America."

Walking is the best way to appreciate the backcountry and cycling the best way to appreciate the parkway. Something new appears every few kilometres: turquoise-colored lakes, castellated mountains and snow-capped summits, glacial valleys, waterfalls, wildlife and tumbling rivers. More than 100 glaciers are visible from the highway and cyclists are protected from traffic, more or less, by the wide, paved shoulder. The cyclist sees and feels what the motorist misses.

Seventeen campgrounds are located along the route between Banff and Jasper. Eight hostels are coveniently spaced for cyclists. The only sure place to get groceries between Lake Louise and Jasper is at the Saskatchewan River Crossing. Their grocery section is small.

Cyclists can bring their bicycles to Banff or Jasper by train, or if boxed, by bus. The Brewster buses which operate every day between Jasper and Banff will take boxed bicycles.

Cyclists tend to average 3 1/2 to 4 1/2 days to travel the 290 km between Jasper and Banff, although it could easily be stretched to a week or more with sidetrips and stops for day hikes. Give yourself lots of time, if you possibly can.

The Bow Valley Parkway northwest of Banff, which is quieter and more scenic than the parallel Trans-Canada, makes a fine route for one-or two-day cycles and most of the roads in the Banff area are excellent for short trips.

The Banff-Windermere Highway between Castle Mountain Junction and Radium is another superb cycling road and can be turned into a 314-km loop if cyclists head north from Radium to Golden, then east again on the Trans-Canada (the hardest section of the trip) into Yoho and over the Kicking Horse Pass, where the Spiral Tunnels were dug, to Lake Louise, then south to Castle Mountain.

In Jasper, cyclists can cross the easy Yellowhead Pass to lofty Mt. Robson or go for short jaunts around Lake Annette and up to Pyramid Lake or down to Athabasca Falls on 93A and back on 93.

You can while away pleasant hours cycling to Jasper Park Lodge, Lake Annette and Lake Edith. Cyclists who don't mind a steep climb could consider going up the Pyramid Lake Road for 7 km and finishing up with a swim.

In Banff, bicycles are available for rent at Park 'N Pedal, 229 Wolf St., (762-3161) or Spoke 'N' Edge, 315 Banff Ave. (762-2854). Bicycle touring clubs in both Calgary and Edmonton conduct summer trips along the parkway.

Mopeds are available in Banff from Mountain Moped for $7.50 an hour and $35 a day: Sundance Mall, 215 Banff Avenue, 762-5611.

In Jasper townsite, bicycles may be rented at Freewheel Cycle on Miette

Avenue in the alley across from the Athabasca Hotel (852-5380); at Mountain Air Sports, 622 Connaught (852-3560) and Sandy's Rentals at Jasper Park Lodge.

For further information, including easy-to-follow directions, see *The Canadian Rockies Bicycling Guide* by the same authors, $8.95, Lone Pine Publishing, Edmonton, Alberta. There's a kilometre-by-kilometre description of the Icefields Parkway with all its facilities and attractions. The book details 60 routes in the mountains, the cities, countryside and forgotten small towns. There are maps of the routes, complete mileages, advice and phone numbers for camping, hostels and private accommodation.

Short Cycling Routes—Banff Townsite Area

- *Vermilion Lakes Drive (12 km, 7.5 miles) (See Walk 19)*
- *Banff Golf Course Loop (12 km, 7.5 miles)*
- *Tunnel Mountain Drive Loop (11.8 km, 7.3 miles)*
- *Banff-Lake Minnewanka Loop (19 km, 11 miles)*
- *Cave and Basin to Sundance Canyon (10.4 km, 6.5 miles)*
- *Banff to Johnston Canyon (48 km, 30 miles)*

Short Cycling Routes—Jasper Townsite Area

- *Jasper to Old Fort Point, Lac Beauvert, Lake Annette, Lake Edith (19 km, 12 miles)*

Kananaskis Country

- *Jasper to Pyramid Lake (14 km, 8.6 miles)*
- *Jasper to Maligne Canyon (23.5 km, 15 miles)*
- *Jasper to Athabasca Falls via 93A and 93 (67 km, 41 miles)*

Short Cycling Routes — Kananaskis Country

The cycling is splendid in Kananaskis Country on the eastern slopes of the Rockies, 60 km southeast of Banff. The shoulders on Highway 40 from the Trans-Canada over Highwood Pass are wide. Grades are mostly gentle and the riding surface excellent. Camping and picnic facilities are perhaps more abundant here than anywhere else in the country. Those who make the ascent of Highwood Pass can conquer Canada's highest paved road. Bicycles can be rented at Mount Kidd RV Park on Highway 40 and at Boulton Creek Trading Post in Peter Lougheed Provincial Park.

- *Ribbon Creek to Wedge Pond (19.6 km, 12 miles return) Bicycle path*
- *Kananaskis Visitor Centre to Elkwood (9.4 km, 6 miles return)*
- *Elkwood to Boulton (9.4 km, 6 miles return)*
- *Boulton to Upper Kananaskis Lake (10 km, 6 miles return)*

Short Cycling Routes — Waterton Townsite Area

Waterton National Park contains only short, though interesting, day trips for the cyclist. In Waterton townsite, bicycles may be rented at Pat's Texaco, (403) 859-2266.

For long distance routes from the Waterton area, you have to head into the U.S. and attempt the awesome ascent of Logan Pass on the Going-to-the-Sun Road. But be warned that the road can be dangerous for cyclists. It is narrow with many blind curves. Traffic volume is extremely high.

- *Waterton townsite to Red Rock Canyon (31 km, 19 miles return)*
- *Waterton townsite to Cameron Lake (31 km, 19 miles return)*

Bicycle Touring the Easy Way: Touring groups handle all the details. They provide meals, accommodation and guide service along the route. A support vehicle is available to carry your gear and give you a lift if you're tired.

- *Ride the Rockies Bicycle Touring Ltd. Box 6866, Stn D, Calgary, Alberta. T2P 2E9. (403) 270-9341*
- *Rocky Mountain Cycle Tours. BOX 895T, Banff, Alberta. T0L 0C0. (403) 678-6770*

Mountain Bikes: Many hikers use mountain bikes to cover the dull stretches, especially when their hike begins with a long slog on a fire road before starting to climb. Fireroads become a joy to travel.

The status of the mountain bike remains uncertain in national and provincial parks, however. Many trails are closed to mountain bikes.

General rules everywhere focus on the environmental impact of bicycles — and make sense. These rules include staying on trails and roadways and generally avoiding fragile alpine areas where a wheelprint can become a channel for water, causing erosion.

When horses approach, cyclists on the trail should dismount and move off the path, preferably to the lower side of the trail. Cyclists should maintain good relations with hikers — who could probably have mountain bikes banned from trails if they complain enough. Stop and let hikers go by on narrow trails. Don't pedal up close behind someone without calling out a warning. ("Hello" is considered better form than "Track!")

When possible, check trail conditions and potential hazards at park offices. They may be able to tell you which trails are muddy and therefore less suitable for cycling and which trails might have a bear nearby.

Cross-Country Skiing

Summer isn't necessarily the best time to travel some of the trails in the mountain parks. In winter, many routes make superb cross-country skiing trails. Under the right conditions, you can cover more ground with less effort on skis. No mosquitoes, no boggy areas; even wooded trails that might seem tedious in summer take on fresh beauty and interest. You haven't totally experienced the mountains until you've skied them in winter or, better still, in early spring.

Be aware, however, that some safe and easy summer trails can be deadly in winter because of avalanche hazard. Untrained skiers without special equipment should try to keep clear of potential avalanche slopes. Check with park wardens or information centre personnel before venturing onto any trail or area not specifically designated for cross-country skiing by the parks. And check every time. A trail that is safe one week can be deadly the next because of snow build-up. In Banff, check trail conditions at the information centre or by phoning (403) 762-4256. The daily avalanche hazard bulletin is relayed on cable television in the hotels and motels. The Warden Office, situated between the townsite and the highway interchange, is open 24 hours a day. Phone (403) 762-4506. In Lake Louise, the Warden Office is (403) 522-3866.

In Jasper, check trail conditions at the Information Centre, (403) 852-6176, or the Warden Office (852-6156). The daily avalanche hazard bulletin is available there and is posted at the Maligne Lake trailhead.

Even some of the designated cross-country trails may pass beneath potential avalanche slopes. Any fairly steep open slope is suspect. Do not linger in these exposed areas.

It's also wise to carry a plastic or aluminum ski tip in case you break the end of one of your skis, a windproof jacket or down parka in a stuff bag, matches, map, compass, suncream, sunglasses and an emergency space blanket. For longer day outings, consider adding a small first aid kit, a change of socks, high energy food, drinks, toilet paper, jackknife with screwdriver blade and, of course, waxes, cork and scraper.

For advanced touring with a party in avalanche country, you'd need an avalanche transceiver, a shovel for rescue and an avalanche probe. (So you'll probably want to stay out of avalanche country.)

Here are a few fairly short, not-too-difficult but enjoyable cross-country trails that, Parks Canada suggests, are usually safe from avalanches, except as noted. These trails are signed by Parks and will usually have set tracks, although drifting and fresh snowfall can obscure any trail.

Banff National Park—*NOVICE TRAILS*

• *Spray River Loop (2.2 km, 1.3 miles). Walk 9.* In Banff townsite, start from Bow Falls parking lot, cross the golf course close to the river and ski up the Spray River, crossing on the first bridge and returning on the fire road on the other side. (Marked as No. 2, then No. 1 on the return.)

• *Banff Springs Golf Course (various lengths).* In Banff townsite, start at Bow Falls parking lot and cross Spray River Bridge, following a network of trails and loops around the edge of gently rolling fairways. (Marked as No. 4, 5, 6 and 7.)

• *Cave and Basin River Trail (1.5 km, 1 mile). Walk 20.* In Banff townsite, start at Cave and Basin parking lot and ski north towards river, looping along Bow and joining Sundance Canyon Road. (Marked as No. 2.)

• *Johnson Lake Loop (8.2 km, 5 miles). Walk 23.* Starts from dead-end road leading off from Lake Minnewanka Road-Two Jack Lake Road north of Banff townsite. Marked as No. 1 with Intermediate portion beyond lake. (Take shortcut on No. 2 to avoid longer, steeper stretch.)

• *Cascade Fire Road (13 km, 8 miles return).* Starts at Upper Bankhead picnic area on Lake Minnewanka Road north of Banff townsite. (Marked as No. 1.)

• *Lake Louise Shoreline (6 km, 3.7 miles return).* From Chateau Lake Louise, follow signs right for Trail No. 4 in trees above lake. Upper route better than summer lakeshore trail. Do not ski on lake. Avalanche area begins beyond end of lake.

• *Moraine Lake Road (16 km, 10 miles return).* Drive 1.1 km (0.6 miles) up the hill on 1A from Lake Louise Village and park at the Fairview picnic area. Ski onto unplowed Moraine Lake Road. (Marked as No. 2.) Avalanche area starts at end of signed trail.

• *Fairview Loop (7.5 km, 4.6 miles).* Start at Chateau Lake Louise parking lot furthest from hotel and follow Trail No. 1 to Moraine Lake Road. Turn left on road (No. 2). Near gate, take Tramline Trail (No. 3) left back to Lake Louise.

• *Pipestone Loops (various lengths).* From the parking area off the Trans-Canada Highway opposite west entrance to Lake Louise Village, take loop No. 1 (12.6 km, 7.8 miles) or shorten the trip by returning on loops 2, 3 and 4.

INTERMEDIATE TRAILS

- *Spray River Loop (10.8 km, 6.7 miles).* In Banff townsite, start from Bow Falls Parking lot and from half-way down the first fairway, take Trail No. 1, ski up Spray River to footbridge. Return on other side on Spray River fire road, crossing two avalanche zones and ending at Banff Springs Hotel.

- *Forty-Mile Creek Loop (9 km 5.5 miles).* See Walk 27 to Cascade Amphitheatre. From Norquay ski road north of Banff townsite, the trail starts from the far end of Parking Lot No. 3. The trail, marked No. 1, passes the Wishbone T-bar and continues on a fire road. Take the right fork (Elk Lake) at km 1.1 (avalanche zone) and loop around by Forty Mile Creek to return again to this point.

Jasper National Park: In Jasper, the best cross-country ski area is at Maligne Lake at the end of the Maligne Lake Road, 48 km southeast of the townsite. There is a variety of trails and terrain. In spring, the snow stays in good condition longer than at the lower townsite area. The chalet at the lake is closed in winter. In winter, there are no services at the lake.

The townsite area is the most convenient for cross-country skiing and has a wide and safe network of trails, both official and unofficial, on the wooded, lake-filled bench above Jasper.

MALIGNE LAKE—NOVICE TRAILS

- *Maligne Lakeside Loop (3.2 km, 1.9 miles).* Walk 100. Start from Maligne Lake Chalet and ski past the boathouse on the left shoreline to a small bay, then loop back through the woods. (Marked as No. 1.)

- *Moose Lake Trail (4.4 km, 2.7 miles).* From the chalet, ski over the Maligne River Bridge to the Bald Hills fire road above the last parking lot. The trail soon branches left from the fire road, then heads down to the lake and loops back along the shore. (Marked as No. 2 Trail. No. 3 is an additional loop that continues from No. 2 and adds 3 km to the total distance.)

INTERMEDIATE TRAILS

- *Lorraine Lake Trail (7.3 km, 4.5 mile loop).* From the chalet ski across the bridge to the Bald Hills fire road above the last parking lot. Climb the road until the Lorraine Lake trail branches right, descends slightly and passes the lake. Turn right on the Skyline Trail which has some interesting, curved descents.

ADVANCED TRAILS

- *Evelyn Creek Trail (13 km, 8 mile loop).* From the chalet ski across the bridge and up the Bald Hills fire road. About two-thirds of the way to the top, the Evelyn Creek trail branches right and continues around the side of the mountain, leading to a steep descent that should be walked by inexperienced skiers. Turn right at the bottom onto the Skyline Trail which has some interesting, intermediate-class curved hills on more gradual descent back to the lake.

JASPER TOWNSITE AREA—NOVICE TRAILS

- *Whistler's Campground Loop (4.5 km, 2.7 miles).* Drive 3.2 km south of Jasper and turn right on the Whistler Sky Tram Road, then left to the plowed campground parking area. The trail follows the campground perimeter road loop and is level and easily followed.

INTERMEDIATE TRAILS

- *Pyramid Bench Trails (various lengths).* Start at the first parking lot on the left up the Pyramid Lake Road from Jasper Townsite (Walk 93). Cross the road and find the wide path through the trees leading to the edge of the bench and up to Pyramid Lake. Portions of this trail are not officially maintained but are still easy to follow.
- *Mina-Riley Loop (6.7 km, 4.1 miles).* Start at the first parking lot on the left up Pyramid Lake Road from Jasper Townsite. The trail loops past Mina and Riley lakes with one long descent to the lakes.

ADVANCED

- *Patricia Lake Circle (5.9 km, 3.6 miles).* See Walk 95. Start from the riding stable parking lot up Pyramid Lake Road from Jasper townsite. The trail crosses the road and loops, sometimes steeply, through varied terrain south of Patricia Lake.

Peter Lougheed Provincial Park: The prepared trails in Peter Lougheed Provincial Park are some of the best in the Canadian Rockies. The park has more than 90 km of trails, most of them rated "easy" or "intermediate." Pocaterra Hut and the Park Visitor Centre are open seven days a week as ski information and warm up centres.

North of the park on Highway 40, the Ribbon Creek Recreational area has 47 km of trails. These trails are at a lower elevation and are more subject to Chinook melting than those in the provincial park.

NOVICE TRAILS

- *Pocaterra Trail (10 km, 6.2 miles).* One of the most popular trails in the park, it rises gradually from Pocaterra Ski Hut and links with nine other trails for a variety of loops.
- *Lodgepole Trail (4.7 km, 2.9 miles).* A pleasant, forested route between Elkwood parking area and Pocaterra Ski Hut without much change in elevation. One short, steep section (which may be walked) near Pocaterra.

INTERMEDIATE TRAILS

- *Elk Pass Trail (7 km, 4.3 miles one way).* From the Elk Pass parking lot, climb gradually on an old fire road to the Alberta-B.C. border. Great views and an opportunity to link up with several other trails for a grand loop.
- *Moraine and Fox Creek Trails (3.8 km, 2.3 miles).* From Boulton ski parking, these two trails offer good views of the Kananaskis Valley and a narrow, winding route along a creek. Makes a good loop combined with Boulton Creek Trail.

Waterton National Park: Few of Waterton's trails are groomed for cross-country skiing. Many of the summer routes such as Cameron Lake, Crandell Lake and the Lakeshore Trail are suitable, however, depending on snow and avalanche conditions. For these routes it is important to check in advance with park staff. The winter information number is (403) 859-2445.

GROOMED TRAILS

- *Snowshoe Trail (8.6 km, 5.3 miles).* Rating—moderate. From the end of the Red Rock Road (which may occasionally be closed because of drifting snow), it follows a fire road through woods and open meadows. Travel beyond Goat Lake is not recommended because of avalanche hazards.
- *Sofa Trail (3.6 km, 2.2 miles).* Rating—Easy. From the Chief Mountain Highway, 6 km from the park entrance, the trail follows old fire roads through forest and meadow under Sofa Mountain. A spur trail at the end can turn this into a 9.1 km route with a moderate rating.
- *River Loop Trail (5.6 km, 3.4 mile loop).* Rating—Easy. From Belly River group campground, 18 km from the park entrance, the trail follows old wagon roads near the Belly River. A cutoff enables skiers to head back after just a 2 km loop if they wish.
- *Belly Loop Trail (5.5 km, 3.4 miles).* Rating—Moderate. The trail

starts close to the River Loop route and parallels the Chief Mountain Highway, passing a couple of viewpoints before returning on a closed-off section of the highway.

Downhill Skiing

Nakiska: Situated on Mt. Allan in Kananaskis Country, Nakiska is Alberta's newest mountain resort and the site of the '88 Olympic Winter Games. The site has been plagued by controversy and lack of snow but there's no doubt that the facilities and the runs are excellent. Vertical rise—918 metres, 1 quad chair, 1 triple chair, 1 double chair. More than two-thirds of the runs on Mt. Allan are intermediate; facilities include a state-of-the art quad chair. Free guided tours are available twice daily in winter. Two day lodges are provided, with lounge and dining services. Annual snowfall 200-250 cm; snowmaking on majority of runs. Call (403) 591-7777 for more information. Snowphone: (403) 270-8680.

Fortress Mountain: Situated up the valley from Nakista, Fortress has 1 triple chair, 2 double chairs and 3 T-bars. While not as lavishly designed as some, it is usually less crowded than other ski areas in the Rockies and offers lower-priced lift tickets. Vertical rise—340 metres. Call 591-7108 for more information. Snowphone: 245-4909.

Mt. Norquay: This area just opposite Banff townsite is noted for its steep, challenging mogul runs, although there is a good lower-angle slope for novices. Vertical rise—396 metres, 2 double chairs, 2 T-bars, 1 platter, 1 rope tow. For more information, call (403) 762-4421. Snowphone: (403) 253-3383.

Sunshine Village: It usually has the longest ski season in Canada from November until the May long weekend, plus the best snow conditions around, 750-1,000 cm a year. Superb spring skiing plus on-hill accommodation. Vertical rise—1,070 metres, six passenger gondola, 1 triple chair, five double chairs, 3 T bars, 2 rope tows. The Sunshine turnoff is 16 km west of Banff townsite. For more information, phone (403) 762-6500. Snowphone: (403) 246-2800. Hotel reservations: 1-800-372-9583.

Lake Louise: Here is the largest ski area in Canada with more than 40 runs and over 2,832 hectares of open bowl and off-track skiing. The runs are long and exciting, although there's an easy way down from each lift. You can ski any one of three individual faces and you'd have to stay a week to ski every run. Views across the Bow Valley to the peaks of the Continental Divide are outstanding. Vertical rise—991 metres, 2 triple chairs, 4 double chairs, 1 T bar, 1 platter, 1 cable tow. Snowphone: (403) 244-6665. Ski packages: 1-800-332-8307.

Marmot Basin: This friendly ski area southwest of Jasper townsite offers outstanding scenery and a good mixture of tree-lined runs and alpine bowl skiing. Vertical rise—720 metres, 1 triple chair, 3 double chairs, 3 T bars. Phone (403) 852-3816. Snowphone: (403) 488-5909.

Fishing

Fishermen who hike or mountain walkers who fish rble advantage. So many fishermen never venture far
fish lakes or streams that lack vehicle access. Obvio
hour or two walking a steep trail to reach a backcou.
likely to be over-fished as one beside the road.

The legend of the almost undiscovered backcountr   ..uc—to a
point. One backcountry disadvantage is that many high-country lakes and
rivers are clouded with glacial silt, not optimum conditions for fish or fishermen. Another problem is that since the water temperature in the high altitude lakes tends to be extremely low, only a few degrees above freezing
in many cases, neither the fish nor the aquatic plants grow fast. And few
of the remote lakes are stocked while there's a regular stocking program
for many of the more accessible lakes.

Some of the high lakes are blanketed most of the year under thick ice
covered by heavy snow. This blocks sunlight and kills aquatic plants. Fish
may die for lack of oxygen. Because of this winter kill, fishing on any particular lake may vary considerably from year to year. Fishermen should
inquire at tackle stores in Banff and Jasper to discover what the best lakes
and streams seem to be at that moment and what's bringing them in.

Jasper, by the way, holds the Alberta record for rainbow trout, a trophy
of more than 9 kg taken from Maligne Lake.

A national parks fishing permit ($4) is required and is available at the parks
information centres and sporting goods stores.

The catch and possession limit is five each for pike, grayling and various
trout and two for salmon. It's 10 for whitefish, except in Jasper where the
limit is only 5. The overall limit is 10, of which five must be other than trout.
No one is allowed to have in their possession more than 10 game fish. The
use of live fish eggs, minnows and such is prohibited.

These regulations even caught up with the Duke of Connaught, who early
this century was advised by a park warden at Consolation Lake of the 15-fish
daily limit, since reduced to 10. "Per angler, per day, perdition," the Duke
sputtered. "My good man, I ask you what is the sense of me being governor of this widespread, far-flung, sea-to-sea dominion if I cannot catch all
the fish I have a mind to?" The warden was unmoved.

Jasper National Park: Fishing is open year-round on some of the major,
lower valley rivers in Jasper: Athabasca, Sunwapta, Maligne (below Maligne
Canyon), Snaring and Miette, plus Talbot Lake.

For most of the lakes, plus Ranger Creek and Rocky River, the season
is Victoria Day to Labor Day: Annette, Beaver, Buck, Christine, Lower
Colefair, Dragon, High Lakes, Long, Lorraine, Marjorie, Mile 9 (Yellowhead
East), Mile 16 1/2 (Icefields Parkway), Moab, Mona, No Name, (Icefields
Parkway-Km 45), Osprey, Princess, Pyramid, Skyline, First Trefoil, Virl,
Maligne and the Fifth (Upper) lake in the Valley of the Five Lakes.

The season doesn't open until Aug. 1 for the beautiful Medicine River

...Maligne Lake and Medicine Lake.

...remainder of the lakes and rivers, with the exception of specific closed ...ers, are open July 1 to Oct. 31.

Closed waters include Cabin Lake and streams emptying into it, all streams flowing into Amethyst Lake, as well as Amethyst Lake close to its outlet, Astoria River between Amethyst lake and a point 400 metres downstream, and the outlet stream from Moab Lake to its junction with the Whirlpool River, including the Moab Lake itself close to the outlet.

Where, among all these lakes and streams, should a fisherman head?

There's not much about fishing in Jasper National Park that the knowledgeable folks at Currie's Tackle, 618 Connaught Dr. (852-5650), Jasper Sports Centre, 622 Connaught Dr. (852-3660) or Online Tackle (852-3630) can't tell you.

They can provide fishing guides, electric motors, rod and reels and most of all, give you advice. Trips are available to Maligne Lake and other spots as well as fly-in trips. They also have boats available at many backcountry lakes: Talbot, Celestine, Marjorie, Hibernia, Dorothy, Yellowhead, Valley of the Five Lakes and others.

Boats and tackle are also available through Maligne Tours, 626 Connaught Drive, (852-3370) or at the boathouse at Maligne Lake. Their Fisherman's Special should appeal to anglers anxious to get away for the day. It leaves the boathouse on Maligne Lake at 8:30 a.m. Fishermen are piloted by small tour boat to Samson Narrows where fishing is often good. They are left for the day with a smaller fishing boat and an electric trolling motor.

Although heavily fished, *Pyramid Lake* on the wooded bench north of Jasper, is regularly stocked and is one of the few in the national parks open to motorboats. Early in the season, you might try casting from shore for rainbow and lake trout. Later, trolling works best. *Patricia Lake* just down the road has rainbow and brook trout up to six pounds and is easily accessible with a (non-motor) boat. Those small, rechargable electric motors may be used wherever boats are permitted.

Medicine Lake on the Maligne Canyon Road is a strange place to fish since the lake drops to a narrow channel by fall because of the underground system that drains water through limestone passages down the valley to below Maligne Canyon. It's known for rainbows and a boat is needed, except in low water.

Maligne Lake, with its extremely cold water, has large brook trout and some rainbows and such scenery as to make fishing only an excuse for being there. *Horseshoe Lake* (Walk 79) is stocked with rainbows and the shore drops off steeply into the water, ideal for casting. *Honeymoon Lake* and *Buck Lake* on the Icefields Parkway are stocked with rainbow and brook trout. *Leach Lake* on Highway 93A is known for its rainbow trout.

Lake Edith (Walk 92) has rainbows and *Annette* has brook trout (Walk 91). *Lac Beauvert* (Walk 87) and the small lakes around Jasper Park Lodge have brook and rainbow trout. Away from the road, try *Wabasso Lakes* (Walk 81) for smaller rainbows and Valley of Five Lakes (Walk 82) for brook and rainbow trout. The first and last lakes are the best and have rental boats.

Amethyst Lake in the Tonquin Valley is renowned for its rainbow trout as well as its scenery. Getting there is either a major backpacking trip or a

horseback trip organized by an outfitter. See Outdoor Adventures—Jasper, Chapter 3.

In winter, *Talbot Lake* is popular for ice-fishing.

Banff National Park: *Lake Minnewanka* is the only lake on which power boats may be used. This beautiful lake north of Banff townsite gets heavy use and can be treacherous in stormy weather. It contains some big specimens indeed, if you can find them—cutthroat, splake, whitefish, rainbows, bull trout and lake trout, the last ranging up to 40 pounds. Boat rentals available.

Jason's Fish Guiding offers fishing from covered and heated motorboats—free coffee and, families are "welcome." Morning and evening trips available on request. The guide has details on where to have your catch cooked in one of the many dining rooms in Banff. Call (403) 762-3108 or write Jason's at Box 2035, Banff, Alta. T0L 0C0.

Minnewanka Tours Ltd., also offers guided fishing aboard 22-foot cabin cruisers equipped with "the most modern sonar and fishing equipment available." Call 762-3473, 9 a.m. to 9 p.m. daily, or write Box 2189, Banff, T0L 0C0.

Fishing equipment is also for rent for those who want to fish on their own. The Banff tackle stores remain your best bet to find out the secrets of where the fish are biting and what they're taking.

Forget about *Lake Louise*. Although there are boats to rent, the lake, according to parks officials, has had it for fishing. That's the price of beauty and glacial silt, one supposes. Lake Louise is visited by about 1.6 million people a year. What chance does a fish have?

Nearby *Moraine Lake* (Walks 42, 43) is still in the game, although the pressure of visitors is intense too. Bull trout reach five pounds, if you can find them. *Consolation Lake* (Walk 44) is a good place to escape the Moraine crowds and you can cast off the boulders that line the shore for pan-sized cutthroat. Across from Lake Louise Village, a 2-km trail leads to unglamorous *Mud Lake* where the fishing for brook trout and cutthroat has often been good.

Closer to Banff townsite, *Johnson Lake* off Minnewanka Road has small rainbows and brookies which must be taken from shore. No boats allowed. Follow our route (Walk 23) and try less-fished spots away from the road. *Two Jack Lake*, also off the Minnewanka Road, is handy to campgrounds but as a consequence gets heavy use from fishermen after its good-size rainbows and lake trout. *Vermilion Lakes*, which have boats for rent, are also extremely popular and a wonderful spot to watch for moose and other game, even if you can't find fish. Its rainbows and brookies are reputed to run up to 8 pounds.

North of Banff, there's *Bourgeau Lake* for small brook trout, although it's a considerable hike in (Walk 30). The same is true for *Boom Lake* (Walk 37). *Smith Lake* (Walk 33) is easier to reach and has smallish cutthroat. The Bow River between Lake Louise and Banff is readily accessible to the Trans-Canada, even the Bow Valley Parkway in many places. See the canoeing section for Bow River trips which will take you to the less-frequented pools.

North of Lake Louise on the Icefields Parkway, *Hector Lake* looks inviting but the trail to it involves a major ford of the Bow River. *Bow Lake*, of course, is famous for its scenery, its lodge and its lake trout and bull trout (Walk 59). *Chephren* and *Cirque lakes*, accessible on moderate walks from Waterfowl lakes Campground (Walks 65 and 66) are worthwhile fishing destinations.

The Bow River south from Bow Lake is open for fishing year-round while the major lakes open Victoria Day and close Labor Day. These include *Minnewanka*, *Ghost*, *Two Jack*, *Johnson*, *Copper*, *Kingfisher* and *Pilo* as well as *Johnson Creek beaver pond* and the three *Vermilion Lakes* and connecting streams and beaver ponds. All other waters, except for the closed areas, are open July 1 to Oct. 31.

Closed waters include *Forty Mile Creek* around the townsite water supply, *Lake Agnes*, *Marvel Lake* within the log jam on the northeast end to the outlet and *Marvel Creek* from its junction with Bryant Creek to Marvel Lake.

Waterton National Park: Waterton's cold backcounty lakes and trout streams can offer exceptional fishing. The three big lakes — Upper, Lower and Middle Waterton provide lake trout of 15 pounds and more, plus smaller rainbows, brook trout and cutthroat. You can rent boats at the marina. Beware of rapidly changing conditions on these lakes, violent winds and big waves can strike without warning, making boating hazardous.

While conditions vary from year to year, some of the top lakes include *Alderson* for cutthroat (Walk 111), *Bertha* for rainbows (Walk 109), and *Maskinonge* for northern pike. *Cameron Lake* has rainbows and brook trout and boats may be rented.

High Crypt Lake is a beautiful spot to fish, although the cutthroat are notoriously hard to catch. Check at the information centre and tackle stores such as Pat's Texaco or Waterton Sports and Leisure in the Tamarack Mall.

One of the best places to fish is, naturally, the least accessible. *Lineham Lakes* above the Akamina Parkway are crystal clear and you may sometimes have a whole lake to yourself. The drawback is that to reach Lineham, you have to continue from the end of the official trail along a narrow ledge, with one short, but potentially-hazardous stretch that is more in the realm of rock climbing than hiking. The ascent to the lake is officialy considered a "hazardous activity" and you have to register for it.

The Dardanelles, *Knights Lake*, *Waterton River* and *Maskinonge Lake* are open for fishing year-round. *Waterton Lakes*, *Cameron Lake* and creek and *Crandell Lake* are open Victoria Day to Labor Day and all others are July 1 to Oct. 31.

Mountain Running

These trails could represent some of the finest running you'll ever do. While the mountains may seem a strange place for this sort of activity, runners who have participated in the gruelling Banff-Jasper Relay held each June along the Icefields Parkway speak of their run with awe. Some regard it as a "spiritual experience": the rhythm of running, the sweat, the joy of achievement, the pure, cool air—and some of the finest scenery in the world.

While runners have even been encountered trying to make it at a jogging pace up steep, slippery scree to the summit of Mt. Rundle, most prefer good footing and relatively level terrain. Many will train only on smooth pavement. Others prefer soft, needle-covered trails which are easier on the feet and knees—and maybe the soul.

Here are a few recommendations for fairly level running routes, both paved and dirt. Distances are the out and back total. For the unpaved trails, we've tried to select routes with fairly good footing, although lugs or waffles on running shoes are a good bet for the mountains, walking or running.

Banff National Park

BANFF TOWNSITE AREA—PAVED

- *Sundance Canyon Approach (6.4 km, 4 miles) Walk 16*
- *Tunnel Mountain Road (9.4 km, 5.8 miles) hilly/Walk 2*
- *Vermilion Lake Drive (9.2 km, 5.7 miles) Walk 19*

BANFF TOWNSITE AREA—DIRT

- *Fenland Trail (2 km, 1.2 miles) Walk 18*
- *Banff to the Hoodoos (9.6 km, 6 miles) Walk 3*
- *Banff Springs Golf Course Road (12 km, 7.5 miles)*
- *Spray River Loop (2.2 km, 1.3 miles) Walk 9*

OUTSIDE BANFF TOWNSITE—PAVED

- *Bow Valley Parkway (unlimited)*

OUTSIDE BANFF TOWNSITE—DIRT

- *Cascade Fire Road (unlimited)*
- *Spray River fire road (unlimited)*
- *Stewart Canyon (2 km, 1.2 miles) Walk 24*

MORAINE LAKE–LAKE LOUISE AREA—PAVED

- *Moraine Lake Road (12.4 km, 7.7 miles) hilly*

MORAINE LAKE–LAKE LOUISE AREA—DIRT

- *Consolation Lake Trail (6.4 km, 4 miles) Walk 44*
- *Lake Louise Lakeshore Trail (3.2 km, 2 miles) Walk 49*

Jasper National Park

JASPER TOWNSITE AREA—PAVED

- *Lake Annette Loop (2.4 km, 1.5 miles) Walk 91*
- *Jasper–Old Fort Point–Lodge (8 km, 5 miles)*
- *Pyramid Lake Road (7 km, 4 miles) hilly*

JASPER TOWNSITE AREA—DIRT

- *Lake Edith Loop (4.5 km, 2.7 miles) Walk 92*

- *Lac Beauvert Loop (3.5 km 2.1 miles) Walk 87*
- *Jasper-Pyramid Lake Trail (14.4 km, 9 miles) hilly, Walk 93*
OUTSIDE JASPER TOWNSITE—DIRT
- *Lower Sunwapta Falls (4 km, 2.4 miles) Walk 77*
- *Valley of Five Lakes (3 km, 1.8 miles) Walk 82*
- *Maligne Lakeside (3.2 km, 2 miles) Walk 100*

Peter Lougheed Provincial Park

- *Kananaskis Visitor Centre to Elkwood bicycle trail (9.4 km, 6 miles return) mostly level*
- *Elkwood to Boulton bicycle trail (9.4 km, 6 miles) level except for one steep portion*
- *Boulton to Upper Kananaskis Lake (10 km, 6 miles) several steep pitches*

Rock Scrambling

Few trails in the mountain parks ever get to the summit of anything. There's little Tunnel Mountain in Banff and the rounded slopes of Sulphur Ridge in Jasper, plus the peaks that have cable lifts.

But officially-maintained trails usually stay in the wooded valleys, rising to cross a rounded pass or ending at a lake or cirque on the very edge of the open alpine terrain. Well, that's certainly adventure and beauty enough for most.

But some hikes need to get to the top, or at least onto high ridges away from the trails. One solution is to hire a guide or take climbing courses and we've listed where you can do that. See Alpine Climbs listings for Banff and Jasper. Yet many of the peaks in the Canadian Rockies can be ascended without much climbing technique, without rope, ice axe or the courage of a Mesner attempting the north face of the Eiger in winter. What you need is an early start, lots of stamina, a bit of map-reading and route-finding ability, common sense and the willingness to turn back, if prudent.

Many of the mountains can be climbed ropeless by those who seek out the easy side. Not all peaks have an "easy" side, of course.

This is a sport which might be called rock scrambling and it's by no means as safe as following a trail. You can get lost, you can fall, you can be hit by rock fall, by snow avalanches. You can get hypothermia, the list is long . . .

On the other hand, you could get hit by a car while walking to the corner store.

The trick in mountain scrambling is knowing when to retreat. Many ridges and other routes may quickly become too steep for ropeless climbing. When a slip could mean a fall of some distance, abandon the climb or find another route. Similarly, be prepared to turn back if the weather becomes threatening.

As a ropeless scrambler, stay completely away from glaciers, even fairly steep snowfields. Don't forget to register your scramble with park authorities. The Warden Service has specific information about many climbs, even ones that can be done without ropes.

It's a matter of examing the mountain, both on the map and from the road. Obviously, a mountain such as Rundle is deadly on one side and easier on the Banff side. Even Cascade has an easy ridge leading to the summit (on the right of the Cascade Amphitheatre) although there's a steep pitch near the end. And, unfortunately, many peaks in the soft Canadian Rockies are little more than a summit sticking its head just above a depressing mound of rock debris. This rotten rock is strictly unreliable and constant vigilance is needed not to knock it down on companions.

Try to use a trail wherever possible to get close to the area you'd like to explore. Seek a trail that leads to timberline to avoid a tiring bushwack through the thick subalpine forest. Five kilometres of trail walking can be much faster than just one kilometre of bushwacking. There are many unmarked and largely unmaintained mountain access trails not listed in the hiking books. Good sources of information are the climbers' guides to the Rockies, although you still need route-finding skills.

Examine 1:50,000 contour maps carefully for white (open) sides of mountains above timberline where the lines are relatively far apart. Even then, be prepared to turn back or find an alternative. Forty-metre contour lines can hide an impassable 30-metre cliff. Wear sturdy boots and long pants and be sure to bring a windproof jacket, gloves, perhaps a parka in a stuff bag, water and some high-energy food.

And, most of all, ask climbers and the Warden Service for advice on routes and access. Many mountains such as Rundle look fairly accessible from Banff. But if you ascend in the wrong place, you may run into impassable cliffs or spend all afternoon searching for the route.

Waterton is an excellent place for the determined scrambler who likes to get to the top of things. Peaks tend to be lower and more eroded than in Jasper or Banff. All of them are accessible with a climbing rope although some are dull slogs and some are potentially dangerous because of loose rock.

Peter Lougheed Provincial Park with its excellent trail system and often accessible ridges offers a wide variety of off trail scrambles. See the comprehensive *Kananaskis Trail Guide*, Rocky Mountain Books.

Rock Climbing

You begin to climb on small, sun-warmed cliffs, belayed safely from the top under the supervision of a qualified instructor. The belayer at the top takes in the climbing rope as you ascend. You could never slip more than a few inches. Gradually you build your skills and your confidence and climbing begins to feel natural and exhilarating.

You may turn your sights to the higher peaks of Alberta's Rocky Mountains. Certified guides are available to take you safely to those lofty summits. Instructors can teach you how to climb frozen waterfalls, take you on extended ski-touring adventures over the glaciers and ice-fields and give you a feeling of self-reliance.

Climbing Schools and Services

• *Banff Alpine Guides.* PO Box 1025, Banff, Alberta, T0L 0C0. (403) 762-2791.

• *The Canadian School of Mountaineering.* Box 723, Canmore, Alberta, T0L 0M0. (403) 678-4134.

• *Jasper Climbing and Guide Service.* Box 452, Jasper, Alberta, T0E 1E0. (403) 852-3964.

• *The Lac des Arcs Climbing School.* 1116-19 Avenue, Calgary, Alberta, T2M 0Z9. (403) 289-6795.

• *Yamnuska Mountain School.* Box 7500, Canmore, Alberta, T0L 0M0. (403) 678-4164.

Where to Climb: Rock in the Canadian Rockies tends to be loose, highly unsuitable for technical climbing. But a few peaks and faces offer superb climbing on steep limestone. Crack systems tend to be erratic. Much of the rock is overhung and route-finding can be tricky.

Yamnuska, north of Highway 1A, 30 miles east of Banff, offers outstanding climbing on a wide variety of routes. See *A Climber's Guide to Yamnuska*, usually available in climbing stores in Banff and Calgary.

In Kananaskis Country, the Wasootch Slabs, just off Highway 40, provide good practice cliffs for all levels of difficulty. It's not unusual to see Sharon Wood, first North American woman to conquer Everest, teaching students here.

Near Banff townsite, various bouldering problems can be found on Rundle Rock on the edge of the golf course. Rundle Ridge above offers longer routes. Some of the lower faces of Cascade Mountain across the Trans-Canada from the Banff interchange offer good routes. See *Banff Rock Climbs* by Murray Toft.

In Jasper, all manner of problems and routes can be had on the slopes of Mt. Morro, east of the townsite and a short walk from where the road crosses the Athabasca.

In Waterton, rock climbing routes are notably lacking because of so much loose rock. The most popular area is Bear's Hump, right behind the townsite, a 150-metre face of limestones and dolomites. Route descriptions are available from the Warden Office where climbers must register.

Whitewater Rafting

Whitewater rafting is wild, wet exhilaration. The spray flies and the rafter plunges down through rock-walled gorges into boiling cauldrons of surging water and over cascades hung with rainbows.

Ahead, you spot two huge, back-curling waves—and you wonder how your raft can possibly get through. Your guide backferries the raft across the river to put it in the best position. For a moment, you hover on the brink, then you begin to accelerate down the smooth water, hitting the middle of the furious V where the two waves come together. The raft rocks madly, one end goes high in the air . . . and in an instant you are through, bobbing gently in a quiet eddy. You take a deep breath, wipe the spray from your face—and begin to wonder what's for lunch.

Rafting expeditions usually range from a half-day to a week or more. And the rivers range from the gentle to the mighty.

You just bring along your own warm sleeping bag, clothing and personal effects. For day trips, you may just need a change of clothes—and your camera.

The upper Red Deer River, flowing out of the foothills, is one of the best all-round whitewater rivers in North America. It was twice the site of the national whitewater slalom championships.

In southern Alberta, the Oldman River also offers classic whitewater thrills, especially at the Gap, a narrow spectacular gorge that constitutes a divide between the Rockies and the foothills. Legend says that this was the playground of Napa (meaning Old Man), the tribal god of the Blackfoot Indians.

The Highwood on the edge of Kananaskis Country southwest of Calgary is perhaps the most outstanding whitewater river in Alberta, although the best sections can only be run for a few weeks of the year when the water levels are ideal.

Access Information

• *Chinook River Sports Ltd.* 93 Lorelei Close, Edmonton, Alberta, T5X 2E7. (403) 454-3878.

• *Clearwater Rafting Adventures Ltd.* 116 Midridge Close S.E., Calgary, Alberta, T2X 1G1. (403) 293- 0959.

• *Hunter Valley Recreational Enterprises Ltd.* Box 1620, Canmore, Alberta, T0L 0M0. (403) 678-2000.

• *Jasper Raft Tours Ltd.* Box 398, Jasper, Alberta, T0E 1E0. (403) 852-3613.

• *Jasper Mountain River Guides Ltd.* Box 362, Jasper, Alberta, T0E 1E0. (403) 852-4721.

• *Mad Rafter River Tours Ltd.* #2 5004 Stanley Road S.W., Calgary, Alberta, T2S 2R5. (403) 282-1324.

• *Mukwah and Associates, Adventure Bound Tours Ltd.* 1216 -16 Ave N.W., Calgary, Alberta, T2M 0K9. (403) 282-0509.

• *Rocky Mountain Raft Tours.* Box 1771, Banff, Alberta, T0l 0C0. (403) 762-3632.

• *River Adventure Float Trips Ltd.* 5678 Brenner Crescent N.W., Calgary, Alberta, T2L 1Z9. (403) 282-7238.

• *WB Adventures River Tours.* 215 Parkvalley Drive S.E., Calgary, Alberta, T2J 4V1. (403) 271-9384.

Wilderness Experiences

Camp in authentic Indian tipis on the edge of the Rockies and experience wilderness living at your own pace. You do your own cooking and learn by doing, under the guidance of one instructor for every five participants. Contact: Camp Apa Cheesta, Box 803, Hinton, Alberta, T0E 1B0. (403) 865-7877.

Mountain sheep

6 Wildlife
Where to Find Them

Animals

The easiest place to see animals in the mountain parks is along the highway. Drive out in the early morning or evening just before sunset and you'll be rewarded. The Bow Valley Parkway, the road along Vermilion Lakes, the Banff-Windermere Highway, the Icefields Parkway, Highway 16 in Jasper, even the shoulders of the Trans-Canada Highway are likely to bring you close to elk, deer and bighorn sheep, maybe even a moose, coyote or bear—if you slow down and look. The best seasons are spring, fall and winter when much big game has moved from the subalpine forest into protected valleys.

But the best places to see game are in the backcountry—at least away from the roads—along many of the walks described in the book. There you encounter animals on their own ground. A highway is a strip of civilization. Animals seem more on display, as if in a zoo. You can't experience much from a car window, with traffic rushing past or a jam of parked vehicles building up beside you.

While big game is harder to spot along the trails, the rewards are greater. You encounter the animals in a more natural environment: a dripping moose emerging from a bog, or perhaps a mountain goat half-way up the cliff above you, treading ledges you'd never dare climb.

Whether walking or driving, try to do some of your travelling in early morning or evening before sunset. That's when many of the larger animals are active and feeding. By mid-morning, they may have retreated to thick forest.

Many of the animals, large and small, appear tame. They'll either pay no attention to people or approach them for food. This can be misleading. **Visitors should be warned that animal-watching is best done at a**

distance. These animals are still wild and unpredictable. Any animal may bite if it feels threatened. Moose in rutting season (the fall) may try to defend their territory. A moose cow can become aggressive to defend her calf if she feels it's threatened. These cautions apply especially to bears. (See Bear Scare.)

Feeding of wildlife is illegal in national parks. Some animals have learned to panhandle for food. You do them no favor by feeding them. This disrupts their natural feeding patterns and makes them dependent on human handouts. It may even make them sick—or kill them—because they're getting the wrong kind of food. Bears that learn to depend on human handouts can turn into "problem animals" and may have to be destroyed. In the beginning, the people who fed the bear were the problem.

Bears: This is probably an animal better seen from your car. While a bear encounter is possible anywhere, it's more likely around the works of humans than in the backcountry. Hikers seldom see grizzlies.

The black bear is the more common sighting. But although hikers do worry, bears usually pick up their scent or sound and take off before they arrive.

You're more likely to see a black bear in campgrounds and along the Icefields Parkway, especially in the early morning. These bears often cause traffic jams. Highway bear encounters can bring out the worst in visitors, who are tempted to get out of their cars and approach the bears or, worse yet, offer them food. One mother allowed her small daughter to coat her hand with honey to attract a bear by the highway. It worked—the girl's hand was bitten off.

Stay in your car and roll the window all the way up if a bear approaches. These bears have learned to tolerate traffic and humans because they associate people with food. They are problem bears, caused by problem people. Such bears are more dangerous and unpredictable than wild ones. Feeding them is illegal, dangerous—and bad for the bear. Between 1971 and 1980, 239 black bears and 54 grizzlies were destroyed in the mountain parks because they had become management problems, a threat to humans and property.

Grizzlies, however, aren't often seen along the roadways and lower trails. You might be able to spot one in spring on the steep avalanche slopes above the Vermilion River in Kootenay National Park.

Bighorn Sheep: While sheep are sometimes confused with mountain goats, it's easy to tell the difference. Both are good climbers and often found in the same range. But sheep are brown and goats white—simple as that. Only the male sheep has the distinctive, heavy, curling horns; the female's are smaller, usually with only a slight curl.

• *Banff.* They're less easy to find in Banff than Jasper. They tend to head for the high country in summer although some traditionally remain on the lower slopes of Mt. Norquay just above the Trans-Canada Highway immediately west of Banff where they've caused thousands of traffic jams over the years. The fencing around the new divided highway will keep sheep separated from cars. Expect close encounters of the sheep kind along the first few kilometres of the Bow Valley Parkway, just west of Banff townsite. Another likely place is around Lake Minnewanka and on the trail past Stewart Canyon (Walk 24). Watch for them on Mt. Wilson and Mt. Coleman in the northern part of the park. You will likely encounter them close up on the ridges of Sulphur Mountain (Walk 13), easily reached by gondola from the Upper Hot Springs.

- *Kootenay.* Big horn sheep are numerous above Radium between the Iron Gates and Sinclair Canyon.

- *Jasper.* It's often difficult to drive east on Highway 16 from the townsite to the park gates without encountering sheep, especially at Disaster Point, 38 km (23 miles) east of the townsite. They are also common around Miette Hot Springs, on the rocky bluffs around Old Fort Point, just south of the townsite and around the Tangle Falls viewpoint near the Columbia Icefield, 99 km south of Jasper townsite.

Caribou: The woodland caribou is about the size of the elk but generally darker in color. In the Arctic, barren-ground caribou travel great distances according to the seasons. In the mountains, caribou migrate vertically, seeking the alpine meadows in summer and descending to protected subalpine forest in winter.

- *Banff.* Caribou have been seen only occasionally in Banff in the deep backcountry, such as Nigel Pass (Walk 71), Dolomite Pass and the Upper Pipestone.

- *Jasper.* In spring, you might spot caribou near the delta on the southern end of Medicine Lake, up the Maligne Lake Road. The Skyline Trail over the Maligne Range is another possibility, although that's a major backpacking trip.

Coyote: This member of the dog family lives on the lower valley slopes and is often seen loping across the road, easy to mistake for a medium-sized domesticated dog. The coyote has a slender muzzle, large pointed ears, and a bushy tail, usually held downwards. It is best seen along the road because this is part of its territory. The coyote patrols the roadway and railway tracks looking for animals killed by traffic. It also nabs small animals such as ground squirrels that live in the lower meadowlands.

- *Banff.* Watch for the coyote especially along the Bow Valley Parkway. Coyotes patrol the area around Vermilion Lakes, attracted by the abundance of small game and are a common sight along the frozen shoreline in winter. In late August, listen for their haunting, nocturnal serenades. The Bankhead area (Walk 21) is a likely spot.

- *Jasper.* You may well see a coyote on any of the roads and highways.

Elk: Few visitors leave the parks without an encounter with elk, also known as wapiti. They are distinguished from other large members of the deer family by their large, straw-colored rump and mere stump of a tail. The bulls have magnificent antlers that may reach four or five feet. They travel in large herds and are numerous in the parks. Elk calves are born in May or June. After that, the herd often migrates to higher terrain for the summer.

• *Banff.* Watch for elk at Sundance Canyon (Walks 16 and 17), and north of Banff at Johnson Lake (Walk 23). Reliable places to spot elk are open, grassy areas along the Bow Valley Parkway and the Icefields Parkway especially in the winter, when they gather in herds of 40 and 50. Even the edges of the Trans-Canada offer good feeding areas for elk, although this isn't as good a location to view them because of the heavy, fast-moving traffic. Along the Bow Valley Parkway, stop at the edge of a meadow, walk a little way into the open woods and examine the aspen trees in these mixed forests. The tree bark is likely to be heavily scarred, the marks of elk teeth. Aspen bark is not the preferred diet of elk; it's too hard to chew and digest. They only eat it in winter when food gets scarce and they might otherwise starve to death.

• *Kootenay National Park.* Over Vermilion Pass, elk can often be found in large numbers all year round in the open grasslands around Dolly Varden Creek picnic grounds, 69 km west of Castle Mountain Junction or nearby at McLeod Meadows. Elk also appear throughout the day at the animal lick close to the highway, 51 km from the junction.

• *Jasper.* Elk are usually plentiful around the Jasper Airfield east of the townsite, in the open woods around Whistlers Campground, just south of town along Highway 93A, especially in the evening, and just east of the townsite. You'll even find them in town, sometimes disputing possession of the sidewalk with pedestrians.

In early fall, the woods around Whistlers Campground can be loud, night and day, with the bugling of courting bull elk. No use complaining to the warden if you can't sleep.

• *Kananaskis Country.* Try the Middle Lake Trail in Bow Valley Park for a good chance of seeing elk.

Moose: These largest members of the deer family are easy to distinguish, though not so easy to find as elk. They are huge, 800 to 1,100 pounds and have a big snout, long legs, humped shoulders, and a flap of skin hanging from the throat, called a dewlap or bell. There's no rump patch. Moose prefer to feed in open or semi-open areas where they can find willow twigs, leaves and aquatic plants. Unlike elk, they are usually solitary, except for a cow and her calves. The calves, usually twins, are born in spring after the cow has driven away her yearling calves. Watch for moose along lake shorelines, in swampy areas and along stream banks.

• *Banff.* A good spot to find moose is Vermilion Lakes, just west of Banff townsite (Walk 19), on the Fenland Nature Trail (Walk 18), or the open, fire-scarred Vermilion Pass burn (Walk 38). Along the Bow Valley Parkway, watch for moose in the semi-open areas, especially Moose Meadows under Castle Mountain. Moose are found on the Icefields Parkway, especially in such marshy areas as the one near Rampart Creek, about 55 km north of the Trans-Canada or at Waterfowl Lakes (Walk 64).

• *Kootenay*. Watch for moose along the Banff-Windermere Highway, especially at the mouth of the Simpson River and at the animal lick, 51 km (31 miles) west of Castle Mountain Junction.

• *Jasper*. Try Cottonwood Slough (Walk 95) just up Pyramid Lake Road on the bench above Jasper townsite. Watch for a stream crossing just past the first parking area and find the slough on the north side of the road. Other moose-watching areas: around Pyramid and Patricia Lakes above Cotton-wood Slough and on the road into Snaring Campground east of the townsite.

• *Kananaskis Country*. Moose are frequently seen in the marshy areas along the road leading into Peter Lougheed Provincial Park, after the Highway 40 turnoff.

Mountain Goats: Goats look best in winter when their coats are white and fluffy. In summer, they moult in great messy patches. Goats, like sheep, can climb to feed on remote, almost inaccessible mountain ledges high in the backcountry.

• *Banff.* Watch for goats on Parker Ridge (Walk 72) near the Banff-Jasper boundary at Sunwapta Pass and on the steep slopes of Mt. Wilson and Mt. Coleman north of the Saskatchewan River Crossing. In Yoho, look for mountain goats on the road into Takakkaw Falls (Walk 56).

• *Kootenay.* The best spot to find them in the mountains is the Mount Wardle Goat Lick, 51 km (31 miles) west of Castle Mountain Junction on Highway 93.

• *Jasper.* You might find goats around Disaster Point on Highway 16 East. The best spot is the goat lick viewpoint, on the Icefields Parkway, 38 km (23 miles) south of the townsite.

Mule Deer: You can tell the mule deer by its large mule-like ears, black-tipped tail and a white rump patch. They are larger than the less common white-tailed deer and tend to migrate higher in the summer. The population levels of mule deer are fairly low in Banff although they can be seen in drier open areas where there are shrubs and broad-leafed plants. The mule deer is more common in Jasper and can often be found right in the townsite.

• *Banff.* In the Bow Valley, look for mule deer on southwest facing slopes and the valley bottoms, part of the Montane zone. Watch for them along the Bow Valley Parkway in open meadows. Mule deer aren't as commonly found on the other side of the valley where the shadier northwest-facing slopes are covered thickly with the typical fir and spruce trees of the sub-alpine zone. Closer to Banff, try Tunnel Mountain (Walk 1), below the mountain along the Bow River (Walk 3), on the road to Mt. Norquay and the trails around it. In summer, mule deer are more likely to be encountered on a trail, higher in the subalpine zone, although some remain in the lower valley.

• *Kootenay.* The Vermilion Valley is a good place to find deer, especially around the animal lick on Highway 93, 51 km west of Castle Mountain Junction and at McLeod Meadows, km 79 (mile 49).

• *Jasper.* Mule deer are well-distributed all over the park at lower elevations, although they tend to migrate higher in summer. An excellent way to see them is to explore the Pyramid bench above Jasper, especially Walk 93 to Pyramid Lake and Walk 95 by Patrica Lake. The Lake Annette and Lake Edith areas also have sizeable populations, most of the time. (See Walks 91 and 92.)

• *Waterton Lakes National Park.* The Crandell Lake Campground is exceedingly popular with deer. They are also frequently seen at Red Rock Canyon.

White-Tailed Deer: More common to abandoned pastureland of the East, white-tailed deer aren't often seen in the parks. They're smaller than the Mule and have long brown tails that are held upright at the sign of danger. When the tail is up, you can see its white underside.

• *Banff.* Watch for them along the Icefields Parkway north of the Saskatchewan River Crossing.

• *Jasper.* You might spot a white-tailed deer along the road to Snaring Campground, east of the townsite or around the Jasper Airfield.

The Secretive Ones: Some animals out there are seldom seen, including the *mountain lion, lynx, wolverine, pine marten, fisher, otter, flying squirrel* and *ermine.*

Wolves aren't often seen although they are making a comeback from the days when they were nearly exterminated, even in national parks. In the 19th century, wolves were shot or poisoned by fur traders and their numbers started to dwindle. In Banff, they were killed during the 1950s in a rabies control program. By 1953, it's thought, only four wolves remained in Banff park although more lived in the remote areas of Jasper.

Fortunately, wildlife experts now realize that the wolf has an important place in the ecosystem. In the parks, it receives the same protection as other animals. The wolf preys on the weaker members of elk and deer herds. Thus it keeps the herds healthy and prevents them from destroying their own grazing environment because of over-population. Contrary to all the fairy tales and stories, the wolf is not a particular threat to humans in the wilderness. Humans are the threat to wolves.

Packs of wolves are sighted occasionally along the river valleys of Banff, but their tendency is to stay in the more remote areas of the park. They are sighted more frequently in Jasper.

The Smaller Ones: Some animals you'll never notice from a car are relatively easy to find when walking the trails. For example, in the forests of spruce and fir above the valley floor, you'll see the *red squirrel* almost everywhere, usually in frenetic motion gathering cones.

Two critters sometimes just labelled "gopher" are the *golden-mantled* ground squirrel and *Columbian ground squirrel* found from valley to timber-line, although the golden-mantled prefers rocky areas and the Columbian sandy soils for its intricate tunnel system. The Ptarmigan Cirque Trail in Peter Lougheed Provincial Park is a good place to see Columbia ground squirrels. Dry, rocky areas are the home of the *least chipmunk*, smallest in North America. Peter Lougheed Provincial Park in Kananaskis Country is home to the *flying squirrel*. Watch for these agile creatures leaping from tree to tree after dark.

On Parker Ridge in Banff (Walk 72) and near the summit of The Whistlers in Jasper (Walk 85), watch for beautifully-camouflaged *ptarmigan*. At Bow Summit (Walk 63) as in many timberline areas, listen for the whistling of the marmot or the high-pitched "eeeep!" of the *pika*, or *rock rabbit*. Major colonies of pikas inhabit the rockslides at Moraine Lake and at the far end of Lake Louise. Pikas are often seen as well on the Rock Glacier Trail in Kananaskis.The marmot is easy to spot with its grizzled back and its habitual upright pose on rocks on the trails. The smaller pika blends in better.

Ground squirrel

You can't miss that most sociable—or pesky—of birds, the *Whiskey Jack*, properly known as the *Gray Jay* with its whitish head and black nape. It seems to be everywhere in the forest and especially haunts campgrounds where it becomes tame and fearless, willing to steal the spaghetti from your lips. Feeding them is illegal, although it's a constant battle not to.

Higher in the subalpine forest, look for *Clark's nutcracker*, slightly larger than the Gray Jay. It is gray with black and white wings and tail, a longer bill and a harsher cry.

Gray Jay, also known as the Canada Jay or Whiskey Jack.

Ruffled grouse live in the montane forest, *blue grouse* and *spruce grouse* in the higher subalpine woods. The park is also permanent home to three kind of *chickadees—black capped, mountain* and *boreal*. Some predatory birds, such as the *osprey*, the *bald eagle* and the *golden eagle* reside in the park in summer. Nigel Pass (Walk 71) or Wilcox Pass (Walk 73) in the Columbia Icefield area are good places for sightings. The Elbow Sheep area of Kananaskis Country is also a good place to spot *golden eagles, bald eagles* and even *peregrine falcons*.

In Banff, the marshlands south of Cave and Basin have a bird blind as part of an elaborate boardwalk tour (Walk 20). Serious bird watching from here should be done in the off-season and off-hours when the place isn't crowded with (human) visitors. Birds you might find include *yellowthroats, ruby-crowned kinglets, red-winged blackbirds, green* or *blue-winged teals, robins, snipe* and a variety of *mallards* and other waterfowl. In winter, the ice-free marsh by the outlet to the hot streams attracts birds such as the *killdeer* which would otherwise fly south.

In Waterton, Cameron Lake is home to the Steller's jay and varied thrush. Carthew Lakes and the Crandell Lake area are also popular bird watching spots.

Columbian ground squirrel

The Bear Scare: Yes, this is bear country! There's something bigger and stronger and faster than you out there. But that fact should be humbling, rather than terrifying. Bears have a bad image. Thousands, maybe millions of visitors to the mountain parks never venture far from the road because of their fear of bears. And if people aren't terrified of bears, they have a cute Disney image of them.

First the terror. The fact is, for all those horror stories of grizzly attacks, studies show that you're really far safer on mountain trails than driving on the highway.

To put the bear scare into statistical perspective, it's estimated that there is only one bear injury for every two million park visitors. Only three human deaths and 71 bear incidents were reported in the four contiguous Rocky Mountain parks between 1929 and 1981, according to a Parks Canada report. More than half those incidents resulted in minor lacerations.

"Considering the millions of people who have visited the park, the average visitor has an extremely low chance of encountering an aggressive bear," says a Parks Canada report on the Natural and Human History of Banff.

So if you allow yourself to be frightened away from exploring the world away from the road, you're missing so much—for so little reason.

Now for the Disney image. All these comforting statistics must not belie the fact that bears, especially when startled or made to feel threatened, can be fearsome, even life-threatening. That's why suggestions for avoiding bear contacts make sense, just as it makes sense to look both ways before crossing the street.

Black bear

It's sensible to make enough noise while hiking to let any bear in the area know you are coming. Some people wear bells; some just talk a lot. Be aware that if you are travelling into the wind, the bear may not get your scent until you are close.

Stay clear of a bear cub if you should happen across one. The mother is probably not far away and she's very protective. Don't leave food or garbage around in the open. Keep your dog at home.

The usual advice, if you should encounter an aggressive bear, is to back away slowly or to "play dead" if the bear should charge. But the truth is that bears are unpredictable and nobody knows for sure what to do.

If camping, minimize the possibility of a bear problem by following these guidelines:

- Keep a clean camp.
- Seal surplus food in airtight containers or clean wrapping material.
- Do not leave food on tables or stored in a tent in open boxes. Back-country campers should suspend their supplies between two trees, out of a bear's reach.
- Burn all garbage and food containers; do not bury them. Backpackers should cart out any litter they can't burn.

See *Bear Attacks: Their Causes and Avoidance* by Stephen Herrero (Winchester Press) for a thorough, landmark study of the bear problem.

Just don't let all those scary bear precautions keep you out of the woods. Nothing important ever gets understood from the parking lot.

Warning / Attention — Bear in the area / Ours dans le secteur — Travel with caution / Avancez prudemment

Tale of the Trees

Identifying trees, at least the most common varieties, isn't as hard as it seems. First of all, simply establish the most likely trees that grow at the elevation reached. Then narrow down the possibilities.

The Montane Zone: This zone is usually below 1,370 metres (4,500 feet) on the valley floor. It goes higher on south-facing slopes than colder north slopes. The common succession forests consist mainly of lodgepole pine with some trembling aspen. Douglas fir is found less frequently, usually in semi-open areas.

• *Douglas Fir.* Not as common as the other trees but can be identified by the thick, gray, deeply-grooved bark on the old trees, many of which have survived a fire. Needles are flat and pointed. Unlike spruce, they don't feel especially prickly.

• *Lodgepole Pine.* Found in areas that have experienced forest fires, they are best identified by their straight, tall trunks, usually with few lower branches. Imagine Indians making tipi poles from these trees. The needles are long and in pairs. The cones are prickly and often stay on the trees for years. They are tightly sealed with resin and may not open to release their seeds without the heat of a forest fire. So they are among the first major trees to re-establish in an open area after a fire.

• *Trembling Aspen.* A common tree of the prairie parkland, it also occurs in dense stands in the mountains and is sometimes mixed with the coniferous trees. It has distinctive, almost round leaves with fine teeth at the edges. The leaves tremble even in a light breeze.

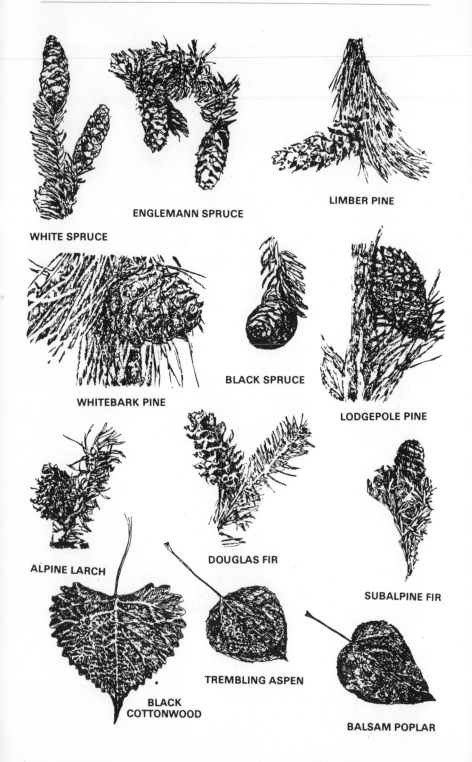

WHITE SPRUCE

ENGLEMANN SPRUCE

LIMBER PINE

WHITEBARK PINE

BLACK SPRUCE

LODGEPOLE PINE

ALPINE LARCH

DOUGLAS FIR

SUBALPINE FIR

BLACK
COTTONWOOD

TREMBLING ASPEN

BALSAM POPLAR

The Subalpine Zone: Above the valley floors, you enter the subalpine zone, usually from about 1,370 metres (4,500 feet) right to timberline. The lodgepole pine occurs in dense stands in the lower part of the zone. White spruce extends from the valleys to about 7,000 feet. Near the top of its range, white spruce is mixed with Engelmann spruce. Around 6,000 feet the spruce trees also co-exist with subalpine fir.

• *White Spruce.* This common tree of the mountainside can be distinguished from the fir by its feel. Its branches feel prickly. The fir is softer. Spruce branches extend almost to the ground and the needles are straight.

• *Englemann Spruce.* This higher-elevation tree tends to have curved needles. Roll some needles in your hand and they smell like camphor. Don't fret too much about telling the Engelmann and white spruce apart because often what you're looking at is a hybrid. The Engelmann tends to be slimmer than the white spruce.

• *Subalpine Fir.* Often found in stunted form high on the slopes, it has branches which feel fairly soft to the touch, unlike the spruce. The needles are flat; unlike the spruce they don't roll between the fingers. The bark is gray and there are usually prominent blisters of resin.

Subalpine fir

Banff Avenue, Banff National Park

7 A Touring Guide
Pick of the Walks

Hikes for the Non-Hiker

Banff Townsite

• *Day One*. If visibility is good, start early with a ride up Sulphur Mountain Gondola Lift. From the teahouse at the top, stroll up the easy trail to the old meteorological station (Walk 12). In the afternoon, you might like to catch the scenic cruise down Maligne Lake or picnic by the lake and stroll to Stewart Canyon (Walk 24). On the way back to Banff townsite, consider stopping at the fascinating Bankhead historical exhibit (Walk 21). The best way to end the day is surely with a soak at the hot springs.

• *Day Two*. Explore the lavishly-done interpretive trails at Cave and Basin: the Marsh Trail (Walk 20) and the Discovery Trail, showing how hot sulphur water here not only changes the environment but led to the creation of Canada's national parks. Visit the Centennial Centre and relax with a plunge in the newly-renovated pool. Later, consider a stroll from Banff Bridge to Bow Falls (Walk 7). Then take the trestle bridge up to the Scottish baronial Banff Springs Hotel for afternoon tea. A fine evening stroll, if you still have energy, is the short Fenland Nature Trail (Walk 18). An excellent spot to view animals before sunset.

Lake Louise

• *Day 1*. Drive to Lake Louise, admire the view with a stroll down the beautiful Lakeshore Trail (Walk 49). Go for tea in the famous Chateau. Later, take the short, scenic drive to Moraine Lake, which many prefer to world-famous Lake Louise. In warm, calm weather, it's delightful to rent a boat or canoe on this magnificent little lake, (pictured on the back of the $20 bill). Alternatively, take a short walk to the top of the rocky hill at the Lodge end of the lake (Walk 42). The view is classic. In late afternoon, the

Post Hotel in Lake Louise Village is a good place for tea.

• *Day Two.* If visibility is good, take the Lake Louise Gondola across the Trans-Canada Highway from Lake Louise Village. It whisks you up to the 2034-metre level of Mt. Whitehorn. There's a stunning overview of Lake Louise and glacier-clad peaks along the Continental Divide.

Bow Valley and Kootenay: Outside Banff, the best drive is along the Bow Valley Parkway, rather than the hectic Trans-Canada. This is an interpretive drive with frequent pulloffs at areas of geological or historical interest and a good chance to see big game, especially in the morning or early evening. Be sure to stop at Johnston Canyon (Walk 31) for a stroll up the paved trail past numerous waterwalls and cascades, cut deep in the limestone walls. At Castle Mountain Junction, turn up Highway 93 to Vermilion Pass. Right at the top on the Continental Divide is the short, surprisingly interesting Fireweed Trail through the burn of 1968 (Walk 38). Drive 7 km more to the deep gorges of Marble Canyon. If you've still time and a little energy to spare, carry on to the Paint Pots, a fascinating area of ochre springs, a sacred place to the Indians.

Yoho: From Lake Louise, take Highway 1A to the Great Divide, a picnic area where a creek divides in two, one part flowing to the Pacific, the other to the Atlantic. Continue to the Trans-Canada Highway and turn west into Yoho. Drive down the steep grade to the historic spiral tunnels of the CPR where a short trail leads to a fine viewpoint. At the bottom of the grade on the right is the turnoff to Yoho Valley. Drive this steep-walled road for 16 km to Takakkaw Falls, one of the highest in North America (Walk 56).

The Icefield Parkway: When driving the Bow Valley Parkway north from Lake Louise, stop at stunning Bow Lake, 34 km north of Lake Louise. Take a least a short walk along the lakeshore past rustic Num-Ti-Jah Lodge (Walk 59). The lodge is a good place to stop after your stroll for tea, home-made muffins and cakes. Continuing up the parkway, pull in at Bow Summit and take the short, paved nature trail to Peyto Lake Viewpoint (Walk 62), among the most stunning views anywhere in the mountains. You might consider walking a little higher in this fascinating timberline zone through the land of marmots and pikas (Walk 63). Another short stroll leads down to Mistaya Canyon Gorge from a parking area on the west side of the Parkway, 71 km north of Lake Louise.

• *Columbia Icefield.* Stop first at the Interpretive and Information Centre opposite the access road to the Athabasca Glacier. Many visitors take the ''Snocoach'' tour up onto the glacier itself. After refreshments at the Icefield Chalet next door, consider the short stroll through rocky desolation to the glacier toe (Walk 75).

• *Icefield Parkway—Jasper.* Sunwapta Falls, 55 km north of Jasper, is an impressive stop and you can stroll down the lower falls (Walk 77) if you're energetic. Athabasca Falls is right by the road at the junction of 93 and 93A, also a good spot for a picnic. The most scenic route north from there is 93A which leads to the turnoff for Mt. Edith Cavell. Don't miss the awesome walk along an old moraine and through the glacial rubble below rumbling Angel Glacier (Walk 83).

Jasper Townsite Area: If the weather's reasonable, a morning trip up the Jasper Tramway to the top of The Whistlers provides a stunning overview of the Athabasca Valley and a glimpse at the barren alpine tundra (Walk 84). Take a warm jacket. In the afternoon, visit luxurious Jasper Park Lodge and stroll at least part-way around elegant Lac Beauvert (Walk 87).

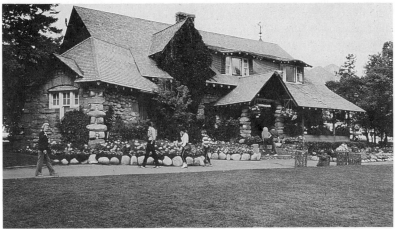

Information Office, Jasper

Maligne Lake: You may want to give the stunning Maligne Lake area a whole day. Stop first at Maligne Canyon, 11 km from Jasper, a deep gorge with an outstanding interpretive trail above it (Walk 97). Continue up the scenic road past disappearing Medicine Lake where the water drains underground into the river below Maligne Canyon. The road ends at Maligne Lake, largest in the Canadian Rockies. Many visitors take the two-hour boat tours past famous little Spirit Island, where all the photographs are taken. After a snack at the chalet, consider the short lakeside trail (Walk 100) which really gives you a feel for this gorgeous area.

Waterton

• *Day One.* Everyone's first choice is the boat trip down Waterton Lake to Goat Haunt in Montana's Glacier National Park. Upon return, stroll up to the Prince of Wales Hotel for lunch, or at least a peek at one of Canada's most picturesque hotels. In the afternoon, take the beautiful drive to Red Rock Canyon and the short nature hike (Walk 114). You might want to cap the evening with a walk along the townsite's lakefront, followed by a visit to Cameron Falls. Nearby, you can attend one of the park's interpretive programs.

• *Day Two.* Start with a drive up the Akamina Parkway with a stop at Oil City. At the end of the road is beautiful Cameron Lakes where boats may be rented. You might enjoy the easy stroll on the north side of the lake. Back at the townsite, consider a walk on the easy and beautiful Bertha Falls interpretive trail (Walk 109), or visit the Waterton Heritage Centre.

Kananaskis: Start with a drive up Highway 40 to Highwood Pass, highest paved road in Canada and one of the easiest ways to reach the subalpine zone. At the top, take a short stroll on the Rock Glacier and Highwood Meadows trails. In the afternoon, descend to Upper Kananaskis lakes and take the Canadian Mt. Everest Expedition Trail for a gorgeous view over the Kananaskis Valley. Stop at the Kananaskis Visitor Centre and attend a park nature program in the evening.

Mt. Fryatt, Jasper National Park.

Pick of the Walks—A Biased Selection

• *Banff Townsite Area.*
  Best Short Family Walk—Stewart Canyon. Walk 24.
  Best Interpretive Walk—Cave and Basin Marsh Trail. Walk 20.
  Best Views—Tunnel Mountain. Walk 1.
  Best Canyon Walk—Johnston Canyon. Walk 31.
  Best Historical Walk—Bankhead. Walk 21.
  Most Strenuous—Cory Pass. Walk 28.

Easiest Way to Subalpine—Sulphur Mountain. Walk 12.
Best Way to See Bighorn Sheep—Sulphur Summit. Walk 13.
Best Nature Walk—Fenland Trail. Walk 18.

- *Lake Louise Area.*
  Best Short Family Walk—Lake Louise Lakeshore. Walk 49.
  Best Views—Lake Agnes, Big Beehive Loop. Walks 53, 54.
  Best Glacier View—Plain of Six Glaciers. Walk 50.
- *Moraine Lake Area.*
  Best Short Walk—Moraine Lakeshore Trail. Walk 43.
  Best Views—Sentinel Pass. Walk 47.
  Easiest Way to Backcountry Lake—Consolation Lake. Walk 44.
- *Kootenay Park Area.*
  Best Short Family Walk—Marble Canyon. Walk 39.
  Best Interpretive Walk—Paint Pots. Walk 40.
  Most Surprising Walk—Vista Lake. (Banff Park) Walk 35.
- *Icefield Parkway (Banff).*
  Best Scenic Lake Walk—Bow Lake. Walk 59.
  Most Dazzling View—Peyto Viewpoint. Walk 62.
  Best Waterfalls—Panther/Bridal Veil Falls. Walk 70.
  Best Walk on Alpine Tundra—Parker Ridge. Walk 72.
  Shortest Walk—Waterfowl Lakes. Walk 64.
- *Columbia Icefield.*
  Best Short Walk—Glacier Toe. Walk 75.
  Best Views—Wilcox Pass Trail. Walk 73.
- *Icefield Parkway (Jasper).*
  Best Waterfalls—Beauty Creek/Stanley Falls. Walk 76.
  Best Short Walk—Angel Loop. Walk 84.
  Easiest Way to Alpine—The Whistlers Mountain. Walk 85.
- *Jasper Townsite.*
  Most Scenic—Old Fort Point. Walk 86.
  Most Elegant—Lac Beauvert. Walk 87.
  Best Picnic Area—Pyramid Island. Walk 94.
  Best Family Picnic/Recreation Area—Lake Annette. Walk 91.
- *Maligne Lake.*
  Most Scenic—Opal Hills. Walk 101.
  Best Lake Walk—Maligne Lakeside. Walk 100.
  Best Short Walk—Maligne Canyon. Walk 97.
- *East of Jasper.*
  Best Views—Sulphur Summit. Walk 105.
- *Waterton.*
  Best Short Walk—Red Rock Canyon. Walk 114.
  Best Views—Bear's Hump. Walk 110.
  Most Relaxing—Lower Bertha Falls. Walk 109.

- *Kananaskis.*
  Best Lake Walk—Upper Kananaskis Lake. Walk 106.
  Best Short Walk—Canadian Mt. Everest Expedition Trail. (See Short Strolls.)
  Easiest Way to Alpine—Ptarmigan Cirque. (See Short Strolls.)

Footwear

When we started hiking many years ago, we wore heavy, stiff climbing boots. They weighed several pounds each—and even after years of breaking in, produced blisters on long trails. Sometimes easy stretches of trail were agony because it hurt to lift those leaden lumps at every step.

A few years later, we shifted to lighter, more flexible hiking boots. Walking felt easier, although an occasional blister still bubbled up. Recently, we've gone even further and abandoned boots altogether for many easy trails.

Running shoes have been a revelation for day hikers. They weigh only a few ounces; no footwear is more comfortable and flexible; they are well-padded under the heel. They never seem to produce blisters and the miles speed by faster and more comfortably than ever before.

Most of the trails in this book can be walked in comfort and safety with running shoes, especially the ones with lug or waffle soles that give a good grip. They don't keep the feet dry like a waterproofed pair of leather hiking boots. But the nylon uppers do dry fast. Carry a change of socks, a practical solution for dealing with wet feet.

For most day walks, running shoes are just fine. And, since almost everybody wears them, they open up mountain trails to the casual stroller. Reasonably lightweight leather walking shoes are also suitable for most trails. The idea is to go in whatever is comfortable and handy and not let lack of special equipment hold you back.

Running shoes certainly aren't ideal in really wet conditions, in mud, over sharp rocks, through scree and snow. They are not suitable for the heavy loads of backpacking. Running shoes could even be dangerous on rough trails and deep in the backcountry where a sprained ankle or bruised foot might seriously hinder one's return to the trailhead. And if it has been raining for three days, the walker is probably better off in boots than running shoes. Similarly, running shoes are seldom pleasant on soggy alpine meadows.

An excellent compromise between the traditional hiking boot and the running shoe are the super lightweight boots made by New Balance and other companies. These are comfortable, sturdy, with good traction and reasonable waterproofing ability. They are expensive, however.

So the general recommendation is to use running shoes or good lightweight walking shoes where possible. Sometimes hikers wear running shoes for long stretches of fire road or easy trail, then change to boots for a rough ascent. If boots are necessary, seek out the lightest, most flexible pair you can find. Each walk in the book contains a footwear recommendation.

What to Bring

For most of these short hikes, it doesn't matter much. Wear whatever you happen to have on. Don't let lack of special gear keep you from a rewarding experience. Many love to hike in shorts, even in fairly cool weather. Legs don't usually feel the cold like hands and feet and shorts provide

freedom of movement. Jeans are adequate for a short stroll, although they tend to be tiring because the relatively stiff, tight material binds the legs when walking uphill. In cold weather, jeans give little protection and they feel especially unpleasant when wet. In cold, damp weather, wool is ideal. Unlike cotton or most synthetic fibres, it still provides insulating warmth when wet.

It's a good idea to bring a sweater and windproof/waterproof jacket, tied around the waist, if necessary. Mountain weather changes fast. You're likely to be warm while walking and cool off fast when you stop.

Here's a list for longer day hikes. No item on the list is strictly necessary:

Day Pack	Rain jacket/windproof
Gloves	Compass
Guidebook	Map
Camera	Sweater or down vest
Wool toque	Lunch
High-energy snacks	Water bottle
Canned drinks	Change of socks
Matches	Toilet paper
Insect repellent	Sunglasses
Sunscreen	First aid kit
Pocket knife	Garbage bags

Maps

The trail and road maps in the book should be adequate for most walkers. For off-trail exploration, for a detailed look at all the features in a particular area, the best maps are the 1:50,000 National Topographic series. They are sold at the Park information centres, bookstores and some sporting goods stores. Across Canada, they are available at federal or provincial government map offices. Maps can be obtained by mail by writing Canada Map Office, 615 Booth St., Ottawa, Ont. K1A 0E9. Maps covering an entire park on a single sheet (with varying scales) are also available.

Be aware that trail lines on some topographical maps are incorrectly shown.

Water

Traditionally, hikers just drank from mountain streams when they felt thirsty. Nothing tasted better than the clear, icy water of a tumbling brook in the backcountry. These days, unfortunately, Beaver Fever *(Giardia Lamblia)* has reared its tiny, ugly head—and taken the romance right out of drinking.

Giardia is a parasite which contaminates water, causing stomach upsets and cramps in humans. It is widespread in Western Canada and the U.S. and recently contaminated the water supply for Banff townsite. The townsite problem has been alleviated by the construction of deep well pumps and a new 18-million-litre reservoir with automatic controls and chlorination.

But Parks Canada says giardiasis continues to be a potential hazard in the backcountry of all the Rocky Mountain parks. They recommend that drinking water taken from rivers, lakes and streams be boiled for five minutes before use.

Day hikers aren't going to bring along a pot and stove for boiling. So the alternative for walks longer than an hour or two is to bring water with you in canteens, supplemented possibly by cans of juice or soft drinks. Take a generous supply of liquid as dehydration is one of the fastest routes to fatigue.

Garbage and Sanitation

Whatever you can pack in, you can also pack out. Take a garbage bag · in your day pack for any leftovers, cans, bottles, foil, paper.

If there are no toilet facilities along the trails (and there usually aren't), defecation should be performed at least 100 metres from water sources. Dig a small hole and cover it afterwards.

Park Regulations

No permit is needed for day walks along the park trails although a park use permit is required for overnight trips. (See backpacking section.) Registration is also recommended (though not usually required) for "risk activities" such as climbing, canoeing, kayaking, skiing outside signed routes or any travel on glaciers. With registration, wardens will know your itinerary, should you fail to return on time. Registration may be done at the park information centres in the national parks and at Warden Service offices. Your portion of the registration notice must be returned by the time and date recorded. After hours deposit boxes are located at the information centres.

Fires aren't permitted, except in designated fireboxes and fireplaces. Dogs are supposed to be on a leash and aren't recommended in the backcountry since they can provoke bears and molest or annoy other animals. It's unlawful to feed wildlife or pick wildflowers or plants or collect rocks or fossils.

Seasons

In winter, walks on paved roads are easily followed. Some of the other lower trails, especially within townsites, may have a beaten path and can be travelled without difficulty. Many of the others are best skied. (See Cross-Country Skiing section.) The snow does linger in the mountains longer than on the prairies. By May, much of the snow has gone from the lower valley forest and some of the south-facing slopes. By June, trails begin to open below treeline, although they can still be extremely wet and muddy, especially at higher elevations and on north-facing slopes. It's a good idea to avoid the alpine or timberline zone until well into July. Even though the snow has melted along most of these high trails, the footing remains extremely wet, slippery and unpleasant. Walkers who use soft trails under these conditions wear down the pathway until it becomes a ditch across the meadows. Then hikers begin to travel on the edge of the ditch and eventually create a second, parallel ditch and then maybe a third. The result is considerable destruction of the delicate environment.

Walking usually remains good through September, although an early fall snowfall can quickly blanket everything. Some years, this melts away. Some years, it doesn't. The hiking can remain fairly warm and dry well into October. But don't count on it.

In the mountains, all you can really count on is change. Weather conditions change, hour to hour, more rapidly than most other places. You can get rain, snow and sunshine all on the same day. In the Rockies, warm moist air from the Pacific often collides with cool, dry air from the plains. This can cause heavy rain or snow in many areas, depending on elevation and the locations of peaks and valleys. The mountains mix up the air flow.

The Columbia Icefield area gets an average of about 640 cm of snow a year and 230 cm of rain. Snow is recorded even in July and August. By contrast, the Jasper Lake area northeast of the townsite has a semi-arid climate, including sand dunes because it is located in a rain shadow. Rain tends to be pushed to either side of this small area or to fall before getting there.

Snowshoeing near Crowfoot Glacier, Banff National Park.

8 Banff National Park
Walks In And Around Banff Townsite

Tunnel Mountain Trail WALK 1

The tiny mountain MAP 5

Highlight: Mountaintop views
Distance: 4.8 km (3 miles) return
Time: 2 to 3 hours
Rating: Moderate
Maximum elevation: 1691 m
(5,550 ft.)
Elevation gain: 275 m (900 ft.)
Footwear: Walking or running shoes
Best season: May to October

An old cougar, so the story goes, lives up on Tunnel Mountain. He doesn't harm anybody; he dines on deer and rabbit and watches over the town from a clifftop vantage. Nobody knows what his reaction is to the hordes pulsing up and down Banff Avenue eating ice cream and fudge.

Tunnel Mountain is not to be compared with Temple, Lefroy, Cascade, Edith or any of the impressive alpine peaks hereabouts. It's merely a rocky protruberance between Mt. Rundle and Cascade Mountain. Once it may have been part of Rundle.

And yet the stroll up Tunnel Mountain is a joy. The climb is relatively steep; the rewards great. The trail is easily accessible right from Banff townsite, an advantage for visitors without cars. Here's one of the few mountain summits in the Rockies that can be readily ascended by the casual walker. The views over the townsite, the Bow Valley, Rundle and Banff Springs Hotel are delightful. Take along drinking water.

Access: Strollers coming on foot from the townsite can reach the trail most easily by walking up Wolf

Street which leads off Banff Ave. just before the Information Centre. After four blocks, turn right at the end of the street, taking the upper fork (St. Julian) towards the Banff Centre. The trail begins from a parking lot just below the centre and climbs steadily through open forest to Tunnel Mountain Drive.

Hikers with cars can save .4 km of steep climbing by taking Tunnel Mountain Road (See Walk 2) up from the townsite. Park at the first viewpoint on the left side above the Banff Centre. The trail begins a few metres further up the road on the right.

Route: From the viewpoint, the trail climbs steadily on a wide, beautifully-maintained trail through a dry forest, views gradually open-

Banff townsite, Banff National Park.

ing up to the townsite below, the Vermilion Lakes and the relatively level Bow Valley.

You begin to catch glimpses of the Scottish baronial splendor of Banff Springs Hotel, set between the distinctive "writing-desk" slope of Rundle and the long wooded ridge of Sulphur Mountain opposite.

A little further up, you can see where the Spray River from the south enters the Bow just below the falls. The trail soon reaches the top of the ridge, now rocky and mostly open. It turns abruptly and swings around to the Rundle side.

Now you can look down the Bow Valley past the vast "city" of Tunnel Mountain campgrounds and the hoodoos above the river. Some may prefer to go no further, although the way ahead isn't difficult. The trail stays close to the edge of the cliffs (but not dangerously close) where climbers often practice. Many of the trees up here are stately old Douglas fir, survivors of fires that downed lesser trees. This climax tree of the Montane zone has thick, fire-resistant bark.

The trail soon reaches the top of the rocky ridge, providing views on both sides. While the high point is partially treed and contains only the footings for a former lookout tower, you can walk a few metres on either side to gain better views. On the west, the whole of the town is at your feet On the other, Rundle rises massively from the golf course. Few other spots away from the roads and mechanical lifts provide such an overview for such moderate effort.

Tunnel Mountain Road

The all-season route

Highlight: Paved road above Banff with views
Distance: 4.7 km (2.9 miles) one way
Time: 1 1/2 to 2 hours
Maximum elevation: 1,493 m (4,900 ft.)
Elevation gain: 90 m (300 ft.)
Rating: Moderate
Footwear: Light walking shoes or running shoes
Season: Year-round

The route is a paved road, not a trail. You could simply drive or bicycle the distance and park at the viewpoints. Yet Tunnel Mountain Drive is popular with strollers who can be found on it any time of the year.

The route is fine in any weather. The road doesn't get blocked by snow like the trails; it doesn't get muddy in the rain; you can never lose the way. Besides, there are good viewpoints over Banff and back towards Banff Springs Hotel. What's more, the road connects downtown Banff and the Banff Centre with the Tunnel Mountain motel village and campgrounds. Automobile traffic is usually moderate and the route is consistently interesting.

Access: In Banff townsite, walk down Banff Ave. and turn left on Buffalo, the last street before the bridge over the Bow River. Strollers might also start from the small parking lot on the right, 2 km up the road at the start of the trail along Bow River to the hoodoos (Walk 3). Or do the route in reverse, starting from the motel village on Tunnel Mountain Drive.

Route: Buffalo Street leads the stroller past some fine old homes overlooking the river. You begin to climb with views opening up to Sulphur Mountain opposite and the long Spray Valley. Soon you come upon one of the most impressive views anywhere of the Scottish-baronial Banff Springs Hotel first built in 1888, then rebuilt in stages over the years.

Beyond is the beginning of the trail along Bow River to the Hoodoos. Consider taking this trail on the return to make a more varied loop.

The climbing gets steeper as you pass the Banff Centre. Visitors might enjoy stopping in at the Walter J. Phillips Gallery in the Studio Building, where Canadian and international artists exhibit paintings, ceramics, weaving and photography. Open year-round, 1-5 pm. Free admission.

Near the top of the slope is a good viewpoint and the trail to the summit of Tunnel Mountain from the townsite (Walk 1). Below, all of Banff townsite, the flat Bow Valley and Vermilion Lakes are spread out before you. Stairs and a switchbacking trail lead back to the town. The drive twists around the cliffs of Tunnel Mountain, descends slightly and reaches a T-junction where there's a store. Left is a direct route back to Banff townsite. Right are the campgrounds and hoodoos and access to the Bow River trail leading back to the townsite.

The Tunnel That Never Was

There's no tunnel in Tunnel Mountain; never has been. When surveyors for the CPR first examined the route up the Bow Valley in 1882, they planned to dig a 275-metre (900 foot) tunnel under the mountain. But C.A.E. Shaw was later commissioned to re-examine the proposed route with an eye towards saving the railway money. He re-routed the line along the Cascade trench where the Trans-Canada Highway now goes. And so the CPR situated Siding 29—the beginnings of Banff—at the foot of Cascade Mountain near the present-day buffalo paddock. But the community of Banff grew up close to the Bow River where the Cave hot pool was the major attraction. The CPR later relocated its station.

Banff to the Hoodoos   WALK 3
Path to pillared giants   MAP 5

Highlight: Hoodoos, Bow Valley views
Distance: 4.8 km (3 miles) one way
Time: 1 to 2 hours
Rating: Moderate
Maximum elevation: 1,417 m (4,650 ft)
Elevation gain: 45 m (150 ft)
Footwear: Walking or running shoes
Best season: June to October

You say you want a scenic, easy trail right from Banff townsite? With an intriguing destination?

Here's a solid recommendation—an appealing walk with constantly changing vistas of mighty Mt. Rundle, the Tunnel Mountain cliffs and the picturesque Bow River Valley—plus the strange earthen pillars called hoodoos. You may also spot coyotes, elk or deer.

The walk can also be done in reverse from Tunnel Mountain campgrounds.

Access: From Banff townsite, drive or walk south on Banff Ave. and turn left on Buffalo, last street before the bridge. Continue up Buffalo for 2 km to the small parking lot on the right at a sharp bend in the road. The trail leads down on steps from the parking lot.

Route: The pine-needled trail descends gently at first, through forest, with Mt. Rundle dominating to the right at 2,864 metres (9,338 ft). The mountain is named for Rev. Robert Rundle, a Wesleyan missionary to the Indians of the Northwest from 1840 to 1848.

Continue through mixed open

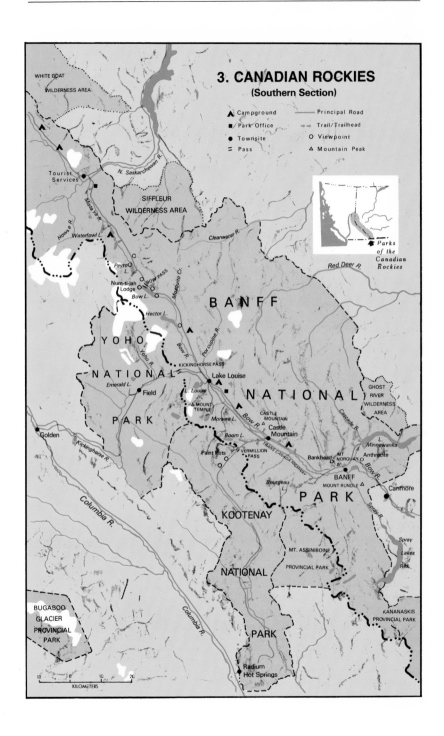

3. CANADIAN ROCKIES
(Southern Section)

⋏ Campground   —— Principal Road
■ Park Office   ⇢ Trail/Trailhead
● Townsite   ○ Viewpoint
= Pass   △ Mountain Peak

WHITE GOAT
WILDERNESS AREA

Tourist
Services

N. Saskatchewan R.

Mistaya R.

Howse R.

SIFFLEUR
WILDERNESS AREA

Waterfowl L.

Peyto
L.

Num-ti-jah
Lodge

Bow L.

Hector L.

BOW PASS

Mosquito Cr.

Clearwater R.

B A N F F

YOHO

NATIONAL

Yoho R.

Bow R.

Porcupine R.

KICKINGHORSE PASS

Lake Louise

Emerald L.

● Field

L. Louise

△ MOUNT
TEMPLE

Moraine L.

N A T I O N A L

Bow R.

CASTLE
MOUNTAIN
△
Castle
Mountain

Cascade R.

GHOST
RIVER
WILDERNESS
AREA

PARK

● Golden

Kickinghorse R.

Boom L.

Paint Pots

VERMILLION
PASS

Bourgeau
L.

TRANS-CANADA HIGHWAY

Bankhead

MT
NORQUAY

BANFF
MOUNT RUNDLE △

L.
Minnewanka

Anthracite

Bow R.

● Canmore

KOOTENAY

Columbia R.

P A R K

Spray R.

Spray
Lakes
Res.

MT. ASSINIBOINE

PROVINCIAL PARK

NATIONAL

BUGABOO
GLACIER
PROVINCIAL
PARK

Columbia R.

P A R K

KANANASKIS
PROVINCIAL PARK

Radium
Hot Springs

Red Deer R.

Parks
of the
Canadian
Rockies

10   0   10   20
KILOMETERS

Hoodoos

forest and tonic alpine air. Numerous branches from the main trail lead to the Bow River, alongside a large island. Sandy beaches along the bank make ideal picnic spots.

The walker is soon under the cliffs of limestone Tunnel Mountain, a popular practice ascent for climbers. Geologists say Tunnel Mountain was once part of Mt. Rundle. There's no tunnel in the mountain, named from early CPR survey maps drawn before an alternate route was chosen around the mountain to the north through the Cascade trench.

Continuing past Tunnel Mountain's rubble-strewn foot, views open behind to the Spray River Valley. Watch for a large flat-topped boulder at a bend in the river, a favorite resting place. Soon the trail

joins the riverside; across are the velvet-green fairways of Banff Springs Golf Course, among the top 10 scenic courses in the world.

The trail follows a side-channel for a while, then climbs a low bluff with excellent views of the Bow Valley, Mt. Rundle and the Spray Valley to the right. Descending, leave the cliffs behind and walk through flat Tunnel Mountain Meadows. This is a good spot for deer, elk and coyote.

Here you'll find an unusual perspective on Mt. Rundle, appearing as just a big gray wall. Rundle's long ridge has seven distinct high points. Only in the last 25 years have all of them been conquered from the frightening east side. This mountain illustrates the typical rock sequence found in the Rockies'

Those Inhospitable Hoodoos

The strange earthern pillars that guard the south side of Tunnel Mountain have long fascinated man.

The Indians thought they were giants who slept by day and awoke at night to throw rocks down on unsuspecting travellers.

Geologists, who tend to have a less poetic, mythic nature, claim that the hoodoos are actually columns of silt, gravel and rocks cemented together by dissolved limestone that seeped down when they were still part of the cliff's edge. The uncemented material around them slowly washed away, leaving the hoodoos.

front ranges. At the top is gray cliff-forming limestone; a middle brownish band is composed of shaley rock known as the Banff Formation. Below it, from base to treeline, is a resistant layer of gray limestone called the Palliser Formation. Many other mountains, including Cascade just north of Banff and Inglismaldie above Lake Minnewanka, display the same sequence.

Now into the trees again. Watch

for purple asters, bunchberry and brown-eyed susan. Note how trees are thinner and more stunted here, exposed to chilling winds. Keep right on the trail near the river bank.

The trail climbs to more views in both directions. Traffic noises intrude well before Tunnel Mountain Road comes into sight.

The path reaches the road and continues on its right to a lookout, before thankfully slipping right into the woods again, away from the road. Limber pine, uncommon in the park, grows on rocky outcroppings here.

The first views of the hoodoos on the south bank appear. An asphalt trail goes to a second and better viewpoint, with a panorama of the Bow and Spray Valleys (Walk 9). Visitors are discouraged from walking any closer to the hoodoos.

An alternate route back to the start is on the road itself. Traffic is heavy until the Tunnel Mountain Motel Village. Turn left on the scenic Tunnel Mountain Drive (Walk 2) and follow the quieter road back to the parking lot.

To walk in reverse from the Tunnel Mountain campgrounds, go west on the asphalt trail on the south side of Tunnel Mountain Road by the campground areas. The trail turns to a dirt path and edges down the hillside towards the Bow River.

Hoodoo Viewpoint

WALK 4

Giants sleep by day

MAP 5

Highlight: Hoodoos
Distance: .8 km (.5 mile) return
Time: 15-20 minutes
Rating: Easy
Footwear: Anything
Maximum elevation: 1,417 m (4,650 ft)
Elevation gain: Negligible
Best season: Anytime

Strange-looking pillars of earth rise along the steep hillside, like sentinels guarding the approaches to Banff. A must for most visitors, this short stroll offers excellent views of the hoodoos, the Bow and Spray Valleys and Mt. Rundle. The more energetic could combine this portion with Walk 3 from Banff townsite.

Access: Start at the viewpoint for the hoodoos, above Banff townsite on Tunnel Mountain Drive south of the Tunnel Mountain campgrounds.

Route: This short interpretive walk begins with a marvellous view over the Bow River Valley. Mt. Rundle dominates. It was named after Wesleyan missionary Rev.

Robert Rundle, who visited the area in 1847. To the right is little limestone Tunnel Mountain, which geologists believe was once part of Rundle. The Bow River is a silvery winding ribbon beneath.

Limber pine, not common in the park, inhabits rocky outcroppings by the viewpoint. This tree often has crooked trunks and large, uneven crowns. The needles are 1 1/2 to 3 1/2 inches long, in bundles of five. Cones are up to eight inches long. Under park regulations, only squirrels are allowed to gather them.

Follow the asphalt path to a second viewpoint, with better views of the hoodoos and Banff Springs Hotel. From this perspective the hotel seems to be nestled in the notch between Mt. Rundle and Tunnel Mountain.

The path loops around a third viewpoint, worthwhile for views back on Cascade and another perspective on the hoodoos.

Central Park East

Easy stroll, instant escape

MAP 5

Highlight: Mellow river walk
Distance: 2 km (1.2 miles) return
Time: 30 minutes
Rating: Easy
Maximum elevation: 1,383 m (4,538 ft)
Elevation gain: Negligible
Footwear: Anything
Best season: April to October

Here's an instant escape to amazing peace and quiet, starting right on frenetic Banff Avenue. Stroll along the fast-moving Bow River on this little outing, suitable for almost anyone. A fine remedy for souls tattered by tourism's more commercial face.

Access: In Banff townsite, start at Central Park on the north side of the bridge on Banff Ave., the main street. Park behind Banff Museum on Buffalo, just off Banff Ave.

Route: Begin on the asphalt path behind the Banff Museum next to the river. Admission to the museum is free. The museum, oldest in Western Canada, has numerous displays of wildlife, including what is perhaps the world's largest stuffed beaver.

The path leads under the bridge, where cliff swallows nest. Note the Indian faces carved into the side of the bridge. Benches and picnic tables are situated beside the Bow River.

At this point, the Bow River goes from tranquil meandering to new momentum for the plunge over Bow Falls. The water is usually silty in early summer and turns a darker green later in the season as silt particles settle. The path leads through trees, past some lovely old houses, then narrows and turns to dirt, offering views of Mt. Rundle with its slanted "desktop" east side and of the more rounded Sulphur Mountain, source of Banff's hot springs.

The trail curves along the river by a cable. You can hear the rumbling falls ahead, and catch glimpses of Banff Springs Hotel, the largest in the world when it was first built in 1888.

The trail pitches up a steep bank where some may wish to turn back. But most should persist—the trail comes out along Tunnel Mountain Drive and rewards the walker with excellent views of the venerable hotel, rising like a castle across the Bow River.

Walkers now have several choices: Return the same way; return on the road which goes past the interesting Banff cemetery (see Rainy Day Diversions-Banff); continue up Tunnel Mountain Drive for a view of Bow Falls and perhaps the highly-recommended walk up to the hoodoos for a longer outing (Walk 3).

Central Park West

The easiest stroll

MAP 5

Highlight: Semi-urban park and museum
Distance: 1 km (.6 miles) return
Time: 20 minutes
Rating: Easy (accessible to wheelchairs)
Maximum elevation: 1,383 m (4,538 ft)
Elevation gain: None
Footwear: Anything
Best Season: Anytime

Instead of surrounding sky-scrapers as in Manhattan's Central Park, you get high peaks and a placid river. The stroll is extremely short, entirely level and—for downtown Banff—peaceful indeed.

Access: In Banff townsite, drive down Banff Ave. and turn right on Buffalo St. just before the bridge. The parking lot is to the right of the Banff museum.

Route: Walk down towards the free museum that looks like a railway station in search of a train. Inside are some stuffed heads, including perhaps the world's largest stuffed beaver, plus more interesting artifacts of the park. The museum was recently renovated and deserves a visit. A reading room and new displays have been added.

Behind the museum, follow the riverside path to the right along the Bow past benches and overhanging trees urging you to stop and con-template this peaceful setting in the

middle of Banff. Cliff swallows nest under the graceful Banff Avenue Bridge and there are usually ducks on the river. The Bow, fed by the glaciers above Bow Lake, Lake Louise and by hundreds of mountain brooks, rises in turbulence, then slows in the relatively level Bow Valley enroute to far-off Hudson Bay. In spring, the river looks thick and brown with mud and glacial silt.

Banff Avenue

Later in the summer, it turns green-blue.

Across the water rises the wooded ridge of Sulphur Mountain whose subterranean depths are the source of the hot springs that were actually responsible for the forma-tion of Canada's first national park in 1885.

Note the warning signs across the river telling boaters to go no fur-ther. The river current soon picks up beyond the bridge and a canoe can be swept over Bow Falls. A few have survived the plunge; others have not.

On the right as you continue past

4. BANFF TOWNSITE

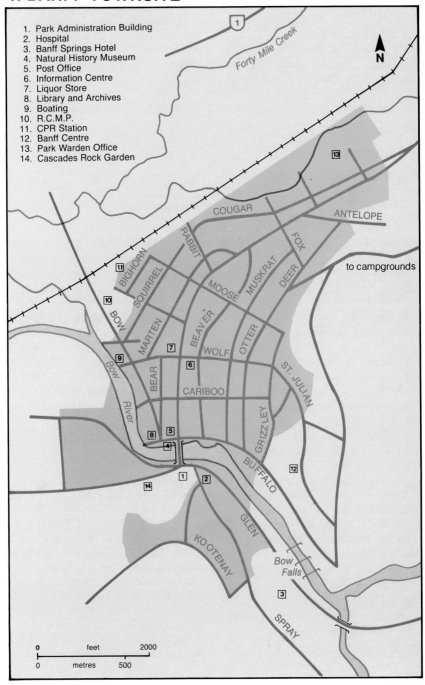

1. Park Administration Building
2. Hospital
3. Banff Springs Hotel
4. Natural History Museum
5. Post Office
6. Information Centre
7. Liquor Store
8. Library and Archives
9. Boating
10. R.C.M.P.
11. CPR Station
12. Banff Centre
13. Park Warden Office
14. Cascades Rock Garden

the park is the Peter Whyte Gallery, with changing displays of photographs and paintings by local and international artists. You also go by some of Banff's most gracious homes along riverside Bow Avenue, a different perspective on the town from throbbing Banff Avenue. The trail soon ends at a boathouse where you can rent a canoe or rowboat and experience it all in another, equally rewarding way.

Bow Falls Trail   WALK 7

Best way to Bow Falls and Banff Springs   MAP 5

Highlight: Waterfall by Banff Springs Hotel
Distance: 1.2 km (.7 miles) one way
Time: 25 minutes
Rating: Easy
Maximum elevation: 1,384 m (4,538 ft)
Elevation gain: Negligible
Footwear: Walking or running shoes
Best season: May to October

Of course, you could drive to Bow Falls and Banff Springs Hotel from downtown Banff. Yet the walk there is so easy, short and enjoyable, it deserves to be the preferred method of approach. The tumbling falls and old-world hotel are perhaps better approached gradually—and savoured.

Access: In Banff townsite, park at Central Park, on the north end of the bridge, just off Banff Ave., or anywhere you can. This walk starts by the Banff Museum.

Route: Walk south across the bridge. At the end you'll find the park administration building and the beautiful Cascade Gardens behind, lush with poppies and delphiniums in summer. This lovely building was not the first to occupy the site—Dr. Robert Brett operated the Brett Sanitorium Hotel and Hospital here until the early 1900s. Wealthy guests enjoyed what they thought to be curative powers found in the hot sulphur water, piped in from the springs above.

The Luxton Museum, which houses one of the best exhibits of Plains Indians artifacts, is just west on Cave Avenue in the fort-like building. Turn right on the other side of the bridge and walk underneath. Note the carefully-imbedded stones and sculpted Indian faces on the side of the bridge. The river is usually silty in early summer and later turns to green-blue. A horse trail winds by on the right while a more suitable foot trail leads close by the river, through lovely groves of fir and patches of bunchberry and wild-

5. BANFF (Southeast)

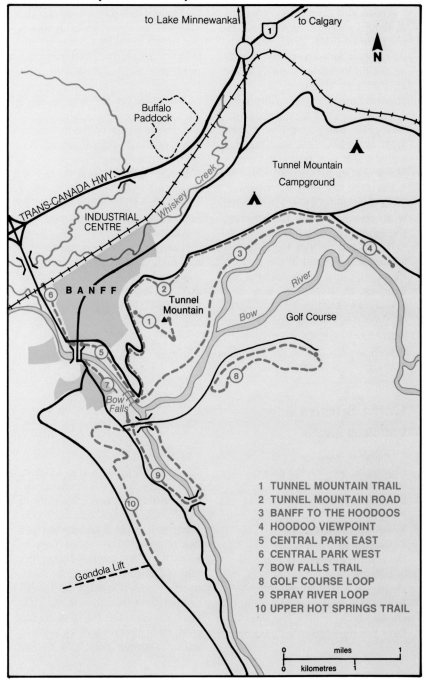

to Lake Minnewanka

to Calgary

N

Buffalo
Paddock

TRANS-CANADA HWY

INDUSTRIAL
CENTRE

Whiskey Creek

Tunnel Mountain
Campground

B A N F F

Tunnel
Mountain

Bow River

Golf Course

Bow
Falls

Gondola Lift

1 TUNNEL MOUNTAIN TRAIL
2 TUNNEL MOUNTAIN ROAD
3 BANFF TO THE HOODOOS
4 HOODOO VIEWPOINT
5 CENTRAL PARK EAST
6 CENTRAL PARK WEST
7 BOW FALLS TRAIL
8 GOLF COURSE LOOP
9 SPRAY RIVER LOOP
10 UPPER HOT SPRINGS TRAIL

miles

kilometres

flowers including yellow cinquefoil.

Ahead you can see the rooftops of Banff Centre on limestone Tunnel Mountain. Mt. Rundle looms to its right. There are views of cliffs on the other side of the river, and of Cascade Mountain north and smaller Stoney Squaw to its left.

The path climbs slightly above the falls. The water roars over rock steps in the river, although the high water levels of spring make it look like a continuous plunge.

Once the falls were much higher. Over thousands of years, they have worn down the rock barrier from the height of the left bank.

Now Banff Springs Hotel comes into view. Descend to the parking lot where there's a promenade and benches.

Walkers continuing to Banff Springs Hotel can go through the parking lot and follow signs up the stairs to the rustic golf clubhouse, and over a beautiful wooden trestle bridge. Enter the hotel near the gorgeous indoor and outdoor pools (for guests only). You can walk back on the road to the townsite, or perhaps pause at Grapes, a wine and cheese lounge on the mezzanine level, or the 24-hour Espresso Bar on the arcade level.

If the walk has really been an appetite rouser, consider sushi or shabu shabu (Japanese version of fondue) in the Samurai Japanese Restaurant.

Hotel tours are held regularly in the high season of summer and winter and usually start between 3:30 and 4 p.m. at the curio shop. Call 762-2211 for details.

Golf Course Loop   WALK 8

Cliffs and greens   MAP 5

Highlight: Velvet fairways, mountain views
Distance: 1.2 km (.75 miles) return
Time: 40 minutes
Rating: Moderate
Maximum elevation: 1,385 m (4,550 ft)
Elevation gain: 30 m (100 ft)
Footwear: Walking or running shoes
Best season: May to October

The Banff Springs Golf Course, with its velvet fairways and magnificent setting between the cliffs of Mt. Rundle and the blue of the Bow River is a magical place—and you don't have to pay green fees to enjoy it. There are trails along the edge of fairways for much of the course, ranked among the top 10 scenic links in the world. Or strollers can take the golf course road, ending up at Devil's Cauldron, where a green pond fills a hole

Banff Springs Hotel

"If we can't export the scenery, we'll import the tourists."

Those famous words, spoken by William Van Horne, general superintendent of the Canadian Pacific Railway, heralded the beginnings of Banff Springs Hotel.

In 1883, the mineral hot springs of Sulphur Mountain were discovered; by 1886 a 10-square-mile block around it had been declared a national reserve and proposals were made to expand the park.

Van Horne foresaw the fabulous tourism potential of the park and predicted that wealthy people travelling by rail would enjoy the mountain playground. In 1887, he made plans for a hotel at the confluence of the Bow and Spray Rivers.

The 250-room hotel was the largest in the world when finished in 1888, but by 1910 it was decided to build anew. Designed in the Scottish baronial tradition, a central stone section was completed in 1913. The original north wing burned down in 1926 and the original south wing was demolished and rebuilt in 1928.

Inside, decor ranges from Spanish in the Alhambra Dining Room to 15th-century gothic in the Mount Stephen Hall. The designers tried to imitate the furniture found in European castles of the time. The oak panelling is from Michigan, the glass in the Riverview Lounge is from Czechoslovakia, the Stephen Hall flagstone from Indiana.

The hotel recently completed a $20-million renovation, and boasts 100 per cent occupancy in its 578 guest rooms from May 1 to September 28. A year-round outdoor pool was completely renovated in 1983, along with a stunning glass-enclosed terrace by the indoor pool, looking out on the Bow River Valley.

The average length of stay used to be a month to six weeks. Now the normal summer stay is two nights, and the winter stay is seven nights on average. Oh, for more leisurely times.

created by a huge, melting block of ice left behind by the retreating glaciers.

Access: Energetic strollers could park their vehicles by Bow Falls in Banff townsite and cross the Spray

River on the bridge, following the road or the trail just beside the road. For a shorter walk, drive over the Spray bridge and continue 1.2 km down the road to a point opposite the No. 4 fairway just before it starts a long dogs-leg to the left. Watch for three boulders on the golf course side of the road and two at the trail entrance.

Route: The trail climbs from the road in a forest of lodgepole pine and white spruce, switchbacking up on a well-graded path with views across to the cliffs of Tunnel Mountain where climbers often practise. There's a feeling of wilderness here, just a few paces from the famous golf course. The trail comes out under the cliffs of Rundle, giving spectacular views back to Banff Springs Hotel. On top of the little

ridge is a grassy spot, fine for a picnic or contemplation of the wild mountains, contrasting with the softness of the fairways.

Below, Shuswap Indians once built their dwellings. Rev. Robert T. Rundle, a Wesleyan missionary, may have been the first white man to view this scene—minus the golf course. In June, 1841, he ascended the Bow Valley, camped near the foot of Cascade Mountain and visited Bow Falls.

The golf course was started in 1911 by the CPR. German prisoners of war extended it to 18 holes during the First World War. But in 1927, the course was redesigned by Stanley Thompson, one of the world's foremost golf architects. Today it's 6,729 yards, par 71. Optical foreshortening,

Banff Springs Hotel

caused by the clear air and the huge mountains towering over the course, often causes golfers to under-estimate the distance to the green, just as hikers misjudge the distance to their destination. The trail continues along the semi-open ridge over the deep green of the golf course and you can now see Mt. Norquay with its ski development on the left, Cascade to its right, and down the Bow River towards Canmore. The trail descends on an old road to the bowl below. At an orange, lichen-covered rock, keep left and descend to the road. Turn left on the road to return to your starting point in just a few minutes.

Spray River Loop

WALK 9

Spray River stroll

MAP 5

Highlight: Peaceful riverside stroll
Distance: 2.2 km (1.3 miles) return
Time: 1 hour
Rating: Moderate
Maximum elevation: 1,371 m (4,500 ft)
Elevation gain: Negligible
Footwear: Walking or running shoes (except in wet conditions)
Best season: May to October

The Spray River Valley just upsteam from Banff Springs Hotel isn't spectacular or exciting. The trail alongside the river simply provides gentle woodland walking easily accessible from Banff townsite.

This route can be easily tailored to one's energy. A pleasant afternoon can be lolled away picnicking along sandy banks, or proceeding 4.6 km (3 miles) further to a picnic spot. Unfortunately, much of this walk is used by horses which churn it into a quagmire in wet weather.

Access: From Banff Information Centre, drive south on Banff Ave. across the bridge, turn left on Spray Ave. towards Banff Springs Hotel and left again at the sign for the golf course. Park at Bow Falls.

Route: Walk over the Spray River Bridge, past a mountain-climbing sheep carrying an ice axe and rope. (Really. His name is Rocky the Ram.) Proceed south on the edge of the lush manicured first green. (This is the most dangerous part—watch for flying golf balls.) Stay close to the river. Don't take the trail that leads off further down the fairway. It is a route for Mt. Rundle and beyond.

A little path in the trees across the fairway leads to the river. Behind looms Banff Springs Hotel underneath Sulphur Mountain; ahead is the Spray River Valley and the incredible slanted slopes of Mt. Rundle are to the east.

The Spray River is relatively tranquil at this point. Its headwaters have been tamed by a hydro-electric development outside the park. You'll soon pass a junction for the Mt. Rundle trail; keep right by the river through the aspens.

Profusions of harebells, purple asters and arnica brighten the bank, compensation for the damage that horses do to the trail. There are pleasant places along the river for picnics on the ground. After 20 minutes or so, cross a wooden bridge. There's an abandoned quarry here where rocks were cut for the building of the Banff Springs Hotel, the Banff Post Office and the Park Administration Building.

Loop north back to Banff Springs Hotel on a less-interesting fire road out of sight of the river. At the junction here, walkers have the option of continuing 4.6 km (3 miles) to the left along the river to a picnic area. The Spray River Youth Hostel is 3 km down the fire road.

To the right, the fire road ends at a locked gate just before the Banff Springs Hotel at the end of Spray Avenue. To return to the Bow Falls parking lot, you could enter the hotel and descend to the arcade level, then out the doors above the pool, following the elevated walkway to the golf club house and the Spray River Bridge, where you started.

Upper Hot Springs Trail

Sweat and soak MAP 5

Highlight: Good soak at the end
Distance: 3.2 km (2 miles) return
Time: 30 to 40 minutes one way
Rating: Moderate
Maximum elevation: 1,584 m (5,200 ft)
Elevation gain: 182 m (600 ft)
Footwear: Walking or running shoes
Best season: May to October

Frankly, this trail isn't much, as mountain routes go. From the Banff Springs Hotel, you pass through fairly thick forest and climb a hill. That's all. What makes the trail worthwhile is its destination—the Upper Hot Springs pool. By climbing the trail rather than driving up the road, you feel you really deserve a soak in the warm, soothing mineral waters. After sweating up the slope, you probably need a swim anyway. And finally, for those without transportation, the trail is more pleasant and less dangerous than walking up to the hot springs on the edge of the long, straight, and somewhat monotonous road from Banff townsite. Don't forget your bathing suit.

Access: In Banff townsite, drive down Banff Avenue across the Bow River and turn left, following the signs to Banff Springs Hotel. Park along the street as close to the hotel as possible (sometimes you won't get too close because it's such a busy spot). Just past the entrance to the hotel, you'll find a parking lot on the oppositefar side marked "24-hour Valet Parking." The trail starts at the far upper corner of the lot where there's a sign.

Route: The trouble with this trail is the maze of intersecting routes. It isn't recommended after dark, at

least the first time through. In daylight, you have only to keep going in the same general upward direction, switchbacking up the moderately steep slope and leading generally left. The trail turns into an old road. At a multi-forked junction near the top, take the uppermost branch to gain the road just below the Rimrock Hotel. (The branch left leads under the Rimrock to the little

known—and not very interesting—Kidney Hot Springs, situated almost directly under the hotel. Water flows to the surface at about 38°C (100°F) and trickles down the hillside, creating a lush ribbon of vegetation.

The main trail leads up to the highway just north of the Rimrock. The Viewpoint Lounge at this hotel has lovely vistas over the Spray Valley and Mt. Rundle, a favorite watering hole, especially if you've just climbed the hill. Otherwise, turn left towards the hot springs parking lot, then up the short road to the pool. On your left, you pass ledges of the sponge-like rock called tufa that form at the outlet of some hot springs from the mineral deposits in the water.

The upper pool has a daily flow of 774,000 litres (172,000 gallons) of filtered and chlorinated water that's usually around 38°C (100°F), although this temperature will vary. We enjoy the pool most in winter when there's snow around it. Mist rising off the hot water gives this otherwise mundane scene a strange unreality. Just don't get so relaxed you can't make it down the trail again.

6. BANFF (Southwest)

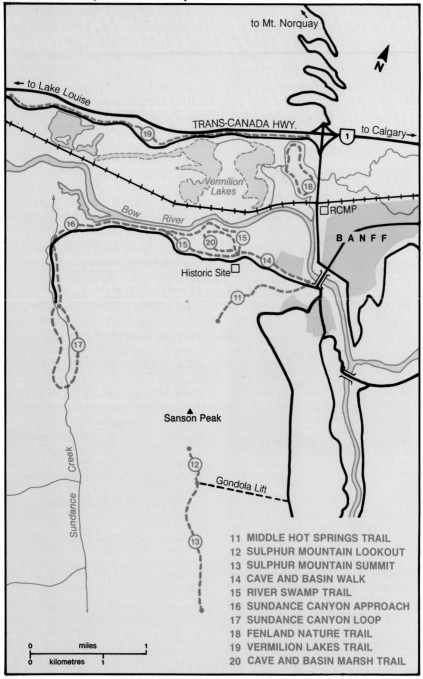

to Mt. Norquay

N

to Lake Louise

TRANS-CANADA HWY.

19

to Calgary→

1

18

Vermilion Lakes

Bow River

RCMP

16

BANFF

15 20 15

14

Historic Site

11

17

Sanson Peak

Sundance Creek

12

Gondola Lift

13

11 MIDDLE HOT SPRINGS TRAIL
12 SULPHUR MOUNTAIN LOOKOUT
13 SULPHUR MOUNTAIN SUMMIT
14 CAVE AND BASIN WALK
15 RIVER SWAMP TRAIL
16 SUNDANCE CANYON APPROACH
17 SUNDANCE CANYON LOOP
18 FENLAND NATURE TRAIL
19 VERMILION LAKES TRAIL
20 CAVE AND BASIN MARSH TRAIL

0   miles   1
0   kilometres   1

Middle Hot Springs

WALK 11

Hot water and unpleasant smells

MAP 6

Highlight: Undeveloped hot sulphur springs
Distance: 3 km (1.8 miles) return
Time: 2 hours
Rating: Moderate
Maximum elevation: 1,490 m (4,900 ft)
Elevation gain: 100 m (350 ft)
Footwear: Walking or running shoes
Best season: May to October

Although little known, the Middle Hot Springs above Banff townsite on the gentle wooded slopes of Sulphur Mountain are a unique place to visit. Here's one of the few undeveloped hot springs in Banff National Park, historically significant and geologically fascinating. Behind them is a cave, examples of the peculiar rock called tufa found around mineral springs and a lush meadow on a plateau offering views over the the Bow Valley.

Access: In Banff townsite, drive down Banff Avenue to the Cascade Gardens and the Park Administration Building straight ahead at the far end of the bridge. There's public parking.

Route: Stroll up through the Cascade Gardens built in 1934 as a Depression-era project. They were originally intended by Toronto architect Howard Beckett to illustrate the successive eras of geological time as represented by rocks of varying ages, all connected by cascades of water. Later research indicates that geologically-speaking, the representation is not accurate. Nevertheless, the gardens are certainly scenic with their decorative pools and streams and thousands of poppies, golden columbine and delphiniums.

Work your way to the upper right edge of the gardens to find the Upper Pergola. Near it is a revolving animal-proof gate in the fence. Whirl through that and follow the

well-groomed trail, avoiding the side route left that leads up to houses just visible through the trees.

There's a potentially-confusing network of trails here and you cross

Sulphur Mountain Teahouse

and re-cross a bridle path. Most of the trails will take you where you're going if you continue generally upward and onward. The easiest way is to follow the signs that say "Footpath," and to stay on the cinders, where you have a choice.

You climb gradually to an old road and begin to smell the distinctive hydrogen sulphide odour of the hot springs. The first one should be visible up the hillside above the road, several small holes in the earth with warm water issuing from them. The little stream below them contains white fronds of algae that grow in the warm mineral water. Above is a shallow cave composed of tufa, the distinctive rock which looks like a sponge and forms at the outlet of hot springs. This has been the main

outlet for the springs.

Tufa (pronounced too-fa) is created when the hot water containing large amounts of dissolved calcium reaches the surface and begins to cool. In a cooler state, it can't hold all its calcium and precipitates the mineral which builds up over the centuries into sponge-like rock.

In front of the caves is a meadow providing good views over the U-shaped, glacier-gouged Bow Valley.

These springs are undeveloped now but were used in the late 1880s when Dr. R. C. Brett, a surgeon connected with the CPR survey team, was given permission to build a sanitorium where the park administration building now stands. The Brett sanitorium eventually burned down.

The hot water from these springs, like the Cave and Basin Springs and the Upper Hot Springs, comes from several thousand metres under Sulphur Mountain. Ground water from snow and rain percolates downwards into the mountain through cracks in the rock and comes in contact with heated rocks at great depths. The hot water dissolves quantities of minerals such as calcium, magnesium chloride and sulphur. It flows to the surface along the Sulphur Mountain thrust fault.

Nobody knows if this mineral water really does anything for your health. But bathing in it is so relaxing you usually feel better, for a while.

You shouldn't try to bathe in the Middle Hot Springs, but you could follow the road from here along to the Upper Hot Springs Road or take the trails directly down to the Cave and Basin springs where the pool is cooler and perhaps more refreshing.

Sulphur Mountain Lookout   WALK 12

Lazy lookout   MAP 6

Highlight: Panoramas of Banff area
Distance: 1.6 km (1 mile) return
Time: 20 to 30 minutes
Rating: Easy
Maximum elevation: 2,316 m (7,600 ft)
Elevation gain: 30 m (100 ft)
Footwear: Walking or running shoes
Best season: Mid-June to October

Here's peak panorama without pain. A short but rewarding walk starts after a gondola whisks the visitor to a futuristic teahouse on top of Sulphur Mountain above Banff townsite. You soon reach a lookout where views can extend 145 kilometres (90 miles) on a clear day, better than an aerial photo. Use a polarizing lens for photos which otherwise tend to turn out hazy.

Curious bighorn sheep, chipmunks, golden-mantled squirrels and Columbian ground squirrels have lost their fear of humans up here. On a warm day, you can picnic at tables provided on top. Just don't expect solitude.

Short interpretive walks are conducted regularly from the teahouse, June 15 to Sept. 15, weather permitting. For more information, call 762-5438 or 762-2523. If you want to walk up to the teahouse from the bottom, a forested trail switchbacks up 4.8 km, an elevation gain of 650 metres (2,132 feet). It starts from the Upper Hot Springs parking area and takes about two hours one way. If you walk up, you can ride down free.

Access: From the Park Information Centre in Banff townsite, drive south on Banff Ave. across the bridge. Turn left on Spray and then take the first right on Mountain Ave. Follow the signs 3.2 km (2 miles) to the Sulphur Mtn. Gondola Lift. The gondola is open year-round.

Route: Starting on the north side of the teahouse, walk down wooden steps to a panoramic view of the Bow Valley. Picnic tables are situated here, and chipmunks, golden-mantled squirrels and bighorn sheep vie for the visitor's attention, sometimes for his lunch. Be hard-hearted. Feeding aninmals in the park is not only illegal, it destroys their natural feeding patterns. It makes them sick and dependent on hand-outs.

The trail winds through stunted fir and spruce, then up a wide, rocky section often exposed to the wind, ending at the site of an abandoned government meteorological station. The station was established in 1902 to study wind and other high-altitude weather conditions.

Here Sulphur Mountain offers its most dramatic views: the wide Bow Valley, the Bow River a slim thread slicing through it, the sharp-toothed Sawback Range across the river, slate-gray Cascade rising to the north and Norquay to its left. Tiny Tunnel Mountain is east; deep-blue Lake Minnewanka shimmers far beyond. The high mountain north of the lake is Mt. Aylmer.

To the south, the teahouse looks somewhat like a concrete spaceship perched on the ridge. There's a cafeteria and licensed restaurant inside. An early bird breakfast is offered—call 762-5438 for times.

Cascade Mountain

Of Squirrels, Stripes and Chipmunks

When is a chipmunk not a chipmunk? Most probably, when it's a golden-mantled ground squirrel. This appealing scamp is often mistaken for a large chipmunk because of its stripes. It can, however, be distinguished by looking to see whether the stripes extend to the head. If they do, the critter is indeed a chipmunk. If not, it's a squirrel. The mature squirrel is also larger than the mature chipmunk.

The golden-mantled ground squirrel can be found in many areas of the parks from valley to timberline, but usually inhabits rocky areas. It is not gregarious and rarely appears in groups of more than two. The Columbian ground squirrel, on the other hand, is larger than the golden-mantled squirrel and has a mottled gray coat and reddish legs. Commonly seen in summer, it also frequents areas from valley to timberline, but prefers sandy soils. It's known for intricate tunnelling, digging an average of 11 entrances to each tunnel system.

The least chipmunk has the distinction of being the smallest chipmunk in North America. It is recognizable by black stripes which extend from its back onto the head and tip of its nose. This chipmunk is also found from valley to timberline, usually frequenting dry, rocky areas.

Sulphur Mountain Summit   WALK 13

Gentle ridge in the clouds   MAP 6

Highlight: Easy ridge walk, some views
Distance: 3.2 km (2 miles) return
Time: 1 1/2 hours
Rating: Moderate
Maximum elevation: 2,346 m (7,700 ft)
Elevation gain: 60 m (200 ft)
Footwear: Walking or running shoes
Best season: Mid-June to Sept.

Start at the Upper Teahouse on Sulphur Mountain for this high-in-the-sky little outing. An eight-minute gondola ride transports you to a designer, space-age teahouse not far below the mountain's summit ridge; the walk follows the ridge south on a dirt trail.

Although views are less spectacular than the shorter stroll north of the teahouse (Walk 12), there are inspiring vistas of the Sundance

Range beyond the Sundance Valley to the west. The trail is usually less crowded this direction, and inquisitive bighorn sheep are apt to tag along behind you. If you want a more strenuous outing, a 4.8-km (3-mile) trail switchbacks through

Bighorn sheep, which associate people with food, tend to follow the visitor.

Parks Canada personnel warn that mountain sheep around here are becoming dangerously undernourished because of reliance on

Mt. Rundle

trees up the side of Sulphur Mountain from the Upper Hot Springs. If you walk up, you can ride down for free.

Access: From the Park Information Centre in Banff townsite, drive south on Banff Ave. across the bridge, turn left on Spray and take the first right on Mountain Ave.; following signs 3.2 km (2 miles) to the Sulphur Mountain gondola lift. It's open year-round.

Route: Follow the dirt path, through stunted fir and spruce (and regrettably sometimes discarded containers and other garbage).

food handouts. They may starve to death on a diet of human snacks provided by well-meaning tourists. If you care for these animals at all, you won't feed them.

Continue left where the trail splits. Squirrels are a common sight. The trail steepens, and excellent views open up east to Mt. Rundle, the Bow River and Lake Minnewanka. Keep on the left side of a large rock outcropping; the trail then leads to the west side of the ridge again, progressing past boulders. Watch your footing in this rock-strewn area. Pick your way up the rocky trail for appealing vistas of the Sundance Range to the west.

A sign indicates the end of the trail. The more intrepid can pick their way up a few more metres onto a high bluff for better views.

Of Bighorns and Mountain Goats

Do bighorn sheep and mountain goats confuse you? Park naturalists have this advice: If it's brown, it's a sheep. Goats are white, and molt in the summer. Simple, isn't it?

About 1,200 bighorn sheep range in Banff National Park. They are the remnant of large herds which dwindled with the settling of the West. Over-hunted, unable to compete with domestic livestock for food, and prone to disease, they retreated to remote parts of their mountain range.

Male bighorn sheep sport magnificent curling horns, while both male and female goats have sharp, pointed horns. Sheep horns remain for life, and grow all year except for a short time in winter. You can tell their age by counting the number of rings—distinct rings mark renewed yearly growth.

Common places to see sheep in Banff National Park are at Sulphur Mountain Summit, on the south-facing slopes above Vermilion Lakes, near Lake Minnewanka and Stewart Canyon. In Jasper National Park, they are frequently viewed along the Yellowhead Highway by Disaster Point.

Banff Avenue to Cave and Basin   WALK 14

Saunter 'n' swim   MAP 6

Highlight: Walk to naturally-heated pool
Distance: 1.6 km (1 mile) one way
Time: 20 minutes
Rating: Easy
Maximum elevation: 1,383 m (4,540 ft)
Elevation gain: Negligible

Footwear: Anything
Best season: May to November

A level woodland path leads from busy Banff Avenue to the historic Cave and Basin Hot Springs. The cave's discovery in 1883 led to the creation of Banff National Park. The pool was renovated in 1985 to its

1914 splendour, right down to rental of 1914-style bathing suits.

You may wish to browse through exhibits at the Cave and Basin Centennial Centre or explore several interesting walks which begin near there. The short Discovery Trail takes you above the Centre to the origins of the hot springs. (See Walks 15, 16 and 20.) Then slip into the waters which have an average temperature of 30-35°C—cooler than the Upper Hot Springs, which averages 40°C.

Access: In Banff townsite, start at the north end of the bridge on Banff Ave.

Route: Begin by crossing the bridge over the Bow River, whose waters turn a darker green as the summer wears on and glacial silt particles settle. Cliff swallows nest under the bridge.

The building at the end of the bridge is the park administration headquarters. The lovely Cascade Gardens behind are worth a visit.

Turn right at the end of the bridge. Walk down Cave Avenue past the Indian Trading Post and the Luxton Museum, an impressive log building. Operated by the Glenbow-Alberta Institute, it contains a remarkable collection which celebrates the Plains Indians. Hours are 10 a.m.-6 p.m. (at least) in summer, 10-5 p.m. in winter, open seven days a week.

The path soon veers into the woods on the river side of the road. It passes some rustic houses and the Brewster Stables and leads through the trees parallel to Cave Avenue, then past the vast parking lot for the Cave and Basin.

When the springs first became known, with their slightly radioactive waters, they were hailed as a cure for everything from syphilis to mercury poisoning. This may have been over-optimistic. In their heyday, however, crutches and canes were nailed to the trees outside by those who attributed cures to the sulphur-laden water.

Cave and Basin Hot Springs

Cave and Basin

The beautiful glistening stalactites that decorated this silent cave were like some fantastic tale of the Arabian Nights... They had attained such perfection, that it must have required myriads of years to shape them to the size they had developed into.

That's how William McCardell described the experience of discovering sulphur hot springs within a misty cave. The year was 1883. He and his companions had found the Cave and Basin.

The three railway workers who made the discovery were not the first men to see these springs—but they were the first to try and profit from them. The Stoney Indians knew of the two mineral hot springs and legend has it that arthritic grizzly bears used to soak their aching bones there.

Soon after their discovery, a dispute arose over ownership that caught the attention of the federal government. In 1885, 25.9 square kilometres (10 square miles) were formally set aside around the springs as a reserve, the beginnings of Canada's superb national park system. In 1887 the area became Rocky Mountains National Park.

That same year, bathhouses were erected beside the Basin and at the entrance to the Cave. In 1914, a large stone building was added. Deterioration prompted closure of this building in 1976.

Fortunately, the Cave and Basin was extensively renovated for the 100th birthday of Canada's national park system in 1985. Visitors may once again enjoy the 1914 building, complete with swimming pool.

The original basin spring has been restored to its 19th-century appearance, bordered by a replica of the original bathhouse. Inside, a photo gallery, Edwardian-style lounge, computer games about the park and multi-image theatre are open year-round.

Most of the Cave and Basin Centennial Centre is accessible to wheelchairs.

Two new interpretive walks also marked the park centennial. The Discovery Trail above the Centennial Centre offers a look at the vent opening to the Cave hot spring, Billy's Lake, a "scratch and sniff" boulder and a quiet resting place by this historic pool. The Marsh Trail explores the edges of the marshland in front of the centre, illustrating the incredible effect of warm water on this environment.

River Swamp Trail

The montane wetland

MAP 6

Highlight: Marshland walk
Distance: 2 km (1.3 mile) loop
Time: 30 to 40 minutes
Rating: Easy
Maximum elevation: 1,383 m (4,540 ft)
Elevation gain: Negligible
Footwear: Walking or running shoes
Best season: May to October

This walk is mostly for swamp lovers: Those who admire wetland habitat and want to see waterfowl, other birds and not too many other strollers. The trail is flat and certainly not spectacular; in fact it's probably less of an obvious attraction than the other routes in the popular Cave and Basin area. The trail is also used by horses, not a point in its favor for the walker. It does, however, provide easy access from Banff to the rich montane wetlands.

Access: The trail starts at the Cave and Basin Hot Springs parking lot, 1.6 km west of the park administration building on Cave Avenue. (See Walk 14 for footpath from Banff Ave.) The trailhead starts below the middle of the parking lot, on the north side.

Route: The trail begins with a walk down towards Bow River, with dramatic views of Mt. Norquay straight ahead. This mountain was named for John Norquay, a former premier of Manitoba.

Slate-gray Cascade glistens to its right, and the spiky Sawback Range thrusts upwards across the Bow River Valley flats to the northwest. The distinctive needle-like pinnacle of Mt. Edith is west of Norquay. The path leads along an old dike bordered by marsh—a continuation of the Montane wetlands of Vermilion Lakes, rich in wildlife and waterfowl. Watch for warblers, juncos and several species of ducks. This is also prime beaver country.

Proceed past a tangle of willows, sedges, water lilies, duckweeds, cattails and rushes, further into the marsh. It curves along the Bow River, slow-moving at this point. Early in the year the river is silt-laden but becomes a darker green as these particles settle.

Cross some little wooden bridges along the riverbank. The lower flanks of Sulphur Mountain are to the left. Four major thermal springs are found on the northeast slope of this mountain. Two, the Cave and Basin and Upper Hot Springs, have been developed. Middle Hot Springs, (see Walk 11) and Kidney Hot Springs under the Rimrock Hotel, haven't been.

Go over another bridge, with views across the river east to Cascade. The trail curves south to an asphalt road, which is closed to traffic. This is the old road to Sundance Canyon, now restricted to walkers, bicycles and official park vehicles. You could turn right for Sundance Canyon (see Walk 16), where coyote and elk are sometimes seen, but the canyon trailhead is almost 3 km further. Turn left to

get back to the parking lot past the renovated Cave and Basin pool.

Sundance Canyon Approach WALK 16
Hard footing along the Bow MAP 6

Highlight: Views of Bow River and Sawback Range
Distance: 6.4 km (3.9 miles)
Time: 2 hours, not including canyon loop
Rating: Moderate
Maximum elevation: 1,463 m (4,800 ft)
Elevation gain: 60 m (200 ft)
Footwear: Walking or running shoes
Best season: April to October

While intended primarily as an access route from Banff to the impressive overhanging Sundance Canyon (See Walk 17), this traffic-free, paved road does offer good vistas along the Bow River and leads past the historic Cave and Basin Springs, now restored as a cool pool. Since the route is paved, it is fine for rainy weather, for wheelchairs and bicycles. At the end, go for a plunge in the Cave and Basin.

Be warned, however, that the mileage above does not include the 2.4-km (1.5 mile) Sundance Canyon Loop. Hikers planning on exploring the canyon should perhaps allow half a day and be

prepared for sore feet. In our experience, walking on a paved road such as this is more tiring than hiking a softer woodland trail. Really, the best way to get to Sundance Cayon, now that the road is closed to motor vehicles, is by bicycle. Bicycles may be rented in Banff.

Access: In Banff townsite, cross the Bow River on Banff Ave. Bridge, then turn right and follow Cave Ave., 1.6 km (1 mile) to the large parking lot at the end. For foot access from the bridge, see Walk 14.

Route: From the parking lot, walk past the naturally-heated springs. This is where Canada's national parks really started. Three prospectors lowered themselves into the cave and enjoyed a soak in the hot water that came from the depths of Sulphur Mountain. Then they built a primitive bath house here and tried to buy the land. But the federal government decided to reserve the land and thus began in 1885 what was to become the largest system of national parks in the world.

Continue past the Cave and Basin

pool onto the old paved road now closed to traffic, except for park vehicles or bicycles.

An excellent, though longer way to approach Sundance Canyon, is to take the River Swamp Trail (Walk 15) which rejoins the paved road about 1.5 km (1 mile) beyond the pool. Otherwise, continue around a locked gate and descend gradually to the Bow River.

The road parallels the river, closely and provides excellent views across to the sharp-toothed Sawback Range. Most prominent in the range is the pinnacle of Mt. Edith directly opposite. The river marshland usually contains waterfowl and it's a fine scene in any weather. Coyote, moose and elk can sometimes be seen along here.

The road curves left away from the river and into the forest, gradually ascending Sundance Creek. It soon reaches a shady picnic area, picnic shelter and toilets. The road ends here and the Sundance Canyon Loop begins.

Sundance Canyon Loop

WALK 17

Wild, romantic canyon

MAP 6

Highlight: Steep-walled canyon and cascades
Distance: 2.4 km (1.4 miles) loop
Time: 1 hour
Rating: Moderate
Maximum Elevation: 1,463 m (4,800 ft)
Elevation gain: 60 m (200 ft)
Footwear: Walking or running shoes
Best season: May to October

An impressive overhanging canyon, waterwalls, cascades, huge boulders, a viewpoint overlooking the Bow Valley and the rugged Sawback Range range behind all make this walk rewarding. Too bad Sundance Canyon is so difficult to reach on foot.

Access: The best and fastest way to reach the canyon on the old, paved road now closed to all except park vehicles is by bicycle. They can be rented in Banff, if you didn't bring your own. Otherwise, the route is a moderately long, but not unscenic walk of 3.2 km (2 miles) each way just to reach the canyon from the parking lot at the Cave and Basin pool in Banff. (See Walk 16.) At Sundance Canyon, the trail begins where the road ends at the picnic area. Sundance Canyon can also be reached on a forested trail that starts from a parking area a short distance up the Sunshine Road from the Trans-Canada, 10 km west of Banff. It leads to Sundance Road near the canyon in 4.6 km.

Route: You pass a sign explaining how Sundance Creek has eroded a soft layer of rock dipping sharply to the west. Large boulders have fallen into the stream because it has undercut the rock. Apparently, long ago a large river flowed out of the canyon where the relatively small Sundance Creek now runs. More recent glacial action diverted its upper drainage basin into the Spray River system on the other side of Sulphur Mountain.

The trail crosses the creek on a footbridge, then climbs past an overhanging cliff, ascending along the creek's cascades. This canyon was part of the setting for a novel by Ralph Connor who depicted it as the site of an Indian sundance ceremony.

The trail ascends steeply on short flights of stairs and crosses the stream again at a fascinating viewpoint with water cascading everywhere in the boulder-strewn stream-bed. A rugged and romantic place, such as Coleridge might have dreamed.

But oh! that deep romantic chasm which slanted
Down the green hill athwart a cedern cover!
A savage place! as holy and enchanted
As e'er beneath a waning moon was haunted
By woman wailing for her demon-lover!

Stone steps take you further alongside the stream. Cross again below another cascade beyond the overhanging cliffs. Cross the creek for the last time and take the trail fork right (the path straight ahead goes nowhere special) to climb gradually above the canyon. The trail continues on the hilltop for a short distance, then reaches a viewpoint over the Bow Valley with the rugged, steeply-tilted Sawback Range behind. Elk, moose and coyote may be seen in this area. Beyond the viewpoint, the trail switchbacks steeply down to the picnic area again.

Fenland Nature Trail

WALK 18

Marshland habitat

MAP 6

Highlight: Self-guiding nature trail
Distance: 2 km (1.2 miles) loop
Time: 30 minutes
Rating: Easy
Maximum elevation: 1,382 m (4,535 ft)
Elevation gain: None
Footwear: Anything
Best season: May to October

This self-guiding nature trail, which loops around a lazy bend in Forty Mile Creek on the Bow River flats, is a surprise. Although it simply traverses unspectacular woodland and marshland on the edge of Banff townsite, the trail is consistently interesting. Moose, deer beaver, red-winged blackbirds and a variety of waterfowl are seen along these pleasant paths. A fine walk for families. Brochures are usually available from a box near the start of the trail describing the area and the gradual, fascinating transition from forest to pond environment. Early evening before dusk is the best time to see animals.

Access: In Banff townsite, take Lynx Ave. north towards the Trans-Canada Hwy, following the signs. Cross the railway track and park in the wide, gravel clearing on the right just beyond the tracks—or back at the station. Walk across the road and find the trailhead a few metres north.

Route: Initially, the wide, level trail winds through thick forest of mostly white spruce. This is an area of rich river-bottom soil inside a loop of Forty Mile Creek which winds across the flat Bow Valley.

Go left at the first fork, the forest growing thinner as the environment becomes moister. This fen environment consists of damp soil, grasses and sedges. An abandoned river channel runs through the middle, now fragmented into ponds, prime habitat for beaver which eat the young growth of aspen trees. Deer and moose keep the shrubs trimmed.

You can see the work of beavers as you cross an old stream bed on a little bridge. Just beyond is a beautifully-situated bench beside the creek under an overhanging tree. Just sitting here, you may be able to see warblers and spot swallows catching insects over the water.

You can look across the creek to the vast marshy area that culminates in the Vermilion Lakes. This semi-open terrain with its aquatic plants and willows is a favored spot for moose who can't find enough to feed on in the dark, thick coniferous forests above.

There's a second bench further on by the clear, sandy-bottomed river and a bridge which leads in a few metres to the beginning of the Vermilion Lakes Drive under the noisy Trans-Canada Highway. See Walk 19. Down here all is peaceful, however. Continue along the river, taking the first fork right back into the forest again. In a few minutes, this will lead you back to the entrance trail. Turn left to return to Norquay Road.

Moose

Moose, largest members of the deer family, are solitary animals, except for the female and her calves.

The mating season is mid-September to November when the bulls turn particularly aggressive. The calves are often twins born in May or early June, weighing approximately 20 pounds. They put on weight fast and remain with the mother all through the summer and the next winter for protection in the deep snow which restricts movement. In spring, the mother drives her yearling offspring away before a new calf is born.

Vermilion Lakes   WALK 19

Moose, muskrats and mergansers   MAP 6

Highlight: Marshy plant and animal habitat
Distance: 9.2 km (5.7 miles) or less return
Time: 2 1/2 to 3 hours
Rating: Moderate
Maximum elevation: 1,386 m (4,550 ft)
Elevation gain: None
Footwear: Walking or running shoes
Best season: April to October

The somewhat busy road edging Vermilion Lakes is well-known as one of the finest short drives in the Banff area; it also makes an unforgettable wetlands walk accessible right from Banff townsite. You can't see or feel this interesting terrain from a car, although a bicycle is excellent here. There's no foot-trail (except for informal paths in some areas) and walkers are forced to use the road. But traffic is slow-moving. The area offers a tremendous range of plant and wildlife habitat, from open water and marshes to meadows and forests, and marvellous views of Mt. Rundle.

Take binoculars and your camera. Early morning or dusk are the best times for both seeing wildlife and taking pictures. The walk is even interesting in winter!

Access: In Banff townsite, take Lynx Ave. north towards the Trans-Canada Hwy, following the signs. Just past the railway station, the main route turns right onto Norquay Road and crosses the CPR tracks. Park your vehicle in the wide gravel clearing just beyond the tracks or back at the station parking lot. Walk across the road and find the Fenland

Vermilion Lakes

trailhead a few metres north.

Route: Initially, the wide, level trail winds through a thick forest of mostly white spruce. This is an area of rich river-bottom soil inside a loop of Forty Mile Creek winding across the flat Bow Valley.

At the first fork, turn right and follow the trail to the creek. Go left and along the creek until a footbridge which leads across and up to the paved Vermilion Lakes Drive.

The road follows the shoreline of the three lakes, connected by ponds and marshland. Knife-edged Mt. Rundle can be viewed here from one of its most dramatic angles. On its right is Sulphur Mountain, believed to be the source of warm springs which surface at Vermilion Lakes.

The wetlands around the three lakes represent a fairly typical feeding site for moose and habitat for beaver, muskrat and many of the park's 238 bird species. Watch for mound-shaped beaverlodges (and their inhabitants). Moose can sometimes be seen feeding here at dusk.

A Bird-Finding Guide to Canada notes that the Vermilion Lakes are probably "the most important area in the park for migrating waterfowl." Between April and late May feathered visitors include tundra swan, common and hooded mergansers and red-necked grebes. The Bald Eagle nests nearby. Some ducks even stay all winter on the warm spring water in the third lake.

Bighorn sheep can frequently be seen on the gravel slopes leading up from the Trans-Canada. With recent highway construction, the sheep were provided with their own underpasses to cross the highway safely. Wardens report that deer, elk, coyote and bear are using the underpasses too.

Lowbush cranberry, red osier dogwood, duckweeds, cat-tails, rushes, sedges, even orchids can be found in this rich habitat. The lakes themselves were formed by water from the Bow River backing up onto the valley flats.

A hot spring enters the lakes on the other side and tropical fish can sometimes be seen darting in its waters—the result of an ecologically-questionable experiment by local aquarium enthusiasts.

In winter, watch for freshly-browsed willow shoots and large hoof prints, the mark of moose. Coyotes prowl the frozen shoreline, and you might see sheep grazing on Mt. Norquay. Nearby should be chickadees, woodpeckers and waxwings plucking berries from scattered juniper bushes.

The road continues to a dead-end and the walker can turn back at any point. Dirt foot-trails appear on the left side of the road in some places and make for more pleasant footing.

If you still have time and energy on the return, head right on the far side of the footbridge over Forty Mile Creek and follow the scenic loop around the creek on the Fenland Nature Trail (Walk 18).

Cave and Basin Marsh Trail   WALK 20

Minnows and Mallards   MAP 7

Highlight: Hot springs flora and fauna
Distance: 1 km (0.6 mile) loop
Time: 20 to 25 minutes
Rating: Easy
Maximum elevation: 1,383 m (4,540 ft)
Elevation gain: Negligible
Footwear: Anything
Best season: Year-round

Watercress growing outdoors in January? Six species of wild orchids? Robins in winter? Find these rewards and more on the Marsh Trail, opened by Parks Canada for the park centennial in 1985.

The lavishly-interpreted trail is a microcosm of the rich marshland warmed by thermal springs from Sulphur Mountain. Your chances of seeing wildlife here are best at dusk. This intriguing loop can be combined with a swim in the naturally-heated waters of the Cave and Basin pool. To stroll here from Banff Avenue, see Walk 14.

Access: In Banff townsite, start at the trailhead sign in front of the Cave and Basin Hot Springs along Cave Ave., 1.6 km (1 mile) west of the Bow Bridge.

Route: Begin on the right-hand boardwalk, soon crossing a tiny, steamy stream. Nature signs explain how warm run-off from Sulphur Mountain's hot springs keeps plants growing here year-round. Bright green moss and watercress thrive alongside snow in

7. CAVE AND BASIN CENTENNIAL CENTRE

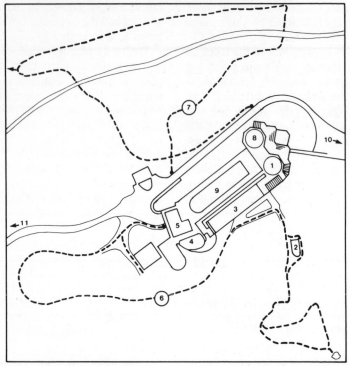

1. Introduction to the Cave and Basin Centennial Centre, and entrance to the Cave hot spring.
2. The Cave hot spring.
3. The story of national parks (exhibits).
4. The Basin hot spring.
5. The 1887 bathhouse, containing a theatre and a 1914-style lounge.
6. The Discovery Trail - the history of the hot springs.
7. The Marsh Trail - the effect of the hot springs on plants and animals.
8. Entrance to the swimming area (summer) and lounge (winter).
9. The swimming pool, open from June to September.
10. To the parking lot.
11. 3.3 km to Sundance Canyon.

winter. Six species of orchids flourish in spring.

Continue to the warm water animal section. Free telecopes are provided to search for animals and birds in the marsh and to scan surrounding peaks, with views ahead of Mt. Norquay to the north and Cascade to its right.

At the bird viewpoint, visitors might spy yellowthroats, ruby-crowned kinglets, red-winged blackbirds, green or blue-winged teals, robins, snipe and mallards. The ice-free marsh attracts non-wintering birds such as the killdeer which would otherwise fly south.

The bird and fish viewing area is a special treat. An elaborate dock-promenade projects into the marsh, where tropical fish thrive even in a northern pond. Here dwell tiny mosquitofish, jewelfish, sailfin molly and the Banff longnose dace, the most commonly-seen species in this habitat. Here, as well, is a chance to dip your hands in the warm sulphur water! There's also a bird-blind at the end of the boardwalk, with peepholes to scan the rich waterfowl habitat at the edge of the Bow River.

The last viewpoint is poignantly named Life Forms No One Loves. Garter snakes, rare in the rest of Banff, live here because it's warm and moist.

Banff's Peculiar Minnow

Many years ago, local aquarium enthusiasts wanted to see what would happen when tropical fish were released into warm waters near the outlet of Banff's famed hot sulphur springs.

What happened was that the tropical fish flourished; their descendents multiplied and the experiment spelled near disaster for the Banff longnose dace, a rare type of minnow specially adapted to warm water.

The minnow—found nowhere else on earth—is now feared to be in danger of extinction from the aquarium fish. A stark reminder, indeed, of the dangers of tampering with nature's delicate balance.

Climbing a frozen waterfall in the Canadian Rockies.

9

Banff National Park
Walks North of Banff Townsite
Walks from Trans-Canada Highway
Bow Valley Parkway
Banff-Windermere Highway

Bankhead Historical Loop

WALK 21

MAP 8

Life in the pits

Highlight: Remains of mining town
Distance: 1.1 km (.7 miles) loop
Time: 25 to 30 minutes
Rating: Easy
Maximum elevation: 1,417 m 4,650 ft)
Elevation gain: Negligible
Footwear: Anything
Best season: May to October

Early this century, a coal mining town called Bankhead flourished under Cascade Mountain near Banff townsite. Yet by 1922, it had become a ghost town.

All that remains now are a few old buildings, some rusting machinery, rubble and grass-covered foundations. Parks Canada recently developed an excellent interpretive trail through this evocative site. Included are exhibits, depicting a miner's life in the pits. Indeed, walking here at dusk can be likened to exploring the remains of a 20th-century cliff community. Recommended for all.

Access: Bankhead is on the Lake Minnewanka Road, 3 km (1.8 miles) north of the Trans-Canada Hwy opposite Banff townsite. There's a sign for the Bankhead parking lot. The trail starts to the right of a viewpoint. Brochures are usually available outlining the mine's history.

Route: The trail descends wooden steps to the main tunnel entrance to the mine, where the coal was extracted on A-Level, B-Level and C-Level, each being a

Slovak Funeral, Bankhead.

8. BANKHEAD (Closeup)

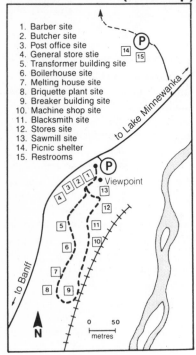

1. Barber site
2. Butcher site
3. Post office site
4. General store site
5. Transformer building site
6. Boilerhouse site
7. Melting house site
8. Briquette plant site
9. Breaker building site
10. Machine shop site
11. Blacksmith site
12. Stores site
13. Sawmill site
14. Picnic shelter
15. Restrooms

sloping tunnel following the coal seams deep under Cascade Mountain. Miners were each assigned a numbered mining lamp at the lamphouse at the beginning of each shift. If a miner's lamp was missing at the end of the day, a search would be initiated.

Mt. Inglismaldie, named after a Scottish castle, is prominent at a height of 2,961 m (9,715 ft) to the northeast.

Keep right over a tiny wooden bridge on an easy cinder trail, up to the transformer building. Peer inside for a depiction of a sooty-faced miner. Workers were mostly immigrants from Poland, Italy, Russia, Czechoslovakia, Germany, Ireland and China. At Bankhead's peak, 275 men worked below ground and 195 above, producing 400 carloads of coal a day.

The trail winds through bare foundations, by the remains of the power house which supplied the electricity for Banff townsite and the briquetting plant. The easily-broken Cascade coal had to be coverted here into a form more easily used for heating.

The trail loops back past slag heaps and the shantytown where the Chinese lived behind the heaps. Wild rhubarb, spread from the abandoned gardens of Chinese workers, grows on the slag heaps.

Today, one can only speculate on the hardships faced by those early Chinese workers. It's said that when the town opened a cemetery, no one wanted to be the first to be buried in it. A friendless Chinese laborer, the town's only murder victim, became its only occupant. His remains were later shipped back to China.

Near the conclusion of the walk is a narrow-gauge coal train.

Bankhead

Once the booming coal mining town of Bankhead thrived beneath the flanks of Cascade Mountain. Today only a few bare foundations and exhibits remain.

Between 1904 and 1922, Bankhead was bigger than Banff. More than 1,200 people lived in 90 homes. There were even tennis courts, a skating rink and a library. Coal production hit 200,000 tons a year.

The boom withered in the 1920s, partly because of the expense of processing the brittle coal, which had to be compressed into "briquettes" to be useable. To these difficulties were added labor problems and poor markets. Mining is no longer allowed in national parks.

The last resident of Bankhead was a Danish caretaker in charge of safeguarding the remaining houses. The story goes that he also scared away a hundred ghosts.

Upper Bankhead Trail

WALK 22

The cutting of miners and glaciers

MAP 9

Highlight: Coal mining ruins, glacial cirque
Distance: 8 km (4.9 miles) return
Time: 4 hours
Rating: Strenuous

Maximum elevation: 1,935 m (6,350 ft)
Elevation gain: 472 m (1,550 ft)
Footwear: Sturdy shoes or light hiking boots
Best season: Mid-June to October

From historic Bankhead, past old coal mine ruins and an overlook of the Lake Minnewanka area up to a cirque deeply cut into the cliffs of mighty Cascade Mountain by ancient, groaning glaciers, this trail has everything—except ease. The route is moderately steep throughout. Bring a canteen.

Access: From Banff townsite, drive back to the Trans-Canada Hwy, then north up the road to Lake Minnewanka. At 3.5 km from the junction just past the turnoff for the Bankhead exhibit, take the entrance left to the Upper Bankhead parking lot, a pleasant picnic area and the trailhead. The trail leaves from the end of the parking lot.

Route: The trail climbs moderately steeply to the upper remains of the once-thriving coal mining operation of Bankhead. The mine shaft entrances and the town are below near the trail head but these are the upper shafts of the tunnels under Cascade Mountain that followed the slanting coal veins.

The trail passes over old coal debris and goes by the concrete shell of an old mine building. Behind are several fenced-off mine shaft holes. Be careful. To the right on another mini-ridge of coal tailings is a good overlook towards Lake Minnewanka and down the Bow Valley towards Canmore. The effort's worth it, even if you only make the journey this far.

The trail continues in the same direction, then turns left into deeper forest, the trees covered with lichen. This subalpine forest is home to deer, elk, moose and bear, among the larger animals, the red squirrel and his enemy the pine marten, among the smaller.

The route leads over a wooded ridge, then levels off as views open up over the valley. Suddenly you round a corner and the cirque looms

Lake Minnewanka

up before you, gray, gloomy and imposing, its massive walls rising above talus slopes.

It's called C-Level Cirque not because of any relation to sea-

9. LAKE MINNEWANKA

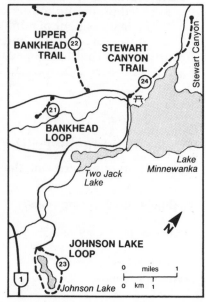

level but because the mine shafts following the coal seams under Cascade Mountain were simply called A-Level shaft, B-Level and C-Level . . .

The main trail ends on a little hillside above a small pond overlooking this boulder-strewn bowl in the rocks, one of several cut into the sides of Cascade by the glaciers. A small pond lies capped in the bottom of the cirque. A rougher trail continues up on the right side of the cirque to provide even better views of this natural amphitheatre, ''a meeting place of the gods.''

The route passes several piles of brown cone scales built up over the years by the red squirrel. The pile is simply the inedible portion of spruce cones which the squirrel tends to chew from the same perch. These squirrels may gather thousands of cones in a single summer, most of them to be cached underground or in a hollow tree for eating in leaner times.

The pine marten feeds on these squirrels, along with his diet of numerous mice and voles. The marten is the best climber among the carnivores and can sometimes outrun a red squirrel in a chase from branch to branch, tree to tree. Sometimes, the marten dive-bombs onto a squirrel or mouse from a tree branch. In winter, it tunnels deep under the snow to get at its prey.

What is a Cirque?

The natural depressions in the sides of mountains tend to be widened and deepened by the freezing and thawing of water. These depressions become natural channels for glaciers which pick up boulders as they travel down the mountain-side and scratch and gouge away the rock at their base. Because the erosion is greatest in the centre of the glacier, a bowl-shaped depression tends to be created under all that ice and snow.

Glaciers in the Canadian Rockies are generally retreating and the ones that created the cirques on the sides of Cascade have long since vanished. In fact, none of the nearby peaks bear glaciers. This is largely because the winter Chinook winds prevent the snowfall accumulation from becoming deep enough to form long-lasting ice.

The most striking peaks in the Rockies such as Assiniboine or Athabasca got their pyramid-like shape largely because of cirque glaciers that cut away the mountain from several angles.

Johnson Lake Loop

WALK 23

Shining water circuit

MAP 9

Highlight: Stroll around pleasant lake
Distance: 3.2 km (1.9 miles) loop
Time: 1 to 1 1/2 hours
Rating: Moderate
Maximum elevation: 1,417 m (4,650 ft)
Elevation gain: Negligible
Footwear: Walking or running shoes
Best season: May to October

The loop around this small fishing lake offers a scenic, undemanding outing, although the route is used by horses and can be hard to follow near the end. The first portion on the south side of the lake would be fine for families. Stroll through the pines and along the shoreline, set against the splendid backdrop of Cascade Mountain. The walk can be capped with a picnic at one of the many pleasantly-situated tables overlooking the lake. (No boats allowed.)

Access: From the Trans-Canada Hwy just east of Banff townsite, turn north at the sign to Lake Minnewanka. After .9 km, turn right at sign for Johnson Lake and continue 3.3 km. Turn right again at another sign and drive to the dead end. We've started the trail just above the parking lot on the south side of lake.

Route: Walk up to the lake and turn right. The trail begins in an open forest of lodgepole pines.

Cascade, a translation of the Indian name meaning "mountain where the water falls" towers beyond the west end at 2,990 m (9,836 ft).

The trail emerges into a power cutline briefly before winding into the forest again. In several spots it veers off to little viewpoints of the lake, ideal for informal picnicking or just day-dreaming. Angling is permitted from shore only. The lake has small brook and rainbow trout and the season runs from Victoria Day and Labour Day. Mt. Inglismaldie with its steep cliffs, named after a Scottish castle, is the dominant mountain to the northeast.

The forest soon thins, offering pretty views back to the lake. Purple asters, Indian paintbrush and goldenrod can be seen in summer. Watch for elk and mule deer as well. Continue near the water's edge.

It takes only 20 minutes or so to reach the end of the lake. On the north side, the path at first leads through a mix of Engelmann spruce and marshy shrubs. Note the dramatic cliffs of Mt. Rundle to the south. West is a panorama of the wide Bow Valley, carved by ice.

The trail follows the shore for about half the distance down the lake on the north side, then veers away. Watch for a lush grassy area by the bank, perfect for sunbathing with its southern exposure. Otherwise, keep on the main trail away from the lake, crossing a small bridge. The trail becomes wide and sounds of traffic remind (or reassure) you that civilization is not far away, after all.

Keep on the main path back to the road, where asphalt paths lead to picnic tables and a wooden walkway over a marshy part of the lake.

Johnson Lake

Stewart Canyon

WALK 24

A little fiord

MAP 9

Highlight: Scenic lake inlet
Distance: 2 to 4 km (1.2 to 2.4 miles) return
Time: 45 minutes to 1 1/2 hours
Rating: Easy
Maximum elevation: 1,493 m (4,900 ft)
Elevation gain: Negligible
Footwear: Almost anything
Best season: May to October

A beautiful inlet, resembling a miniature fiord. A shady path along the lakeshore, the shimmering blue of Lake Minnewanka and the gray and white of the mountains visible through the forest. Such is Stewart Canyon, not spectacular or awe-inspiring, as the Rockies go, yet surely a fine family stroll.

Access: The interchange for Lake Minnewanka Road is 3.2 km east of Banff townsite. Drive the 7 km up to the lake and park in the large lot for the Minnewanka day use area. Walk down the road above the boat ramp past the snack bar.

Route: Follow the asphalt path through a grassy picnic area near the lake, a pleasant spot with scenic coves to explore and boulders for children to climb. Some of the limestone rocks hereabouts contain fossil imprints. The views across the lake, largest in Banff (24 km long and 1.5 to 3 km wide), to the gray cliffs of Mt. Inglismaldie (on the right) and Mt. Girouard are inspiring. The first mountain is named for a Scottish castle; the second for Col. Sir Edward P. Girouard, a prominent officer during the Boer War.

At the far end of the picnic area is a trail sign indicating a wide path through lodgepole pines, an easy, appealing route. To the right is a gravel beach covered with driftwood, often swept by large waves. You begin to catch sight of the beginning of the canyon. The whole scene—the robin's egg-blue water seen through the pines—appears more Mediterranean than subalpine.

Minnewanka is an Indian name meaning Lake of the Water Spirit. The route along the north shore was once used by Indians travelling into the mountains from the plains through the gap at the far end.

The cold lake usually supports a sizeable population of loons and other waterfowl in spring and fall. Watch for mountain bluebirds along the trail.

The trail reaches Stewart Canyon in less than 1 km and crosses it on a scenic bridge. Here are the best views of this interesting inlet, sheer gray walls of rock rising up from the water. This canyon was carved out of the limestone by the Cascade

River which does not naturally flow into Lake Minnewanka. In earlier days, the lake did not extend this far down the valley. When the level of Minnewanka was raised in 1941 to provide hydro-electric power, the head of the lake was pushed south and the river canyon became a steep-walled inlet.

Though many will go no further than the bridge, good views of the canyon can be obtained by taking a rough path left on the far side of the

bridge and following up the river—until you tire. The main path straight ahead leads down the lake and to lofty Aylmer Pass above.

Above the bridge, notice how the somewhat murky lake water suddenly turns clear where it meets the flow from Cascade River. The further you go up the canyon, the faster-moving the water is. This is a good place to spot Bighorn sheep. In about a kilometre, the trail finally descends to the river at the end of the canyon, a favorite place for trout fishermen. A rocky clearing beside the river provides a natural area for a backcountry picnic.

Stoney Squaw Lookout

A little lookout

WALK 25

MAP 10

Highlight: Good view of Bow Valley
Distance: 2.4 km (1.5 miles) return
Time: 1 1/2 hours
Rating: Moderate
Footwear: Walking or running shoes
Maximum elevation: 1,883 m (6,180 ft)
Elevation gain: 580 ft (176 m)
Best season: June to October

Stoney Squaw is just a pimple of a mountain visible from Banff townsite, nestled between Mt. Norquay on the left and Cascade on the right. While the trail to the lookout is mostly through forest, it's relatively short, easy and well-suited to families, except when covered with snow when it can be impossible to follow.

The payoff? A superb panorama of the Banff area. Those wishing to

10. BANFF (North)

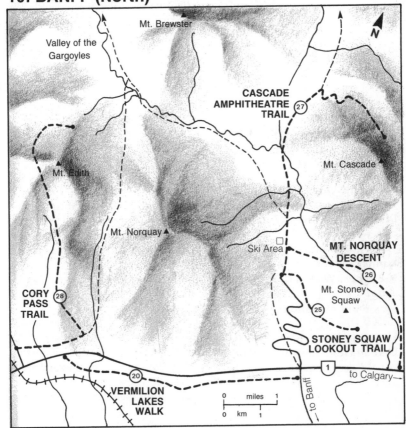

make a half day or more of it, and who can arrange transportation, could walk back to Banff townsite after completing this trail (Walk 26).

Access: The trail starts near the entrance to parking lot No. 3 on Mt. Norquay, 5 km north from Banff townsite on Mt. Norquay Road. Mule deer and bighorn sheep are commonly seen along this drive. The trailhead is at the entrance to the large parking lot, just as you turn in.

Route: The pine-needled path starts through mixed forest, moving up the west side of Stoney Squaw on a moderate grade. The name refers to a Stoney Indian woman standing beside her Stoney Chief—the former name for Cascade Mountain directly east.

Continue through stands of Douglas fir and white spruce until the trees thin out and views begin to appear of Banff townsite and the Spray Valley to the south.

The path proceeds on to the lookout, where the forest breaks to an excellent view of 2,998-metre (9,839-foot) Cascade Mountain. To its south and west, the striking outlook encompasses the Bow Valley, tiny Tunnel Mountain, Mt. Rundle, Spray Valley, Sulphur Mountain and the Trans-Canada Highway. The view from here represents a good way for the visitor to learn the geographical and man-made complexities of the townsite area.

Mt. Norquay Descent

WALK 26

Downhill walk

MAP 10

Highlight: Gentle downhill walk, few views
Distance: 4.4 km (2.7 miles) one way
Time: 1 1/2 hours
Rating: Moderate
Footwear: Walking or running shoes
Maximum elevation: 1,676 m (5,500 ft)
Elevation loss: 287 m (940 ft)
Best season: June to October

Stoney Squaw, the mite of a mountain between Norquay and Cascade, provides that rarity—a trail that's downhill all the way. The pine needle-softened path begins at the Mt. Norquay ski area, winds around the north of Stoney Squaw and down to the highway near the Buffalo Paddocks.

Disappointingly, it yields fewer views than might be expected; nevertheless, trees do clear further down for vistas of the Bow and Spray Valleys. The catch, of course, is the need to arrange transportation to the

Banff's Bison

From the safety of their cars, visitors to Banff can come almost face-to-face with a herd of plains and wood bison wandering through 100 acres, in a fenced area just north of the Trans-Canada Highway opposite the townsite.

Parks Canada hopes that the bison may one day be released to range freely in the parks, as they were before mass slaughter threatened their extinction. The idea is being studied.

The tale of bison in North America is a sad one: bison population may have exceeded 60 million in 1790. By 1890 only about 1,090 remained—the result of "the largest slaughter ever witnessed in the world," according to Parks Canada.

The federal government finally moved to conserve the bison. In Banff, Plains bison donated from private herds have been kept captive since 1897.

Bison, largest land mammals indigenous to Canada, are fairly docile except when provoked or during mating season, mid-July to mid-October. They spend most of their time grazing or wallowing— rolling about in dust pits to relieve sexual frustrations and itching from insects and their shedding coats.

Bison have a strict social order. The main herd is composed of mature cows with calves, immature bulls and immature cows. Mature cows are at the top of the pecking order in these matriarchal bands, immature cows at the bottom. Mature bulls go off on their own or with small herds for most of the year.

The Buffalo Paddock is 1 km west of the Banff Avenue interchange on the Trans-Canada Highway.

top. We can't recommend this trail as an approach to the Cascade Amphitheatre route. It makes for too long a day.

Access: From Banff townsite, drive north 5 km up Mt. Norquay Road to parking lot No. 3 for the ski area. Drive to the far end of the large parking lot, where the trail begins on an old road.

Route: Walk down the narrow road, keep more or less straight past a maintenance shed and the Wishbone lift. The road leads into the trees again beyond the ski area. At .6 km, turn right where a sign points the way to the Trans-Canada. You have 3.8 km (2.2 miles) to go.

The trail progresses behind Stoney Squaw in thick mixed forest, with views of slate-gray Cascade Mountain on the left, and then past limestone bluffs. Cross a bridge, descend a short, steep pitch and go through more open bowers of lodgepole pine.

The path gradually opens onto a south-facing bluff of Stoney Squaw. Pause and admire views of the Fairholme Mountains to the east, Mt. Rundle with its slanted desk-top side above Banff, tiny Tunnel Mountain, Sulphur Mountain to its right

and the Goat Range south. On a sunny day, this is a good spot for a picnic or nap.

The trail follows Forty Mile Creek, ending at the Trans-Canada just west of the buffalo paddocks. If you haven't left transportation nearby or arranged for a pickup, cross the highway and cut across into Banff townsite.

Cascade Amphitheatre   WALK 27

Playground of the gods   MAP 10

Highlight: Rocky cirque in mountainside
Distance: 12.8 km (7.9 miles) return
Time: 6 hours
Rating: Strenuous
Maximum elevation: 2,194 m (7,200 ft)
Elevation gain: 610 m (2,000 ft)
Footwear: Light hiking boots
Best season: July to September

While the Cascade Amphitheatre route is longer and tougher than most in this book, it leads to an extraordinary and beguiling bowl cut deep into the limestone cliffs of Cascade Mountain, that striking, turreted sentinel overlooking Banff townsite. Here's a location that invites the more experienced hiker to wander the edges of its steep talus slopes and boulder fields or seek the high ridge above. Good

views open back towards Mt. Brewster and the Sawback Range and grassy meadows invite picnicking.

Access: From Banff townsite or the Trans-Canada Hwy, take the Mt. Norquay turnoff north and drive up the steep, switchbacked road— which offers fine views—to the start of the ski area. Park in the No. 3 parking lot on the right. The trail begins at the far end of this vast lot.

Route: Walk down the narrow road from the parking lot and keep going, more or less straight past a maintenance sked and the Wishbone lift. The road leads into the trees again beyond the ski area. At .6 km from the parking lot, a sign gives assurance that you're on the route. Another trail leads off left for Mystic Lake.

Keep straight on the old road which descends gradually through a pleasant forest. In 1 km, a trail leads left up Forty Mile Creek. Keep right and descend to the vigorous creek which is crossed on a bridge at km 3.

The road becomes more of a trail and begins to climb in earnest, switchbacking up the western flank of Cascade with occasional views across the valley to Mt. Norquay and a glimpse up Forty Mile Creek to the striking tower of Mt. Louis. At km 4 (2.5 miles), the trail to Elk Lake continues straight ahead. The Amphitheatre route goes right, climbing more steeply now and switchbacking steadily through a lodgepole pine forest. It feels wonderful when the trail finally levels off and the trees begin to open, revealing the amphitheatre ahead.

The trail follows the edge of the trees, now turned to subalpine fir and Engelmann spruce. You can begin to see up this remarkable U-shaped valley to the limestone heights of Cascade. A rough trail leads right to the crest of the Cascade Ridge, a route to the summit that is considered a climb. Park wardens recommend that you register such climbs for your protection. Walkers, who have no need for registration under ordinary circumstances, will be content with the barren splendors of the meadows and amphitheatre ahead. Rev. Robert Rundle, the first white man to pass through the Bow Valley, camped at the base of Cascade in 1841.

Continue through meadows mixed with occasional trees and boulders, the terrain growing more desolate as you enter the amphitheatre, a cirque hollowed out by glaciers that have long since retreated. Behind, views open up to Mt. Brewster. The trail wanders on for a while, gradually becoming indistinct among the large boulders. You might wish to explore a little further up this valley or climb one of the slopes a short distance for better views.

Watch closely among these rocks for marmots and pikas. The marmot has a high-pitched whistle while the smaller pika lets out a shrill "eeeep!"

The marmot weighs between 10 and 30 pounds, and has grizzled hair on its back, although the rest of its body may be fairly brown. The chubby, small-eared pika is about the size of a hamster and is otherwise known as the "rock rabbit." Its gray coloring blends with the rocks it lives on.

Sulphur Summit

Cory Pass

WALK 28

A glimpse of the gargoyles

MAP 10

Highlight: Rugged pass, striking rock formations
Distance: 13.5 km (8.3 miles) return
Time: 6 hours
Rating: Strenuous
Maximum elevation: 2,371 m (7,780 ft)
Elevation gain: 981 m (3,220 ft)
Footwear: Light hiking boots
Best season: Mid-July to late September

A wild, desolate pass, topped by jagged rock formations that sometimes resemble gargoyles. Wide views over the Bow Valley and most especially behind the pass to the magnificent spike of Mt. Louis, one of the most striking mountains in Banff. This trail has everything—except ease. The ascent is long and steep, the trail rough in places, often with snow lying over the path on the final section even in midsummer. For those with the stamina, however, Cory Pass is highly recommended.

Access: From Banff townsite, drive west on the Trans-Canada Highway for 6 km (3.8 miles) to the Bow Valley Parkway. Turn onto the parkway and stop at the Fireside picnic area just past the junction where a new trail begins.

Route: The route parallels the Trans-Canada, climbing slightly. In about 1 km, the route reaches a patch of Douglas fir where the Cory Pass Trail branches left while the

trail to Edith Lake continues straight. The left branch begins to climb steeply and relentlessly, soon gaining the crest of a semi-open, grassy ridge of Mt. Edith (2,554 m, 8,380 ft). The mountain is named after Edith Orde, who visited Banff in 1886 with Lady MacDonald, wife of Canada's first prime minister. Mt. Cory (2,790 m, 9,154 ft) is named for William Cory, deputy minister of the interior from 1905 to 1930.

The lung-pounding ascent is partly compensated for by the expanding views, with Vermilion Lakes and much of Bow Valley visible below, and the distinctive writing-desk formation of Mt. Rundle to the left beyond Banff townsite. The route levels off slightly at the top of the ridge but climbs again as it traverses along towards Mt. Edith, views now opening up into the valley below between Mt. Cory and Edith.

The trail goes over several rocky knobs, descends steeply for a few metres through a crack in the rock (the route can be obscure here) and climbs again. The terrain gradually opens up as you begin the long ascent above the Cory Valley, the pass visible ahead, looking inhospitable even on a sunny day. There are few switchbacks as the trail ascends the pass under the crumbling cliffs of Mt. Edith where snow patches may lie across the trail well into July.

The top, which is above timberline, is a spectacular, rugged and usually cool place which funnels the winds between Mt. Cory on the west side and Mt. Edith to the east. You can climb a little higher on the ridge to the right for better views of the rock needles over the other side which might be compared to gothic carved gargoyles.

These mountains are part of the aptly-named Sawback Range whose rocks stick up almost vertically. Most dramatic of these spires is Mt. Louis, visible on the other side of the Gargoyle Valley, a most challenging ascent for rock climbers. Far beyond Banff, you can see the lofty pyramid of Mt. Assiniboine.

Rock Isle Lake
Subalpine splendour

WALK 29

MAP 11

Highlight: Delicate alpine tarn and meadows
Distance: 3.2 km (2 miles) return
Time: 1 1/2 hours
Rating: Moderate
Maximum Elevation: 2,280 m (7,480 ft)
Elevation gain: 90 m (295 ft)
Footwear: Running shoes
Best Season: July to September

While Sunshine handles 400,000 skiers each season from November to June, the summer season is relatively tranquil. These alpine meadows are by no means deserted — about 30,000 visitors came in a recent summer. Yet few alpine areas in the Canadian Rockies are so accessible to the day hiker. The Sunshine Meadows contain more than 300 species of alpine flowers. The well-graded and smooth path to Rock Isle Lake is the easiest and most popular of the hikes from

Sunshine Village.

Access: From Banff, drive west on the Trans-Canada Highway for 8 km to to the Sunshine Access Road. The 8-km road ends at the Bourgeau Gondola Station. Bus service is also available from Banff. Call 762-2241 for information. The gondolas take 20 minutes to travel up the valley, saving the hiker five km of uphill slogging. Call 762-4000 for gondola operating schedule.

Route: Start at the Sunshine Village interpretive centre and follow the path past the Strawberry Chairlift (not operating in summer). You begin a moderately steep ascent out of this timberline valley, making a quick and easy transition from subalpine forest of larch, fur and spruce to the bare meadows of the alpine region.

The trail soon levels off in the meadows and rolls past wet hollows containing moisture-tolerant plants. Some of the hollows may be

11. ROCK ISLE LAKE

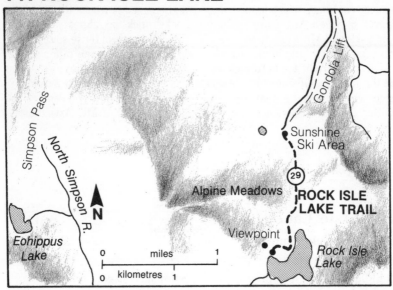

covered with snowdrifts even in mid-summer. A yearly snowfall of 6 1/2 m (22 ft) is not uncommon. The small plants at the top of the mounds must survive in thin, dry and dusty soil, buffeted by strong winds for much of the short summer.

Views begin to open up to the imposing peak of Mt. Assiniboine to the southeast and the trail climbs over a small rise marking the Continental Divide and the boundary between Alberta and British Columbia. Beyond, the tiny alpine streams all flow towards the Pacific.

A trail leads off left into Mt. Assiniboine Provincial Park and the Rock Isle Lake Trail begins to descend slightly past the burrows of hundreds of aggressive ground squirrels to the small lake, a gorgeous spot on a sunny day.

Benches and an observation deck

have been built above the lake or hikers can follow the trail around the side of it. Do stay on the trail. Alpine areas are particularly fragile and this area gets heavy use.

Hikers with the time and energy could explore the stunning plateau further by continuing on the trails (no longer as wide or as well-maintained as before) to Grizzly Lake or Larix Lake a kilometre or two further, although these involve a descent (and an ascent on the return) back into the subalpine forest.

Rock Isle Lake

Bourgeau Lake

WALK 30

Land of the rock rabbit

MAP 12

Highlight: Alpine lake, meadows
Distance: 15.2 km (9.5 miles) return
Time: 6 hours
Rating: Strenuous
Maximum elevation: 2,148 m (7,050 ft)
Elevation gain: 747 m (2,454 ft)
Footwear: Light hiking boots
Best season: July to mid-September

While the climb to Bourgeau Lake is fairly long and steep, the day walker passes waterfalls and cascades along the way, finally attaining a gorgeous timberline meadow and a small lake set amid rugged rock walls and scree slopes.

The trailhead is close to Banff townsite and there are good views for much of the ascent. It is recommended for strong hikers only.

Access: From Banff townsite, drive 11.4 km north on the Trans-Canada Hwy to the Bourgeau Lake parking lot which is marked with a prominent sign.

Route: The trail climbs easily at first above Wolverine Creek through a lodgepole forest, gradually entering the steep valley. Views open up as the trail crosses old slide areas. You can also see back across the Bow Valley to the sharp-toothed Sawback Range whose rocks are laid nearly vertically.

The lodgepole forest gradually

12. BOURGEAU LAKE

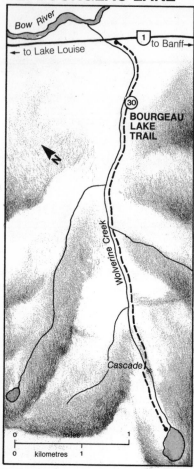

through a series of rock bands to get above the cascades.

Views open up again in most directions and the trees become more stunted as you gain the upper floor of the valley, a grassy meadow under impressive, rugged slopes set between a continuation of Mt. Brett to the right and Mt. Bourgeau to the left (2,918 m, 9,575 ft). The first mountain is named for Dr. R. G. Brett, a CPR doctor and Banff pioneer who became lieutenant-governor of Alberta. The latter is named for Eugene Bourgeau, botanist with the famous Palliser expedition.

This valley is a typical glacial cirque, carved out by the ice. The glacier has long since retreated, leaving a lake where it created a depression in the rock.

The trail continues over the meadows spangled with wildflowers and home to ground squirrels. You reach icy, boulder-strewn Bourgeau Lake under forbidding limestone rock walls and steep scree slopes. The rocks around here shelter colonies of pikas, among other small animals. The rabbit-like pika is difficult to spot because it blends in with the local rock. They're easy to hear, however; their call is a piercing "eeep!"

You can sometimes discover where pikas live by looking for the little "haystack" which they spend the summer gathering: a fine collection of grasses and other plants, even marmot droppings, often hidden in the shelter of an overhanging rock. Don't disturb it. The pika relies on this material for its winter meals, taken in peace under the snow.

turns to spruce as elevation increases and you cross a stream on a rough log bridge. This is about the half-way mark in terms of distance, although the hardest climbing is yet to come. The trail works its way up well above the stream, passing under the broken, brown cliffs of Mt. Bourgeau on the left. A series of spectacular cascades looms ahead and you cross the stream below them on a rough plank. The climbing gets steeper as the trail switchbacks

Johnston Canyon Trail

Seven waterfalls

WALK 31

MAP 13

Highlight: Narrow canyon and waterfalls, cool pools
Distance: 1.6 km (1 mile) return to Lower Falls
• 4.8 km (3 miles) return to Upper Falls
• 11 km (7 miles) return to Inkpots
Time: 40 minutes to Lower Falls
• 1 1/2 hours to Upper Falls
• 4 1/2 hours to Inkpots
Rating: Easy to Lower Falls
• Moderate to Upper Falls and Inkpots
Maximum elevation: 1,647 m (5,500 ft) at Inkpots
Elevation gain: 243 m (800 ft) to Inkpots
Footwear: Anything to Lower and Upper Falls
• Light hiking boots to Inkpots
Best season: Mid-May to October

Johnston Canyon, a narrow, dark gap cut by rushing, crystal waters, is probably the most visited canyon in the Canadian Rockies. Yet relatively few venture beyond the first cascade, and that's a pity. The path from Lower to Upper Waterfalls features seven waterfalls, an optional walk through a wet tunnel and a chance to stand near the base of the magnificent Upper Falls, twice the size of the Lower Falls. For those with extra energy, the half-day hike to the jade-green Inkpots is an interesting option.

Access: Johnston Canyon is 25 km (15 miles) north of Banff townsite on Hwy 1A, the Bow Valley Parkway. The trail starts past the lodge.

Route: The wide asphalt trail starts up gently through lush, mossy forest, beside vigorous Johnston Creek. Interpretive signs

13. JOHNSTON CANYON

explain how the canyon was formed by the forces of glaciation and landslides over the eons, and how no rock can withstand the power of water.

Far above, Johnston Creek flows parallel to the Bow River Valley for several kilometres, then cuts suddenly southwest across the mountains, plunging down Johnston

Canyon to empty into the Lower Bow Valley.

The path is fairly steep at first. In this narrow canyon, the world seems to consist only of rock, water and the sound of swirling water. In some places, canyon walls are more than 30 m (100 ft) high and less than six m across. The trail follows a concrete ramp bolted onto the side of the cliff, with guardrails, part-way up the canyon wall. Watch your head.

Black swifts, found only in a few places in Alberta, nest in the canyon walls. Look for them in early morning or at dusk, especially by the lower falls. Watch also for American dippers.

Soon the trail reaches one of the deepest parts of the lower canyon. Each year, rushing water wears away two millimetres of limestone, carving the canyon's face into myriad shapes. Some claim to see carved animal heads.

Benches are situated all along the walk to Upper Falls, which progresses through lodgepole pine and spruce. Pass under an overhanging cliff of solid limestone to the Lower Falls which swirl into a green pool from copper-colored cliffs. These falls once plunged from the top of the cliff directly into the pool.

Almost everybody will want to cross the small bridge to the other side of the canyon and go through a tiny, dark rock passage for a thrilling close-up of the falls. Water or mist from the walls usually coats the visitor at this unusual vantage point. As a water-soaked visitor you begin to gain the true feel of a water-scoured canyon.

Continue past pretty Twin Falls, keeping to the right to the impressive, cascading Upper Falls. Walk down a steel ramp and partway across the stream on the dead-end bridge to a point near the base of the falls—close enough to feel its spray and sense the power of the rushing water. Algae is imbedded in the damp leached rock on canyon walls.

Backtrack to the junction for the Inkpots and take the right path up.

Inkpots: Continue up the wide pathway away from the falls until you reach a fireroad, and turn right. The fireroad cuts uphill through thick forest. Calypso orchids (or Venus slipper) bloom here in June, their purplish-pink flowers delicately shaped like tiny slippers. Asters, arnica, Indian paintbrush and other wildflowers adorn the trail and meadows ahead. A clearing offers views of the Bow Valley.

The path descends and the trail narrows before opening out into a beautiful, wide valley. You reach a sign indicating the end of the ski trail to the Inkpots. Keep going in the same direction. The Inkpots are only a few steps further.

These are small natural springs, usually bright blue or jade in color. The water in the pools is a constant temperature of 1°C (35°F). The color is from glacial "rock flour."

The glaciers have since retreated and disappeared but glacial till is everywhere. Water which flows into the Inkpots probably travels through this till, picking up the rock flour ground up by ancient glaciers. This flour is suspended in the water and catches the light, changing the color of the water on the surface to stunning shades of blue or jade.

The spiky Sawback Range dominates the eastern flanks of the valley. In fair weather, this is a fine place to lunch, sketch or explore the valley.

Silverton Falls

WALK 32

The unknown falls

MAP 14

Highlight: Waterfall
Distance: 2.5 km (1.6 miles) return
Time: 45 minutes
Rating: Easy
Maximum elevation: 1,524 m (5,000 ft)
Elevation gain: 76 m (250 ft)
Footwear: Walking or running shoes
Best season: May to October

Silverton Falls are slightly higher and more spectacular than anything in tourist-crowded Johnston Canyon nearby. Yet they aren't often visited by the thousands who travel Bow Valley Parkway between Banff townsite and Castle Mountain Junction. These high falls are off any main trails and are seldom mentioned in park literature. So the stroller can approach them with a sense of discovery. This is an easy trail which loses its snow faster than many others in the spring. The ideal time for a visit is in late spring-early summer when the creek's water volume is highest.

Access: In Banff National Park, take the Trans-Canada Hwy to Castle Mountain Junction, 28 km north-

14. CASTLE MOUNTAIN AREA

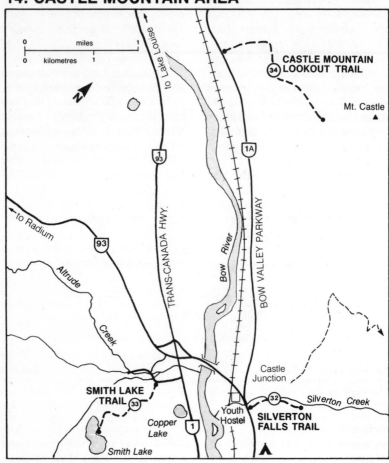

west of Banff townsite at the intersection with Hwy 93. Turn east and at the store and cabins, turn right onto the Bow Valley Parkway. Less than .05 km south of this junction, turn beside a warden station into the parking lot for the Rockbound Lake Trail.

Route: Continue up the wide trail for Rockbound Lake for about 200 m. Watch for a smaller trail leading right that may be unmarked. The trail heads through a thick growth of lodgepole pines to Silverton Creek and a rough bridge. (Don't cross the stream. The trail on the far side leads to the bottom of the falls but there's scarcely any view from down there.) From the stream, take the wide trail left which ascends the slope and switchbacks up along the open bank of the creek.

Soon, the trail ends abruptly at a fine viewpoint half-way up the falls and separated from the wild rush of water by only a few metres. Above, water is forced through a narrow gap in the rock and down five waterfalls in the cliff, although the last plunge is out of sight. This creek, named for the silver mining boom that hit this area in 1883, drains Rockbound Lake behind Castle Mountain.

The boom started in 1882 after a Stoney Indian showed prospector J.J. Healy a chunk of ore high in silver and copper. Healy staked a claim and word got around, as word always does. By 1883, there were 175 wooden buildings down there, including five stores, three hotels, two saloons and three butchershops, plus numerous tents in what was called Silver City. But no silver.

By 1885, Silver City was a ghost town. The water still plunges over Silverton Falls.

Smith Lake

WALK 33

A plain old mud pond

MAP 14

Highlight: Quiet woodland lake
Distance: 3.2 km (1.9 miles) return
Time: 1 hour
Rating: Moderate
Maximum elevation: 1,544 m (5,100 ft)
Elevation gain: 121 m (400 ft)
Footwear: Walking or running shoes
Best season: June to October

Don't come here looking for spectacular scenery. Smith Lake is as plain as its name. Visited mostly by fishermen after trout, it nestles snugly into a gentle fold of hills on the lower, wooded slopes of Storm Mountain. No cliffs, no mightly glacial cirque, just a woodland pond, fairly close to the Trans-Canada. Yet maybe that's a little attraction by itself: a cozy, easily attainable alternative to all those drafty alpine expanses, good for fishing or just escape.

Access: Drive the Trans-Canada Hwy 28 km NW of Banff townsite to the intersection of Hwy 93 at Castle Mountain Junction. Just south of the interchange, watch for a dirt road on the west side (the left if travelling from Banff). Follow this road for a few m, then take the first left. Just after the first bend in this road and before crossing a stream, park your vehicle. The Smith Lake Trail leads off on the left side of the road, beginning as an old road. There's a sign about 50 metres in.

Route: About 100 m after the sign, turn left off the old road and up a narrow trail. Suddenly you're free of the noise and bustle of the

Trans-Canada as you ascend through a pleasant mixed forest, past two tiny ponds bounded by Indian paintbrush and Labrador tea. The terrain turns to the subalpine forest of spruce and fir, far darker and thicker on these cold northeast-facing slopes than on the other side of the valley. Over there, the warmer, dryer slopes support a more open montane forest of mostly lodgepole pine and some aspens. Grazing animals such as moose, elk and deer naturally prefer the other side because the snow is less deep in winter and at all seasons, grass, and broad-leaved plants are easier to find.

The trail ascends gently and you soon find yourself on a little bluff overlooking tranquil Smith Lake. The trail leads left steeply down to the lake, named after Joseph Smith, who came to these mountains in 1882 after hearing of a silver strike near Castle Mountain.

Smith got here early and built a two-storey hotel near the base of the mountain in what became Silver City. By 1883, there were 175 wooden buildings there. At the time, it was larger than Calgary.

But the mines never did produce any silver and by 1885, Silver City was a ghost town. Smith stayed on at his cabin as a trapper until 1937 when, overtaken by old age and partial blindness, he was persuaded to enter the Lacombe Home in Midnapore. He died a few months later.

Castle Mountain Lookout   WALK 34

To the castle walls   MAP 14

Highlight: Viewpoint halfway up Castle Mountain
Distance: 7.2 km (4.5 miles) return
Time: 3 1/2 hours
Rating: Moderate
Maximum elevation: 1,900 m (6,233 ft)
Elevation gain: 436 m (1,433 ft)
Footwear: Walking or running shoes
Best season: May to October

Castle Mountain is among the most magnificent peaks in Banff with its towers, terraces and sheer walls. The lookout trail won't take you up the castle ramparts—that's the province of experienced climbers and fairy princesses—but it does climb to the base of the great walls. And it provides outstanding views over the wide Bow Valley up towards Lake Louise, down towards Banff and across to the great mass of Storm Mountain cut by deep cirques.

Access: From the Trans-Canada Hwy, turn east at Castle Mountain Junction, 28 km (18 miles) NW of Banff townsite, then left on Hwy 1A, the Bow Valley Parkway. At

Castle Mountain

about the 5-km (3-mile) mark from the junction, turn right on a paved road leading in 100 metres to a parking area. The trail starts beyond the gate at the end of the pavement.

Route: The hiking is moderate at first on a fire road. It becomes steeper and passes the remains of an old cabin as the trees begin to open to reveal the valley below. The road reverts to a narrow trail and begins to switchback up rocky, mostly open slopes and meadows below the cliffs.

At about 3.6 km, the trail finally pushes through a band of rock, levels off atop a rock pitch and reaches what used to be a fire lookout. Lookouts have been replaced with aerial patrols and the old place burned down, anyway. This is still a wonderful spot to contemplate the glacier-gouged Bow Valley and such impressive peaks across it as rugged Storm Mountain—which often seems to create its own bad weather.

The peak you are on had long been called Castle Mountain until following the Second World War when it was named Mt. Eisenhower after the American general and president. When told of the honor, he is said to have replied that there already was a mountain named after him: "Old Baldy." Only recently has the name reverted back to Castle Mountain, although the first and most prominent rocky spire on the south end of the ridge is still called Eisenhower Peak.

Castle Mountain is a perfect example of a layer or castellated mountain composed mostly of horizontally-laid sedimentary rock.

Erosion creates the great towers and pinnacles. The softer rock gradually drops away, leaving an upstanding core of more resiliant rock.

Vista Lake

WALK 35

The magnificent desolation

MAP 15

Highlight: Lake and forest fire devastation
Distance: 2.8 km (1.7 miles) return
Time: 1 1/2 hours
Rating: Moderate
Maximum elevation: 1,700 m (5,577 ft)
Elevation loss: 130 m (427 ft)
Footwear: Walking or running shoes
Best season: June to October

This short trail descends through the fascinating devastation of a 1968 forest fire to a vivid green lake set under the imposing heights of Storm Mountain. The trail is short and open to grand views all the way. The hard part is at the end when you have to climb back up to your car.

Access: From the Trans-Canada Hwy at Castle Mountain, junction, 28 km NW of Banff townsite, take Hwy 93 for 4 km up Vermilion Pass, past Storm Mountain Lodge. Near the top of the hill is a scenic turn-off on the left from where Vista Lake may be seen below.

Route: From the viewpoint, the trail begins to edge down the side of the steep hill through the burn. Ahead looms the imposing bulk of Storm Mountain, its reddish-brown quartz sandstone deeply cut by great cirques. This mountain does seem to gather the storms; it's often enclosed in dark cloud when other peaks around are clear.

Luxuriant new growth appears through the gray dead trees, the bright magenta of fireweed dotting the hillside. This is not a depressing environment, as you might expect, but a demonstration of nature renewing itself.

On July 9, 1968, lightning struck this area and the resulting fire burned 6,160 acres. Now, animals and a new succession of plants and trees have invaded the burn and the forest is slowly returning. Large browsing animals such as moose depend particularly on clearings in the sub-alpine forest produced by fires.

Only in such areas in the coniferous forest—plus avalanche tracks and areas of poor soil or drainage that can't support trees— can moose find enough of the willow and aspen twigs and broad-leafed

15. BOOM MTN./STORM MTN.

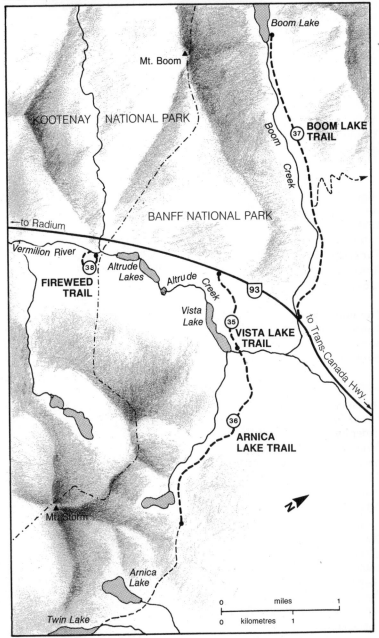

plants they need. So ironically, the traditional national parks policy of using manpower and machines to stop forest fires has deprived animals of their natural browsing areas. This parks policy is being studied. It's expected that wardens will continue to fight fires vigorously in the front country but may tend to let other fires burn far away from the normal haunts of man.

The route passes a small hoodoo composed of conglomerate material—clay and stone—that has remained cemented together while the soil around it has eroded. The trail soon reaches the lake where cutthroat trout might be caught. The trail follows the shore to the outlet which is crossed on a bridge. (See Walk 34 to Arnica Lake for continuation of the trail.)

Arnica Lake Trail
A burnt-out scene

WALK 36
MAP 15

Highlight: Bare ridge, good views, subalpine lake
Distance: 10 km (6.2 miles) return
Time: 5 hours
Rating: Strenuous
Maximum elevation: 2,133 m (7,000 ft)
Elevation gain: 550 m (1804 ft)
Footwear: Light hiking boots
Best season: July to October

From near the top of Vermilion Pass dividing Banff and Kootenay national parks, the day walk passes through the fascinating devastation of a 1968 forest fire, climbs a bare ridge with gorgeous views, passes under the gloomy cliffs of Storm Mountain and ends at a small, subalpine lake. While the way is relentlessly steep, views are nearly constant. Strollers could turn back at any point along the route and still

have an enjoyable outing. Strong hikers could continue on from Arnica Lake to remote Twin Lakes.

Access: From the Trans-Canada Hwy at Castle Mountain Junction, 28 km NW of Banff townsite, take Hwy 93 for 4 km up Vermilion Pass, past Storm Mountain Lodge. Near the top of the hill is a scenic turn-off on the left side, providing a view of Vista Lake amid the burned-out forest.

Route: The route begins from the viewpoint as a highly-unusual mountain trail—downhill. (See Vista Lake Walk 35 for more details.) The lake is reached in 1.4 km and you cross the outlet on a little bridge. Now the work begins. The trail begins to climb gradually through the burn. You can see waterfalls on the cliffs above. At an unmarked junction, the trail from Storm Mountain Lodge enters left just as you leave the burn. Keep straight, returning to the burn area again, climbing more steeply towards a rounded ridge below the cliffs of massive Storm Mountain.

Now the trail is completely in the open with striking views down Vermilion Pass into Kootenay Park. To the left, back towards the Bow River the great ramparts of Castle Mountain dominate the horizon, one of the finest sights in these mountains. Across the Banff-Windemere Highway is the steep-walled Mt. Whymper, named for the conqueror of the Matterhorn who also climbed in this region.

The 3,148-metre Storm Mountain above is a massive quartz sandstone peak with deep glacial cirques or bowls cut into its sides. The way remains steep as the trail ascends the open ridge. Finally, the trail enters the trees again, leaving the burn, skirting an open area of rocks and gravel, eventually leveling off in thick forest to reach Arnica Lake where cutthroat trout may be taken, July 1 to Oct. 31.

Behind the lake, steep scree slopes lead up to the barren heights of Storm Mountain. Although the trail continues for 4.3 km (2.7 miles) further to the Twin Lakes, the scenery remains more or less the same and most strollers will probably be content with Arnica Lake as their destination.

The name "arnica" refers to a common wildflower of this subalpine, spruce-fir forest. The heart-leafed arnica, the most widely-distributed, is a member of the daisy family and bears yellow, daisy-like flowers from stems up to 2 feet high.

The golden fleabane has a similar-looking, yellow daisy-like flower. But it is usually found at higher elevations, especially in alpine meadows. The fleabane is only a few inches high and has hairy leaves for protection against the extreme alpine climate.

Boom Lake Trail

WALK 37

Boom of beauty

MAP 15

Highlight: Dramatically-set alpine lake
Distance: 10.2 km (6.3 miles) return
Time: 3 to 3 1/2 hours
Rating: Moderate
Maximum elevation: 1,892 m (6,210 ft)
Elevation gain: 185 m (610 ft)
Footwear: Light hiking boots
Best season: June to October

Clear Boom Lake is dramatically set below Chimney Peak, Boom Mountain and Mt. Quadra, framed by dark timber and a white glacier. The outing is reasonably short without major climbing and could be suitable for families. While the approach to the lake is easy, views along the way are non-existent. The lake makes up for this subalpine confinement in the forest.

Access: From Banff townsite, drive 28 km (17 miles) northwest on the Trans-Canada Hwy to Castle Mountain Junction. Turn left on Hwy 93 and travel 6.2 km (4 miles) up Vermilion Pass. Boom Lake parking lot is on the right at a picnic area. Start at the north end, crossing over a wooden bridge.

Route: The walk begins on a wide road, veering left for a short steep section onto a trail embowered by lodgepole pine, white spruce and fir. Behind are tantalizing views of Storm Mountain, named by G.M. Dawson in 1884 after the storm clouds so often seen

on the summit.

The trail soon crosses a wooden boardwalk, then levels off. The air here seems especially fragrant, a tumbling stream echoes below; an "away from it all" feeling prevails at last.

The junction for Taylor and O'Brien Lake is at the 1.4-km mark. Keep straight. The wide main trail continues uneventfully through deep woods. Shortly before the lake, the walker has a choice of going right through a small rock slide area, or continuing left on the wide trail. They both go the same way, although the left-hand route is easier. Boom Mountain rises on the left at 2,758 m (9,048 ft); Chimney Peak is to its right.

Cross a boardwalk, on the narrowing trail, and descend on the last, somewhat rough section down to the lake. Boom Lake is long, narrow and aqua-green, forested at its edges and strewn with rubble on the north side. Small cutthroat and rainbow trout can be taken here. Early in the season, avalanches drop from Boom Mountain on the south side. Mt. Quadra dominates the panorama to the northwest, and to the right are the forested lower slopes of Bident Mountain.

Fireweed Trail

WALK 38

A terrible beauty

MAP 15

Highlight: Forest fire devastation
Distance: .8 km (.5 mile) loop
Time: 20 minutes
Rating: Easy
Maximum elevation: 1,640 m (5,382 ft)
Elevation gain: Negligible
Footwear: Walking or running shoes
Best season: June to October

Life from ashes, blossoms from blazing forest fires—that's the vivid lesson in forest ecology provided by the unusual Fireweed Trail. The little path wanders through the devastation left by a huge 1968 forest fire at Vermilion Pass right on the Continental Divide and the boundary between Alberta and British Columbia. Surprisingly, the walk is anything but depressing, with bright magenta fireweed and other new growth surging everywhere.

Access: From Banff townsite, drive 28 km (17 miles) north on the Trans-Canada Hwy and turn left on Hwy 93 to Vermilion Pass at Castle Mountain Junction. The trail starts 9 km (6 miles) further, on the right of the prominent Continental Divide sign which marks the division between Banff and Kootenay national parks, as well as the eastern and western watersheds.

Route: On July 9, 1968, lightning struck the Vermilion Pass area and burned 6,160 acres. Since 1969, scientists have been studying the

effects of fire on a mountain environment. This walk is a glimpse into that living laboratory.

The walk, through young pine and fir and the skeletons of trees, illustrates how the burnt area is renewing itself. New plants and animals have taken hold to such an extent that Parks Canada calls the result "a more dynamic community than previously existed here."

The first "pioneer" species to colonize a burn area are light-loving trees such as trembling aspen or lodgepole pine. Many of the resin-sealed cones of the lodgepole pine remain on the tree for years and never open except in the extreme heat of a forest fire.

These pioneering trees' affinity for light means they are not able to reproduce themselves indefinitely since they begin to shade each other, blocking the growth of new trees which require sunshine. But spruce or subalpine fir can grow in these shady surroundings. So they begin to invade the forest and gradually the pioneer trees die out. Not a speedy process—it may take 200 years. Here are the beginnings.

A narrow path leads through trees that are devastated but still standing. The habitat is ideal for many animals, including moose, because it provides both food and shelter. The moose usually can't find enough to eat in the dense coniferous forest and depends on the clear areas produced by forest fires for the twigs and broad-leaved plants it needs.

Blue grouse and northern hawk-owls nest here and small animals and rodents abound. Few places in the Rockies offer a richer sight than the renewing forest decorated with magenta fireweed (or "great willow herb") in summer. This plant is easily recognizable by its long spike, brilliant blossoms and affinity for forest clearings and burns. Watch also for yellow columbine and various mosses and berries.

Follow the path up by a trail registry. Then loop up under the shadow of Storm Mountain to the east, past a bench wrought out of one of the fire victims—an excellent place to contemplate the view west to Mount Whymper, named for the famous conqueror of the Matterhorn who visited the Canadian Rockies many times.

The trail descends from here and can be slippery in wet weather. You are right on the Continental Divide where water may flow eastward into the Saskatchewan River system and thence to Hudson Bay, or into the Vermilion River, Columbia and ultimately the Pacific.

The Light Dawns on Fire Management

Before the Rockies became parks, fires crackled through the lower Bow Valley every 20 or 30 years, and a series of fires blazed throughout much of the Athabasca Valley.

At the beginning of this century, however, park wardens began a rigorous program of fire suppression. But years of man's intrusion took a toll on forest ecology. Because regular fires no longer thinned the forest, the stands became dense, wildlife dwindled and dead wood accumulated on the ground, creating the danger of fueling larger-than-ever fires.

Parks Canada has now instituted a series of experimental burns to test the possibility of more widespread burning programs. In remote areas, natural fires are allowed to burn as long as they do not threaten the rest of the park.

"The whole subject of controlled burning is presently under study," states a Parks Canada report on the natural and human history of Banff National Park.

Marble Canyon

WALK 39

A marble salad bowl

MAP 16

Highlight: Dramatic limestone canyon
 Distance: 1.6 km (1 mile)
Time: 30 to 40 minutes return
Rating: Easy
Maximum elevation: 1,432 m (4,700 ft)
Elevation gain: Negligible
Footwear: Anything
Best season: May to October

The scalloped limestone walls of Marble Canyon, eroded by rushing water, are almost an art exhibit. The deservedly-popular walk along the rim of this narrow chasm, ending at a striking outlook at the head of the falls, is enjoyed by all ages.

You could loll away a pleasant couple of hours by combining this walk with a visit to the nearby Paint Pots (Walk 40), and the Fireweed Trail (Walk 37).

Access: From Banff townsite, drive north on the Trans-Canada Hwy for 28 km (17 miles) to Castle Mountain Junction. Turn left here on Hwy 93, and climb Vermilion Pass, crossing into Kootenay National Park. The Marble Canyon parking lot is 16 km (10 miles) from the junction.

Route: A gravel path starts by dipping down to water's edge, near the junction of Vermilion River with Tokumm Creek, then leads gradually up. The water is an unforgettable milky turquoise. The trail is fringed with wildflowers in

summer—purple asters, daisies, arnica . . . Picking is prohibited.

Cross over First Bridge, where

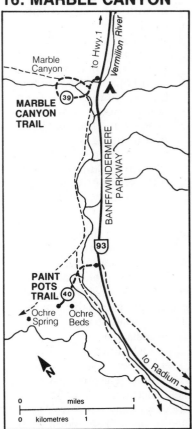

16. MARBLE CANYON

the canyon is widest. You can see the river disappearing ahead into the limestone rock, cut down over the centuries. Continue up steps—the only steep part—where the effects of the 1968 Vermilion Pass burn are

Lichen

The black, green and gray splotches that appear on many of the rocks and limestone canyons of the mountains certainly don't look like forces of destruction.

Yet this form of growth, called lichen, often is such a force. The splotches are actually two kinds of plants living in a mutually-beneficial relationship. Each lichen is composed of a fungus and an alga. The fungus absorbs and stores water, while the green alga produces food.

Lichens, which have no leaves, stems or roots, are often the first plants to grow on bare rocks. When numerous lichen accumulate on a rock, they produce a film of soil which helps mosses to start growing as well. Larger plants are then attracted to the rock, then sometimes small trees which send roots down into cracks in the rock . . . and the rock begins to disintegrate.

More than 15,000 known kinds of lichen have been identified. Apple-green lichen has a growth rate of about one centimetre in diameter for the first thousand years. Not an ideal houseplant.

apparent on the right.

The canyon walls contain a strata of white and gray marble running through the predominant gray limestone. When Sir James Hector and his party passed this way, some of the soft white stone was taken for pipe manufacture.

The rushing waters of Tokumm Creek, which drains Prospector Valley, have chiselled and carved these limestone walls. At Second Bridge the canyon is narrow and 17 metres deep. Peer down at the ferns and mosses growing in the "salad bowl" scooped out by eons of pounding water. The rising mist creates a lush, damp environment.

You can walk on either side of the canyon, crossing over the bridges. At Third Bridge the depth is 28 metres and only a step or two

across. The steepest portions of the canyon are at Sixth Bridge and Seventh Bridge, both at a dizzying 36 metres (118 ft).

If the railings seem overly cautious along parts of the canyon edge, consider that at least three persons have fallen to their deaths down here, two because they backed too close to the edge when having their pictures taken.

Seventh Bridge is an impressive spot, with dramatic views of the rumbling 21-metre (70 ft) waterfall plunging into a foaming turqouise pool at the very start of the canyon.

Return on the opposite side—it doesn't really matter which. Picnic tables are situated in the woods just north of the parking lot. An information centre also operates in summer.

The Paint Pots

WALK 40

Place of the red clay spirit

MAP 16

Highlight: Ochre beds
Distance: 1.6 km (1 mile return)
Time: 30 minutes
Rating: Easy
Maximum elevation: 1,432 m (4,700 ft)
Elevation gain: Negligible
Footwear: Anything
Best season: May to October

To the Indians, this was a place of great spiritual significance—the place where the Red Clay Spirit is taken. It was a practical place too. Here Indians obtained the ochre color they used to decorate tipis, clothing, bodies and rock paintings. This short, fascinating trail crosses the Vermilion River on a suspension bridge, leads past old mining equipment and ochre-colored meadows, up an ochre-colored stream to the paint pots which are cones formed by mineral deposits in the spring water. The stroll has historic and cultural significance and is a unique sort of walk to boot.

Access: The large parking area for the Paint Pots is in Kootenay National Park on Hwy 93, 19 km (12 miles) west of Castle Mountain Junction and 85 km (53 miles) east of the park gate at Radium Hot Springs. The trail leaves from the far side of the lot, near a large sign explaining what the paint pots have meant in recent history.

Route: The path to the suspension bridge is paved and easy. The Vermilion River is fast-moving and its banks provide good views of the surrounding peaks. You move onto the flat, low-lying ochre beds, colored red-brown by the deposits. Indians travelled here from the prairies to obtain "red earth." They mixed the ochre with water, kneaded it and shaped it into flat cakes. These were baked in a fire. The hardened cakes were ground into powder and mixed with fish oil or animal grease for use as paint.

The trail soon leads past old mining equipment. Around 1900, the white man dug up the ochre by hand and hauled it in sacks to the nearest railway—across Vermilion Pass at Castle Mountain Junction. Then it was shipped to Calgary for use as a pigment in paints. Later, machinery was brought in to increase production. Horse-drawn scoops replaced the shovels while other machines ground up the ochre. Ochre production stopped in 1920 when Kootenay became a national park and the mining equipment was left to rust, eventually becoming much the same color as the ochre beds.

Continue past the unusual yellow-red clearing up the ochre-colored stream to a "choked cone," a dried-up mound of iron oxide, formed by what used to be a "paint pot" until it was blocked by its own mineral deposits. Ahead are the paint pots themselves.

The pots are formed because the heavy concentration of iron in the

water from underground springs forms a natural ring around the outlet. The iron oxide rim gets higher and higher until the water, always seeking the easiest route, forms another outlet elsewhere.

Taylor Lake Trail

WALK 41

Woodland walk to a bell

MAP 17

Highlight: Green cirque lake
Distance: 12.6 km (7.8 miles) return
Time: 4 hours
Rating: Moderate
Maximum elevation: 2,057 m (6,750 ft)
Elevation gain: 579 m (1,900 ft)

Footwear: Light hiking boots
Best season: Mid-June to October

To be perfectly upfront about this walk, forget about any views until Taylor Lake is reached. Expect, instead, a long, long uphill trudge through thick subalpine forest. . . and more thick subalpine forest.

So why do it? The reason is to enjoy Taylor Lake's dramatic

17. TAYLOR LAKE

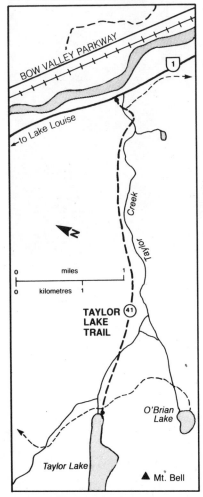

setting under the backdrop of Mt. Bell—and that's probably reason enough. The trip may also be extended 2 km to O'Brien Lake. Just remember, in this case getting

there is not half the fun.

Access: From Banff townsite, drive 36 km (22 miles) west on the Trans-Canada Hwy, or 8 km (5 miles) west of Castle Mountain Junction. Start at the Taylor Creek picnic area and parking lot. Cross over a wooden bridge; the trailhead is to the right.

Route: The trail starts on the level through mixed forest, along rushing Taylor Creek. The undergrowth is typical of the lower subalpine: horsetails, grasses, wildflowers, buffalo berry and labrador tea (so named because Indians and early explorers made tea from its leaves).

In a few minutes the walker begins a gentle ascent, with a few brief glimpses of the peaks ahead. Switchback up on some steep portions. The trail can be mushy in places.

The path crosses Taylor Creek on stones and heads into an upper subalpine area where the forest of fir and Engelmann spruce becomes more stunted.

After so much forest trudging, the walker may be relieved when dramatic views open to Mt. Bell on the left and the Panorama Ridge on the right. Cross a small log-bridge over a creek. Pick through a potentially mushy meadow before coming to a camping area in the trees and then to Taylor Lake—a small, gem-like, forest-fringed cirque.

Cirques are natural depressions in the sides of mountains which were slowly widened and deepened by the freeze-thaw action of water. Heavy snow accumulation was compressed into ice and the scouring and gouging action of the glaciers carved cirques to a much greater size. Many of the mountain lakes, like Taylor, occupy abandoned cirques.

While the trail also leads 2 km further to O'Brien Lake, the way can be difficult. Most day walkers should be content to picnic at Taylor Lake before heading back.

10 Banff National Park
Walks by Lake Louise and Moraine Lake

Moraine Lake Viewpoint WALK 42

Rubble with a view MAP 18

Highlight: Gorgeous lake views
Distance: .7 km (.4 miles) return
Time: 15 to 20 minutes
Rating: Easy
Maximum elevation: 1,950 m (6,395 ft)
Elevation gain: Negligible
Footwear: Walking or running shoes
Best season: June to October

The walk up to Moraine Lake viewpoint is one of the shortest in this book; the panorama it offers is not to be missed. Starting at the bustling parking lot, the path leads up masses of rocks under the imposing Tower of Babel to a magnificent vantage point on the turquoise-green lake framed by jagged peaks. This is the same view that's depicted on the back of the $20 bill. Here it's free.

Access: From the Trans-Canada Hwy at the Lake Louise intersection in Banff National Park, turn west on Hwy 1A and drive 1.1 km (.7 miles) up the hill towards Lake Louise. Turn left (south) on the Moraine Lake Road which ends in 12.4 km (8 miles) at a large parking lot. The trail begins at the south end of the parking lot, near the toilets, at the sign for Consolation Lakes.

Route: The walk starts in a dramatic setting, under the reddish, aptly-named Tower of Babel. Geologists now believe that the rock debris which dams this end of the lake fell from this mountain. However, Walter Wilcox, who named the lake in 1893, believed the debris to be a moraine, a deposit of debris carried by a glacier or pushed ahead by it. Hence, Moraine Lake,

18. LAKE LOUISE (South)

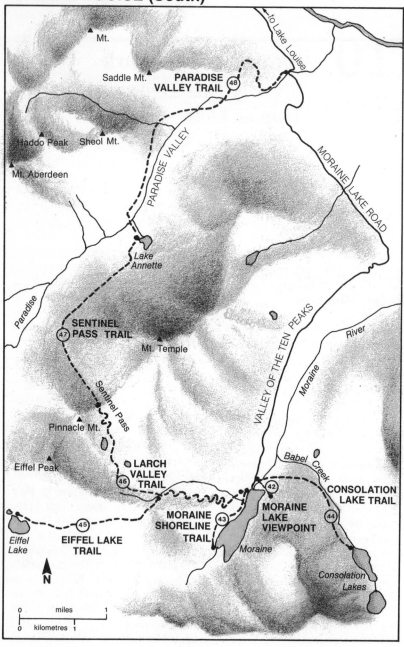

Mt.

Saddle Mt.

PARADISE VALLEY TRAIL (48)

to Lake Louise

MORAINE LAKE ROAD

PARADISE VALLEY

Haddo Peak   Sheol Mt.

Mt. Aberdeen

Lake Annette

Paradise

(47) **SENTINEL PASS TRAIL**

Mt. Temple

VALLEY OF THE TEN PEAKS

River

Moraine

Sentinel Pass

Pinnacle Mt.

Babel Creek

Eiffel Peak

(46) **LARCH VALLEY TRAIL**

(42)

CONSOLATION LAKE TRAIL

(45) **EIFFEL LAKE TRAIL**

Eiffel Lake

MORAINE SHORELINE TRAIL (43)

MORAINE LAKE VIEWPOINT

(44)

Moraine

Consolation Lakes

N

0   miles   1

0   kilometres   1

a good name, even if scientifically wrong.

Walk over a little wooden bridge and up a fairly steep stretch. This section, with its boulder-strewn surface, resembles a prehistoric battlefield.

At the sign for Consolation Lakes, turn right to walk up to the viewpoint. After another steeper stretch, the path opens out onto a panorama of Moraine Lake.

The 10 dazzling peaks, east to west, are: Fay, Little, Bowlen, Perren, Septa (Peak Five), Allen, Tuzo, Deltaform (the tallest), Neptuak and Wenkchemna.

There is no formal picnic area here, only a bench. You can climb right down to the water's edge if you want. Fishermen can often be seen at the shoreline, at dawn or dusk, trying for trout.

This can be a blustery and cold spot. On a sunny day, however, it's a lovely place to sketch, read, or just soak in the splendour, though not the solitude.

While you may just stay a few minutes, pikas live here year-round. The pika, or rock rabbit, is about the size of a hamster and blends in with the rock. You can hear his shrill "eeeep!" and sometimes find the "haystack" he gathers for food to eat under the snow in winter.

Moraine Shoreline Trail   WALK 43

The happiest half hour   MAP 18

Highlight: Pleasant woodland walk
Distance: 3.2 km (2 miles)
Time: 30 to 40 minutes
Rating: Easy
Maximum elevation: 1,900 m (6,233 ft)
Elevation gain: Negligible
Footwear: Walking or running shoes
Best season: Mid-June to October

Turquoise Moraine Lake, set in the commanding Valley of the Ten Peaks, is regarded by many as more dramatic, more striking than its more famous sister, Lake Louise.

A pretty lakeshore stroll, suitable for all ages, meanders along its wooded west shore. The path is just long enough to stretch your legs or work off dinner.

Views are fewer than one might expect, however. If panoramas are a priority, take the short stroll to Moraine Lake Viewpoint, Walk 42, or the longer Larch Valley trail, Walk 46.

Moraine Lodge serves a special hiker's breakfast and dinner is served to 8 p.m. Canoes can be rented and fishing is permitted in season with a parks permit.

Access: From the Trans-Canada Hwy at the Lake Louise intersection in Banff National Park, turn west on Hwy 1A and drive 1.1 km up the hill towards Lake Louise. Turn left (south) on the Moraine Lake Road which ends in 12.4 km (8 miles) at a large parking lot. The walk starts on the asphalt path at the south end of the parking lot.

Route: For a change, the most fabulous views are at the beginning, even before you reach Moraine Lake Lodge. The spectacle of the green lake set against the magnificent backdrop of the Valley of the 10 Peaks is exquisite indeed.

Walter Wilcox, an explorer-alpinist from the Yale Lake Louise Club, came upon Moraine Lake in 1893. He mistook the rubble at the south end of the lake for a glacial moraine and therefore named the lake Moraine.

"I stood on a great stone of the moraine where, from a slight elevation, a magnificent view of the lake lay before me, and while studying the details of this unknown and unvisited spot, spent the happiest half hour of my life," Wilcox wrote.

The path goes by the lodge and dock, where canoes can be rented for half an hour or more. On the other side of the boat launch, take the lower trail left at the junction with the trailhead sign for Larch Valley.

Mt. Fay, the first of the 10 numbered peaks, is to the left. To its right are Little, Bowlen, Perren, Septa (Peak Five), Allen, Tuzo, Deltaform (the highest), Neptuak and Wenkchemna. The pink rock pile visible on the east shore is composed of shales and quartz sandstone.

The pleasant path is strewn with wildflowers in summer, and winds through an open forest with lake views. Moraine's color, the result of suspended rock particles, seems to change as one walks, from teal blue to turquoise and green.

Backless benches are located at several points along the trail, which progresses over some little brooks, then edges right along the lake once

Moraine Lake

again. Note the fir valiantly hugging the cliffs of Mount Babel across the lake.

Dippers and harlequin ducks can sometimes be seen on the lake. The forest becomes mossy and marshy, and better views of hanging Fay Glacier appear ahead. Near the end, you may hear the rumble of a glacial stream. The trail heads into cool, dense forest before ending at a small clearing near the end of the lake.

Consolation Lake

WALK 44

Rock hoppers delight

MAP 18

Highlight: Subalpine lake under impressive peaks
Distance: 6.4 km (3.9 miles) return
Time: 2 1/2 hours
Rating: Moderate
Maximum elevation: 1,950 m (6,400 ft)
Elevation gain: 94 m (310 ft)
Footwear: Walking or running shoes
Best season: Mid-June to October

Most of the spectacular subalpine lakes in the Banff backcountry require hours of hard uphill slogging to attain. Consolation Lake, as scenic as any of them, is easily reached on a wide, gentle trail from popular Moraine Lake, south of Lake Louise. It's a good way to escape the crowds that drift through the Lake Louise-Moraine Lake area in summer, and you don't have to strain yourself to do it.

Access: From the Trans-Canada Hwy at the Lake Louise intersection in Banff National Park, turn west on Hwy 1A and drive 1.1 km up the hill towards Lake Louise. Turn left (south) on the Moraine Lake Road which ends in 12.4 km (8 miles) at a large parking lot. The Consolation Lake Trail begins from the lower parking lot near the washrooms.

Route: The trail climbs briefly over part of the huge rock pile that blocks the end of the lake. The Consolation Lake trail soon branches left away from the rocks while the route straight ahead continues to a viewpoint overlooking the gorgeous lake. (See Walk 42).

The Consolation Lake route traverses a boulder field under the imposing and crumbling heights of the Tower of Babel. Behind is the sprawling mass of Mt. Temple (3,547 metres, 11,636 feet), a most imposing pyramid.

The trail ascends gradually up vigorous Babel Creek and enters a good forest of spruce and subalpine fir.

At .9 km, the trail to Taylor Lake forks left. Keep straight, climbing gradually on the wide and usually dry trail. It soon levels off as views open to the craggy heights on the right. The valley here is wide and open and the lake soon comes into view.

The trail terminates in a vast area of boulders at the end of the lake. Long scree slopes descend to the lake on the right while gorgeous, Mt. Bident and Mt. Quadra tower behind it.

Actually, this is the lower of two lakes. Determined hikers could reach the second one by walking far enough back down the creek to gain the other side, then following a rough trail along the left shore and over the moraine that divides the

two small lakes. Most hikers, however, should console themselves with lower Consolation Lake, so named by Walter Wilcox's exploratory party in 1899.

They called the Valley of the Ten Peaks "Desolation Valley," after seeing it first from its desolate upper reaches. The valley, Wilcox said, appeared "like a veil of desolation and death." But the party appreciated the green valley southeast of Moraine Lake and so thought it only fair to name it "Consolation Valley."

Eiffel Lake Trail

WALK 45

The barren lakes above

MAP 18

Highlight: Alpine lakes, stunning views
Distance: 11 km (6.8 miles) return
Time: 5 hours
Rating: Strenuous
Maximum elevation: 2,270 m (7,450 ft)
Elevation gain: 384 m (1,260 ft)
Footwear: Light hiking boots
Best season: Mid-July to October

"The peers of any lakes in the Rocky Mountains." The first white exploration party into this upper valley in 1899 thus described the barren Eiffel Lakes among the last stands of larches and the desolation of rubble under the wall of the Wenkchemna Peaks, otherwise known as the Valley of the Ten Peaks.

While popular, these gorgeous lakes and the open country beyond them aren't visited as much as nearby Sentinel Pass. But the lakes are considerably easier to reach. The approach from the Larch Valley junction after a sweaty climb from Moraine Lake cleverly follows the contours of the hillside and is almost level. And the views down into the upper, rubble-strewn valley are gorgeous, the sparkling lakes reflecting the steep turrets of the Ten Peaks. Altogether, for stronger hikers, there's no better place to admire the valley in its entirety— and this valley is one of the finest in Banff.

Access: From the Trans-Canada Hwy at the Lake Louise intersection in Banff National Park, turn west on

Hwy 1A and drive 1.1 km up the hill towards Lake Louise. Turn left (south) on the Moraine Lake Road which ends in 12.4 km at a large parking lot. The trail to Eiffel Lakes begins near the lakeside just beyond the lodge. Take the right fork up the hill.

Route: The initial trail is wide and well graded as it switch-backs up the steep slopes, offering occasional views down to the stunning emerald green of Moraine Lake and across the lake to Wenkchemna Glacier, its ice hidden and protected from the sun under rockfall and dirt accumulated over the years. This covering keeps the ice from melting at the same rate as most other glaciers. At km 3.2 (2 miles), the Sentinel Pass trail leads off right. Stay straight for Eiffel Lake, the trail neatly following the contour of the hillside under crumbling Eiffel Peak without much gain or loss of elevation. The valley floor below is gradually rising to meet the trail. Among the usual alpine fir and Engelmann spruce are larches which turn a most spectacular yellow in fall before losing their needles, the only coniferous trees to do so.

There are wonderful views back to Moraine Lake and the trees gradually open up, revealing the glacial rubble and rockfall below. The hillside becomes more rocky and rugged as you go along, now passing under the broken cliffs leading up to trailless Wastach Pass and Paradise Valley beyond. You round a corner and Eiffel Lake comes into view below the trail. There are actually several of these alpine lakes. From here on, there are few trees to block the spectacular views.

Follow the trail as it climbs slightly above the lake, crossing a rock slide which may obscure the route for a few metres. There's an excellent natural rock bench with a back-rest on a pitch above the lake right on the trail, a perfect spot to contemplate this stunning alpine area.

The Stoney Indian name Wenkchemna which is given to the mountain range opposite simply means '10'. The peaks, all visible from this vantage, are, in order from Moraine Lake: Fay, Little, Bowlen, Perren, Septa (Peak Five), Allen, Tuzo, Deltaform, Neptuak, and on the other side of Wenkchemna Pass ahead, Wenkchemna Peak. The name "Eiffel" comes from the rock tower above which could be compared, if you squint a bit, to the Eiffel Tower of Paris.

Little Eiffel Lake is set among enormous boulders which tumbled down from Neptuak Mtn. This is the view, more or less, that explorer Walter Wilcox saw when he first encountered this area in 1893 and named it "Desolation Valley." Had he seen Moraine Lake first, his designation might have been different.

Strong hikers still feeling energetic can continue up the valley from the lakes, climbing only slightly as the trail follows the right edge of the valley. It works its way along an old lateral moraine, keeping well away from the avalanche-prone slopes on the side.

The ultimate destination is visible 4 km (2.5 miles) above Eiffel Lake:

Wenkchemna Pass at the top of broad, rocky meadows. To the right are crumbling tower-like crags with little waterfalls coming off them. Across the valley rises Deltaform and Neptuak. The trail curves left towards the middle of the valley floor, passing near more rock-bound ponds and beginning its ascent of the pass. These rocky meadows may be snow-covered until mid-summer and the snow cover often returns early in the fall.

In good weather, the route is unmistakeable, zig-zagging steeply up to the low point in the barren, windswept pass. Views are grand back down the whole valley and west into Yoho National Park, to the barren Eagle Eyrie and the icefield leading to Opabin Pass and Lake O'Hara.

Larch Valley

The golden meadows

WALK 46

MAP 18

Highlight: Beautiful subalpine meadows
Distance: 8 km (5 miles) return
Time: 3 to 3 1/2 hours
Rating: Moderate
Maximum elevation: 2,275 m (7,463 ft)
Elevation gain: 375 m (1,230 ft)
Footwear: Light hiking boots
Best season: July to October

This popular trail rises rapidly above Moraine Lake to delightful subalpine meadows, set against the jagged backdrop of the Valley of the Ten Peaks. Families would find it an ideal way to enjoy sublime mountain views. In September, when the larches have turned gold and the sun is shining, Larch Valley is one of the most exquisite spots in the Rockies.

Those in good physical shape could continue 2.4 km further to Sentinel Pass for a stupendous mountain panorama (Walk 47).

Another adventurous option is the day trip over the pass to Paradise Valley (Walk 48).

Access: From the Trans-Canada Hwy at the Lake Louise intersection in Banff National Park, turn west on Hwy 1A and drive 1.1 km up the hill towards Lake Louise. Turn left (south) on the Moraine Lake Road which ends in 12.4 km (8 miles) at a large parking lot. From here, follow the asphalt path past Moraine Lodge, following the sign to Larch Valley and turning right at the second sign to Wenkchemna Pass, Larch Valley and Sentinel Pass.

Route: The first part of the trail bolts up fairly steeply, with tantalizing glimpses through the trees of Moraine Lake below. In 1893 explorer Walter Wilcox climbed a ridge and recorded "one of the most beautiful lakes I have ever seen. . . No scene has ever given me an equal impression of inspiring solitude and rugged grandeur.''

The lake was Moraine and its colors of mingled robin's egg blue and green make it equally beautiful today. At the 3.2-km mark, the trail reaches the junction with the Eiffel Lake Trail. Keep right, through the subalpine environment of alpine larch, feather mosses, arnicas, bunchberries and heathers. The larches are not evergreen and turn yellow-gold in autumn before shedding their needles. These needles come in bunches of 30 to 40 on dwarfed, knob-like branches. In Banff National Park, larches are found only in a restricted range at timberline and do not grow north of Hector Lake.

Views soon open onto the lower Larch meadows. Mt. Fay with its hanging glacier dominates the skyline among the jagged 10 peaks.

Cross a small stream and continue to the upper Larch Valley, gradually leaving the trees behind to emerge into an area of meadows, delicate pools and, for a short time in summer, tiny alpine flowers. You could lunch, sketch or just soak in the sun for hours in this popular valley. Just don't expect much solitude on a sunny day in summer.

Eiffel Peak and Pinnacle Mountain dominate views on the left. On the right is Mt. Temple, highest mountain in the Lake Louise area, first climbed in 1894 by Wilcox.

The trail works its way towards the base of Temple, past a pond and begins to ascend the bare, rocky slopes of Sentinel Pass. You can see the trail high above as a faint "Z" zig-zag on the remarkably steep slope that's often partially snow-covered well through July.

Casual hikers, however, will want to turn back before the steep ascent begins, especially in bad weather. This valley is so gorgeous, it should be enough.

Sentinel Pass and Paradise Valley WALK 47

Alpine path to paradise MAP 18

Highlight: Stunning views from mountain pass
Distance: 20.1 km (12 miles)
Time: 7 hours
Rating: Strenuous
Maximum elevation: 2,600 m (8,530 ft)
Elevation gain: 700 m (2,296 ft)
Footwear: Light hiking boots
Best season: Mid-July to September

Peak-rimmed alpine meadows, a pinnacled mountain pass, delicate lakes, pools—those are the rewards of the popular Sentinel Pass trail. In autumn when the larches turn gold above blue-green Moraine Lake, the demanding all-day hike over the pass is one of almost indescribable beauty, plus considerable toil.

Sentinel Pass can be adapted to most walker's schedules. If you don't want to cross the pass, or can't arrange transportation on the other side, you could go only as far as Larch Valley (Walk 46), or take an extra two hours to climb to the top of the pass and return the same way.

One difficulty with this marvellous walk is the need to arrange transportation back to Moraine Lake from Paradise Creek Parking Area. While we don't especially recommend hitchhiking, necessity has sometimes dictated it here. An enjoyable alternative is to hide bicycles in the woods (locked to a sizeable tree near the Paradise Valley parking lot. Leave your car at Moraine Lake at the start of the route. At the end, cycle back to the lake. A trail leads from near the end of the Paradise Valley route back to Moraine Lake parallel to the road. Forget it. After that long a walk, you'd have to be crazy to tackle such an extended, uninteresting slog through the woods.

Snow can last well into summer and cover the other side of the pass by early September. Take plenty of drinking water.

Access: From the Trans-Canada Hwy at the Lake Louise intersection in Banff National Park, turn west on Hwy 1A and drive 1.1 km up the hill towards Lake Louise. Turn left (south) on the Moraine Lake Road which ends in 12.4 km (8 miles) at a large parking lot. From the parking lot, follow the asphalt path past Moraine Lodge. Turn right in about 50 metres on the trail to Larch Valley.

Route: The wide trail heads up through spruce forest for about 20 minutes before revealing gorgeous views of Moraine Lake now a

considerable distance below. The mingled greens and blues of the lake are caused by glacial rock particles reflecting the sun's rays like a spectrum. When early mountaineer Walter Wilcox first came across Moraine Lake in 1893, he declared it "one of the most beautiful lakes I have ever seen."

The path switchbacks—10 times if you're counting—to the junction with the Eiffel Lake trail (Walk 45) at 3.2 km (2 miles). From here it's 2.4 km (1.4 miles) to the top of the pass. Follow signs right, through stunted alpine larch with irregular, gnarled branches. The larch is not an evergreen, so its soft needles turn gold in autumn before dropping like leaves. This timberline species grows in a fairly restricted range around Lake Louise and on higher slopes in the Bow Valley.

The trail opens up into the magical subalpine meadows of Larch Valley, rimmed with the tops of the Ten Peaks. The Wenkchemna Glacier drapes these peaks. Deltaform, named after a Greek letter, is the tallest of the 10 peaks at 6,981 metres (11,235 feet). The peaks, all visible from a slightly higher vantage are, from the left Fay, Little, Bowlen, Perren, Septa (Peak Five), Allen, Tuzo, Deltaform, Neptuak, and Wenkchemna.

Cross logs over a small stream to reach the upper meadows. Here, alpine flowers bloom briefly in summer, and it's delightful to stop for a break by one of the tiny ponds before heading up to the pass.

Up towards the pass, Pinnacle Mountain dominates views on the left while Mt. Temple looms on the right. This latter mountain at a massive 3,647 metres (11,636 feet) is the highest in the Lake Louise area and the 10th highest in the Canadian Rockies. Named for Sir Richard Temple, a visitor to the Rockies in 1884, it was first climbed in 1894 by members of the Yale Lake Louise Club, a merry band of alpinists who explored extensively in the area. The forbidding north face was not conquered until 1966 when a party led by Brian Greenwood of Calgary forced a route.

The increasingly-rugged trail heads past a small beautiful pool under Pinnacle Mountain at the bottom of the amazingly steep pass. Head right and cross a small creek to begin the hard slogging on the Mt. Temple side of the pass. The trail ahead is visible as a huge

Sentinal Pass

zig-zag up the bare slope, as if someone carved the mark of Zorro upon the mountainside. The trail begins its arduous switchbacking through rubble to Sentinel Pass. Snow often lies across the trail into summer, although there's usually a well-stamped trail across steep patches. Walkers will have to judge the safety of a crossing for themselves. This is a route best undertaken in August or early September.

Wilcox wrote: "The last few steps to a mountain pass are attended by a pleasurable excitement equalled only by the conquest of a new mountain. The curtain is about to be raised, as it were, on a new scene, and the reward of many hours of climbing comes at one magical revelation."

Indeed. The top of the pass offers such a "magical revelation"—a tremendous view ahead to Paradise Valley and back over the Valley of the Ten Peaks. When the sun is shining and the wind light (a rare day, indeed), this is an inspiring place to stop for lunch.

The walk over the pass down to Paradise Valley can be treacherous. Snow usually remains on the initial steep and rugged descent as late as early July and returns as early as Labor Day. This shady north face holds the snow later than the Moraine Lake side.

Pick your way carefully down the steep slope before descending to an old avalanche area. The sentinels, strange needle-like formations of Pinnacle Mountain, add a gothic touch. The trail keeps to the right side of the valley. Watch for a line of cairns.

Below, north, lies Paradise Valley, named by the Lake Louise Club which explored it in 1894. They termed it a "sunlit fairyland."

The valley hasn't changed at all. Shining Horseshoe Glacier drapes the foot of Ringrose Peak at the west end of the valley. To its right are Mount Lefroy, the Mitre, snow-frosted Mount Aberdeen, Haddo Peak and Sheol Mountain.

On warm afternoons in early September, the valley booms with the sound of avalanches. The route descends gently through larches and spruce, then switchbacks more steeply down. Near the bottom, watch for signs for Lake Louise to the right.

(Those with extra time or energy would enjoy taking the trail left, which leads to the Giant Steps, a cascading waterfall on Upper Paradise Creek. The path loops back down the valley to eventually rejoin the main trail.)

The way is mostly level or downhill now, through subalpine forest. This part can be mushy. Mt. Temple towers above and Pinnacle Mountain behind resembles a gothic tower.

The trail crosses a large avalanche area. This is a fine place to stop for a break and enjoy scenic views east and west of valley—the last such panorama on this walk.

A high-pitched whistle among the rocks may be the hoary marmot. The small pika also lives in this habitat, but its call is less a whistle and more like a shrill "eeeep!"

The trail then descends through more open forest to Lake Annette. This small lake is dramatically located under the gloomy, awesome, sinister cliffs of Mt. Temple. On a sunny summer afternoon, one can witness huge avalanches.

Don't expect views from here down to the Paradise Valley parking lot, 5.6 kms (3.4 miles) further. The flower-fringed trail passes over tumbling Paradise Creek. Sheol Mountain and Saddle Mountain flank the left side of the trail. Cross several bridges to a large sign.

Keep right and walk 0.6 km further to the parking lot.

The parking lot is situated on the Moraine Lake Road, 2.4 km (1.5 miles) south of the junction with the Lake Louise access road—1A. It's 10 km (6.2 miles) from the parking lot back to Moraine Lake. Don't plan on walking 10 km on a paved road after that long trail. Your feet will die a thousand deaths.

Paradise Valley   WALK 48

The most awesome sight   MAP 18

Highlight: Subalpine lake under imposing mountain
Distance: 11.2 km (7 miles) return
Time: 4 to 4 1/2 hours
Rating: Moderate
Maximum elevation: 1,975 m (6,479 ft)
Elevation gain: 150 m (492 ft)
Footwear: Light hiking boots
Best season: June to October

Lake Annette is snuggled beneath the imposing, sinister north face of Mt. Temple, highest mountain in this area. The walk to it is through mixed forest and along rushing Paradise Creek with few views until you reach the lake. On warm afternoons the lakeshore can be a safe and dramatic seat for viewing lacy avalanches plummeting down the dark north face of Mt. Temple.

Those wishing a longer walk into Paradise Valley might continue 4.9 km (3 miles) further to Giant Steps,

an unusual waterfall resembling a natural stairway.

Access: From the Trans-Canada Hwy at the Lake Louise intersection in Banff National Park, turn west on Hwy 1A and drive 1.1 km up the hill towards Lake Louise. Turn left on the Moraine Lake Road and drive 3.2 km (2 miles) to the Paradise Creek parking area on the right.

Route: Head up through the trees, keeping right at the first junction at 0.4 km and turning left just ahead at the large log sign for Paradise Valley. The first part of the trail is somewhat tedious, through thick forest and past numerous streams.

Ahead are the first views of Mt. Temple, which dominates the Lake Louise region at 3,647 metres (1,196 feet). This predominant peak seems suitably named. Actually the name isn't descriptive; it has a more prosaic origin. It is named for Sir Richard Temple, president of the economics and statics section of the British Association for the Advancement of Science who visited the Rockies in 1884. Ten years later, a group led by alpinist-explorer Walter Wilcox climaxed explorations in this area by climbing Temple, recording that they had "stood on the highest point then reached in Canada."

The trail crosses Paradise Creek several times, opening occasionally on open meadows dotted with wildflowers in late summer.

Massive Mt. Temple, one of the 10 highest in the Canadian Rockies, is unmistakeable ahead. Its dark north face is renowned among climbers as "the most awesome sight in the area." One look at the hanging glacier on its shadowy north face explains why. Only highly-skilled climbers attempt it. On the opposite side of the valley are Aberdeen, Haddo Peak and Sheol Mountain.

Keep left at the next junction at the 4.1 km mark, following signs to Lake Annette. The trail can be sloppy at this point. Continue through dark lodgepole pine to reach the little lake.

Lake Annette's shore, with its sunny southern exposure, can be a fine place to lunch, sun, sketch, or just enjoy the fabulous scenery. You could also pick your way around the lake.

On warm summer afternoons, walkers can sit and watch avalanches tumble down Temple. Those who continue upwards for a few minutes on the same trail will reach an open avalanche area that offers inspiring views over Paradise Valley and the peaks that border it. Hikers could also continue on over Sentinel Pass, a major undertaking. See Walk 47 and do it in reverse.

Lakeshore Trail   WALK 49

The most beautiful lake   MAP 19

Highlight: Stunning glacial lake
Distance: 3.8 km (2.3 miles) return
Time: 40 to 60 minutes
Rating: Easy
Maximum elevation: 1,732 m (5,682 ft)
Elevation gain: Negligible
Footwear: Anything
Best season: July to October

"As a gem of composition and coloring it is perhaps unrivalled anywhere," Sir James Outram wrote of Lake Louise. His assessment endures—a Florida newspaper recently called Lake Louise "the most beautiful lake in the Western hemisphere." The shimmering peacock-blue lake, with the sun catching Victoria Glacier at one end and stately Chateau Lake Louise at the other, simply IS the Canadian Rockies to many.

19. LAKE LOUISE (North)

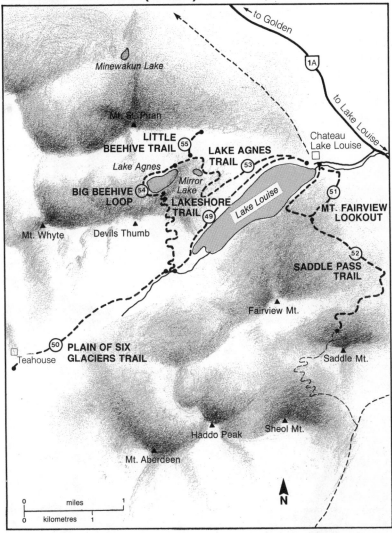

Yet you can't really appreciate the lake and its surrounding peaks and glaciers amidst the milling crowds in front of the Chateau. A much better way is to arrive in early morning (when picture-taking is best anyway) and stroll along its right shore.

This walk is for anyone. Mothers have pushed prams through the rougher section at the end.

Just don't expect solitude on this short, pine-scented walk—the lake has been visited by more than 100 million and more than 1.6 million are drawn here annually.

Canoes are available for rent at the boathouse to the left of the chateau and there is a dock at the southwest end of the lake. You can also rent horses.

Access: From the Trans-Canada Hwy at the Lake Louise Village intersection, drive 8 km (5 miles) up the steep road to Lake Louise. From the big parking lots, walk down to the lake and turn right on the asphalt path in front of the hotel.

Route: Walk past the Chateau gardens, which in summer are spangled with the reds, oranges and yellows of Icelandic and Shirley poppies, as well as lilies, purple

Lake Louise

delphiniums, violets and many others. Mt. Victoria and the gleaming Victoria Glacier overwhelm the landscape. On the immediate left is Mt. Fairview and to the right, The Beehives.

In 1882, Tom Wilson, a CPR worker, was camping at Laggan, as the former Lake Louise station was called, when he heard the sound of distant thunder. The thunder, the Stoney Indians told him, came from an immense white mountain nearby, above "The Lake of Little Fishes." Intrigued, Wilson decided to investigate. The next morning, he became the first white man to see Lake Louise. It's said Wilson recalled the wonder of gazing on Lake Louise that morning for the rest of his life.

"For some time we sat and smoked and gazed at the gem of beauty beneath the glacier," he wrote. Wilson renamed the lake Emerald Lake, and the name was changed to Louise in 1884 after Princes Caroline Alberta Louise, daughter of Queen Victoria and wife of the governor-general of Canada.

Keep on the lower lakeside trail, where the formal gardens give way to an asphalt path fringed by daisies, asters and other wildflowers.

The color of the lake seems to change constantly, the result of rock flour particles from Victoria Glacier catching the sun's rays like a spectrum. Early summer sees the lake a clear blue; it turns progressively greener through the season as more silt accumulates in the lake.

The path hugs the shoreline. This lake, along with many others in the Rockies scooped out by glaciers, is finger-shaped. It's less than half a kilometre wide and 2 1/2 km long and up to 75 metres (250 feet) deep. The water never warms up in summer.

Benches are situated all along. Views soon emerge back to the chateau, the old gray lady of the Rockies perched on the old moraine like a duchess on a beach chair. The CPR first built a one-storey log building here in 1890, and quickly followed it with a full-scale Tudor wooden chateau. All except one section, the concrete Paynter Wing, burned down in 1924 and was replaced by the current brick addition. The 375-room hotel has recently been renovated and is now open year-round except for a few weeks around Christmas.

Pause to enjoy the semi-circle of mountains surrounding the lake. From left to right: Saddle, Fairview, Sheol, Aberdeen, Lefroy, Victoria, Whyte, Niblock, St. Piran and Little Beehive. From the walker's perspective, Fairview looms closest across the lake on the left. The lookout above the lake under Fairview makes a wonderful destination from which to view everything (see Walk 51).

Continue on the path, going by a boat dock. You can see the chateau and the runs of the internationally-known Lake Louise ski area to the north. The path becomes a bit rougher here, following along a rock wall of pink-stained quartzose sandstone.

Golden-mantled ground squirrels, often mistaken for chipmunks because of their stripes, frequent this area. They are usually only seen in pairs. Look to see if the stripes extend to the head. If they do, it's a chipmunk, if not, it's a squirrel.

At the end of the lake, a profusion of braided glacial streams pour in amidst a mass of glacial rubble. Note the color contrast as the clear meltwater enters the opaque lake.

Plain of Six Glaciers Trail

WALK 50

Six glaciers, half-dozen biscuits

MAP 19

Highlight: Panoramas of glaciers, famous lake
Distance: 11 km (7 miles) return
Rating: Moderate
Time: 5 hours
Maximum elevation: 2,263 m (6,900 ft)
Elevation gain: 471 m (1,218 ft)
Footwear: Light hiking boots
Best season: July to October

Six glaciers, the starkness of glacial rubble, panoramas of turquoise Lake Louise, the startling thrust of great peaks and deep rumbling avalanches—these are some of the rewards awaiting the walker on this classic choice.

The appetite-rousing walk leads up to a rustic teahouse near the top which serves teas, homemade soups, hot baking powder biscuits and other goodies. If you only have time for one walk in the Rockies—and don't mind sharing it with horses and many other hikers—this would be an excellent choice.

Access: From the Trans-Canada Hwy at the Lake Louise intersection, drive 8 km (5 miles) up the steep road to Lake Louise. From the large parking lots, walk down to the lake and head right along the shore past the flower gardens and snack bar concession. The trail starts at a sign just right of the chateau.

Route: The trail begins on a lakeshore path skirting the right side of Lake Louise. Mt. Victoria and the Victoria Glacier dominate high above the lake's end. Mt. Fairview is on the left of the lake and The Beehives on the right.

The first section along the lake is on an asphalt path; views emerge back to Chateau Lake Louise, rebuilt after fire destroyed all except one concrete wing in 1924.

Pass a dock where the path becomes a bit rougher, following under a rock wall of pink-stained quartzose sandstone.

A delta has formed at the end of the lake where Louise Creek drops its glacial debris. Note the color change in the lake where the smokey, silt-laden creek meets deep water.

You now leave the lake and enter an area of fir, spruce and wild strawberries. The trail is steep and muddy for a short stretch.

The trail passes an overgrown

avalanche area. Some tiny paths lead to clearings by the glacial stream: a pleasant place to relax before the next push. Continue past shrubbery laced in summer with yellow cinquefoil, harebells, Indian paintbrush, western anemone and purple saxifrage.

The next portion ascends gradually through trees. The walker starts to reap the rewards of toil. The trail enters a vast, open plain of deadfall and lateral moraines, deposited here by Victoria Glacier as it receded during the last century. The scene is one of stark and desolate beauty.

The next portion is rough, like a trip through a gravel pit. Progress can be slow because of foot and horse traffic. Don't drink water from the streams hereabouts, which may be polluted.

The trail now switchbacks briefly through the trees before arriving at the teahouse. Here is one of two surviving teahouses in the Canadian Rockies built at the turn of the century by the CPR. The other is nearby, at Lake Agnes.

Supplies are packed up here by horse and baking is done on a wooden stove. The menu includes home-made soups, sandwiches, hot baking powder biscuits with strawberry jam, a cake of the day, tea, coffee, lemonade and hot chocolate. The teahouse is open from late June to early September.

An alternative is to picnic in the clearing by the teahouse, where views are beautiful, though winds can be cold. Toilets are to the right of the teahouse.

While weary walkers may be tempted to turn back at the teahouse, they should probably persist for another 30 minutes to the end of the trail. The going is not difficult, except for the last portion and views are tremendous.

Cross a little bridge past the teahouse. You may hear the crashing of avalanches from the Upper Lefroy and Upper Victoria Glaciers on warm summer afternoons. Chateau Lake Louise is visible in the distance, a world away from this desolate grandeur.

The last few steps, over the ridge of a lateral moraine, require care. The trail stops on a barren south-facing slope at the end of the moraine. Vistas are stupendous. Looming ahead, from left to right, are the black Mitre, shaped like a bishop's hat, lofty Lefroy at 3,420 metres (11,220 feet) and snow-benched Mt. Victoria at 3,464 metres (11,365 feet). The six glaciers visible from here are, from left to right: Aberdeen Glacier, Upper Lefroy Glacier, Lower Lefroy Glacier, Upper Victoria Glacier, Lower Victoria Glacier and Pope's Glacier.

The sharp-eyed will spot the Abbot Hut between Victoria and Lefroy. The hut was the highest building in Canada when it was constructed in 1922 for $30,000. It was named after Phillip Abbot, an attorney for the Wisconsin Central Railway who plunged to his death in this pass on August 3, 1896, becoming the first recorded climber to die in the Rockies. The glacier going up to the hut, a refuge for serious climbers, has the reassuring name of "Death Trap."

Fairview Mountain Lookout

WALK 51

The early morning splendor

MAP 19

Highlight: View of Lake Louise
Distance: 3.5 km (2.1 miles) loop
Time: 1 to 2 hours
Rating: Moderate
Maximum elevation: 1,825 m (5,990 ft)
Elevation gain: 93 m (305 ft)
Footwear: Walking or running shoes
Best season: Mid-June to October

The splendor of Lake Louise is best seen at sunrise before the hordes of tourists begin to stir. Mist still curls over the water and the early light etches Victoria Glacier and mountains beyond in startling clarity. The Beehives and other high vantage points are probably too difficult to reach before breakfast, the Fairview lookout can be attained in about 30 minutes, even in dim light. The trail is just long enough to build a breakfast appetite, a splendid spot to observe the unbelievable colors of Lake Louise and the wide expanse of the Bow Valley beyond—before breakfast, lunch or dinner.

Access: From the Trans-Canada Hwy at the Lake Louise intersection in Banff National Park, drive 8 km (5 miles) up the steep road to Lake Louise. From the vast parking lots, walk down to the shore of the lake and and turn left along the shore towards the boathouse. Before you reach the boathouse, a wide trail enters the trees and begins climbing.

Route: From the lake, the trail begins as the main route to Saddle Pass, climbing gradually through a thick,

mossy forest. In a few minutes, at .4 km, take the right fork and ascend, sometimes steeply, through the forest under the cliffs of Mt. Fairview.

The trees open up at a good viewpoint with an observation platform high above the lake. The views are inspiring, to say the least.

Lake Louise is a hanging valley above the wide, U-shaped Bow Valley trench. The lake, hollowed out by glaciers, is up to 75 metres (250 feet) deep in places and the water temperature doesn't rise much above freezing. Its dazzling color is attributed to the lake's depths and the "rock flour" suspended in the water. The glaciers high on the slopes of Lefroy and Victoria grind up rock as they move gradually down the slopes. When the ice melts at the bottom, the streams carry this rock flour into the lake, changing Louise's color, as a tablespoon of milk changes the color of a glass of water.

In summer, when the ice finally goes out, the lake is a robin's egg blue. Later, it seems to turn greener or aquamarine, delectable shades that are best appreciated from such vantage points as these.

The easiest and shortest way back is the route you arrived on. For more variety, a true loop can be made by descending steeply from the lookout down to the Lake Louise shoreline. Turn right at the bottom and follow the trail, much quieter than the tourist-clogged route on the far side, back to the boathouse and the chateau.

Saddle Pass

More than a fair view

MAP 19

Highlight: Good views across to Mt. Temple
Distance: 7.2 km (4.4 miles) return
Time: 4 hours
Rating: Strenuous
Maximum elevation: 2,300 m (7,545 ft)
Elevation gain: 570 m (1,865 ft)
Footwear: Light hiking boots
Best Season: July to October

The pass between Saddle Mountain and Mt. Fairview, while not the most popular choice for day walks in the Lake Louise area, does provide extraordinary views across to the awesome north face of Mt. Temple and the cliffs of Sheol Mountain. The pass is a meadow, lush with wild flowers. The trail to it is fairly steep.

Access: From the Trans-Canada Hwy at the Lake Louise intersection, drive 8 km (5 miles) up the steep road to Lake Louise. From the vast parking lots, walk down to the lake and turn left along the shore towards the boathouse. Before you reach the boathouse, a wide trail enters the trees and begins climbing.

Route: From the lake, the trail climbs gradually through a thick, mossy forest. You'll soon pass a large heap of brown scales near the base of a tree on the left. This is the midden of the red squirrel, a widely-distributed inhabitant of the subalpine forest. The pile consists of the inedible portion of spruce cones, accumulated over the years.

The red squirrel is usually the one

you hear chattering madly. It's in frantic motion all day long, harvesting these cones, storing thousands underground or in hollow trees for the lean days of winter. The squirrel also eats and caches mushrooms.

The side trail to Fairview lookout heads right at .4 km. Continue straight, the trail beginning to switchback more steeply before levelling off somewhat along open avalanche paths which provide views of the Bow Valley. The route zig-zags around these lower slopes of Fairview, then turns straight for little Saddle Mountain. The trail divides, but both forks will take you up towards the pass and in about the same distance.

The terrain opens up in rocky meadows below Saddle, home of numerous ground squirrels, pikas and marmots. Subalpine wildflowers grow lushly here.

The route rises gradually almost to timberline through this beautiful meadow, reaching the top of the pass at km 3.6 (2.3 miles). The black mass of Temple looms before you. While it first appears that Temple rises up from the top of the pass, you soon discover that the base of it lies some distance away, separated from Saddle Pass by the wide Paradise Valley (see Walk 48).

Temple at 3,647 metres (11,636 feet) is an imposing, symmetrical pyramid crowned by a dazzling white snowfield. Closer at hand are the imposing black cliffs of Sheol Mountain. While a trail continues down the other side of Saddle Pass into Sheol Valley and Paradise Valley, most walkers will probably be content with these glorious heights and inviting meadows.

Strong hikers could turn either left or right from Saddle Pass to ascend, at least partway, either of the low-angled peaks. Saddle Mountain, to the left, is much the easier and offers stunning views in all directions, except up the valley beyond Lake Louise.

Mt. Fairview is a stiffer ascent on loose scree slopes and the views from the barren top are simply magnificent up to Mt. Victoria, Huber, Lefroy and Aberdeen and down to Lake Louise itself. For strong, experienced hikers only.

Lake Agnes Trail

WALK 53

The most popular hike

MAP 19

Highlight: Subalpine lake, tea-house, Lake Louise vistas
Distance: 8 km (5 miles) return
Time: 4 hours
Rating: Moderate
Maximum elevation: 2,125 m (6,971 ft)
Elevation gain: 400 m (1,312 ft)
Footwear: Sturdy shoes or light hiking boots
Best Season: July to October

The hike to Lake Agnes is reputed to be the most popular in the Canadian Rockies—and it's easy to see why. It departs from what may be Canada's most visited natural tourist attraction next to Niagara Falls: the famous Lake Louise. It ascends for 4 km (2.5 km) on a wide trail to a fascinating, scenic subalpine lake where there's a rustic teahouse offering homebaking and, of course, tea, amenities more common to Europe than Canada.

There are stunning views back to the Bow Valley and the incredible milky-blue of Lake Louise itself. Plus a gorgeous waterfall-cascade just below the teahouse which the hiker reaches by stairs. Once refreshed at the teahouse, the lake itself and the nearby Beehives offer excellent areas to explore. It is the starting point for Walk 54 and Walk 55. The disadvantage, of course, is that you'll find little solitude here-abouts, except by comparison with the Lake Louise scene.

Access: From the Trans-Canada at the Lake Louise intersection in Banff park, drive 8 km (5 miles) up the steep road to Lake Louise. From the vast parking lots, walk down to the lake, then along the shore past the hotel grounds. The Lake Agnes Trail leaves the paved lakeshore trail just past the hotel's open air snack bar concession.

Route: The Lake Agnes trail is wide and well-graded through thick subalpine forest with occasional glimpses of Lake Louise. The route soon crosses the horse trail to Plain of the Six Glaciers and begins a couple of switchbacks past an open slide area.

The ascent is gradual and un-eventful until you reach Mirror Lake at about km 3, a tiny tarn set below the cliffs of the Big Beehive. The lake is sunken enough so that little wind usually reaches it and the water reflects the cliffs above. There's a vigorous stream running into the far end of this little pond but no surface outlet.

From here, the left-hand trail takes a high-level route along to the Plain of Six Glaciers. Take the right hand route which switchbacks up into more open country, views im-proving every minute. Behind is the wall of Mt. Fairview towering over Lake Louise, its ridge rising into the glaciated and sharper peaks of Mt. Aberdeen and Haddo. You can also see up Louise Creek to the glacier-capped heights of Mt. Victoria and the great thrust of Mt. Lefroy.

Ahead, a waterfall tumbles down from Lake Agnes under the Big Beehive. That's where you're heading. At the first junction above Mirror Lake, keep straight and traverse along under cliffs towards gorgeous Bridal Veil Falls, then ascend the cliff by the falls on stairs.

The teahouse at the top of the stairs—whose menus once des-cribed it as the "highest tea room in Canada"—usually offers a home-made soup and a wide assortment of teas, including wild strawberry, black currant, apricot, raspberry,

lemon, lime, Irish breakfast and others. You can get sandwiches on home-made brown bread, cookies and cake. Don't worry about the calories. If you've made it this far, you deserve it.

Pioneer explorer and map-maker Walter Wilcox called Lake Agnes "a wild tarn imprisoned by cheerless cliffs." He, didn't have the advan-tage of sitting on a teahouse balcony eating cookies and sipping herb tea, something to brighten any cliff in the mind's eye.

The lake was named for Lady Agnes Macdonald, wife of the first prime minister. To the left as you look down the cirque lake, once carved out by a small glacier, rises the distinctive, conical Big Beehive, a huge, gray horizontally-layered rock wall that would hold some rather large insects indeed. For the trail to the Big Beehive, see Walk 54.

Behind the teahouse, on top of the falls, is a stunning view down to the marvellous greenish blue of Lake Louise, one of the most beau-tiful sights in the Canadian Rockies. and behind it the Slate Range which includes Mt. Whitehorn and all its ski development.

The stroll down the lake from the teahouse is highly recommended. It provides changing perspectives on the beehives. The rocky boulder field at the end is a pleasant place to sit and enjoy the panorama and observe marmots, pikas and, on a warm summer's day, the unending flow of walkers.

Lake Agnes

Big Beehive Loop

WALK 54

View from a beehive

MAP 19

Highlight: Best views of Lake Louise
Distance: 11.5 km (7 mile) loop (variations possible)
Time: 6 hours
Rating: Strenuous
Maximum elevation: 2,235 m (7,335 ft)
Elevation gain: 504 m (1,655 ft)
Footwear: Light hiking boots
Best season: Mid-July to October

"I have never seen this glorious ensemble of forests, lakes and snowfields surpassed in an experience on the summits of more than 40 peaks and the middle slopes of as many more in the Canadian Rockies." Walter Wilcox, an early explorer of these regions, was writing about his first view from the Beehive area.

To experience what Wilcox felt, you must journey beyond the cozy, gorgeous confines of Lake Agnes and the teahouse above Lake Louise. You must toil up at least one of the unusual "beehives" from the lake, a steep grind and a challenge for many—but what a reward!

The trail past the largest and best Beehive can be combined with a loop back to Lake Louise on the lower stretch of Plain of Six Glaciers Trail, then along the shore of Lake Louise, a route consistently varied and interesting. There are so many trails and options in this fascinating area. You can tailor your route to how you feel, how much time you have or how the weather's holding up. You would never know from below that there's so much of interest up here.

Access: From the Trans-Canada Hwy at the Lake louise intersection in Banff park, drive 8 km (5 miles) up the steep road to Lake Louise. From the vast parking lots, walk down to the lake, then along the shore past the hotel grounds. The Lake Agnes Trail leaves the shore just past the hotel's pool/snack bar concession.

Route: The Lake Agnes trail is wide and well-graded through thick subalpine forest with occasional glimpses of Lake Louise. The ascent is uneventful until you reach Mirror Lake at km 2.8, a tiny tarn set below the cliffs of the Big Beehive. The lake is sunken enough so that little wind usually reaches it and the water reflects the cliffs above.

At Mirror Lake, the left-hand trail takes a high-level route along to the Plain of Six Glaciers. Take the right-hand route which switchbacks up into more open country, the views improving every minute.

Ahead, a waterfall tumbles down from Lake Agnes under the Big Beehive. That's where you're heading. At the first junction above Mirror Lake, (km 3.4) keep straight and traverse along under cliffs towards gorgeous Bridal Veil Falls, then ascend the cliff by the falls on stairs.

The teahouse (km 3.6) at the top of the stairs usually offers a home-made soup and a wide assortment of teas, plus sandwiches on home-made bread.

To the left of the cirque lake, carved out by a small glacier, rises the distinctive, conical Big Beehive, a huge, gray horizontally-layered rock wall that would hold some rather large insects indeed. That is your destination on this loop, 2.1 km ahead.

From the teahouse, follow the trail around the right side of Lake Agnes, past the trail right that leads to toilets and Little Beehive. The trail by the lake crosses rock slides

Big Beehive

and gaining ever more impressive views of the gray, broken slopes of Mt. Whyte and Mt. Niblock soaring steeply above its dark green waters. The trail crosses a large scree slope and stays mostly in the open.

From here, the trail switchbacks very steeply up the side of Big Beehive, passing between the Beehive and a promontory known as the Devil's Thumb. The exertion is rewarded with grand views back over the lake and the heights of Mount St. Piran, one of the most easily climbed peaks around.

From the flat, larch-covered top of the semi-wooded Beehive ridge, a sidetrail wanders left to the Big Beehive viewpoint. Don't omit it. The short sidetrail is somewhat indefinite here but it doesn't matter. Keep generally to the right and pick your own route to the edge of the Beehive 150 metres (500 feet) above Lake Agnes, as the rock drops.

Near the edge of the cliff is an open sided, red-roofed log shelter providing views from safety and comfort. Even better views can be obtained just below and closer to the edge, if you don't feel nervous about the drop. Lake Louise is a marvel from here, maybe the best spot of all to contemplate this milky masterpiece, considered one of the top 10 natural landscapes in the world. This is the place to appreciate it, not the crowded shores in front of the hotel where cameras click like a woodpecker on an old tree.

Across the lake rise the cliffs of Mt. Fairview and behind them, the dark, threatening north wall of Mt. Temple. Directly below is tiny Mirror Lake. Down Lake Louise are the great glaciated walls of Lefroy and Aberdeen. Chateau Lake Louise, a huge gray structure in the French chateau style, is such a dignified dowager in these rough-cut surroundings.

Walk back towards the main trail and, on your way, stop again for a look down at tiny Lake Agnes. What a contrast to Lake Louise. Louise is so milky and opaque, bearing glacial silt from Mt. Victoria, Huber, Lefroy and Aberdeen, the rock ground up into flour and suspended in the waters to catch the light. Little Agnes, her water unsullied by glacial grindings, sparkles as a dark green gem.

From the junction with the main trail (km 6.7), you could turn back to the teahouse the way you came, but we recommend an alternate loop back to Lake Louise, unless you urgently require more tea.

Turn left and descend the other side of the Big Beehive, dropping steeply through the subalpine forest to the Highline Trail, 3.1 km from Lake Agnes. The left fork will take you back to Mirror Lake and the descent to Lake Louise again. It saves a couple of kilometres of walking.

For a loop with more variety that's slightly longer, go right on this well-maintained and mossy trail heading gradually downhill and providing occasional views ahead to Victoria Glacier at the end of the Lake Louise valley.

You'll reach a trail junction in .7 km. While the route straight ahead goes on to the Plain of Six Glaciers viewpoint, that would make for a total loop of almost 20 km (12 miles), an extremely long day indeed. Most walkers who have already come over Big Beehive prefer to take the left branch, and descend steeply on switchbacks for almost a kilometre down to Louise Creek and the Plain of Six Glaciers Trail. See Walk 50 for continuation of trail up the Plain of Six Glaciers.

Go left at the bottom back towards Lake Louise on the wide, heavily-travelled route that leads down the vigorous stream to the gravel flats at the end of the lake.

From here, the trail leads under some steep cliffs and on a busy, well-manicured trail along the lakeside back to the hotel, an inspiring stroll that thousands take every summer.

Little Beehive Trail

WALK 55

A beehive of hikers

MAP 19

Highlight: Spectacular view of Bow Valley
Distance: 1.8 km (1.1 miles) return from Lake Agnes
Time: 1 hour from Lake Agnes
Rating: Moderate
Maximum elevation: 2,246 m (7,368 ft)
Elevation gain: 121 m (400 ft) from Lake Agnes
Footwear: Light hiking boots
Best season: Mid-July to October

For the day walker who has already reached scenic Lake Agnes and the cozy teahouse above Lake Louise, the side trail to Little Beehive involves less than 1 km each way and provides perhaps the best view anywhere of the wide, U-shaped Bow Valley and hundreds of peaks north to the Columbia Icefield and south towards Banff townsite. It also offers views down to the astonishing turquoise of Lake Louise, one of the finest sights in the Canadian Rockies.

Access: From the Trans-Canada

Hwy at the Lake Louise intersection in Banff park, drive 8 km (5 miles) up the steep road to Lake Louise. From the vast parking lots, walk down to the lake, then along the shore past the hotel grounds. The Lake Agnes Trail leaves the shore just past the hotel's pool/snack bar concession.

Route: See Lake Agnes trail description for 3.6-km route to Lake Agnes Teahouse. (Walkers bound directly for the Little Beehive may take the trail right .6 km above Mirror Lake for a shortcut that leads in 1.3 km to Little Beehive.)

Otherwise, begin from the teahouse at the end of the Lake Agnes. Take the trail that leads right up the hill, away from the lake just behind the teahouse. Soon views open up back to Lake Louise with tiny Mirror Lake almost directly below. The trail climbs gradually. Keep straight at the trail junction at .2 km as the route works its way along the edge of the ridge. Directly across Lake

Louise is Mt. Fairview which strong hikers can climb without ropes from Saddle Pass (See Walk 52). Behind Fairview is the black, terrifying north face of Mt. Temple which is a difficult climb even with full alpine equipment. The ridge to the right of Fairview leads to the glacier-hung peaks of Haddo, Aberdeen, and at the end of the valley, the imposing Lefroy.

The Little Beehive trail ascends through old slide areas over boulder-strewn fields vivid with wildflowers in summer. Along the top of the ridge are stands of larch, especially beautiful in fall when their needles turn yellow. The alpine larch stands out from other conifers because it is not an evergreen. It sheds its needles, as a tree drops its leaves.

All along this spectacular ridge are views of Lake Louise, an unbelievable shade of green/turquoise/blue-green/milky blue depending on the time of year, time of day, weather and your own sense of color. Don't be surprised if you find the lake a rather dull steely-gray. Ice lingers on the lake until early summer, although the snow melts on the surface.

The trail soon reaches the edge of Little Beehive. Here's an abandoned fire lookout and cabin and you can see why this site was selected—for the wide vistas. Directly across the Bow Valley is the Lake Louise ski area and the Slate Range. Below is the village complex and you can look down at all the activity around Chateau Lake Louise, grand dame of Rocky Mountain hotels.

To the left, the Trans-Canada Highway branches west and out of sight to climb the easy Kicking Horse Pass. North is the Icefields Parkway and Mt. Hector, its snow-fields out of view on the other side. Beyond, wave after wave of mountains lead up to Bow Summit and beyond to the Columbia Icefield.

Right, the Bow River winds down towards Banff along the relatively flat valley, carved out by the glaciers. Long ago, the rivers carved the Bow Valley into a "V" shape and the glaciers finished the job, changing "V" to "U." Once great glaciers flowed over what is now Lake Louise right down to the valley and joined the main valley glacier. At one time, the glacier must have ended just below. Chateau Lake Louise is perched on an old terminal moraine left by the receding ice.

Takakkaw Falls (Yoho National Park) WALK 56

Minute amble to magnificent falls MAP 20

Highlight: High waterfall
Distance: 1 km (0.6 miles) return
Time: 25 minutes
Rating: Easy
Maximum elevation: 1,524 m
(5,000 ft)
Elevation gain: Negligible
Footwear: Anything
Best season: June to October

While the trail to Takakkaw Falls in Yoho National Park is nothing more than a short amble, getting there is half the fun. The spectacular falls, set in the striking Yoho Valley, is among the highest in North America.

Access: From Banff townsite, drive 56 km (34 miles) west on the Trans-Canada Hwy to the junction with the Icefields Parkway. Continue straight on the Trans-Canada Hwy 22.5 km (14 miles) into Yoho National Park. Turn right at the sign for Yoho Valley.

The road ahead is extremely steep and narrow. A drop-off area near the information bureau is provided for trailers. Mountain goats can sometimes be seen on the road up. It ends at a parking lot where a wide asphalt trail on the east side goes to the falls.

Route: Takakkaw means "magnificent" in Cree, and the falls, named by Sir William Van Horne, do not disappoint. While lacy streamers of spray can be seen from the parking lot, everybody has to get closer.

The interpretive path leads by a relief map of the area, showing how

the falls originate from meltwaters of the Daly Glacier. This glacier is in turn fed by the vast Waputik Icefield that straddles the continental divide.

Cross a bridge over the Yoho River, the roaring of the falls beginning to dominate. Signs explain Indian myths relating to the falls. The majestic peak of Mt. Ogden is prominent on the right (south). Looking north, you can see the Yoho Glacier.

The trail soon comes to an end, although one could scramble further

20. TAKAKKAW FALLS

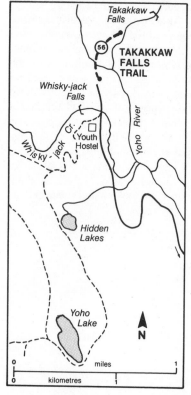

on the rocks closer to the falls—and potential rockfall. The falls drop several hundred feet, making them among the highest in North America.

Takakkaw Falls

Yoho Valley and Highline Trails

Valleys and high places

WALK 57

MAP 21

21. YOHO VALLEY

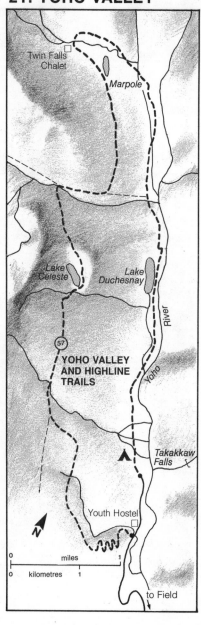

Highlight: Beautiful valley, lakes, waterfalls, lofty views

Distance: 15.4 (9.5 miles) to Twin Falls and return via Yoho Valley: 19.1 km (11.8 miles) to Twin Falls and return via Highline and Yoho Pass Trails

Time: Full day

Rating: Strenuous

Maximum elevation: 2,050 m (6,725 ft)

Elevation gain: 540 m (1,771 ft)

Footwear: Hiking boots

Best season: Late June to September

This fascinating hike opens with a wonder of nature—Takakkaw Falls—and never lets you down. You head through spruce into the lovely Yoho Valley, ending at the Twin Falls Chalet which offers meals and snacks for hikers, as well as accommodations. Strong hikers have the option of returning on the high route, a subalpine traverse under Emerald Glacier and Michael Peak that provides the ultimate views of the Yoho Valley.

Access: Begin at Takakkaw Falls, 14 km north of the Yoho Park Information Centre on the Trans-Canada Highway, 3 km east of Field.

Route: The hike starts at a walk-in campground, an excellent place for early starters to stay overnight. (Some sites have views of the falls.) A panorama of peaks opens before you, dominated by Yoho Peak to the north and Whaleback to its left. The hiking is almost level and the trail soft and dry.

Laughing Falls, a pluming, lacey cascade, is reached at 4.8 km; the Laughing Falls Campground offers sites by the river. Continue along the Little Yoho river, climbing steadily to gain your first views of Twin Falls. At the end of the valley, the Yoho Glacier Trail heads off right and the main trail begins to ascend. To the left is the Twin Falls Campground. Continue switchbacking up to reach the Twin Falls Chalet. Situated at an elevation of 1,813 metres, the cozy log-cabin hut offers a hiker's special, soup, sandwiches and such treats as pound

Mt. Burgess, Yoho National Park

cake. Overnight accommodation is available. Phone (403) 269-1497, summer only.

Continue across the bridge on the Marpole Lake Trail for views of Twin Falls. The trail passes pretty Marpole Lake, then under steep cliffs to an open avalanche area. You soon reach the Little Yoho Valley Trail. The fastest way back is to turn left and descend to the main Yoho Valley Trail that you started on. But hikers with energy would appreciate making this a true loop and returning on a spectacular high-level route.

For an elevated return, head right on the Little Yoho Valley Trail and continue for 0.8 km to the Highline. Turn left up the Highline and begin a well-graded ascent up to pretty Celeste Lake fringed with arnica. The ascent from the lake takes you to the highpoint and there are sweep-ing views of the whole Yoho Valley from atop an overgrown morraine.

The trail leads through flower-filled meadows, past the junction with the Skyline Trail and then across a vast desolation of boulders and scree under Emerald Glacier, a inspiring place for a rest stop. The views across the valley to Takakkaw Valley are first rate. You can see what the tourists down by the parking lot always miss: the Waputik Icefield above the falls, highest in Canada.

Take the cutoff at the sign for Takakkaw Falls. This continues as a spectacular walk across a series of old laterial morraines. In the trees, you descend on a smooth, improved trail that switchbacks smoothly down to the Whiskey Jack Youth hostel on the Takakkaw Falls road, just a short distance above the falls parking area.

Emerald Lake Circuit

WALK 58

More for your money

MAP 22

Highlight: Tranquil stroll around forested lake; good opportunity to observe big game
Distance: 5.2 km (3.2 miles)
Time: Two hours
Rating: Moderate
Maximum elevation: 1,312 m (4,304 ft)
Elevation gain: Negligible
Footwear: Walking or running shoes
Best season: June to October

The beauty of Emerald Lake was considered grand enough to adorn the back of the $10 bill for many years and it's certainly grand enough for a rewarding hike. Although the lakeside is deeply forested, the lake itself is a stunning blue-green and many clearings offer splendid views of rugged Mt. Burgess. The animals along the lakeside are accustomed to seeing people and you may have a better chance of seeing moose, deer and sheep here than in many other

22. EMERALD LAKE

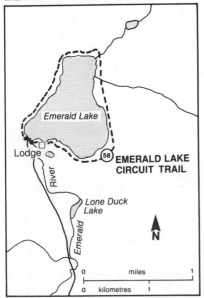

Emerald Lake

Lodge

River

58 EMERALD LAKE CIRCUIT TRAIL

Lone Duck Lake

Emerald

N

0   miles   1

0   kilometres   1

portions of the national parks. And a circular trail is always a special delight; no need to turn back on the same route.

Access: Four kilometres past the Field townsite turnoff, turn right off Trans-Canada Highway, 40 km west of Lake Louise. Drive 10 km to the end of the road.

Route: Begin your stroll by heading down the left side of the lake on a popular self-guided nature trail. You pass some of the best-situated picnic tables to be found anywhere. The grassy area overlooks the lake and the great walls of Mt. Burgess, (behind the lodge) and to its left, Mt. Wapta. Michael Peak is straight ahead.

Soon the pavement turns to soft spruce-needles and you cross open (winter) avalanche slopes that are often bright with asters and fireweed. A few benches close to the lake invite you to meditate upon this tranquil scene. The lake gets its color partly from the suspended glacial silt washed into it from the heights of the President Range. You notice that the forest on this side of the lake is less dense than opposite under the shadow of Burgess. This side gets less rain than the opposite and the gravel soil around here quickly carries away surface moisture.

Straight ahead through the trees, you catch glimpses of Emerald Glacier. Keep right when another trail leads off to Emerald Basin.

Soon you cross an old alluvial fan where a creek enters the lake. Cross a bridge and enter the lush forest of the far shore. The air feels cooler and damper along here and a boardwalk spans some of the soggier sections. This is a world of thick moss, jungle-like undergrowth and massive trees. Some of the lush plants are more common to the wet British Columbia coastal ranges than to the Rockies.

The path gets muddier when the horse trail re-joins the hiking trail for a while but views back to Emerald Glacier compensate for what is underfoot. Near the end of the lake, you can head off left on a high trail that leads by Peaceful Pond before returning to the parking lot. Or continue by the lake past renovated Emerald Lodge. The main building was constructed in the early 1900s of hand-hewn timber with massive stone fireplaces. A day lodge is open to hikers and offers a sundeck and a barbecue menu at the self-serve restaurant.

Canoes are available for rent opposite the parking lot and provide an alternative for those who don't want to hike all the way around the lake. Just divide your party in half and arrange to have the canoe meet the hikers by the open area at the end of the lake. At that point the canoeists can become hikers while the hikers become canoeists—offering two different perspectives on this very special lake.

Emerald Lake

Bow Lake

11 Banff National Park
Walks from Icefields Parkway

Bow Lake Trail WALK 59

A trail among trails MAP 23

Highlight: Lakeside walk and alpine views
Distance: 6.8 km (4.2 miles) return
Time: 3 hours
Rating: Moderate
Maximum elevation: 2,042 m (7,000 ft)
Elevation gain: 91 m (300 ft)
Footwear: Walking shoes or light boots (can be wet)
Best season: Mid-July to October

A stroll right along the edge of one of the most gorgeous lakes in the Canadian Rockies, then over braided gravel flats through a gorge, past a natural bridge to a vast open alpine area topped by glaciers and a huge waterfall, a journey made without much exertion. Here is a trail among trails.

Access: The turnoff to Num-ti-jah Lodge is 36 km (22 miles) north of the Trans-Canada Hwy on the Icefields Parkway or 40 km (25 miles) south of the David Thompson Hwy. The trail begins just beyond the lodge building on the lake side from the parking lot marked "Guests only."

Route: The route leads across the grassy flats, crossing a stream on a rough bridge and leading down to the lakeshore. The going is often muddy along here.

The lake is spectacular, a gorgeous glacial blue, reflecting the white glaciers of Crowfoot Mountain across the water. The meadows at this elevation not far below timberline are flush with flowers in season and the red-roofed lodge behind adds a vivid splash of color.

The lodge was built by pioneer guide and outfitter, Jimmy Simpson, who established a cabin here when

23. PEYTO AND BOW LAKES

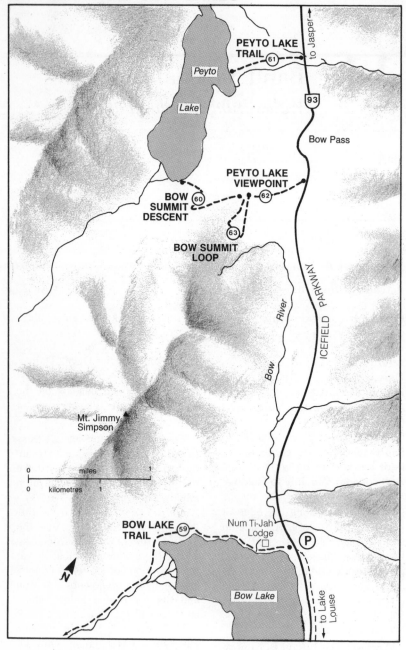

the route from Lake Louise was nothing more than an arduous horse trail.

Ahead, the tongue of Bow Glacier dips down from the vast snowfields above, part of the Waputik Icefield which straddles the Continental Divide. Out of sight below the glacial tongue is a small lake. Water from the lake plunges over the cliff in a brilliant white curtain. The massive rock walls on the right of the glacier belong to Mt. Thompson.

The trail, which remains within a metre of the water, passes under the cliffs rising to a ridge of Mt. Thompson. Twenty minutes from the highway and it's a wild, rugged and quiet world. You may be able to hear Bow Falls far above, the sound mixed sometimes with the deep rumble of an avalanche.

Notice that the low-lying land close to the lake is open meadow while the heights above remain forested. This is partly due to temperature inversions in which cold air from the glacier and the alpine heights drains down into the valley bottom at night, creating a cool climate, less receptive to trees.

The trail soon reaches the gravel flats at the end of the lake. Even if the stroller only makes it this far, he'll be amply rewarded. This is a delta created by the boulders, pebbles and silt brought down from the glacier and falls above. When the creek loses momentum in the lake, it can carry its load no further and drops it here.

You cross the edge of the gravel and follow the inlet stream up the valley, climbing a hillock, returning to the flats, then back again into the trees for another short climb. The trail ascends a third hill, then returns to the flats. The route can be obscure on the flats but the stroller can just continue in the same general direction, heading for the stream canyon ahead. Stay on the right of the stream, the beginnings of the Bow River.

The trail reaches a canyon that the creek has cut in the hillside and climbs very steeply for a short distance to get above it. There's a thunderous roar from below and you can peer over and see the stream forced through narrow cracks and under a natural bridge created when a huge rock fell across the gorge.

The trail suddenly comes out into the open atop an old moraine. Ahead is a vast open area of gravel, boulders, scree, streams and meadows leading up to the base of Bow Falls, source of the lovely Bow River and the South Saskatchewan River system. Less than 100 years ago, Bow Glacier extended right down into this valley. But all glaciers of the divide area have been retreating due to a general warming of the climate.

Most strollers will prefer to go no further, especially since the views don't really improve as you proceed. The trail does wind downwards and then picks its way through the vast rock bowl to the base of the falls.

Bow Summit Descent

Drop down, crawl back

WALK 60

MAP 23

Highlight: Descent to beautiful lake
Length: 5.6 km (3.5 miles) return
Rating: Strenuous
Time: 3 hours
Maximum elevation: 2,133 m (7,000 ft)
Elevation loss: 304 m (1,000 ft)
Footwear: Light hiking boots
Best season: July to October

Turquoise Peyto Lake is so dazzling as seen from the crowded viewpoint at Bow Summit that some might want to examine it more closely. But we can't wholeheartedly recommend this hike for most casual walkers. The trek down to the lake is steep, and it's a hard, steep, unrewarding climb back up. And this section of the lake lacks the sandy shoreline of the other end of the lake, reached more easily via Walk 63. This descent is not without merit, of course. It does enable the stroller to wander the vast and desolate gravel flats at the lake's south end up towards Peyto Glacier or merely to contemplate the view down the lake towards Mt. Patterson, which is stunning.

Access: Bow Summit is situated 42 km (26 miles) north of Lake Louise on the Icefields Parkway or 37 km (23 miles) south of Saskatchewan River Crossing. At the top of the pass, turn at the exhibit signs. Parking is at the lower lot, except for buses and the disabled. The trail starts at the northwest end of the parking lot.

Route: Follow the paved, busy Bow Summit viewpoint path upwards from the parking lot. The trail begins its steep descent just left of the spectacular viewpoint overlooking the lake.

The trail provides good footing as you descend from near treeline over a pleasant, needle-covered path. Openings in the subalpine forest of spruce and fir offer occasional glimpses of the lake below. Strollers who would rather not hike all the way down but merely seek to escape the crowds above can easily find open areas atop bluffs just right of the trail. These private viewing areas offer spectacular vistas over the lake to the heights of Mistaya Mountain and massive Mt. Patterson to the right.

The descent continues through thick forest, finally emerging in the open on a rocky slide area above the lake. The trail zig-zags down, the footing nowhere as good as before, ending up at the edge of the extensive gravel flats with stream channels constantly shifting.

The lake used to extend further up this valley but the silt and gravel brought down from the glacier and deposited here has gradually taken over. Some day, it may turn all of beautiful Peyto Lake into one long gravel bed. You can see the process occurring as the fast-moving water suddenly meets the calm of the lake. Only the finest particles, the "rock flour" ground up by the glacier above, remain suspended in the smoke-colored outlet water. It is

Peyto Lake

gradually dispersed in the lake, helping to create magnificent shades of green, blue, or turquoise, according to the season.

The strong hiker can follow a rough route over the flats up towards Peyto Glacier. On no account should the untrained hiker venture onto a glacier without proper equipment and knowledge of crevasse rescue.

Have a good rest by the lake for the hardest is yet to come. You still have to ascend that steep and unrelenting slope. Be thankful it was all so gorgeous.

Peyto Lake Trail

Peyto's paradise

MAP 23

Highlight: Picturesque lake with pebbled beach
Distance: 3 km (2 miles) return
Time: 1 to 1 1/2 hours
Rating: Moderate
Maximum elevation: 1,950 m (6,397 ft)
Elevation loss: 100 m (300 ft)
Footwear: Light hiking boots recommended
Best season: June to October

The truth is that Peyto Lake looks best from the popular viewpoint at Bow Summit. Close up, the lake seems to lose much of its intense color and drama. But the relatively short trail to the end of the lake from the Icefields Parkway is a good choice for a family outing or summer picnic. A mellow woodland trail descends to a pretty mountain lake where gnarled driftwood and a pebbled beach invite sketching, fishing, contemplation or further ambling.

Access: The Peyto Lake trail begins at a parking lot 2.1 km (1.3 miles) north of Bow Summit or 35 km (22 miles) south of Saskatchewan River Crossing on the Icefields Parkway. The unmarked trail starts as a deceptively small footpath at the north end of the parking lot.

Route: The trail starts through a mass of daisies and purple asters. There are splendid views of the dark-forested Mistaya Valley stretching to the North Saskatchewan River.

The trail descends quickly along a tiny stream to a fireroad. Continue on it for about five minutes, enjoying good views of Mt. Patterson ahead. Watch for an arrow on the ground made out of stones and logs, which indicates the junction where the trail turns left into the forest away from the road.

Once you leave the fireroad, exposed roots, some deadfall and boggy patches may slow you down. This section, however, is fairly short.

You'll soon arrive at Peyto Lake, named after one of Banff's most colorful and eccentric guides, Bill Peyto.

The color of Peyto Lake changes according to the season, depending on the proportion of settled rock particles in the water. Peyto Glacier is visible at the end of the lake, with Peyto Peak and Mistaya Mountain to its right. You can stroll a bit further along the eastern shore, or perhaps sketch driftwood, or just relax. Fishermen should note that the lake, open for fishing (with parks permit) from July 1 to October 31, has a natural population of cutthroat trout, best caught in early season. Unfortunately, the lake is too cold for swimming.

Don't try to walk down the lake all the way to the end in hopes of taking the trail upwards from the delta to Bow Summit, as one of the authors did. While the lakeside looks easy and begins as a wide gravel beach, the walker soon finds himself skirting bogs, climbing over lakeside cliffs and tiresome heaps of driftwood.

Peyto Lake Viewpoint

Lake of liquid jade

WALK 62

MAP 23

Highlight: Beautiful lake
Distance: 1.2 km (.7 miles)
Time: 20 minutes return
Rating: Easy
Maximum elevation: 2,133 m
(7,000 ft)
Elevation gain: 45 m (150 ft)
Footwear: Anything
Best season: July to October

There are almost as many beautiful lakes in the Canadian Rockies as there are castles in England and pubs in Ireland. Peyto Lake, along with Lake Louise and Moraine, is popular, often crowded—and one of the best.

This short interpretive stroll gently ascends to a stunning viewpoint of the beautifully-hued lake, set against high peaks and the forested Mistaya Valley. Detailed signs along the way offer an excellent mini-lesson in alpine and subalpine terrain. A fine leg-stretcher for all. Combine it with the Bow Summit Loop (Walk 63) for an enjoyable introduction to life at timberline—which is like life nowhere else.

Access: Bow Summit is 42 km (26 miles) north of Lake Louise on the Icefields Parkway, or 37 km (23 miles) south of Saskatchewan River Crossing, at the top of the pass. Parking, except for vans and the disabled, is in the lower parking lot, where the trailhead begins.

Route: As you begin this walk, look into the distance at how the timberline appears on surrounding mountains. Note how it seems to be a firm line. When you get up close,

as you will soon, you'll see that the transition is actually gradual, not sudden. This transitional band usually extends about 300 metres (1,000 feet) from the edge of forest to the lone remaining stunted trees. The walk ahead goes through such a transition zone. If you choose to continue on the Bow Summit Loop, you'll see the transition line extend to an area of tree islands near the upper limit of treeline.

On the way up, interpretive signs show how to distinguish Engelmann spruce, lodgepole pine and fir, which are among the toughest trees in the world. Here's a chance, as well, to view the phenomenon of krummholz, German for the "crooked wood' often seen at treeline: twisted, gnarled and dwarfed by fierce winds.

You'll soon reach the viewpoint where Peyto Lake (pronounced Pee-toe) glistens far below beyond the boardwalk and railings. The lake's color changes with the season. The water is dark blue in spring. Melting glaciers, however, bring with them tiny particles of rock which cloud the water at the head of the lake. The largest rock particles gradually settle, with the remaining suspended particles giving the lake its colors, according to depth of water, time of day, weather and the amount of suspended particles. This amount varies as the summer goes on. Hues run from dark blue and opaque turquoise to gorgeous jade green.

The Mistaya Valley extends nearly 30 kilometres north, and the forks of the North Saskatchewan River can be seen from here. Benches are provided at the viewpoint.

Peyto Glacier is at the end of the lake and below it a desolate area of rock and rubble which geologists say is the way Bow Summit must have looked 7,000 years ago. At that time, the entire area up to 500 metres above the viewpoint was covered by Peyto Glacier, one tongue of the Wapta Icefield. Peyto Peak is to the right of Peyto Glacier. Next to this peak, from left to right, are Mistaya, Barbette and Mt. Patterson.

Continue left on the upper trail for the Bow Summit Loop, or return the same way.

Wild Bill's Lake

One of the most colorful lakes in the Rockies is named after Bill Peyto, one of the most colorful of the early Banff guides. Peyto and alpinist-explorer Walter Wilcox passed through here in 1895 and paused at the sight of this exquisite lake. Who wouldn't?

Later, the story goes, Peyto found conditions too crowded at his usual campsite at Bow Lake. Usually a quiet, withdrawn man among strangers, he would suddenly announce while sitting around a campfire at Bow Lake: "There's too darn many people around here, I'm going where there's some peace and quiet."

He would then retreat to a camp on Bow Pass above what people began to call Peyto Lake.

Bow Summit Loop   WALK 63

Where summer is short   MAP 24

Highlight: Adaptation of flora to alpine zone
Distance: 1 km (.6 miles) loop
Rating: Easy
Time: 15 to 20 minutes

Maximum elevation: 2,173 m (7,129 ft)
Elevation gain: Negligible
Footwear: Anything
Best season: July to October

24. PEYTO LAKE (Closeup)

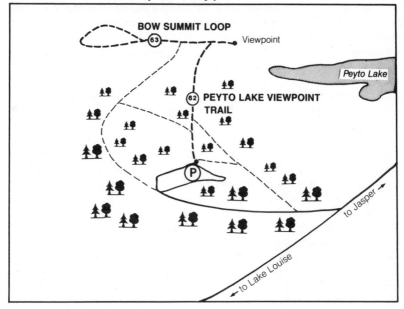

Bow Summit is one of the few timberline zones in the Canadian Rockies traversed by a highway. A short interpretive nature trail just off the Icefields Parkway shows how plants survive this brutal habitat. Snow can fall any day of the year.

This popular, asphalt trail is easy enough for almost anyone. Combine it with the Peyto Lake Viewpoint (Walk 62).

Access: Bow Summit is 42 km (26 miles) north of Lake Louise on the Icefields Parkway, or 37 km (23 miles) south of Saskatchewan River Crossing, at the top of the pass. Parking, except for vans and the disabled, is in the lower parking lot. To reach the trailhead from the lower parking lot, follow the Peyto Lake Viewpoint and take the upper trail to the left after the viewpoint.

Route: The trail starts at an interpretive sign, where an informative booklet about Bow Summit can usually be obtained. This area is one of the newest and most fragile of the world's natural landscapes. As recently as 7,000 years ago, Peyto Glacier filled these valleys up to 500 metres above the viewpoint. Pioneer trees and plants required thousands of years to gain a foothold on these windswept ridges. Gradually, islands of spruce, pine and fir began to take root in protected locations.

Interpretive signs explain how this landscape is frozen most of the year. Alpine zones, where the trees give way to heather and tiny, ground-hugging plants, have a severe climate. The average yearly temperature up here is less than -4°C and the growing season may be less than 60 days. Areas such as Bow Summit also endure high winds, deep snow and high solar radiation—which dries out plants without thick bark or furry stems.

Alpine plants have to adapt to survive. White mountain avens, for example, grow close to the ground to escape the wind and have waxy leaves to retain moisture. Some plants, such as moss campion and the umbrella plant, grow in the form of pincushions, with low, compact tops attached to a central tap root. The wind can't get at them.

Alpine flowers are usually brightly-colored shades of reds and purple. These colors are thought to screen out much of the higher levels of ultra-violet radiation at these elevations.

"Where someone picked a flower two years ago, it will be eight more years before that plant produces another," Parks Canada cautions.

This area became so damaged by visitors that in 1977 Parks Canada rerouted paths and now requires visitors to stay on these trails. The old damage is still visible.

A few minutes up the trail, views open onto a meadow with splendid views of Mt. Thompson. There are a few benches.

Golden-mantled ground squirrels and hoary marmots live up here. Marmots weigh between 10 and 30 pounds and have grizzled gray hair on their backs. Highly social, they live among the boulders in colonies filled with tunnels, and emit a high-pitched whistle at any sign of danger.

Watch also for hermit thrushes, Clark's nutcracker and white-tailed ptarmigan. The latter live here year-round, feathers changing from brown in summer to white in winter. Note also the phenomena of "tree islands"—clumps of trees growing together to protect themselves from the dry winds and deep snow.

Peyto Lake Viewpoint

Upper Waterfowl Lake

WALK 64

A leg-stretcher

MAP 25

Highlight: Beautiful lake, wildlife habitat
Distance: .75 km (.5 mile) return
Time: 10 minutes
Rating: Easy
Maximum elevation: 1,828 m (6,000 ft)
Elevation loss: Negligible
Footwear: Anything
Best season: July to October

25. WATERFOWL LAKES

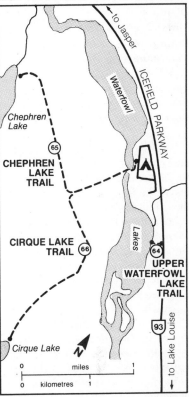

While the amble down to Upper Waterfowl Lake is among the shortest in Banff, it's worth stretching your legs for. The lake is a rich habitat for observing birds and animals of the subalpine forest. This is a good spot to see moose and waterfowl, especially in early morning or at dusk.

Access: The trail starts 1.2 km south of Waterfowl Lake campground on the west side of the Icefields Parkway. The campground is 20 km (12.5 miles) south of Saskatchewan River Crossing and 57 km (35 miles) north of the Trans-Canada Hwy. Just take the dirt trail down from the interpretive sign at the pull-out.

Route: Only a few minutes take you to a world far away from the rushing highway. Marshes fringe the edge of Waterfowl Lake. This is a fine place just to sit and listen. Gray Jays, Clark's nutcrackers, juncos, sandpipers, gold-eyes and teals are among the birds often sighted here.

The lake is also an excellent place to spot moose. The largest members of the deer family, they weigh

between 800 and 1,100 pounds, although some bulls do get considerably larger. They are solitary animals, except for the female and her calves. Moose feed in the lake's shallows and in the open area along the shore.

Even without the chance to see wildlife, this little stop provides a fine opportunity to gaze on the glories of Mt. Chephren, black and towering on the right. Many consider Chephren to be one of the finest mountains in the Rockies.

Chephren Lake Trail

To a black pyramid

MAP 25

Highlight: Scenic subalpine lake
Distance: 8 km return (5 miles)
Time: 2 1/2 to 3 hours
Rating: Moderate
Maximum elevation: 1,798 m
(5,900 ft)
Elevation gain: 150 m (500 ft)
Footwear: Light hiking boots
Best season: July to October

"No ripple of worry from the outside could touch us . . . It was hard to go from that beautiful place, to leave the little lake to the butterflies, the gophers, the ducks, the bears and the flowers." Thus wrote Mary Schäffer, an early explorer in the area, of a spot near the Columbia Icefields.

Such an idyllic scene awaits at Chephren Lake, situated under the purplish-black towers of Mt. Chephren (pronounced KEF-fren), one of the most dramatic mountains in the Rockies. The walk in, though easy, is somewhat tedious through dense forest and mushy swamp-like meadows. Nevertheless, Chephren Lake is a fine destination, especially for those staying at Lower Waterfowl Lake Campground, one of the most beautifully-situated in the park. Take an extra pair of socks.

Access: Start at Waterfowl Lake campground on the Icefields Parkway, 20 km (12.5 miles) south of Saskatchewan River Crossing or 57 km (35 miles) north of the Trans-Canada Hwy. Follow the campground road down to where the Mistaya River meets the lake. A small parking area is situated in front of a signboard indicating the trail.

Route: Take the well-manicured trail leading away from the lake up the Mistaya River on the edge of the campground. In a few minutes, the trail leads over the river on a wooden bridge. Down the river, beyond the lake and the Mistaya Valley, the Kaufmann Peaks and Mount Sarbach dominate. Across the bridge comes the only uphill portion of the route, through a mixed forest of lodgepole pine, spruce and fir on a smooth, improved trail. At 2 km is a T-junction, the trail to Chephren lake heading right. Cirque Lake is the left branch.

Things look easier now—the grade is level and the path, although massed with large roots, is wide. But it soon narrows and there are several boggy portions to skirt the rest of the way. Through thinner parts of the forest, beautiful views emerge of jagged Augille Peak and Mt. Synge.

The trail goes through thick forest, the vegetation mossy and spongy. Watch for labrador tea (which natives used to make tea from), buffalo berry, Indian paintbrush and arnica.

After an hour or so, the walker may have to cross a stream the adventurous way—by hopping. You may hear the echoes of avalanches thundering down surrounding peaks.

In a clearing on the right commanding views emerge of massive Mt. Murchison on the east side of

Waterfowl Lake. Sir James Hector, in his 1858 expedition, named it after his patron, Sir Roderick Murchison of the Geological Survey of Britain. Petrified trees are said to have been found on Murchison.

Brown-eyed susans, bluebells, asters and micklemass daisies form a colorful carpet on the meadows. From here it's a short, steep descent down to the green lake huddled under the towering buttresses of Mt. Chephren, 3,266 metres (10,715 feet.) The mountain was named Black Pyramid by Mary Schäffer but a conflict with a mountain in Jasper resulted in it being renamed in 1918 after an Egyptian

pharaoh. The summit is usually cloaked in clouds.

Picturesque driftwood adorns the shore. Brook, cutthroat and rainbow trout are said to inhabit the lake. Fishing is allowed with a parks permit from July 1 to October 31. Impressive Howse Peak, 3,292 metres (10,800 feet) is to the left of Chephren, and a hanging glacier can be seen at the far end of the lake. West of Howse Peak out of sight is the pass used by fur trader Joseph Howse in 1810.

After slogging through all that forest, do find a rock or log and enjoy the the view before heading back down.

Cirque Lake Trail   WALK 66

Slippery route to a peaceful lake   MAP 25

Highlight: Subalpine lake
Distance: 10 km (6.2 miles) return
Time: 3 1/2 hours
Rating: Moderate
Maximum elevation: 1,828 m (6,000 ft)
Elevation gain: 182 m (600 ft)
Footwear: Light hiking boots
Best season: July to October

From a peaceful, milky-green lake, gouged out by glaciers, great cliffs rise above huge boulders and scree slopes to the hanging icefields of Stairway and Midway peaks. An inspiring spot, though a harder and longer trip than to nearby Chephren Lake.

The trail leading to Cirque Lake is often wet and covered with slippery roots, creating relatively uninspiring slogging through heavy forest. The lake, however, makes an interesting subalpine destination, especially for fishermen or anybody staying at Waterfowl Lake campground in Banff National Park where the route begins.

Access: Drive to Waterfowl Lakes campground 20 km (12.5 miles) south of the Saskatchewan River Crossing or 57 km (35 miles) north of the Trans-Canada Hwy. Follow the road down to where the Mistaya River meets the lake. A small parking area is situated in front of a signboard indicating the trail.

Route: Take the well-maintained gravel trail leading away from the lake up the Mistaya River on the edge of the campground. In a few minutes, the trail leads over the river on a wooden bridge and gradually up the forested hillside on a wide, smooth improved trail. At 2 km is a T-junction, the trail to Chephren Lake heading right. Cirque Lake is the left branch.

Initially, the left-hand trail leads gradually downhill, across a stream and into a bog meadow. The footing is usually damp. The trail crosses numerous small streams as you hop from rock to rock or balance on a few slippery poles until you finally come to the creek that drains Cirque Lake itself.

The route climbs steeply along the stream, passing a miniature waterfall and cascade. The footing for most of the way tends to be either on damp ground or on roots which are often slippery. The trail soon flattens out and you can sense the lake ahead beyond this rough, boggy area.

The trail reaches the end of the lake and heads along the right side, disappearing in an impressive jumble of boulders by the lakeside.

From here, the view's great— Midway and Stairway Peak hem the lake in a horseshoe vise at the far end. Snowfields and a small hanging glacier rise above the rubble immediately beyond the lake. Rainbow and cutthroat trout are among the attractions of the lake itself. Even from this distance, you can hear the torrents of water coming off the glacier and cascading down into the lake.

Mistaya Canyon

WALK 67

A pot-holed gorge

MAP 26

Highlight: Water-carved gorge
Distance: 1.5 km (.9 miles) return
Time: 30 to 40 minutes return
Rating: Easy
Maximum elevation: 1,525 m (5,000 ft)
Elevation loss: Negligible
Footwear: Walking or running shoes
Best season: May to October

"This is neither the longest or deepest canyon in the parks, but it is one of the loveliest," says Travel Alberta. Mistaya Canyon is indeed a spectacular, pot-holed gorge, delicately carved from limestone by the rushing waters of the Mistaya River. A good family leg-stretcher.

Access: The trail starts at the Mistaya Canyon parking lot in Banff National Park, 13.6 (8 miles) north of Waterfowl Campground or 3.2 km (2 miles) south of the Saskatchewan River crossing on the Icefields Parkway. The trailhead is on the north side of the parking lot.

Route: The trail descends on an old road and turns left away from the highway. To the southeast across the highway soars mighty Mt. Murchison with its wide base and one of the few icefields on the east side of the Parkway.

The Mistaya River, which originates on a glacier high above Peyto Lake, can be heard rumbling into the depths of the canyon from far up the trail. "Mistaya" is an Indian word for grizzly. The path descends through a fragrant subalpine forest to the remarkable narrow canyon. Small trails lead in either direction on the other side of the bridge.

Stop for a rest and contemplate the unusual sight of a flat-bottomed Mistaya River suddenly plunging over limestone canyon walls, almost vanishing from sight, twisting and curving the soft rock into beautiful, smoothly-scalloped formations.

26. MISTAYA CANYON

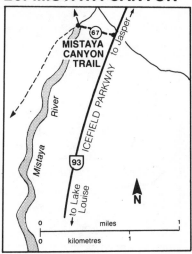

Directly west is Mt. Sarbach, frosted with a beautiful hanging glacier on the south. Both Sarbach and the Kaufmann Peaks to its left are named for Swiss guides employed by early alpine climbers.

Sunset Lookout Trail

WALK 68

Slog to a sublime lookout

MAP 27

Highlight: Striking mountain views
Distance: 9.5 km (6 miles) return
Time: 4 to 4 1/2 hours
Rating: Moderate
Maximum elevation: 2,050 m (6,725 ft)
Elevation gain: 590 m (1,930 ft)
Footwear: Light hiking boots recommended

Best season: July to October

There are lookouts, and then there are lookouts. Sunset Lookout, although rewarding the persistent walker with a fabulous view of mountains and the braided river channels of the North Saskatchewan and Alexandra rivers, demands a great deal of slogging up a steep

27. SUNSET LOOKOUT

forested ridge. Once there, however, alpine meadows are easily accessible, and a delightful afternoon can be spent exploring. Just don't expect much scenery on the way up. Take a canteen.

Access: The trail starts at a parking lot on the east side of the Icefields Parkway, 34.5 km (21 miles) south of the Icefield Centre, or 4.5 km (2.7 miles) northwest of the Rampart Creek Hostel. Begin at the northwest end of the parking lot, across a tiny swamp crisscrossed with logs.

Route: The trail bolts up fairly steeply, through a mixed forest of fir, lodgepole pine and spruce, and soon crosses a little stream. Watch for asters, bearberry, harebells and strawberries which spangle the sides of the trail in mid-summer. The path, which is used by horses, can be boggy and in poor condition here.

The forest soon thins out a bit and

the trail pitches up a steep rocky section, then slogs relentlessly up. Views open on gigantic Mt. Amery which dominates the view to the west at a height of 3,335 metres (10,941 feet), its flat top gleaming with a huge snowfield. This mountain is named after Leopold Stewart Amery, a former secretary of state for Dominion Affairs, who in 1928 was the first to ascend it. Mt. Saskatchewan soars to its right.

The trail switchbacks through patches of aspen. Stop for a view of Norman Creek, which tumbles through a steep gorge to the right of the trail. This would make an appealing picnic stop for those who wish to go no further.

The forest thins in places to give views of the North Saskatchewan and Alexandra River. Keep left where the trail splits at the 3-km mark, the right-hand trail going to Sunset Pass, Norman and Pinto Lakes.

Terrain can be somewhat tedious from here to the lookout. Watch for tiny sub-alpine flowers amidst the mossy forest carpet. Eventually you'll pass a wooden sign on the left for "Waterhole No. 2." Keep straight, descending steeply to the lookout. All that remains of it is some foundation and rubble.

The view, however, is commanding. Mt. Amery and Mt. Saskatchewan dominate the landscape; below is the confluence of the Alexandra River, from the west, and the North Saskatchewan River to its right. Glacial waters like these carry large deposits of sediment from the continental divide. The rivers are said to be "braided" when their current splits into several channels which divide and unite depending on the water volume. From here the North Saskatchewan will make its way across the Great Plains to Hudson Bay.

Those with energy to spare may backtrack to the Waterhole sign and turn left for a kilometre to reach appealing meadowlands. They are dominated by the summit of Mt. Coleman on the left, named for A. P. Coleman, a professor of geology at the University of Toronto who travelled here in 1893. A pleasant hour or two could be spent hereabouts exploring, reading or sketching.

North Saskatchewan Canyon   WALK 69

A river begins   MAP 28

Highlight: Narrow canyon
Distance: 2.4 km (1.5 miles) return
Time: 1 hour
Rating: Moderate
Maximum elevation: 1,737 m (5,700 ft)
Elevation gain: 60 m (200 ft)
Footwear: Walking or running shoes
Best season: Mid-June to October

The North Saskatchewan River, just downstream from its point of origin, has torn a great cleft through limestone, a canyon so deep and narrow the water disappears altogether at some places. Here is the "source" of the mighty river that bisects Edmonton and traverses northern Saskatchewan and Manitoba on its way to Hudson Bay. The trail, while short, is extremely steep and passes close to the edge of sheer drops. It is not for the fainthearted or young children.

Access: The route begins at the unmistakable "big bend" on the Icefields Parkway in Banff National Park just below the Big Hill, 16 km (10 miles) south of the Icefield Centre or 34 km (21 miles north of the Saskatchewan River Crossing. There's a small turnoff in the middle of the bend.

Route: Walk across the gravel flats to the trees and follow the edge of the forest towards the obvious cleft in the cliff ahead on the right side of the river as you face upstream. While there's usually little sign of a trail here, the way is open and level. Near the cleft, where the North Saskatchewan River rushes out of the rocks, a rough trail leads steeply up the bank.

Follow the trail which leads close to the edge of the narrow canyon. The canyon becomes deeper and narrower, the river cutting through more than 12 metres (40 feet) of limestone. The force of the rushing water has smoothed and rounded the rocks below, creating pot holes and sculptured formations.

The trail leads to a viewpoint at 1.2 km (.75 miles) although walkers might want to turn back at the top of the first pitch which provides fine views by itself.

The river, of course, doesn't actually start in this canyon. It really comes from the melting glacial waters of the huge Saskatchewan Glacier, about 4 km (2.5 miles) up the valley. And that glacier is only a tongue of the great Columbia Icefield higher up.

Panther and Bridal Veil Falls   WALK 70

The leap of a great cat   MAP 28

Highlight: Two waterfalls
Distance: 1.6 km (1 mile) return
Time: 30 minutes
Rating: Moderate
Maximum elevation: 5,950 ft
Elevation loss: 45 m (150 ft)
Footwear: Almost anything
Best season: July to October

Panther Falls leaps 180 metres (600 feet) out of a deep limestone canyon with the grace and beauty of a cat. Spray from this awesome falls drifts far up the valley. On the other side of clear Nigel Creek, a tributary stream pushes over a cliff in a slim column—the beautiful Bridal Veil Falls. This trail leading to a viewpoint for both these falls is short, although fairly steep on the return. No one should regret the small effort.

Access: The trail starts from the large paved area on the east side of the Icefields Parkway on top of what is known as the Big Hill, 38 km (24 miles) north of the Saskatchewan River Crossing or 13 km (8 miles) south of the Icefields Centre. It's the uppermost of the two stunning viewpoints over the North Saskatchewan River Valley far below. The trail, which can be hard to find, descends steeply from the lower end of this parking lot near the sign showing mountain profiles.

Route: The trail is narrow and descends in a couple of switchbacks through a mossy, boulder-strewn forest. The falls get louder as you progress, although you can't yet see them. The route passes under a small cliff and you begin to see the impressive gorge below.

The way suddenly opens up. Panther Falls come into view high above. The whole force of Nigel Creek springs from the rock and over the cliff in a spectacular plunge. Mist from these falls is often picked up by the wind and carried well across the trail you've reached.

To the right is the narrow plume of Bridal Veil Falls whose water originates in an icefield high above.

28. PANTHER AND BRIDAL VEIL FALLS

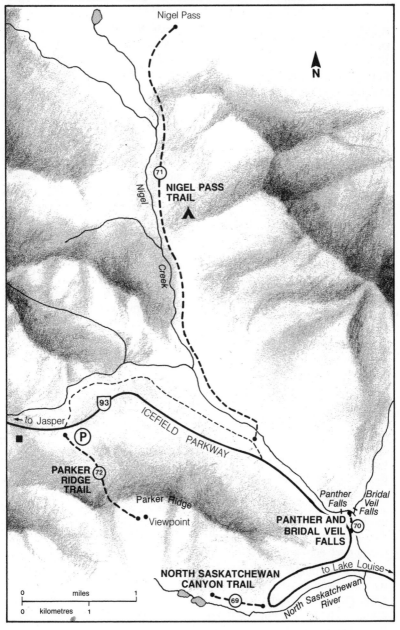

Nigel Pass

N

71

NIGEL PASS TRAIL

Nigel Creek

93

ICEFIELD PARKWAY

← to Jasper

P

PARKER RIDGE TRAIL 72

Parker Ridge

• Viewpoint

Panther Falls

Bridal Veil Falls

PANTHER AND BRIDAL VEIL FALLS 70

to Lake Louise →

North Saskatchewan River

NORTH SASKATCHEWAN CANYON TRAIL 69

0 — miles — 1
0 — kilometres — 1

Nigel Pass

WALK 71

Paradise at a price

MAP 28

Highlight: High pass, good views
Distance: 16 km (10 miles return)
Time: 6 hours
Rating: Strenuous
Maximum elevation: 2,225 m (7,300 ft)
Elevation gain: 365 m (1,200 ft)
Footwear: Sturdy shoes or light boots (trail often wet)
Best season: Mid-July to October

A beautiful valley with high peaks and cliffs above subalpine meadows, lush with wildflowers, a clear creek running through it. At the top, a bare, rocky pass offering views back to the glacier-carved heights of Mt. Athabasca and over to the desolation of the Upper Brazeau Valley. There's a price, of course, for this paradise and that is 16 km (return) of walking, sometimes along soggy or muddy trails. A longer, more strenuous day than most of the routes in the book. On the other hand, the walk isn't particularly steep except for a short pitch near the top.

Access: The trailhead is 12 km (7.5 miles) south of the Icefields Centre and 38 km (23.5 miles) north of Saskatchewan River Crossing. Turn off the Icefields Parkway onto an old road just north of the Big Hill. The trail starts a few metres past the barrier across the road.

Route: From the old road, once the main Banff-Jasper highway, turn right and cross Nigel Creek on a bridge. The trail climbs through trees and soon emerges on a wide avalanche track. The ascent is gradual with one open area following another, providing good views. These avalanche meadows are often flush with Indian paintbrush.

The views back towards Parker Ridge get better as you ascend. At a junction, keep to the right.

The forest gives way to mostly upland meadow. From here on, the views are uninterrupted. The cliffs opposite, part of the ridge leading up to Nigel Peak, were named for Nigel Vavasour who assisted an 1898 climbing expedition in the region. You can see ahead to the pass, low point at the end of the valley.

At 5.6 km, the trail passes a tiny backcountry campground. The trail continues straight ahead, crossing numerous small streams. Much of the trail, which remains on the right side of sparkling Nigel Creek, is deeply eroded in these damp meadows but passage isn't difficult. If you walk beside the eroded trail, as most will, you'll create another erosion ditch and, before long, the meadow will be bisected by a series of these trenches.

The last kilometre is steeper, with an elevation gain of 275 metres (900 feet) as you climb the final rocky ridge to the top of the pass, km 8 (mile 5).

Once on top, you can gain better views by wandering left over the rocks. The valley to the right leads up to an impressive boulder field and a lake at the end of the Brazeau River. The pass marks the boundary between Banff and Jasper national parks. This is the land of the golden eagle, which can be distinguished from the bald eagle by its dark head and tail and feathered legs.

On the far side, you can see the trail descending towards Brazeau flats through a desolate landscape of rocks and scree. Behind you, bare Parker Ridge leads up to the glaciated heights of Mt. Athabasca.

Nigel Pass

Parker Ridge

WALK 72

Tundra and glaciers

MAP 28

Highlight: Alpine tundra, view of Saskatchewan Glacier
Distance: 5 km (3 miles) return
Time: 2 to 4 hours
Rating: Moderate
Maximum elevation: 2,255 m (7,400 ft)
Elevation gain: 215 m (700 ft)
Footwear: Sturdy shoes or light hiking boots
Best season: Mid-July to Mid-September

Journey to the Arctic in less than an hour. Pass from the forest to a land of tundra, ptarmigan, great glaciers, treeless ridges and bright wildflowers. This inauspicious-looking ridge offers one of the easiest and most rewarding opportunities in the mountain parks to view alpine terrain. The huge Saskatchewan Glacier, out of sight from the highway, glistens on the other side of the ridge. Mountain goats can often be seen. An afternoon can easily be lolled away wandering alpine meadows or just soaking in the panorama, so much more striking than what the motorists get to see.

Note that the recently-improved trail is often crowded by mid-afternoon on warm summer weekends. Congestion can usually be avoided by starting in mid-morning. Be sure to take extra clothes as you may never realize from the parking lot how cold and windy the ridge gets. Bring water if you plan to stay awhile.

Access: The trailhead parking lot is 117 km (72 miles) north of Lake Louise and 113 km (70 miles) south of Jasper townsite on the Icefields Parkway. It's 8.8 km (5.4) miles south of the Icefield Centre.

Route: Start up a wide path, with the dramatic horn of Mt. Athabasca to the northwest, its sides deeply cut by cirque glaciers. Parks Canada has recently worked to restore this fragile area, trampled by thousands of hikers. So slowly do plants grow here that the damage of a single boot may take years to recover.

About 350 million years ago, when a shallow inland sea covered this part of North America during the Devonian Age, a coral reef built up on the flat ocean bed. The ocean floor rose to become the Rocky Mountains and today, fossils of the primitive coral creatures can be found in the rocks.

The appetite-rousing path twists upward, gaining elevation quickly, with ever-changing views back over Sunwapta Pass to Mt. Nigel and Mt. Wilcox. The almost-level pass below Wilcox was once surveyed for the Banff-Jasper road. In those days the Athabasca Glacier extended down to where the highway goes today.

The vegetation as you ascend is typical of upper subalpine terrain—feather mosses, heathers and grouseberry. Purple asters, arnica and a multitude of other alpine flowers edge the trail at lower levels. As you ascend, the trees become tiny and stunted. Listen for the squeak of pikas.

The walker enters the alpine zone, characterized by cold, deep snow ranging from 40 to 60 inches a year and winds which typically blow three times as hard as in the valley. Note how frost has churned up the soil. Midsummer briefly sees these meadows starred with white mountain avens, alpine vetch, delicate blue alpine forget-me-nots, red and white heather and moss campion. Frost may descend any day of the summer.

At the top of the ridge (where it's usually a good idea to add a layer or two of clothing) is a tremendous panorama of the Saskatchewan Glacier, largest valley glacier in the Columbia Icefield system. This, the source of the North Saskatchewan River, is nearly two kilometres wide. Its surface is said to be unusually smooth because of the gentle underlying bedrock. Along with the other glaciers in the Rockies, this one has been receding for the last 150 years because of a general warming of the climate.

Beyond the glacier is Mt. Castleguard, known for its extensive cave system. To the south are Terrace Mountain, Mt. Saskatchewan and Mt. Coleman.

Watch for mountain goats. These nimble ungulates, with skidproof soles and flexible toes, are at home on remote ridges such as this. They can feed undisturbed on grasses growing from narrow ledges on the cliff walls, although you'll also find them on easy ground like this.

Also at home on the high ridge is the white-tailed ptarmigan, hard to spot even when you pass close by because of its clever camouflage of mottled brown in summer and white in winter.

If weather permits, walkers may enjoy meandering up inviting grassy slopes to the north; on a sunny day there could be few finer spots to laze the time away.

12 Jasper National Park
Walks from Icefields Parkway and Highway 93A

Wilcox Pass

The best view of all

MAP 29

Highlight: Alpine pass, icefields vistas
Distance: 12 km (7.4 miles) return
Time: 5 hours
Rating: Moderate
Maximum elevation: 2,377 m (7,800 ft)
Elevation gain: 335 m (1,100 ft)
Footwear: Light hiking boots
Best Season: Mid-July to late September

The Wilcox Pass Trail provides the most spectacular views around the awesome Columbia Icefield. The trail has almost no tedious stretches, no unrewarding slogging. Although fairly long and containing some steep stretches, it is open and exposed for virtually the entire distance, providing probably the best views of the Athabasca Glacier and elegant, lofty Mt. Athabasca that can be had anywhere, at least from a trail.

Then, without much additional ascent, the route leads into the pass itself, a treeless alpine world of wildflowers and summer snowbanks, a fascinating region that's almost flat, though bounded by high peaks. Here's one of the most rewarding open places to see game from grizzlies—at a distance, you hope—to marmots, moose, bighorn sheep and golden eagles.

Access: Drive to the Icefield Information Centre, 104 km (64 miles) south of Jasper on the Icefields Parkway (Hwy 93). The trailhead is 2.5 km (1.5 miles) south of the centre at the entrance to Wilcox Pass Campground, the second campground after the

29. ATHABASCA GLACIER

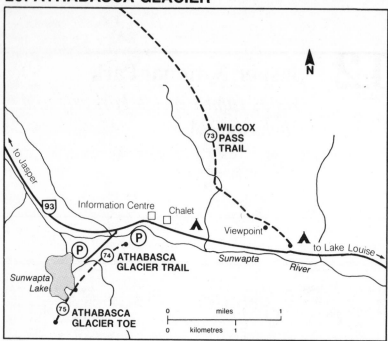

centre. Coming from Lake Louise, the trailhead is 2 km (1.2 miles) north of the Banff-Jasper boundary.

The trail starts on the left only a few metres up the road from the highway and campground gates, although there's no place to park. Park .4 km up the road at a pull-off area just before the campground bulletin board and walk back down to the trail.

Route: The trail climbs steeply at first through an open forest with occasional views back towards Sunwapta Pass as you edge up the slope above the highway. You soon come out on the bare edge of the hillside. From here on up, the views are continuous and always changing.

Directly across the valley is the inspiring pyramid of glacier-clad Mt. Athabasca (3,490 metres), a favorite of experienced climbers, its sides cut deeply by glacial cirques. Climbers usually ascend from the creek that crosses the glacier tour access road above the Icefield Chalet. They travel up over the moraine to the glacier, then right towards the northwest ridge, then behind the lower peak to the main summit.

Left are yellow-green meadows leading up to Sunwapta Pass and bare Parker Ridge. Below right is the red roof of the Icefield Chalet, one dot of color amid this gray and white landscape of rock, glaciers and rubble.

Above is Athabasca Glacier itself and you can see all its famous features from here: The glacial melt lake at the bottom of the toe, the icefall above rising to the snowy heights of the vast Columbia Icefield and to Snow Dome behind and to the right. From the cliffs under Snow Dome, the steep Dome glacier plunges to the barren valley below.

The trail now leads up through delightful subalpine meadows, dotted with only a few stunted Engelmann spruce below the steep ridge of Nigel Peak. Even if strollers go no further, they will have been amply rewarded. A grassy knoll overlooking the valley is a fine spot for a picnic.

The trail steepens briefly as it climbs along the edge of a gully, at last moving away from the valley's edge and into the pass, named for pioneer explorer Walter Wilcox, who may have been the first white man to traverse it. The rock exposed on the hillsides is sandy limestone of the early Paleozic age. Some of the beds contain marine fossils such as bracchiopods.

You soon leave behind even the scattered islands of trees. Note that this area is unprotected from the elements and can be extremely cold and windy, even in summer. If you're experiencing any difficulty with the weather, especially with the visibility, turn back now. The valley is usually extremely soggy because of its flatness. The heavy snowfall continues to melt, even

into early summer.

The trail climbs to a low rise marked by a cairn and some larger boulders, looking like a miniature Stonehenge. This high point, between the ridge of Wilcox Peak on the left and Nigel Peak on the right, might be as far as many strollers wish to go.

From here, the valley ahead is mostly flat for more than a kilometre, dotted with ponds and slow-moving streams. Among them are many distinctive round patches of campion moss, looking like a light green pin cushion. The dominant vegetation is closely-cropped "sheep grass."

The grasses and flowers in this high pass must withstand the weight of heavy snows in winter and flower in the short summer as soon as the snow banks retreat in July. Some years, there's not enough time for plants to produce seeds before the snows return.

The visitor could walk up the low ridge to the left for the definitive view of Athabasca Glacier or simply explore some of this fascinating valley, once used as the main route between Banff and Jasper and surveyed for the Banff-Jasper Highway.

Only 80 years ago, the Athabasca Glacier extended right across the valley below. To avoid it and the difficult passage along a deep gully cut by the Sunwapta River, outfitters took the low-level Wilcox Pass and descended again by Tangle Creek on the far side into the Sunwapta Valley from the end of the pass.

Beyond the high point, the trail is often indistinct in this grassy alpine meadow, although the way is clear in good weather. Ambitious hikers could continue to the end of the pass and follow the cairns down to the trees and the trail which descends Tangle Creek to Hwy 93, for a total distance of about 10 km. But you'd need to arrange transportation back to your vehicle.

Most visitors will want to linger in the pass—one of the best places to spot moose, bighorn sheep and ptarmigan in the area—and then return the way they came. This wind-swept, bare valley seems so remote, such a different world from the teaming Icefield Centre area only a short distance below where more than 750,000 visitors pass by every year. Most of them will never know the splendors above.

Athabasca Glacier Trail

WALK 74

An icy approach

MAP 29

Highlight: Walk over desolate, glaciated landscape
Distance: 2 km (1.2 miles) return
Time: 50-60 minutes
Rating: Moderate
Maximum elevation: 1,981 m (6,500 ft)
Elevation gain: Negligible
Footwear: Light hiking boots recommended
Best season: June to September

The Athabasca Glacier creeps out of the Columbia Icefield in a dark and gloomy landscape almost overpowering in its immensity. Beyond is a crevasse-ridden river of ice, with mighty wedges at its toe (or tongue, or snout, whatever you prefer.) Such cold grandeur is best approached gradually, on this easy walk through glacial debris. (Those with less time or energy would prefer the shorter toe trail, Walk 75). Even on a hot day, the wind rolling down from the glacier can be chilly. Wear several layers.

Access: The Columbia Icefield is 125 km (78 miles) north of Lake Louise and 105 km (65 miles) south of Jasper townsite. Turn west at the sign for Athabasca Glacier. A parking area with an orientation sign appears just off the highway.

Route: The trail leads through a landscape that looks almost lunar. This is glacial debris created by the retreating Athabasca Glacier. The glacier has been shrinking since the late 1800s, and in recent years has averaged a retreat of between one to three metres a year.

The path, which is all through rubble, crosses a little bridge over a glacial stream, and then becomes rougher and more narrow. Fireweed, purple vetch, small spruce and willows struggle to grow on the outer edges here, hardy pioneers among the plants beginning to establish themselves in inhospitable post-glacial terrain. Up here, the growing season is so short that even tiny plants may take years to grow and flower.

Pause to contemplate the stupendous proportions of the landscape. On the far left is the noble head of Mount Athabasca at 3,940 metres (1,292 feet). To its right, just to the left of Athabasca Glacier, Mt. Andromeda soars at 3,444 metres (11,300 feet). Note the icefall draping down from Andromeda in the foreground. The great tongue of the Athabasca, one of many glaciers emanating from the Columbia Icefield, is flanked on the right by a peaked spur, and behind it is Snow Dome.

That insignificant-looking hump is actually what is called the hydrographic apex of the continent. Water from it drains three ways: to the Athabasca River flowing north and northeast to the Mackenzie River and then the Arctic Ocean, the North Saskatchewan River flowing to Hudson Bay and the Columbia to the Pacific. The Dome Glacier spills out below Snow Dome; to its right is Mt. Kitchener.

Just below the Athabasca Glacier is a meltwater pond created by the glacier. Its levels can change daily, depending on the ice melt.

The trail starts to descend fairly steeply and the first parking lot comes into view. Continue walking down part of a moraine. The huge ridge of rubble to the left, between the road and the glacier, is a classic example of a lateral moraine, formed on either side of a glacier by debris carried by the ice.

The trail follows along the glacial stream, then across a bridge and along a self-guided nature trail right up to the toe (see Walk 75).

Columbia Icefield

The Columbia Icefield

The view that lay before us in the evening light was one that does not often fall to the lot of modern mountaineers. A new world was spread out at our feet; to the westward stretched a vast icefield probably never before seen by human eye, surrounded by entirely unknown, unnamed, unclimbed peaks.

So wrote Scottish chemistry professor Norman Collie in August, 1898, after overlooking the icefield from the summit of Mt. Athabasca, then the highest mountain climbed in the Rockies.

The largest icecap south of the Arctic Circle, it covers 325 square kilometres or about the area of Vancouver. Six major glaciers creep from it, but only three—the Dome, Stutfield and Athabasca—can be seen from the parkway. By far the most accessible is the Athabasca Tongue. A fourth glacier, the massive Saskatchewan, can be viewed by walking up Parker Ridge.

The Icefield area is a walker's delight. A stroll to the toe is a must (Walk 74 and 75). Perhaps the best way to enjoy the icefield glaciers, though, is to back up a bit in order to appreciate their immensity. Wilcox Pass (Walk 73) has the most dramatic views of the icefield. Parker Ridge, overlooks the more massive Saskatchewan Glacier (Walk 72).

The Icefield Centre across the highway from the glacier offers films and displays, including a scale model of the entire icefield. Park personnel are available to answer questions.

Those who want a closer look could take a "snocoach" tour of the Athabasca Glacier, including close-up views of its crevassed surface. Tours run from about May 24 to the end of September, 9 a.m. to 6 p.m., with the last tour at 5 p.m. Reservations for groups of 10 or more. Call 762-2241.

The glacier is said to have more than 30,000 crevasses—a good reason for leaving close exploration for experts and guided tour groups. See Alpine Courses section in both Banff and Jasper Outdoor Adventures.

Athabasca Glacier Toe

WALK 75

Tiny trail, tremendous toe

MAP 29

Highlight: Visit to toe of glacier
Distance: 1 km (.6 miles)
Time: 20 minutes return
Rating: Easy
Maximum Elevation: 1,981 m (6,500 ft)
Elevation gain: Negligible
Footwear: Walking or running shoes
Best season: June to September

The Athabasca Glacier, stemming from the Columbia Icefield, is the most accessible glacier in North America. This short self-guided walk takes you right to its hulking, cracking, melting toe. Here you can touch ice formed from snow that may have fallen before you were born. The more energetic would probably enjoy Walk 74, a more gradual approach to a truly awesome spectacle. The winds can be cold, so be prepared to bundle up—even in July.

Access: The Columbia Icefield is 125 km (78 miles) north of Lake Louise and 105 km (65 miles) south of Jasper townsite. Turn west off the Icefields Parkway at the sign for Athabasca Glacier. Take the right fork at the junction. The parking lot is just to the left of the large glacial melt pond. (On this drive, watch for the markers and recessional moraines indicating the retreat of the glacier over this century.) Start by going over the bridge.

Route: The short path to the glacier is through a desolate, gloomy landscape. Yet it's full of interest.

The glacier you're approaching has been shrinking since the late 1800s and in recent years has averaged a retreat of between one to three metres a year. Glacial time is definitely life in the slow lane— snow falling on the icefield today will not reach the glacier toe for another 150 years.

Just below Athabasca Glacier is a meltwater pond created from the glacier. Its levels can change daily, depending on degree of ice melt. The muddy color is caused by "rock flour" ground by glacial ice.

The end of the trail is an excellent spot to see "millwells"—where surface water has cut into fractures on the surface, funnelling water down into the ice. Watch out for "glacial goop": powdered rock and ice water mixed into quicksand-like patches along the trail.

The tip of the toe is a fascinating spot to contemplate the strength of these rivers of ice. Watch also for bits of snow which in summer might be bright red, from red snow algae. The glacier's surface usually appears a dirty-white close up, laden with dust particles, not surprising considering its age. But when deep ice is exposed, it glows a beautiful pastel blue. The color is caused by ice particles in the deep layers, which reflect only blue light.

Stanley Falls

A beauty of a creek

WALK 76

MAP 30

Highlight: Series of waterfalls
Distance: 6.4 km (3.9 miles) return
Time: 2 hours
Rating: Moderate
Maximum elevation: 1,680 m (5,511 ft)
Elevation gain: 110 m (360 ft)
Footwear: Walking or running shoes
Best Season: June to October

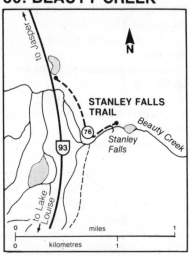

30. BEAUTY CREEK

It is a beauty, a little-known trail that passes eight waterfalls within a couple of kilometres, ending at impressive Stanley Falls. This route is best in the late spring or early summer when the water volume in the creek is heaviest. The ascent isn't terribly strenuous; there isn't a single dull stretch on the trail. The only hard part is finding the trailhead.

Access: If travelling north, look for the trailhead 15.2 km (9.4 miles) north of the Icefields Centre, or 5.8 km (3.6 miles) beyond the Stutfield Glacier viewpoint. If approaching from Jasper, it's 88.5 km (55 miles) south of Jasper townsite. On the braided, gravel flats of the Sunwapta River, watch carefully on the east side of the highway for two large culverts beside a dike, a man-made strip of land across the flat, wet ground about 200 metres long. There's a tiny pulloff beside the dike.

Route: Walk down the dike towards the trees at the far end. This is an inspiring spot with Diadem Peak, crowned by ice, and Mt. Woolley rising across the valley. Ahead is the steep length of Tangle Ridge and down the valley begins the long symmetrical slopes of the Endless Chain Ridge. On these valley flats, the Sunwapta River has slowed, and dumped the gravel and silt it carries, forming numerous braided channels.

At the end of the dike, there are two paths leading through the trees. Take either one. They both go the same place, to an old road, the former Banff-Jasper highway, its pavement now severely broken by the frost, a striking example of what happens when a road is left unmaintained.

Turn right along this road and follow it on the level for about a kilometre, as far as you can go. The road ends at fast-moving Beauty Creek where the bridge has broken away. At this point, you'll see a narrow trail leading left up the bank.

The trail, which may not be as well-maintained as more heavily-used routes, follows above Beauty Creek which begins to turn into a limestone gorge. Soon you come to the first waterfall, the water disappearing through a narrow crack. Although not far from the highway, this area feels wild and remote.

Be warned there are no handrails along this fairly primitive trail. Hold on to small children.

The next falls is more of a cataract while No. 3 flows impressively into a deep pool which you can walk down to. Along here are a number of potholes in the rock created by the scouring action of the water. The trail leads past No. 4 which drops into a round pool and No. 5 with a cascade about seven metres long in a narrow gorge.

No. 6 and No. 7 are close together, two waterfalls plunging down into a gorgeous, deep aquamarine pool.

The last is Stanley Falls, tallest and most impressive, all the water from Tangle Ridge and icefields high on the Banff-Jasper boundary plunging through a narrow opening in the rock and thundering down into a large pool.

Lower Sunwapta Falls
WALK 77

Beyond the turbulent tourists
MAP 31

Highlight: Waterfalls, cascades
Distance: 4 km (2.4 miles) return
Time: 1 1/2 hours
Rating: Moderate
Maximum elevation: 1,400 m (4,593 ft)
Elevation loss: 80 m (262 ft)
Footwear: Walking or running shoes
Best Season: May to October

All summer, tourists by the busload converge daily on Upper Sunwapta Falls, walking only a few metres from the parking lot to the upper falls. Yet only a few take the scenic hike down to the lower series of falls. While these falls may not be any more spectacular than the upper set, they are truly off the beaten path and feel more exciting. Strollers savour them because they have walked a little—on a most pleasant path—to get there. The walker becomes part of the scene, an explorer in a small sense, not just another tourist crowded behind a chain-link fence.

Access: The turn-off road to Sunwapta Falls is 55 km (34 miles) south of Jasper on the Icefields Parkway and 175 km (108 miles) north of Lake Louise. Drive to the end of the short side road and take the busy trail to the upper falls.

Route: After exploring the upper

31. SUNWAPTA FALLS

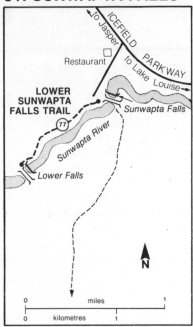

falls with its deep canyon and dark roar of water where the river makes an abrupt change of direction, take the well-marked route to the lower falls on the right (north) side of Sunwapta River, as you face downstream. Don't confuse this with the long trail to Fortress Lake across the bridge on the far side of the river.

The trail to the lower falls is soft and wide as it gradually descends within earshot of the river though a pleasant forest of lodgepole pine. A view opens up across the river.

Within 30 minutes or so, at about the 2-km mark, the stroller reaches the lower falls. The water, as above, plunges through a narrow gap and over a ledge, creating deep potholes in the rock, working its way down to the more level Athabasca Valley a kilometre beyond. A short distance below this waterfall is another, which is equally impressive. Hold young children by the hand.

You can truly understand how the river got its name—Sunwapta is an Indian word meaning "turbulent water."

Athabasca Falls

Thunder and mist

Highlight: Athabasca Falls
Length: 1.4 km (.9 miles) return
Time: 45 minutes
Rating: Easy
Maximum elevation: 1,173 m (3,848 ft)
Elevation gain: Negligible
Footwear: Anything for first part, sturdy shoes beyond
Best Season: May to October

WALK 78

MAP 32

Few visitors to Jasper National Park miss the fabulous sight of Athabasca Falls boiling and foaming, the water plunging 25 metres (82 feet) into a narrow gorge. Instead of being content with the first viewpoint, take this short saunter with interpretive signs explaining geology, and a visit to a now-abandoned river channel where the falls used to be.

Access: Athabasca Falls is 32 km (20 miles) south of Jasper and 198 km (123 miles) north of Lake Louise. It is also the point where Hwy 93A rejoins the Icefields Parkway. Starting from the southwest side of the parking lot, just follow the usually crowded asphalt path to the falls.

Route: Stop at the first viewpoint, a dramatic spot to enjoy the spectacle of the river plunging into the deep gorge. The river eats away at the underlying quartz sandstone cliffs, gradually moving the falls further upstream. Each year the pounding water cuts the lip back a few millimetres.

Go over the pedestrian bridge and turn left to a second viewpoint on the other side of the falls. Here you are close to the mouth of the steep canyon. Mist from the thundering falls rises above your head.

Sir James Hector travelled here in February, 1859, looking for a way across the mountains. But he had to turn back after his guide, Tekarra, hurt his foot. In 1893, A.P. Coleman, a professor of geology from Toronto, passed through looking for Mt. Brown and Mt. Hooker, which were erroneously believed to be the highest in the Rockies. Coleman's journey opened the trail between Sunwapta and Jasper. At Athabasca Falls, the party sat on a rock overlooking the torrent and "for a while forgot about slimy muskegs, tormenting blackflies, burnt trees and stifling heat," he wrote.

Towering Mt. Kerkeslin dominates the landscape to the southeast, and Mt. Fryatt and Mt. Christie are to the south. Look for

32. ATHABASCA FALLS

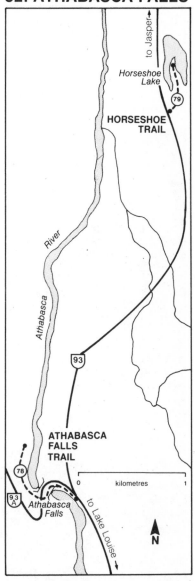

the unusual angle offered here of Mt. Edith Cavell, to the west.

Turn back to the pedestrian bridge and continue straight past it through a narrow, abandoned gorge, from the days when water extended much higher than it does today. It can be muddy. In a few minutes, the walker reaches an excellent viewpoint of the canyon, gorgeously honed and streaked with orange rock. Below is the milky Athabasca River, its opaque color due to the fall's churning action which stirs up the glacial rock flour in the water.

At the sign, you can descend to the rubble-strewn river. Watch your step here. This dramatic setting is a popular launching place for kayakers shooting Grade III rapids between here and Old Fort Point.

Athabasca Falls

Horseshoe Lake

Echoes and ecology

MAP 32

Highlight: Clear woodland lake
Length: 2 km (1.2 miles) return
Time: 45 minutes
Rating: Easy
Maximum elevation: 1,250 m (4,101 ft)
Elevation gain: Negligible
Footwear: Walking or running shoes
Best season: June to September

The short trail to rockbound Horseshoe Lake offers a fine mini-outing, especially for those who want to stretch their legs after the rigours of parkway driving. The lake is somewhat unusual for this area, a valley-floor basin fringed with rocky outcroppings reminiscent of the Canadian Shield. A mellow afternoon could be lazed away on its rocky shoreline, picnicking, sketching, fishing, taking pictures—or bouncing echoes off Mount Hardisty.

Access: Horseshoe Lake parking lot is 29 km (18 miles) south of Jasper townsite and 204 km (126 miles) north of Lake Louise, on the east side of the Icefields Parkway.

Route: Follow the wide trail, fringed with wildflowers, to the tip of the lake's "horseshoe." A network of trails all lead from here to the lake. Perhaps the most scenic approach is to continue across the middle of the "horseshoe," then make your way left to the lake, where the banks drop steeply off into deep water, a good place for casting from shore.

Across Horseshoe Lake are the forest-fringed, reddish quartz sandstone slopes of Mt. Hardisty, named for Richard Hardisty, chief factor of the Hudson Bay Company for Edmonton district between 1857 and 1858. The flat, rocky ledges along the lake invite wandering and picnicking—on the rocks, that is; there are no picnic tables. Fishermen report catches of rainbow trout here. If there's no one else about—and you don't feel too silly—bounce a few echoes against Hardisty.

On the return, you might head right along the shore to where the trail curves back into the woods past a huge boulder where kids could have a good time. You can even walk through it, if you're not the claustrophobic type.

Geraldine Lake Trail

Fish and Mt. Fryatt

MAP 33

Highlight: Subalpine lake
Distance: 4 km (2.5 km) return
Time: 1 1/2-2 hours return
Rating: Moderate
Maximum elevation: 1,650 m (5,413 ft)
Elevation gain: 150 m (492 ft)
Footwear: Light hiking boots
Best season: June to September

Frankly, for the expenditure of energy involved plus wear and tear on your vehicle on a rough access road, there are many more scenic day hikes in Jasper National Park than the fairly steep, often boggy trail up to the first of three Geraldine Lakes. But the lake is an undeniably pretty spot and has been noted for its large rainbow trout, making it popular with fishermen. The sharp-eyed will enjoy tiny wildflowers blooming along the path in mid-summer. Be sure to bring mosquito repellent.

Access: The trailhead starts 37 km (23 miles) south from Jasper Information Centre. Drive south on the Icefields Parkway 8.5 km (5.2 miles), to the junction with Hwy 93A. Turn right and follow it 22.5 km (14 miles) south to the Geraldine fire road. This road leads up 6 steep, narrow and bumpy kilometres to the trailhead just below the gate. There's a small slanted clearing for parking.

Route: Start through a forest of thick lodgepole pine on a soft needle-carpeted trail. The route soon progresses more steeply through a cool bower of trees. Parts of the trail are mushy in wet weather and gnarled roots can make footing difficult.

Continue through lower subalpine vegetation, including grasses, horsetails, labrador tea and buffalo berry. Watch for calypso orchids, Indian paintbrush and yellow arnica.

After 20 minutes or so, you may catch sight of Mt. Fryatt ahead to the left, named after Capt. Fryatt who was killed by the Germans in 1916 on charges of trying to ram

a submarine.

A vigorous stream pours down from the lake, where the approach can be rocky and wet.

The serene view of the tree-rimmed lake, with Mt. Fryatt dominating the landscape to the south at 3361 metres (11,027 feet) and a waterfall at the other end, is soothing indeed.

33. GERALDINE LAKE

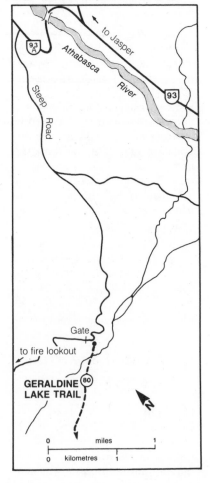

Wabasso Lake

A modest piece of tranquility

MAP 34

Highlight: Peaceful woodland lake
Distance: 6 km (3.7 miles) return
Time: 2 hours
Rating: Moderate
Maximum elevation: 1,250 m (4,101 ft)
Elevation gain: 50 m (164 ft)
Footwear: Walking or running shoes
Best season: May to October

34. JASPER (Southeast)

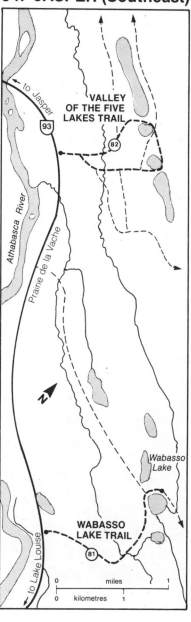

Wabasso Lake is no big deal. All you get is tranquility, meadows filled with flowers, a pretty stream and a green, placid lake, set under the Maligne Range. The access trail is appealing and doesn't involve much climbing.

Access: From the Jasper Information Centre, drive 15 km (9 miles) south on Hwy 93, the Icefields Parkway, to a parking area on the left side of the highway where the trail departs.

Route: The wide trail parallels the highway for a short distance, provides a view of the Athabasca River snaking below, then turns into the trees, passing rock slabs and climbing over a series of ledges. This is the typical, dry Montane forest, retreat for deer, elk and sheep during the winter when the subalpine snows become too deep and the climate too harsh.

Here the lodgepole pines are mixed with aspens. The lodgepole pine has few lower branches and its trunks are tall and straight, the needles one to three inches long.

The aspen is best identified by its gray-green bark and its leaves which flutter in the slightest breeze. Both the lodgepole pine and the aspen require lots of light and gradually crowd each other out.

They are often the first trees to grow after a forest fire. The pine has cones tightly sealed with resin that may stay on the tree for years waiting for the heat of a firest fire to open them up. The aspen spreads after forest fires because the heat may foster production of an abundance of suckers. Many of the aspens show black scars on their trunks. This is caused during severe winters when starving elk, or wapiti as they are called, are forced to chew the bark for food.

The lodgepole pine-aspen forest opens up in meadows called Prairie de la Vache. The trail crosses a stream which it follows upwards, climbing briefly to a scenic crag, then past a little cascade. The footing becomes somewhat rough and rocky but the trail quickly reaches the lake at about the 3-km mark and follows along the west side of this peaceful retreat.

There's a picnic area with fire box (no camping) halfway along. The lake, named for an Indian word for rabbit, is reputed to have rainbow and brook trout. The trail continues beyond the lake to ascend the ridge to the Skyline Trail, one of the few places in the park where caribou are sometimes seen. Another branch leads to the Valley of Five Lakes and back to Jasper townsite.

Most strollers will be content right here, the deep blue of the lake contrasting with bright-red Indian paintbrush, purple asters, golden fleabanes and yellow heart-leafed arnica along its shores. The place invites relaxation.

Horseshoe Lake, Jasper National Park.

Valley of the Five Lakes

WALK 82

Five lakes in one jaunt

MAP 34

Highlight: Series of small lakes
Length: 6 km (3.7 miles) return
Time: 2 1/2 hours
Rating: Moderate
Maximum elevation: 1,100 m (3,608 ft)
Elevation gain: 30 m (100 ft)
Footwear: Walking or running shoes
Best season: May to October

For an easy family outing, a tranquil picnic by a woodland lake or fishing, this low-key walk is a gem. It's one of the most accessible near Jasper townsite.

The trail loops by all five lakes—most of them little more than ponds—with very little climbing. This is a route for the short of breath. The forest path is mostly dry and soft-carpeted with pine needles. There are views of the high peaks beyond the Athabasca Valley and agreeable glades beside the lakes, some with fire boxes for a barbecue or warming campfire. The lakeside is bright with flowers in early summer. The first and last lakes can be good for fishing and row boats are available for rental. Pick up a key at Jasper sporting goods stores.

Access: Drive 11 km (6.8 miles) south of Jasper townsite on Hwy 93, the Icefields Parkway, to the sign for Valley of the Five Lakes trail and turn into the parking area on the east side.

Route: The wide, well-maintained trail winds through an open forest of lodgepole pines with a few aspens and scattered patches of wildflowers. There's a boardwalk across a shallow stream dammed by beavers and a short climb up an open meadow (keep straight at junction) with views back towards the snows of Edith Cavell and down the wooded Athabasca Valley.

Enter the woods again, through a grove of aspens, bright with Micklemas daisies, Indian paintbrush and goldenrod. Turn left at the junction (sign to first and second lakes). The route descends steeply to pass between the first and second lakes. The first is the largest and there are picnic areas along its far side.

After crossing between the two lakes, turn right (the left fork leads back to Jasper townsite) on a well-graded trail that leads through meadows above the second lake, then on towards the third and fourth lakes. There's a pleasant picnic area and viewpoint on a little peninsula which you'll share with asters, fleabanes, dwarf dogwood, everlasting and heart-leafed arnica.

With little gain in elevation, the trail reaches the fifth and last lake where there's a scenic clearing and picnic area. Rowboats are locked here. From the fifth lake which contains rainbow and brook trout, the trail loops back to pass above the fourth and third lakes with a few ups and downs over rocky knolls. It rejoins the original route.

Path of the Angel Glacier Trail

The splendour of an angel

MAP 35

Highlight: Walk through glacial retreat area
Distance: 1.6 km (1 mile) loop
Time: 45 minutes return
Rating: Easy
Maximum elevation: 1,768 m (5,800 ft)
Elevation gain: 30 m (100 ft)
Footwear: Walking or running shoes
Best Season: July to September

Few walks in the Canadian Rockies afford such grandeur right from the parking lot. Even a leisurely stroll of a few hundred metres rewards the visitor with a panorama of Mt. Edith Cavell, the devastation of a retreating glacier and the bluish-green splendour of Angel Glacier.

Access: From the Parks Information Centre in Jasper townsite, drive west on the main street (Connaught) as it turns onto Hwy 93, the Icefields Parkway. Keep going south on 93 until the 93A turnoff right at km 8.5 (mile 5.2). Go up the hill until the Mt. Edith Cavell Road turnoff at kilometre 13.8 (mile 8.5). The scenic road ends at a parking lot at km 28 (mile 17.4).

Route: Start climbing up the asphalt path, with views of Mt. Edith Cavell becoming more impressive. The trail leads beside a brook, over a little wooden bridge and across the tumbled boulders of an old moraine. There are benches conveniently placed along the way.

Four hundred years ago, a worldwide cooling trend started a "little Ice Age" in mountain regions. Glacier ice advanced to the site of the present-day parking lot. Warm weather more recently has caused a retreat. The rubble and debris before you is its legacy.

Continue straight at the trail junction (the left turn here leads to Cavell Meadows (Walk 84). Cavell looms ever more imposing above as the walker progresses over the moraine. Photographs are best taken in the morning when the low-angle light gives the glacier and rock wall depth and detail.

The Angel Glacier—bluish-green with a layer of debris on top—spreads her wings on Cavell's inhospitable face, with waterfalls tumbling below. Her forbidding north face, above Angel Glacier, was first climbed in July, 1961, by a party including Yvon Chouinard, the California climber who founded the Patagonia line of outdoor gear. Constantly falling rock inspired Chouinard to call the face "a shooting gallery."

Thankfully, this walk isn't nearly so hazardous. Watch for pikas, golden-mantled squirrels and fat marmots.

The trail leads down past massive boulders to Cavell Lake, a glacial melt pond where it's usually chilly even in summer. This is an incredible place, the closest and most awesome vantage point to Angel Glacier, a magnificent cirque glacier. Ice breaks over the cliffs to create her 40-metre-thick wings. The remaining ice plunges down the steep valley, completing her white skirt.

Right across the lake is Cavell Glacier, whose ice feeds the lake. Sometimes ice is shorn away in flat sections, allowing you to see the vertical crevasses of its interior. Each summer, a little more of its toe is nibbled away by a slightly warmer lake, forming icebergs and ice caves.

Follow the trail down along Cavell Creek back towards the parking lot, through an area covered with glacial ice as recently as the 1950s, back towards the parking lot. Life is slowly returning here after the devastation of the glacier. Patches of purple mountain heath and willow shrubs struggle to gain a foothold. Moose find the willow shoots irrestible during the long, cold subalpine winter. Scientists say it will take several hundred years before the valley is completely reforested.

35. CAVELL AREA

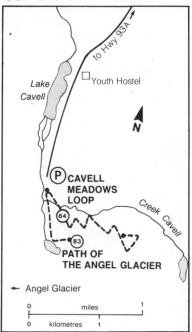

Who Was Edith Cavell?

Edith Louisa Cavell, born Dec. 4, 1865 in Norfolk, England, began her nursing career in a London hospital in 1895. In 1907, she became the first matron of the Berkendael Medical Institute in Brussels, later turned into a Red Cross hospital at the outbreak of the First World War.

She began to help wounded French and English soldiers who were first hidden at a chateau near Mons by Prince Reginald de Croy. The soldiers were conveyed to Cavell's house and those of her friends and given supplies to reach the Dutch border. About 200 soldiers found assistance this way.

It all ended on Aug. 5, 1915, when Cavell was arrested and imprisoned. She was shot on Oct. 12, despite efforts of the United States minister in Brussels.

"Patriotism is not enough," she remarked as the final sacrament was administered. She never saw this mountain.

Angel Glacier

Angel Glacier-Cavell Meadows Loop   WALK 84

Angel spreads its wings   MAP 35

Highlight: Subalpine meadows, glacier views
Distance: 8 km (5 miles) return
Time: 4 hours
Rating: Moderate to strenuous
Maximum elevation: 2,103 m (6,900 ft)
Elevation gain: 335 m (1,100 ft)
Footwear: Sturdy shoes or light hiking boots
Best season: Mid-July to September

Deep rumbles and sharp cracks break the stillness of spruce and fir as the walker ascends the switch-backed trail opposite the cliffs of Mt. Edith Cavell, which might be called the Mt. Fujiyama of Jasper. The sounds are Angel Glacier ''spreading its wings'', its snow and ice cracking and avalanching down from the heights. From a safe vantage perch across the Cavell valley you can watch these avalanches—terror of climbers—most of the summer, particularly on warm afternoons.

The higher you go, the better the views get. And in an hour or so, walkers can reach rolling subalpine meadows where stunted, twisted spruce and fir give way to the tundra country, where for a few weeks each summer, a riot of wildflowers blossom.

Even those not inclined to venture far from the parking lot can still experience the grandeur of the setting. Just go as far as you please and turn back. Note that because of lingering snows and wet footing, the high portion of the route in the meadows is usually not in good condition until at least mid-July.

Access: From the Parks Information Centre in Jasper. drive west on the main street (Connaught) as it turns onto Hwy 93, the Icefields Parkway. Keep going south on 93 until the 93A turnoff right at km 8.5 (mile 5.2). Go up the hill until the Mt. Edith Cavell Road turnoff at km 13.8 (mile 8.5). The scenic road ends at a parking lot at km 28 (mile 17.4).

Route: From the parking area at the end of the road, take the asphalt trail on the right leading a few steps up onto a slope affording views of Angel Glacier, the forbidding, 1500-metre north wall of Edith Cavell and the desolation of tumbled rock and ice below.

The trail leads along the top of a lateral moraine, the debris pushed to the side—as a plow pushes snow into two lateral ridges—by the glacier that covered this area as recently as 1950. Strengthened by a cooling trend, the ice pushed down the valley as far as the present-day parking lot, carrying with it rock from higher up the mountain. The warming trend since then has reduced the glacier severely.

As you ascend, the glacier views begin to improve. Here are benches for peaceful contemplation of the rocky desolation, punctuated by the blue-green glacial melt pond below. The wings of Angel Glacier come into view.

At a junction and the end of the

pavement, take the left branch that switchbacks up the moraine, then climbs slowly behind it, tumbled rocks on one side, deep forest on the other.

The route leads up into fragrant, tangled woods of spruce and fir, climbing steadily, at times steeply. While there aren't many views for the moment, hikers should persevere. The best is to come.

Soon, the trees begin to open into meadows filled with Indian paintbrush, yellow arnica, golden fleabane and a multi-colored carpet of heather, the flowers blooming bravely in the growing season which may not last more than a month, not much time to reproduce. A lookout at about the 3-km mark affords a spectacular view of Angel Glacier on the north face of Edith Cavell.

Edith Cavell at 3,363 metres (11,032 feet) the dominant peak of the area, consists of Lower Cambrian and Precambrian quartz sandstone. It was named for the heroic British nurse who was executed for helping prisoners of war escape from the Germans in the First World War.

Although the mountain itself was climbed by the west ridge in 1915, the great north face before you wasn't ascended until July, 1961, when the well-known climbers, Yvon Chouinard and Fred Beckey and cinematographer Dan Doody, first established a route. They climbed the ice-covered rocks to the left of the Angel Glacier tongue, beseiged by nearly-constant falling ice. Then up over the centre portion of the glacier to the rounded buttress just above, then more or less straight up, the rock getting more difficult as they went, the bombardment of rockfall never letting up. They bivouacked on a small ledge 300 metres below the summit and made the top on the second day.

"Never have I felt so happy as that day on the summit with my friends," said Chouinard.

For a look at a similar sort of climb, watch Challenge, the film that plays daily at the Chaba Theatre in Jasper.

From the viewpoint, the walkers' humble and safer route winds up into timberline meadows of heather where snow lingers into early summer. Across the valley, waterfalls plunge from the black-brown cliffs. On a warm, sunny day, there's no finer place to picnic.

Heed the warning signs, however, and keep to the trails. The damp alpine carpet of flowers, mosses, lichens and small shrubs is far too fragile to stand the footprints of the many who pass this way. In the short growing season, the damage of a single bootprint can take years to disappear.

The trail loops up, around and back through the higher meadows, where boulders provide refuge for pikas and hoary marmots.

What is a Wapiti?

The elk of this area are called wapiti, to avoid confusion with the European moose which are also referred to as elk.

Larger than deer and smaller than moose, wapiti have a nondescript knobby tail and a large, straw-colored rump patch. They are the most common hoofed animals in Banff and Jasper National Parks and may often be seen grazing beside the highways at sunrise or sunset. The wapiti once ranged widely across the U.S. Eastern herds were killed off by hunters. Rocky Mountain wapiti came close to the same tragic end and were almost extinct by the end of the last century. In 1917, 250 were imported from Yellowstone National Park for restocking of the mountain parks. Most of the elk seen in these Canadian parks today are their descendents.

Wapitis are gregarious animals which congregate in herds of up to 80 in mating season which starts in early September. The male works to attract females at this season by shaking its horns in the bushes, rolling in the mud and bugling.

Tramway to Whistlers Summit   WALK 85

Jasper from the summit   MAP 38

Highlight: Alpine summit, spectacular views
Distance: 3 km (1.9 miles return)
Time: 1 1/2 hours
Rating: Moderate
Maximum elevation: 2,464 m (8,085 ft)
Elevation gain: 199 m (653 ft)
Footwear: Walking or running shoes
Best season: July to September

The easiest way to reach a barren, fascinating alpine area in the national parks is the Jasper Tramway which ascends 973 metres in a few minutes to an upper terminal above timberline. The terminal is only a short, although fairly steep, walk from the actual summit of The Whistlers through a typical and vast area of Arctic tundra, wildflowers and natural rock gardens. The views open in all directions and are magnificent.

Access: From the Park Information Centre in Jasper, drive west and south for 4 km (2.4 miles) on Hwy 93 to The Whistlers Mountain Road. Drive another 4 km to the end of the road and the parking lot for the lower terminal. Bus service is also available from Jasper. The tramway is usually open from mid-April to Thanksgiving, although the lofty trail to the summit itself might not be pleasant until the warmer days of summer.

Route: Many visitors, having passed from the montane through the subalpine to the high alpine zone in seven minutes, will understandably be tempted to go no further than the upper terminal. They're missing a lot; it's almost like the difference between watching a travelogue on television as opposed to travelling yourself. The views improve immensely as you ascend The Whistlers. What's more, the relatively easy trail allows the walker to experience a true alpine area, something you can't quite get from a balcony at the terminal's restaurant and gift shop.

The trail to the rounded dome of the summit is well-marked and there are rock stairs in some of the steep places. Although some will find the ascent steep, every step is worth the effort, even if you don't make it to the top.

Up here, only miniature plants a few inches tall can grow. Some take 25 years to flower so don't spoil it for others by picking them or trampling on them. The most prominent alpine flowers include yellow alpine cinquefoil, white dryas and round moss campion, the last looking like a green pincushion with pink and lavender flowers growing through it.

There are sidetrails in several spots affording closer views in each direction. Be warned that fat ground squirrels and marmots patrol these trails, expert at begging food from the visitor. These tame beasts have been hopelessly corrupted.

Another inhabitant is the pika or "rock rabbit" which is about the size of a hamster and blends in with the color of the rocks. On the other, less crowded, side of the mountain roam caribou and mountain goats.

The trail climbs steeply, then levels off briefly before turning right for the final push to The Whistlers summit, named for the whistling of marmots. Marmots are much easier to find than the smaller pika. They love to sit upright on rocks when they're not eating, building up a thick layer of fat to carry them through winter hibernation.

The large summit area is level. There's a log book and direction finder. North is Morro Peak at the beginning of its long ridge called the Colin Range, stretching back towards Jasper and culminating in the sawtooth peaks of Hawk and Colin. Closer at hand to the northeast is the rounded mass of Signal Mountain, beginning the long Maligne Range on which a splendid backpacking trail winds.

South in the direction of the Columbia Icefield are Mt. Kerkeslin, Christie and Brussels Peak. Turning southwest, you see the imposing mass of Edith Cavell with its spectacular glacier. To the west in the distance is the white pyramid of Mt. Robson, monarch of the Canadian Rockies at 3,953 metres (12,972 feet) and usually enveloped in clouds of its own making. Northwest is Monarch Mountain, Snaring

36. JASPER TOWNSITE

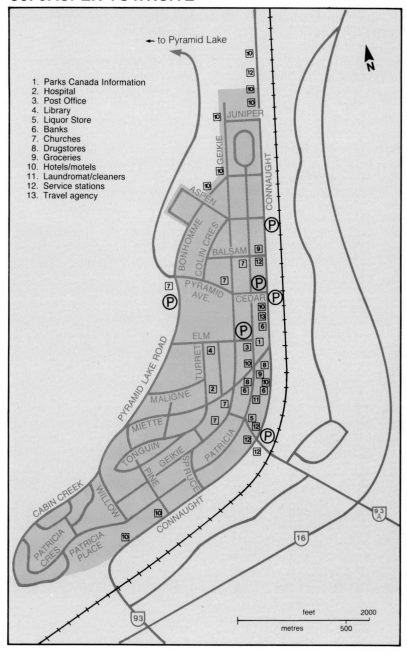

- to Pyramid Lake

1. Parks Canada Information
2. Hospital
3. Post Office
4. Library
5. Liquor Store
6. Banks
7. Churches
8. Drugstores
9. Groceries
10. Hotels/motels
11. Laundromat/cleaners
12. Service stations
13. Travel agency

N

JUNIPER
GEIKIE
CONNAUGHT
ASPEN
BONHOMME
COLIN CRES
BALSAM
PYRAMID AVE.
CEDAR
ELM
TURRET
MALIGNE
MIETTE
TONGUIN
PINE
GEIKIE
SPRUCE
PATRICIA
PYRAMID LAKE ROAD
CABIN CREEK
WILLOW
PATRICIA CRES
PATRICIA PLACE
CONNAUGHT

93
16
93 A

feet 2000
metres 500

and Pyramid, the latter built, the locals joke, 2,000 years ago by the ancient Egyptians.

Closer at hand, the complexities of the Athabasca and Miette Valleys are revealed and you should be able to spot most of the 50 lakes in the region. Once, two mighty glaciers met near the site of present-day Jasper, one coming down the valley from the Columbia Icefield, the other from what is now Yellowhead Pass. When the glaciers began to melt, large chunks of ice remained.

When this ice finally melted, it left depressions in the gravel which were filled with water.

The especially energetic could really experience the mountain by hiking all the way down to the road in a few hours. The 4.5-km trail heads down the wide trail to the upper terminal, then left to loop down towards the trees, under the tramway, ending near the youth hostel, 0.9 km down the road from the lower terminal. Now that's experiencing a mountain.

Mt. Edith Cavell, Jasper National Park.

Why Do the Trees Stop?

At timberline, the trees begin to thin. Within 300 metres, the trees grow shorter and eventually to mere dwarfs. Then there are only "islands" of low shrubs, a dense mass of crooked, twisted wood called "Krummholz." Then there is nothing, just bare rock, a few tiny plants hugging the ground.

The subalpine becomes the barren alpine as if one travelled from the forested Canadian Shield to the tundra of the High Arctic.

The reasons for this transition are complex. There isn't a single cause and the factors are interlocking.

First of all, it's colder up there. Temperature drops as you ascend. You may have climbed the mountain on a warm day in July or August but the average temperature year-round is only about -4°C (24°F). Frost can occur any day or night of the summer and the growing season may be much less than two months. Strike one against a tree.

There's more precipitation up here, most of it snow. Drainage is usually poor. The snow may not melt until late in July, scarcely providing any time for the plants to grow and spread.

For trees, it's simply impossible to get established and stay alive. In the short growing season, they can't grow enough protective bark, so they lose too much moisture to the strong winds and intense radiation from the sun.

And because everything grows and decays so slowly in the frigid temperatures, little soil is built-up over the rock base, making it hard for roots to get established. The frost breaks up the soil. Winds blow it away. The rock base may be scree that is constantly shifting.

What chance does a poor tree have?

So timberline around here is about 2,150 metres (7,053 feet), although that varies depending on how exposed the hillside is.

To survive, you've got to be something really tough and adaptable: one of those beautiful, seemingly-fragile alpine plants. They know how to exist in marginal conditions through their low profile, their ability to grow fast, their hairy or waxy leaves that prevent moisture loss—and often the ability to spread by runners without producing seed. The meek shall inherit the earth!

37. CANADIAN ROCKIES
(Northern Section)

▲ Campground   ⇥ Trail/Trailhead
■ Park Office   — Principal Road
● Townsite   ○ Viewpoint
⊐ Pass   △ Mountain Peak

Parks of the Canadian Rockies

WILLIAM SWITZER
PROVINCIAL PARK

● Hinton

J A S P E R

● Pocahontas

Athabasca R.

Jasper Lake

Miette
Hot Springs

N A T I O N A L

JASPER ■
Miette R.

Maligne R.

Medicine L.

Brazeau R.

Whistler Cr.

Astoria R.

Athabasca R.

△ MT. EDITH CAVELL

Athabasca Falls

Whirlpool R.

P A R K

Maligne
L.

Southesk R.

Geraldine L.

△ MT. FRYATT

ICEFIELD PARKWAY

Sunwapta R.

△ MT. BRAZEAU

Brazeau R.

Brazeau L.

HAMBER

PROVINCIAL

PARK

Fortress L.

△ MT. ALBERTA

Beauty Cr.

NIGEL PASS

SUNWAPTA ○

WHITE GOAT
WILDERNESS
AREA

Wool R.

Icefield
Information
Center

Panther
Falls

△ MT. COLUMBIA

Columbia R.

△ MT. AMERY

N. Sask. R.

10   0   10   20
KILOMETERS

Old Fort Point Trail

WALK 86

A knobby knoll

MAP 38

Highlight: Views of Athabasca Valley
Distance: 6.4 km (4 miles) return
Time: 1 1/2 to 2 hours return
Rating: Moderate
Maximum elevation: 1,160 m (3,805 ft)
Elevation gain: 130 m (426 ft)
Footwear: Walking or running shoes
Best season: June to October

A grassy knoll, sweeping views of the Athabasca Valley, a pinch of history and a peck of scenery combine to make Old Fort Point a super outing. This stroll is for those who don't care to venture far from Jasper townsite. The trailhead can be reached by foot from the townsite in about 30 minutes. It's especially appealing in fall, when

brilliant yellow aspens are set against deep green-forested valleys.

Access: From Jasper Information Centre, turn west on the main street (Connaught). At Hazel Ave., turn left (south), cross the tracks and Hwy 16, continuing about .75 km until the sign for Lac Beauvert Road. Follow it to the parking lot just beyond the bridge over the Athabasca River. The trail starts on the west side of the parking lot, up steep wooden stairs.

Route: The steep stairs lead to a cairn commemorating fur trader and geographer David Thompson. He and 10 men passed through on a hard and wintry trek in 1810-11, which resulted in the discovery of Athabasca Pass and the Columbia River.

Scenic rewards come early—the

38. JASPER (South)

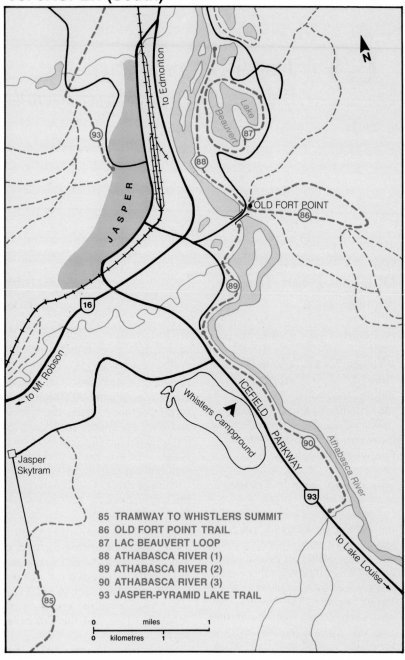

85 TRAMWAY TO WHISTLERS SUMMIT
86 OLD FORT POINT TRAIL
87 LAC BEAUVERT LOOP
88 ATHABASCA RIVER (1)
89 ATHABASCA RIVER (2)
90 ATHABASCA RIVER (3)
93 JASPER-PYRAMID LAKE TRAIL

turquoise Athabasca River bends and oxbows to the south; on a clear day Mt. Edith Cavell gleams prominently to the west. Behind the townsite is distinctive Pyramid Mountain, reddish-orange from its quartz sandstone cliffs.

Follow up a bedrock ridge, with excellent views back to Jasper townsite, to reach a grassy meadow. Nearby shrubs, aspen and spruce groves are excellent grazing terrain for bighorn sheep. The males sport impressive curling horns with distinct rings which indicate their age. Each ring marks one year's growth.

The dirt path, marked with cairns, leads into groves of aspen and pine. Just before the third cairn, climb a high shale bluff for fine

perspectives on Jasper Park Lodge, aqua-green Lac Beauvert, Pyramid Mountain and Jasper townsite.

No one is really certain how Old Fort Point got its name, since it is improbable that a structure would have been built on the ridge, which is off the main trail and has no water. The name may be a corruption of "Old Ford Point", since there may have been a ford on the river below. Another possibility is

that Henry House, a small shack erected by North West fur trader William Henry around 1811, may have been situated nearby, and the name simply transferred to the knoll.

It's said that Mary Schäffer, an early explorer to the Rockies, passed by here in 1908 en route from Maligne Lake. The story goes that she astonished early Jasper resident John Moberly, who hadn't seen a white woman around here for 15 years.

Descend among juniper, aspen and bearberry. Thrushes and grouse inhabit the aspen groves. Signal Mountain slopes immediately to the left, with Mt. Tekarra and Amber Mountain behind. Now it's up once again. Bluffs on the left provide the last good viewpoint to let the quiet wash over you.

Even off the rib, the woodland walk is delightful. Almost a kilometre away from the summit, the trail comes to a junction with the route to Valley of Five Lakes. Keep left for the trail that circles back to the starting point. The trail descends steeply at first and leads back through pleasant woodland.

Lac Beauvert Loop

WALK 87

A civilized stroll

MAP 38

Highlight: Scenic lakeside trail
Distance: 3.5 km (2.1 miles) loop
Time: 1 hour
Rating: Moderate
Maximum elevation: 1,020 m (3,346 ft)
Elevation gain: Negligible
Footwear: Walking or running shoes
Best season: May to October

From the elegant, groomed grounds of Jasper Park Lodge to the tranquil green lake and cool forest around it, to the velvet golf course by the water, this is a serene, leisurely stroll, pleasant in almost all weather. The footing is good, grades minimal and you can relax afterwards in front of a huge fireplace at the lodge.

Access: From the Park Information Centre, drive east to Hwy 16, turn left and continue to the Maligne Road turnoff and bridge at km 4 (mile 2.4), then follow the signs right to Jasper Park Lodge. Leave your car in the visitor's parking lot on the left and walk down to the lake. Turn right towards the main lodge building.

Route: The lakeside trail leads past the lavish lodge. Right by the water is a concession with boat and bicycle rentals. Continue around the lake on an asphalt trail with views across the water to The Whistlers and the snowy layered pyramid of Edith Cavell. This is one of the best places in the evening to photograph the alpenglow effect on Edith Cavell.

Lac Beauvert, which means "beautiful green" in French, is shaped like a horseshoe. Pavement ends just past the lodge and the trail continues close to the lake through appealing groves of spruce and pine. There are several log rest areas on the edge of the lake with tables and chairs for contemplation of these surroundings, at once elegant and rustic. The water is remarkably clear and changes quickly depending on sun, cloud and wind to a variety of peacock greens and green-blues.

The route curves into a cove, briefly rejoins the lodge buildings, then descends to the lake again and crosses the outlet on a wooden bridge.

From here, the route becomes a forest path, usually close to the lake, providing views back towards the lodge, a tranquil setting indeed, among patches of Indian paintbrush, dwarf dogwood, asters and fleabanes. There are benches close to the shore.

At the end of the lake, the trail connects with the paved road to Old Fort Point. This end of the lake is a favorite spot for scuba divers who enjoy the lake's clear waters, although they wear wet suits for protection from the cold.

Stay close to the lake until the trail leads up through the golf course, past an elegant wooden gazebo, then turning back towards the lodge. Follow the signs and descend again to the lake and a delightful needle-carpeted trail leading back to the lodge.

Lac Beauvert

Along the Athabasca River (1)

Sandbars to picnics

MAP 38

Highlight: Riverside walk
Distance: Maximum 5 km
(3.1 miles) return
Time: 1 1/2-2 1/2 hours
Rating: Moderate
Maximum elevation: 1,030 m
(3,379 ft)
Elevation gain: Negligible
Footwear: Walking or running
shoes
Best season: May to October

This short walk has no hills what-soever, a rarity in the mountains. While not a scenic marvel, it leads along the banks of the Athabasca River, past riverside sandbars ideal for picnics or children's play. It connects with the elegant Lac Beauvert route (See Walk 87). It can be made as long or short as the walker wishes—and you never have to retrace your steps. Visitors without vehicles can walk to Old Fort Point from Jasper townsite and combine the little hike with a visit to Jasper Park Lodge.

Access: From the Jasper Information Centre, turn west on the main street (Connaught) to Hazel Ave., the first left. Go left (south) and continue over the railway tracks. After crossing Hwy 16, take the first left, heading downhill to the old bridge across the river at Old Fort Point. There's a parking area just across the bridge and the trail starts down by the river.

Route: The route is a horse trail that remains close to the river. There are numerous side trails leading off but you can't go wrong by taking the left or riverside branch. Not much grows close to the river, except hardy shrub willow in the sandy soil of the floodplain. The forest further back is typical of the fairly dry montane zone. This trail becomes free of snow earlier in the spring than the shaded paths in the forest.

The trail crosses a couple of stream beds that are usually dry and passes areas along the river where long sandbars have formed. While the river is fast-moving here, it's still considerably slower than the other side of the bridge. From here to the east end of the park, the valley is wide and almost flat.

To turn back, the walker can just take one of the trails to the right into the forest. These quickly lead to the road from Old Fort Point or to the edge of Lac Beauvert. The road beyond leads back to Old Fort Point.

Walkers who continue along the riverside trail for about 2.5 km will end up on the Jasper Park Lodge road east of the luxury resort. Return by following the road to the lodge, then take the lakeside trail and the road back to Old Fort Point.

Along the Athabasca River (2)

WALK 89

Riverside walk

MAP 38

Highlight: Riverside walk
Distance: 2.5 km (1.5 miles) one way
Time: 45 minutes
Rating: Moderate
Maximum elevation: 1,040 m (3,412 ft)
Elevation gain: Negligible
Footwear: Walking or running shoes
Best Season: May to October

This trail along the banks of the Athabasca River is a handy route from Old Fort Point to the cabins and motels south of Jasper townsite along Highway 93A. There are views along the fast-moving river and down the Athabasca Valley. The route connects with river trails and scenic hikes on both ends.

Access: From the Jasper Information Centre in Jasper townsite, turn west on the main street

(Connaught) to Hazel Avenue, the first left. Go left (south) and continue over the railway tracks. After crossing Hwy 16, take the first left, heading downhill to the bridge at Old Fort Point. There's a parking area across the bridge. The trail, however, starts on the north side of the river, just before the crossing of an old stream bed. The route heads off on the west side of the road.

Route: The trail enters the woods, turns towards the Athabasca, then climbs a short, steep ridge with views ahead to The Whistlers and back towards Signal Mountain and rocky Mt. Tekarra. The route crosses a beautiful high bluff behind Tekarra Lodge where a sign shows the location of prominent peaks. The view down the forested Athabasca Valley to the pyramid of Mt. Hardisty is especially impressive. Below, the river steepens into rapids, the last on the Athabasca, until it leaves the park en route to the Arctic Ocean. On the

river gravel bars, you'll sometimes see Harlequin ducks, along with more common waterfowl. Moose, wapiti and mule deer are often seen below, especially in the early morning and evening.

The trail turns onto paved Highway 93A, crosses a bridge over the clear Miette River and resumes again 50 metres further on the left, leading back to the silt-laden Athabasca.

Thousands of years ago, this area was the junction point for two huge glaciers, one coming down what is now the Miette Valley from Yellowhead Pass, the other from the Athabasca Valley to the south. They brought with them huge accumulations of rocks and gravel which make up the benches on which the townsite is situated.

Beyond the bridge, the trail follows the top of an old embankment, a metre or so above water level, finally ending at 93A again opposite Alpine Village near the junction with Hwy 93, the Icefields Parkway.

Along the Athabasca River (3) WALK 90

A short evening stroll MAP 38

Highlight: Scenic riverside trail
Distance: 3.5 km (2.1 miles) one way
Time: 1 hour
Rating: Moderate
Maximum elevation: 1,060 m (3,477 ft)
Elevation gain: 30 m (100 ft)

Footwear: Walking or running shoes
Best season: May to October

This little-known trail follows the high banks of the scenic Athabasca River and connects with the vast Wapiti Campground. It is accessible to the larger Whistlers Campground across the highway, plus several commercial bungalow resorts. The trail, while not a scenic marvel, is suitable for a short evening stroll or as a connecting route. There's even a sandy beach, most years at least. The trail also connects with the riverside trail to Old Fort Point. See Walk 86.

Access: The trail starts near the intersection of Hwy 93—The Icefields Parkway—and Hwy 93A, 3.5 km (2.1 miles) south of the Parks Information Centre in Jasper townsite. The trailhead is just east of Hwy 93 near the edge of the river.

Route: Don't follow the power line but keep left on the soft trail close to the river. Views are good up the valley towards majestic-looking Mt. Hardisty. The river moves fast with

occasional rapids. The trail enters a forest of mostly lodgepole pines, passes a couple of picnic tables at a scenic location overlooking the river, then runs behind Jasper Bungalows. From there it descends to what in some years, depending on the shifting sands, is a beautiful sandy area close to the river, perfect for a picnic. Deer and wapiti can often be seen in these semi-open woods.

The trail climbs the river bank again and passes close to the outdoor theatre for Wapiti Campground. Then it runs more or less straight on the high bank above the fast-moving river that's laden with glacial silt. To the right are the loops of the vast Wapiti Campground. Whistlers Campground is across the highway, a little closer to Jasper townsite.

After a few ups and downs, the trail reaches a stream at the edge of Wapiti. Most walkers won't bother to go further since the trail gets rough from here on.

To continue, follow the stream up from the river a few metres where you may find a few poles stretched across as a rough bridge (if the floods haven't washed it away—this isn't an officially maintained trail). The trail gets less use on the other side and can be obscure. Just keep going parallel to the river.

Soon you'll encounter the major obstacle on the trail: Whistlers Creek, a vigorous stream draining much of Marmot Mtn. and Manx Peak above the Athabasca Valley. There's usually no bridge so you can either wade it or follow the rough trail up the creek to the highway. Just beyond the creek is Becker's Bungalows and Becker's Rapids, one of the most exciting on this stretch of the Athabasca.

Lake Annette Loop   WALK 91

A lazy lakeside amble   MAP 39

Highlight: Walk around woodland lake
Distance: 2.4 km (1.5 miles) loop
Time: 30 minutes to 1 hour
Rating: Easy (wheelchair accessible)
Maximum elevation: 1,019 m (3,343 ft)
Elevation gain: Negligible
Footwear: Anything
Best season: May to October

A leisurely loop around a pretty green lake on an asphalt path that's good in any weather. A loop that's almost level, accessible to wheelchairs and easy for all ages.

This walk, which has interpretive signs, can't be called spectacular. Never mind. It offers mountain vistas, a sandy beach with swimming and changing areas, a chance to see squirrels, elk, coyotes, ravens and gray jays and even a quicksand bog. Anglers report brook trout here, and the clear lake is popular with scuba divers. The path, although paved, is off-limits to bicycles.

Access: To drive from the Jasper Information Centre, go east on the main street (Connaught) to Hwy 16, turn left and follow it east 4 km (2.5 miles) to the Maligne Road Junction. Cross the bridge and turn right to Jasper Park Lodge. The Lake Annette road soon heads off left. The parking lot is about 2.5 km (1.5 miles) further on the right.

Route: It doesn't matter which way you choose to go around the lake. This route describes a clockwise approach.

You may see red flags on the water indicating scuba-divers below. Divers like the clarity of Lake Annette's water. Visibility in early fall can be as much as 30 metres

39. JASPER (North)

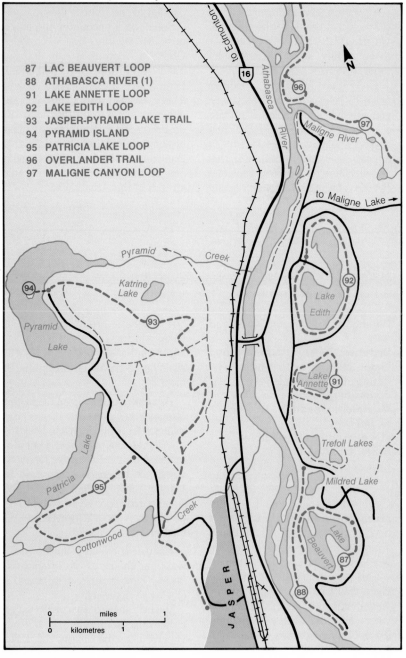

87 LAC BEAUVERT LOOP
88 ATHABASCA RIVER (1)
91 LAKE ANNETTE LOOP
92 LAKE EDITH LOOP
93 JASPER-PYRAMID LAKE TRAIL
94 PYRAMID ISLAND
95 PATRICIA LAKE LOOP
96 OVERLANDER TRAIL
97 MALIGNE CANYON LOOP

(100 feet), comparable to what you'd expect underwater at a tropical coral reef.

The lake is spring-fed. Close to the shore, the lake bottom is silt-covered and the water light in color. Parts of the lake bottom are littered with medium-sized boulders. Deeper water looks black because of the heavy vegetation on the bottom.

The trail meanders along the lakeshore past spruce and thick shrubbery, the edges of the path dotted with asters and other wildflowers. You soon approach a marshy area on the right, fringed with clusters of goldenrod and rosebushes. Here are well-situated picnic tables and views of the lake.

The trail then opens onto a small, sandy beach. Lake Annette is one of the warmest swimming holes hereabouts, although it's still chilly by swimming pool standards.

Lake Annette was named after the first wife of Colonel Maynard Rogers, one of Jasper's early park superintendents. In 1981, the Year of the Disabled, the trail was tailored for wheelchairs through a $90,000 grant from the Clifford E. Lee Foundation.

The trail goes by a fenced area of quicksand, which is actually loose silt caused by the constant motion of water flowing out of a spring into light sediment. Although not deep, it is enough to cause real problems for the unwary, park naturalists warn.

After the beach, the path ascends slightly and leads through open forest, where you may see squirrels, ravens, or gray jays in the branches. Interpretive signs indicate the boundary between the Rocky Mountain main ranges on the left and the front main ranges on the right. The walk continues through a dry open montane forest, dominated by white spruce and Douglas fir, back to the parking lot where you started.

Lake Edith Loop WALK 92

Cabinside and Lakeside loop MAP 39

Highlight: Scenic lakeside loop
Distance: 4.5 km (2.8 mile) loop
Time: 1 1/2 hours
Rating: Moderate
Maximum elevation: 1,020 m (3,346 ft)
Elevation gain: Negligible
Footwear: Walking or running shoes
Best season: May to October

The loop around Lake Edith near Jasper townsite is an anomaly among national parks routes: partly residential. But what residences! Gorgeous old log homes with large stone fireplaces right on the lake. The trail is a mix of lakeside strolling and woodland walking. It can be done either as a loop right around the lake or a short jaunt for a kilometre or two on either side. Lake Edith is also one of the warmest swimming lakes around Jasper. There's a beach right at the start and swimming areas at a couple of other spots. The lake is a fairly long walk from Jasper townsite but can be reached easily from Jasper Park Lodge.

Access: From the Parks Information Centre in Jasper townsite, drive east to Hwy 16. Turn left and continue to the Maligne Road turn-off

and bridge at km 4. Keep right beyond the bridge and take the next left. This side road leads past Lake Annette (See Walk 91) and ends at a parking lot and well-sited picnic area at the south end of Lake Edith. Walk down to the lake and turn right.

Route: Walk past the swimming area around the end of the lake. There are good views across the lake to the sharp peak of Mt. Colin and the rest of the Colin range. The lake water is strikingly clear for those accustomed to muddy prairie ponds. You soon reach a paved bike path and there are more picnic tables on the right.

The route leads onto a traffic-free road which gradually moves away from lakeside, although there are rough trails closer to the water. Many strollers will want to follow the lake for some distance, then cut back

to the road. Pick your own way; you can't get lost.

The limited-access road soon reaches the first of many graceful old log homes. These homes, which predate park policy restricting such buildings outside the townsites, never come on the open real estate market.

The stroller can continue around the end of the lake following the road in the front of the houses or by staying close to the lake itself. The lakeside route is a public right-of-way. The north end of the lake offers a striking view of snowy Edith Cavell.

The road on the other side of the lake carries a little residential traffic. A side road leads down to another beach area. Walk down to the lake and follow a trail right beside the water. The trail passes a few more homes, crosses the outlet stream on a wooden bridge and lands you back at the beach area where you started.

Jasper-Pyramid Lake Trail

WALK 93

A bench above the valley

MAP 39

Highlight: Views over Athabasca Valley
Distance: 7.2 km (4.5 miles) one way
Time: 3 hours
Rating: Moderate
Maximum elevation: 1,320 m (4,330 ft)
Elevation gain: 300 m (984 ft)
Footwear: Sturdy shoes or light hiking boots
Best season: May to October

Among all the tangled networks of trails on the wooded bench behind Jasper townsite, this is a favorite. Some of the bench trails, while handy to Jasper, are little more than secluded woodland routes with few views to speak of, except for a pleasant pond at the end. But the Pyramid trail begins right from the townsite and follows the edge of the bench providing fine views across the Athabasca Valley and down to the townsite. It leads through semi-open meadows and up a rocky ridge, ending at one of the most beautiful picnic areas in Jasper—on an island.

Hikers planning on walking all the way to Pyramid Lake, could make arrangements for a ride back to Jasper townsite. The return trip otherwise is long and tiring. A bicycle secured in the woods at the end of the Pyramid Lake Road would make for a nearly effortless return. Or get a ride to the end of the road and do the route in reverse.

Access: From the Parks Information Centre in Jasper, drive one block east to Cedar, turn left and keep straight as Cedar turns into Pyramid Ave. At Pyramid Lake Road on the upper edge of town, turn left and park opposite the recreation centre.

…l leaves where the steep begins.

oute: The trail, marked No. 2, …dges gradually up the side of the steep hill, climbing above the town. As close as you are to Jasper, this can be an excellent place to see deer, elk and other game. Views across the valley to Mt. Hardisty and east to the Colin range improve as you climb the needle-covered path.

The trail enters the woods, levels off and in 1.8 km reaches the Pyramid Lake Road at a parking area. This is a good alternate place to begin the route. The trail resumes on the other side, crosses Cottonwood Creek on a footbridge and parallels the Pyramid Lake Road for a while. This is a good area to spot such birds as the northern waterthrush, Wilson's warbler and the rufus hummingbird.

The trail, here an old road churned up by horses, gradually veers right. At a junction, take Trail No. 2. It heads slightly downhill and then begins to ascend a ridge, climbing another steep grassy hill. Views open up over the whole valley and townsite. Across is rounded Signal Mountain where the old road to a fire lookout is now being "rehabilitated" back to nature. Behind it is the more craggy Tekarra Mountain, named after an early Indian guide. West is The Whistlers with its aerial tramway.

The route continues along the edge of the bench through beautiful open forest and meadow, offering excellent picnic spots. Ancient Douglas firs guard the path, survivors of fires which devastated lesser trees. Now you can see right down the Athabasca Valley and up to the snowy heights of Mt. Edith

Cavell, the Fujiyama of the Jasper area.

Close at hand, the somewhat confusing terrain in the townsite area comes into focus: Lac Beauvert with Jasper Park Lodge at one end. To the left are Lakes Annette and Edith and beyond them the Maligne Valley and the steep Colin Range. The dry, open montane forest below and on the bench constitutes an important winter range for deer, elk and moose. The snow cover is lighter than in the higher subalpine forest. Its easier for grazing animals to dig through the snow for grass and plants. The climate is less severe.

The trail turns left to skirt a ravine that cuts into the bench, then resumes on the other side without loss of elevation. Eventually, it turns left and plunges into the trees again, reaching a junction. Trail No. 2 straight ahead will take you more directly back to the Pyramid Lake Road.

Try 2A, if you have time. It leads right, and into the open again, then begins to climb a rocky ridge to the left. The way ahead is open, providing views over the wooded bench. At the top is a good viewpoint for Pyramid and Patricia lakes, the latter shaped somewhat like a human foot. Behind is the distinctive quartz sandstone peak of Pyramid Mountain with its microwave tower.

If you are turning back to Jasper, this is the place. For those going on to Pyramid Lake, the trail descends steeply, ending at the Pyramid lookout fire road. Turn left on the fire road and in a few metres you come to the parking area at the end of the Pyramid Lake Road. Below the parking area is the bridge to Pyramid Island.

Pyramid Island

WALK 94

An island sojourn

MAP 39

Highlight: Island in Pyramid Lake
Distance: 0.6 km (0.3 miles) return
Time: 15 minutes
Maximum elevation: 1,180 m (3,871 ft)
Elevation gain: None
Footwear: Anything
Best season: June to October

Pyramid Island, reached by a footbridge at the end of the road above Jasper townsite, is an irresistible spot, looking more like a scene from a Tom Thomson painting of the Canadian Shield than part of the Rockies. The island has shady groves, a rustic gazebo-picnic shelter and lots of picnic tables, all of them with stunning views over the lake or to the heights of Pyramid Mountain.

Access: From the Jasper Information Centre, drive one block east to Cedar. Turn left and keep straight as Cedar becomes Pyramid Ave., then curves right above the townsite. Drive to the end of the 6.5-km (4-mile) Pyramid Lake road

north of Jasper. The route begins at the bridge below the parking area.

Route: Simply cross the bridge to the island and explore the semi-open terrain at will. Each side of the island provides good views, especially across the lake to the red and orange quartz sandstones of distinctive Pyramid Mountain (2,766 metres, 9,076 feet) and capped with a microwave tower.

Bring a lunch; there's probably no more scenic picnic area in all of Jasper. The lake is known for its fishing and is regularly stocked with lake trout. Pyramid Lake is one of the few in the national parks open to motorboats. Everything aquatic happens here: water-skiing, windsurfing, sailing, even demonstrations of fearless seamanship in pedalboats. Practically everything can be rented just down the lake. You can swim as well but the water remains fairly cold all summer and most prefer warmer lakes Edith or Annette in the valley near Jasper Park Lodge.

Patricia Lake Loop

WALK 95

Woodland, Wapiti and Warblers

MAP 39

Highlight: Woodland walk through wildlife habitat
Distance: 4.8 km (2.9 miles) return
Time: 1 to 1 1/2 hours
Rating: Moderate

Maximum elevation: 1,220 m (4,002 ft)
Elevation gain: 70 m (230 ft)
Footwear: Walking or running shoes
Best season: June to October

Patrica Lake

Here's a mostly woodland stroll near Jasper townsite to gladden the eye and delight a closet naturalist. The trail loops past Patricia Lake on the wooded bench above Jasper townsite, where moose are sometimes seen and marshes are rich with waterfowl and beaver. The walk is a particular treat in autumn when the aspens turn to gold. Canoes can be rented and fishing is permitted with a parks permit. Take along mosquito repellent in summer.

Access: From the Jasper Information Centre, drive east one block to Cedar Ave. Turn left. Keep straight on Cedar which turns into Pyramid Ave. and then Pyramid Lake Road. Follow it for 3.5 km (2.2 miles) to the Pyramid Riding stables. The parking lot is on the right side of the road. The trail starts across the road, on the west side.

Route: Begin ascending a gentle knoll, through mixed forest of jackpine, aspen and occasional isolated Douglas fir. In early October, the sound of wapiti bugling and geese honking punctuates the silence.

After about 10 minutes, you reach a junction—keep right and descend to Patricia Lake. It honors Princess Patricia, daughter of a former Canadian governor-general, the Duke of Connaught.

You can walk right down to the opaque green lake for views of Pyramid Mountain, a colorful spectacle of mulberry and reddish-quartz sandstone. This 2766-metre (9074 foot) mountain was first climbed in 1911 by Conrad Kain, conqueror of Mt. Robson, and George Kinney, both early climbers in this area. It isn't a difficult ascent.

Patricia Lake was used by scientists during the Second World War for some strange schemes indeed. One called Operation Halakkuk involved the use of ice for a ship's hull. The ultimate aim was to use ice to construct airfields in the North Atlantic. In Jasper, one structure was built, composed of an ice hull and a wooden superstructure. Before the research could be put to use, however, the war ended.

These days, the lakeside is a pleasant spot to sketch or perhaps just contemplate the stillness—the only sound may be the gentle lap of waves on the shore. Rainbow trout can be caught here.

You can follow a shoreline footpath to the end of the lake, past a green cove. The trail then veers left away from the lake, over a rustic bridge and down into a small valley along Cottonwood Creek and Cottonwood Slough. This is a popular birdwatching area, with hummingbirds, warblers, yellowthroats and thrushes among summer sightings. Moose can sometimes be seen in the marshy areas in early morning or evening. In spring, watch for baby ground squirrels.

Keep left at a junction. The trail continues along the side of a bare bluff with pretty vistas and flat rocks convenient for resting. Stay left at another trail junction, enjoying the panoramas, before heading into the woods briefly and back to the trailhead.

Overlander Trail

WALK 96

Route of the gold seekers

MAP 39

Highlight: Riverside walk
Distance: 6 km (3.7 miles) return
Time: 3 hours
Rating: Moderate
Maximum elevation: 1,030 m (3,379 ft)
Elevation gain: Negligible
Footwear: Walking or running shoes
Best season: May to October

This modest route which follows the Maligne and Athabasca Rivers for a little way is used mainly by fishermen seeking rainbow, brook trout and pike, although it connects with the river trail coming from Old Fort Point (Walk 86).

Hikers who persevere will end up at the historic old Moberly farmstead. There's a sense of history along here for this constituted part of the old Overlander Trail, used in 1862 by gold seekers from the east seeking their personal El Dorado across the divide in the Caribou country of British Columbia. The route is pleasant, but not especially scenic.

Access: From the Park Information Centre in Jasper, drive east to Hwy 16, turn left and continue until the Maligne Road turnoff and bridge at km 4 (mile 2.4). Keep left after the bridge and at km 6.3 (mile 3.9) turn left on the Sixth Bridge—Warden Headquarters road. Follow the signs for the picnic area. The trail starts at the bridge over Maligne River.

Route: Beyond the bridge, turn left and follow the narrow river, which seems to move like an express train. Much of this water came through limestone underground passages from Medicine Lake high in the Maligne Valley. Open meadows and shady groves by the river offer places to linger amid asters, bunchberry and wild roses.

When the Maligne River meets the Athabasca, the trail turns right along the big river, then heads more inland, following an old river channel. Strollers who venture further should be aware that Jasper residents tend to shun this area because it has gained the reputation as a route for grizzly bears.

Bears have long frequented the area because of natural food sources. When garbage from Jasper townsite was for years dumped into an open landfill across the river, that became an added attraction. Now the landfill is bear-proof behind an electrified fence, but the bears still remain in the area. Jim Todgham, chief park naturalist in Jasper, recommends that hikers do the route in late fall if they definitely want to avoid bears: "This is the only trail where I've found fairly fresh bear tracks every time I've hiked it," he said. Your chances of actually meeting a bear are still slim but this would definitely seem to be a place to wear bells, make noise, leave your dog behind and be aware of the bear precautions explained earlier in the book.

The route follows meadows and crosses a stream on an old wooden bridge, entering the woods on the far side. You reach a T-junction.

At the junction, the left fork continues above the Athabasca to the old farmstead where John Moberly's cabin, built in 1898, is situated. He was the son of Henry Moberly, factor at Jasper House until 1861. John, like his brother Ewan, homesteaded in the valley until the national park was established. Then they sold their holdings to the government and moved to Grande Cache.

At the T-junction, the other fork leads back towards Sixth Bridge, passing the wardens' horse corrals. The recommended route back is the same way you came.

The trail represents more or less the route of the gold-seeking Overlanders in the 1860s. Gold was discovered in the Fraser River and some came west on a long, arduous trail from Fort Garry through Edmonton and finally reached Jasper House, ragged and worn, on their way over the divide.

14 Jasper National Park
Walks in the Maligne Area and East of Jasper

Maligne Canyon Loop

The awesome canyon, quickly

MAP 41

Highlight: Dramatic limestone gorge
Distance: .8 km (.5 mile) loop
Time: 20 minutes
Rating: Easy
Maximum elevation: 1,160 m (3,805 ft)
Elevation loss: negligible
Footwear: Anything
Best season: May to October

Pounding water swirls, pummels and shapes Maligne Canyon into a narrow, potholed gorge as delicate and powerful as a fine work of art. This short loop takes you over and alongside the limestone canyon from its deepest point—where the vertical walls are 30 times the height of a person—to its most shallow point, all in 20 minutes.

While the longer, one-way walk to

Fifth or Sixth Bridge is recommended for those with more time, this walk should be short and easy enough for everyone, and no visitor to Jasper should miss it.

Access: From Jasper Information Centre, it's 11.5 km (7 miles) to Maligne Canyon. Drive east on the main street (Connaught) to Hwy 16, then turn left (east) on Hwy 16. After 4 km (2.5 miles), turn right across the bridge to Maligne Road, which leads to the Maligne Canyon parking lot.

Route: Begin at the exhibit at the lower end of the vast parking lot. It shows details about the topography and origin of this fascinating canyon and whole Maligne lake area.

The walk descends through open forest on a wide trail, giving little hint of the drama ahead. Suddenly, you reach the Second Bridge.

Here the narrow gorge drops 50 metres (164 feet). This is the deepest part of the canyon. The limestone walls are being worn down by water half a centimetre a year, slow by human standards, but a breakneck pace in mountain time. Water-bearing sand and silt swirls against the rock walls.

The steep escarpments provide homes for some small creatures such as pack rats and field mice. The canyon is also one of the few places in Alberta where black swifts nest.

Turn left after the bridge and head gradually uphill along the canyon's edge which has been securely fenced. A few unfortunates have met their end along here. One visitor apparently tried to jump the canyon—and failed.

Fine views continue up the slope as the steep canyon becomes smaller. Below, ferns and mosses live in the potholes, an ideal damp environment. The trail stays close to the canyon edge to First Bridge where the drop is 38 metres (124 feet). Just above the bridge is a dramatic waterfall. But as you near the teahouse, the canyon is only a

40. MALIGNE AREA

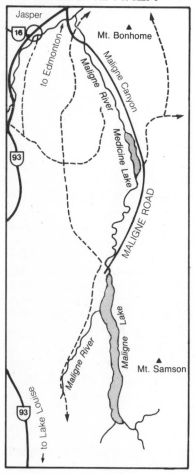

41. MALIGNE CANYON

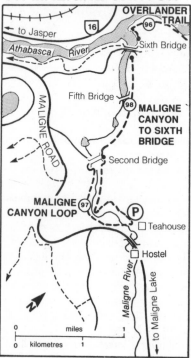

few feet deep. The rocks contain fossilized remains of marine creatures which lived 350 million years ago.

The walk ends at the tea house where you'll find various teas, of course, black forest cake, muffins, chili and other food.

Maligne Canyon to Sixth Bridge   WALK 98

The awesome canyon   MAP 41

Highlight: Dramatic limestone gorge
Distance: 3 km (1.9 miles) one way

Time: 1½ hours
Rating: Easy
Maximum Elevation: 130 m (426 ft)

Bald Hills

Footwear: Walking or running shoes
Best Season: June to September

Of all the canyon walks in the Rockies, Maligne Canyon is the longest and perhaps the most interesting.

You could, of course, view the deepest part of the canyon in a short, interpretive loop (see Walk 97). You would miss the wilder lower canyon, however, which shows how the gorge interacts with plants and animals and provides outlets for a large underground river.

The difficulty with this popular walk is the need to arrange transportation from the dead-end roads to Fifth or Sixth Bridge. Cyclists could make a bike-and-hike loop, leaving a bicycle hidden and locked in the trees at the top, then driving their vehicle to the Sixth Bridge and walking up—and perhaps indulging at the teahouse before coasting back down the road.

In winter, guides offer fascinating cave crawls into the canyon. The canyon is potentially hazardous in winter, so visitors should not attempt to enter it alone if unequipped or unskilled.

Access: From Jasper Information Centre, it's 11.2 km (7 miles) to Maligne Canyon. Drive east on the main street (Connaught) to Hwy 16, then turn left (east) on Hwy 16. After the 4 km (2.5 miles) point, turn right across the bridge to Maligne Road, which leads to the Maligne Canyon parking lot.

Route: Begin this walk by the Maligne Teahouse. The name Maligne comes from a French word meaning "bad"—apparently because of a wicked ford near the mouth of the Maligne River. On this walk, you need not worry about fords; you have your choice of six bridges.

At this point, the canyon is only a couple of feet deep, with water flowing over smooth limestone. The rocks contain fossilized remains of marine creatures which lived 350 million years ago.

The scalloped canyon quickly deepens. What you are seeing is a continuous sculpturing process, begun more than 10,000 years ago, wearing down limestone half a centimetre a year.

You begin to understand the water's force. At First Bridge, where the canyon is 38 metres (124 feet) deep, a thundering 23-metre (75 feet) waterfall plumes and boils into the gorge. Differences in rock resistance have formed the rock into the shape of a bulb in the canyon.

In a few minutes, the stroller reaches Second Bridge. Benches are located along the edge.

The steep escarpments provide homes for small creatures such as pack rats, field mice and other small rodents. Ravens have built nests here to escape egg-stealers.

At Third Bridge, cross into a damp, misty environment on the right side of the canyon. After this point, there are no more safety barriers or asphalt and the walk feels more adventurous. The path continues close to the canyon, by a waterfall, to Fourth Bridge.

You soon approach one of the larger seepages of Medicine Lake. Water takes at least 70 minutes, and

A Wicked River and a Bad Lake

Where did all that water come from? That's a natural question for walkers along Maligne Canyon, see a Maligne River swell from a few feet at the mouth of Maligne Canyon to a wide river at its lower end.

The answer won't meet the eye but it's one of Jasper's most fascinating geological phenomenon. Fifteen kilometres above, Medicine Lake acts like a sink without a plug, draining water into what is believed to be one of the biggest inaccessible cave networks anywhere.

In fall and winter, Medicine Lake literally disappears, leaving a soggy clay basin. The Indians called the vanishing lake "Bad Medicine."

The lake has long fascinated residents. One park warden went so far as to dump two truckloads of Saturday Evening Posts into Medicine Lake to see where the water went. The results were messy and inconclusive. It wasn't until 1956 that a French scientist, Jean Corbel, first identified a sinking river.

Later, researchers from McMaster University used fluorescent dyes to determine where the water went and to prove the physical characteristics of the underground complex.

If the underground passages keep enlarging, scientists say that one day the underground system could handle all the water flowing into the Medicine Lake basin.

often several days, to flow 15 km (9 miles) through a series of underground channels in the limestone from Medicine Lake to the lower canyon. The increase in water volume as you go from the top of the canyon to Fifth and Sixth bridges is a direct result of the springs and is the most obvious early in the season and in fall.

The trail now winds higher, past serrated rock cliffs. Pyramid Mountain rises impressively to the north. In summer, the edges of the path are dotted with goldenrod, yarrow, labrador tea and purple asters.

At a junction, walkers who have had enough can turn left and cross the Maligne at Fifth Bridge. A road leads from the bridge back to the Maligne Road. Otherwise, continue straight for Sixth Bridge, where the path suddenly veers into a shady, dewy forest which can be boggy.

The walk goes past cliffs, strewn deadfall, a little stream and under rocky knolls. Soon the walker passes park warden buildings on the left, across the river. The trail ends at Sixth Bridge where there are nicely-situated picnic tables by Maligne River. You may see kayakers going by. Be assured they didn't start in Maligne Canyon but at Fifth Bridge.

Maligne Lake Road to Summit Lake

The summit of adventure

WALK 99

MAP 42

Highlight: Narrow valley leading to scenic lake
Distance: 9.6 km (6 miles) return
Time: 4 hours
Rating: Moderate
Maximum Elevation: 1530 m (5,019 feet)
Elevation Gain: 90 m (295 ft)
Footwear: Walking or running shoes
Best Season: June to September

A wide path up a narrow valley between steep limestone ranges, a gentle ascent and two lakes within a few kilometres, that's what you get. While Summit Lake has the sound of alpine grandeur, the reality is more modest. For most day walkers, it should be enough.

Access: From the Jasper Information Centre, drive east to Hwy 16, then left until the Maligne Lake Road at km 4 (mile 2.4). Keep left towards Maligne Lake. The trailhead is at km 31.7 (mile 19.6) at the far end of Medicine Lake, by the parking lot for a picnic area.

Route: From the parking area, the trail parallels Beaver Creek on a dirt road, passes a vehicle barrier, a cabin and corral before starting a gradual climb up the gentle wooded valley. Beaver Lake is reached in 1.5 km, a secluded woodland pond with picnic shelter, home for much waterfowl and fish including the loon, Barrow's goldeneye and trout.

The trail continues past the lake and soon begins to level off as you attain the first Summit Lake, nestled

between the gray, steeply-tilted Queen Elizabeth (right) and Colin (left) ranges. These rocks contain traces of marine life from 600 million years ago when seas covered everything, the mountains not yet formed.

42. MEDICINE LAKE

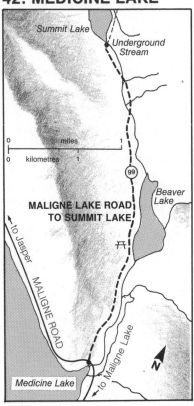

There's a grassy clearing at the lake's end. Note that although this is the lower end, there's no outlet into Beaver Creek. Like Medicine

Lake below, Summit Lake has underground passages in the limestone that connect its drainage to the vast subterranean system hereabouts.

The main path leads through the forest on the right of the lake. The second Summit Lake is not far ahead and the trail continues for about six kilometres more to Jacques Lake. That makes for a long day hike, however, and first Summit Lake is just as interesting.

Maligne Lakeside Loop

Trail of the legendary lake

MAP 43

Highlight: Beautiful lake views
Distance: 3.2 km (2 miles) loop
Time: 1 to 1½ hours
Rating: Easy
Maximum Elevation: 1,700 m (5,577 ft)
Elevation Gain: Negligible
Footwear: Walking or running shoes
Best Season: June to September

This short, popular loop goes down the shore of Maligne Lake, largest in the Canadian Rockies and surely one of the most beautiful. An excellent family stroll.

Access: Maligne Lake is 48 km (30 miles) from Jasper townsite. From the Jasper Information Centre, drive east on the main street (Connaught) to Hwy 16, turn left and proceed 4 km (2.5 miles) to cross over the Maligne Road Bridge on the right. Turn left after the bridge and continue up the valley to the lake. Park on the east side of the lake and chalet. The trail begins by the lake, just in front of the boat house.

Route: Walk down the asphalt trail along the lake, keeping on the lower path, past a rustic boathouse built in 1926. Rowboats, canoes, and motorboats may be rented here. Or you can take a guided cruise down the Narrows.

Mt. Charlton, at 3,209 metres (10,528 feet), and Mt. Unwin at 3,270 metres (10,728 feet), soar in the south, both part of the Queen Elizabeth Range. H.R. Charlton was the general advertising agent for the Grand Trunk Pacific Railway. Locally, these two mountains are called "the sweater girl."

To the left is a forest of lodgepole pine, identified by their long needles,

43. MALIGNE LAKE LOOP (Closeup)

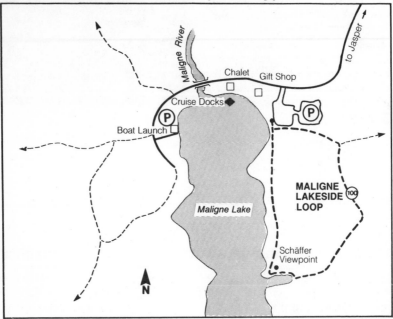

mixed with a few short-needled Engelmann spruce. Lodgepole pine covers most of the lower Maligne Valley.

The easy asphalt path leads past some of the most beautifully situated picnic tables in Jasper. It then narrows to dirt, offering only glimpses of the lake through the trees. Moose, elk and mule deer are frequently seen, and the upper alpine meadows of the Maligne Valley are the southern-most grazing grounds in the Canadian Rockies for caribou. The Maligne Valley is said to be home to more than 60 kinds of birds, including American Dippers.

Walkers who are tempted to wade in the lake on a hot day will quickly discover that it never warms up in summer. Surface temperature rarely exceeds 11° C (51° F).

An exhibit tells the story of Mary Schäffer's party reaching the lake by way of Maligne Pass in 1908. Benches are provided, and it's a marvellous spot to absorb the scenery.

At this point, walkers have the option of retracing their steps along the lake, or following the loop trail by a peaceful, clear green cove popular with fly fishermen trying for trout. The record rainbow trout for Alberta was caught in Maligne in 1980 and weighed in just over 9 kilograms (20 pounds).

At the end of the cove, keep

straight, heading inland from the lake. (There is a rough trail continuing down the lake, used mostly by fishermen.)

Keep left on the path at a junction, traversing an area of meadows and small pines with views of reddish-brown Opal Peak, named by Schäffer. Ascending through an open forest of lodgepole pine, the trail reaches an open meadow filled with low mounds. These are kames,

formed by rock and gravel that were washed into depressions in the glaciers that once covered this area. When the ice melted, the debris was deposited in these mounds. They are the opposite of kettles.

The trail soon leads past a kettle. These bowl-shaped holes in the earth were caused by huge block of ice breaking off from a glacier. When the ice melted, it left a kettle-shaped hole.

Mary Schäffer's Magnificent Lake

Early in this century, when men were men and white women were a rarity in this part of the Canadian Rockies, a feisty Philadelphia widow who spent her summers in the Rockies heard Stoney Indians speak of a mysterious lake.

The widow, Mary Shäffer—whose Quaker background emphasized equality between the sexes—resolved to find it. She set off in 1908 from what is now Lake Louise with 22 horses, six riders and a dog, Muggins.

The party searched for three weeks before discovering beautiful Maligne Lake. Schäffer, who named several of the peaks in this area after members of her party, thus became the first white woman to set eyes on the legendary lake. She returned for further explorations in 1911.

"There burst upon us that which all in our little company agreed was the finest view any of us had ever beheld in the Rockies," she wrote of her approach on the south side.

The successful expedition even had a romantic ending—Schäffer later married her guide, Billy Warren.

Opal Hills Loop

A hidden alpine valley

MAP 44

Highlight: Alpine meadows, distant views
Distance: 8 km (5 miles) loop
Time: 4 hours
Rating: Strenuous
Maximum Elevation: 1,985 m (6,512 ft)
Elevation Gain: 305 m (1,000 ft)
Footwear: Sturdy shoes or light hiking boots
Best Season: July to September

You round a corner and there, hidden from sight until the very end, is an open valley of lush alpine meadows, bright flowers and deep gullies high above Maligne Lake. All you have to do to reach this Shangri-la is...sweat. While no other trail in the stunning Maligne Lake area leads in a relatively short distance to the alpine, there is a price: The access trail is relentlessly steep.

Access: From the Jasper Information Centre, drive east to Hwy 16, then left to the Maligne Lake Road at km 4 (mile 2.4). Keep left after crossing the bridge and follow the road to Maligne Lake at km 48 (mile 30). The trail begins from the upper side of the upper parking lot.

Route: The trail descends slightly, connects with a path from the lake and leads through a meadow filled with kames.

The route climbs steeply through a lodgepole pine forest. The trail divisions you encounter are just routes made by hikers cutting across the switchbacks, not a recommended practice since it erodes the mountainside. The trail levels off slightly and passes a trail junction. Follow the sign and keep left, as this represents the easier ascent.

44. MALIGNE LAKE

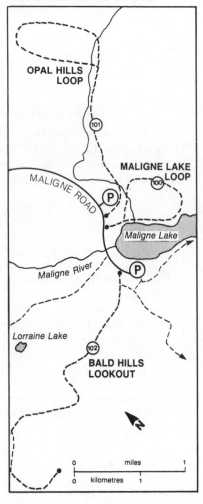

The climbing grows easier as the route edges along the hillside and the forest opens up into shrub meadows filled with wildflowers. Views begin to appear back across the valley to Bald Hills and the Maligne Range and you can just make out the end of Maligne Lake.

The best is yet to come as you go round a corner with the Bald Hills opening up before you, green at the

base and brown along the top of the ridge where the climate can't even support grass. Below, only a few scattered islands of Engelmann spruce and subalpine fir survive here and there. Only by growing together in clumps can these trees survive the wind and cold.

The hills are cut by deep gullies and to the right is Opal Peak, so named because of its pink patches. Up there, snow patches usually linger into August. The trail turns

right to wind back through this delightful valley, home of ground squirrels and marmots.

This rodent, the marmot, which weighs between 10 and 30 pounds, is related to the woodchuck and is easily spotted among the boulders with its grizzled back or gray hair. The highly social animal lives in colonies combed by tunnels among the boulders. It lives mainly on grasses. Grizzlies feed on them; but human encounters with grizzlies are fairly rare. Only a small number of grizzlies inhabit the Maligne Valley.

The trail leads through the valley, although you might consider climbing the low hills on the right for excellent views of Maligne Lake. This open country is an excellent place to spot wapiti and moose, or even an occasional wolverine, a solitary, frightening-looking member of the weasel family about the size of a bear cub and notorious as a vicious fighter. It eats almost everything, from roots and berries to small mammals and birds. But it will stay clear of hikers.

At the end of the valley, the trail crosses a gully and climbs the other side. Here an unofficial trail leads left further up the hills for those inclined to exploration. The main trail turns right along the top of the gully. Views open to Maligne Lake and its surrounding peaks. Down the lake, on the far side, the dominating peaks are Mt. Unwin and Mt. Charlton.

Closer to this end of the lake, Maligne Range is more gently rounded, hospitable enough to allow a fine backpacking trail—The Skyline—to traverse much of its length back towards Jasper.

Take the first descending trail leading back into the trees. The descent is steep until you reach the trail junction (sign) where you began the loop.

Bald Hills Lookout

Bald hills, beautiful views

MAP 44

Highlight: Panorama of Maligne Lake and peaks
Distance: 10 km (6 miles) return
Time: 3½ to 4 hours
Rating: Moderate
Maximum Elevation: 2,170 m (7,119 ft)
Elevation Gain: 490 m (1,607 ft)
Footwear: Walking or running shoes
Best Season: June to September

This fire road walk leads to what is probably the finest view of Maligne Lake. While views are limited on the way up, wildflowers fringe the path in summer. Pick a clear day and plan to ramble on the subalpine meadows. Bring warm clothing and take a canteen.

Access: Maligne Lake is 48 km (30 miles) from Jasper townsite. From the Jasper Information Centre, drive east to Hwy 16, turn left and proceed 4 km (2.5 miles) to the Maligne Road Bridge. Turn right across the bridge and continue up the valley to the lake. At Maligne, follow the main road over the Maligne River to a parking lot. The signed trailhead starts just right of the sign for the warden station.

Route: The road passes a few old buildings near the beginning, used by Parks Canda for their horses. The Bald Hills appear briefly above the tree tops.

The trail follows along a brook, winding gently upward, then, in the quirkish way of mountain routes, alternately levelling off and becoming steep.

To the northeast, the light-gray, limestone Queen Elizabeth Range rises against the skyline. The range is composed of Devonian limestone more than 300 million years old.

After about 30 minutes, views open to the east to reveal the Opal Hills. Mt. Unwin, named by Mary Schäffer for her second guide, soars dramatically on the right side of the lake at 3,270 metres (10,728 feet).

You could rest on a rock here but the panorama is more pleasing a little higher. You soon leave lower subalpine terrain for the peak-rimmed, open meadows of timberline. Watch for feather mosses, grouseberry and heathers.

Not far now. The fire road winds upwards, the views getting better all the time. The trail ends at a high viewpoint, once the site of a forest lookout tower. Now all that remains are two cement foundations. This can be a fine place, if the weather

Maligne Lake

cooperates, to picnic, explore alpine meadows above, or just enjoy the panorama.

Maligne Lake, 22.4 km (13.9 miles) long, is dazzling in the distance, a milky emerald-and-aqua gem surrounded by jagged peaks. Leah Peak is prominent across the lake on the left and Samson Peak on the right. The latter is named after the Stoney Indian whom Schäffer met in what is now Banff National Park. He drew a map showing her how to reach the lake. She became the first white woman to see it.

Morro Trail

WALK 103

Above the historic valley

MAP 45

Highlight: Viewpoints above river
Distance: 2 to 4 km (1.2 to 2.5 miles) return
Time: 45 to 90 minutes
Rating: Moderate
Maximum Elevation: 1,067 metres
Elevation Gain: 61 metres
Footwear: Walking shoes or light boots
Best Season: June to October

This short trail underneath gray, steep-walled Mt. Morro provides stunning views over the Athabasca River and the ranges beyond. You ascend to an excellent rocky viewpoint on a steep trail and continue around the base of Morro, a favorite "practice" mountain for climbers. You might even see mountain goats. Bighorn sheep are more common.

Access: The trail begins on Hwy 16, 21 km (13 miles) east of Jasper townsite just past the bridge over the Athabasca at the parking area for a cold sulphur spring, which is located at the base of the cliff.

Route: The trail climbs very steeply at first to get above a short cliff by the highway, enters mossy woods and switchbacks up the slope. It soon comes out into the open and

45. MORRO TRAIL

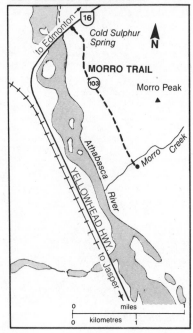

Mountain goats

These nimble mountaineers prefer a rugged, remote habitat. In Banff National Park, they can often be seen on Mount Coleman, on Parker Ridge, and on the rock face below the "big hill" onthe Sunwapta Pass section of the Icefields Parkway. In Jasper National Park, they are often viewed at the goat lookout between Sunwapta Falls and Athabasca Falls, and also by Mt. Morro on the Overlander Trail.

Skidproof soles and flexible toes enable them to climb steep mountain slopes and cross ledges separated by several metres of open space.

Frequently, visitors confuse mouuntain goats with female bighorn sheep. The difference is easy to define: If it's brown, it's a sheep. Goats sport luxurious white coats in winter; in summer they're a molting (white) mess.

Although billies are larger, the nannies are dominant in mountain goat circles—except in rut, the mating season. Females and their kids often stay together in summer. The billies are more solitary.

While fights are rare during rut, they can be vicious, with billies goring each other with their sharp horns. Indeed, males literally develop thick skin to help protect them in these battles.

the views down the broad Athabasca Valley are impressive. Across is the rock wall of the Palisades. The landscape, so close to the highway, seems wild and rugged here and you feel a sense of the tremendous forces that shaped the mountains.

Walkers might decide to go no further than the bare knoll overlooking the valley that provides outstanding views for such little elevation gain. The trail descends slightly intot he woods, then opens up again, crossing another rocky knoll above the railway and highway. The trees are stunted and twisted on these rocky ledges. The route continues mostly level. Most of the traffic along here is from climbers gaining access to the mountain's varied rock pitches.

Beginners can often be seen on the short rock pitch just above the river on this side of the bridge. They learn to climb the relatively smooth rock slab with the safety and assurance of a "top rope," a belay from a climber at the top of the cliff who takes in rope as his partner asccends. If the belay is done properly, the climber shouldn't fall more than a few inches, should he lose his footing. Don't try this without instruction. Climbing lessons can be arranged in Jasper.

The trail continues on above the valley to Morro Creek. For there, it's a rougher, less-frequented woodland walk along the south side of the Athabasca to the Sixth Bridge at Jasper, a route too long for this book.

Miette Hots Springs Trail

WALK 104

Source of the sulphur

MAP 46

Highlight: Sulphur hot springs
Distance: 400 m (1,300 ft) return
Time: 10 minutes
Rating: Easy
Maximum Elevation: 1,378 m (4,520 ft)
Elevation Gain: Negligible
Footwear: Anything
Best Season: May to October

The stroll takes only 10 minutes or so and you need not walk more than a few hundred metres. Yet the little trail behind the old Miette hot pool takes you up a narrow, interesting valley past unique rocks that look like huge gray sponges and are formed only in areas of hot springs. Beyond, the boardwalk crosses to where one of the hot springs issues from the side of the mountain. You can put your hand in the water and feel heat brought up from deep in the earth's crust.

Access: The Miette Hot Springs Road is 42 km (26 miles) east of Jasper on hwy 16. Drive the Miette Road for 17 km (10 miles) to the end. The road starts from the very end of the road along the creek past the old pool.

Route: Follow the boardwalk up Sulphur Creek, past large rocks of tufa (pronounced TOO-fa), composed mostly of calcium precipitates and found primarily at the outlets to hot springs. This spring water has a high calcium content, about 366 parts per million, while sulphur runs up to about 1,085 part per million,

enough to create a considerable odor.

Centuries ago, the outlet to these springs was much higher on the mountainside. As the hot, calcium-laden water cooled at the surface, it no longer could retain all the minerals. So the calcium was precipitated and built up as the solid, swiss-cheese sort of rock called tufa. Eventually some of this tufa broke off and avalanched down into the creek bed.

Ahead is the source of one of Miette's four hot springs, rushing from a hole in the rock wall. The sulphur smell of rotten eggs is almost overpowering but everybody lingers long enough to put their hand into the water to feel its temperature.

The average temperature of this water is 53° C (129° F), making the Miette hot springs among the warmest in Canada. They are still much cooler than at Yellowstone National Park where the springs approach 100° C (212° F)—which is boiling.

Sometimes, when earthquakes occurred elsewhere in North America, these hot springs have gushed black, murky water into the pools.

Trappers and fur traders ventured up this creek in the late 1800s and apparently built circular bath pools along here to relieve their tired muscles just as the visitor does today in the big pool. There are four springs with a flow of about

568,000 litres (125,000 gallons) a day. The trail continues up the clear, sparkling creek where trout can be taken, although the board-walk soon ends and most visitors will turn back.

46. MIETTE HOT SPRINGS

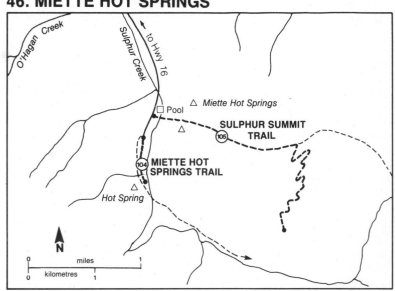

Sulphur Summit

WALK 105

The summit of adventure

MAP 46

Highlight: High, rocky summit
Distance: 9.5 km (5.9 miles) return
Time: 5 hours
Rating: Strenuous
Maximum Elevation: 2,062 m (6,765 ft)
Footwear: Light hiking boots
Best Season: July to September

From the barren summit of Sulphur Mountain, the wild peaks stretch back to the horizon like ocean waves—one of the highest and best views from a trail in Jasper National Park. Although the climb is steep and fairly long to the rounded top of Sulphur Ridge, the reward for your exertions is great indeed. A fine walk for experienced hikers.

The Sulphur Ridge hike is the outstanding route in the Miette area. The bare ridge, however, should be avoided in bad weather. Walkers also have the treat— especially welcome on a cold, windy day— of soaking in the hot springs at the bottom of the trail after their toil. A new pool and pool house has been constructed as part of a complete upgrading of Miette.

Access: The Miette Hot Springs

Road is 42 km (26 miles) east of Jasper on Hwy 16. Drive the Miette Road for 16 km (10 miles) to the end. The trail starts on an old road behind the new hot springs pool.

Route: The road enters the trees and climbs gradually, passing a horse trail on the left. The trail steepens and views open up to Capitol Mt. on the Miette Range west of the hot springs. Ahead to the left are the steep rock slabs of an unnamed ridge, while the less dramatic Sulphur Ridge rises on the right.

At 2.4 km (1.5 miles), turn right at a junction. The trail straight ahead follows the Fiddle River for 8 km (5 miles) to Mystery Lake. To the right, the Sulphur Mountain trail switchbacks steeply up the ridge. The views improve as you climb higher into the subalpine zone through stunted firs and Engelmann spruce, into a world of steep rock and scree. The red squirrel thrives among these trees, harvesting spruce cones all day long, storing thousands of green ones underground. With that supply to sustain him, he's active all winter, despite the rough conditions.

What appear to be trails high on the opposite side of the valley are actually animal paths. This is a good area for spotting bighorn sheep.

The trail levels off briefly in a col that offers the trees—and hikers—protection from the wind and passes a grassy clearing. The trail then climbs the steep ridge to the right. Now you can begin to see over the other side to the steep, remote Fiddle River Valley where few hikers ever venture. You pass the treeline and part way up the ridge come across a large white quartz rock, looking like an imposing tombstone. This is a glacial erratic, carried here long ago by the ice and deposited far from its place of origin.

The trail climbs steeply to the cairn marking the top of the ridge, a few steps from the bare, rocky Sulphur Summit. Views are spectacular over to Utopia Mountain to the south and to the craggy tops of Ashlar Ridge above the Miette access road.

This is the true alpine zone. Notice how almost all the vegetation in this zone of high winds and loose rocks has anchored itself in cracks or in the shelter of boulders. An exception is the campion moss. It has such a low profile and wide base that it can hold on where other plants are blown away.

Up here, the growing seasons for plants may be less than 60 days a year and frost may descend any day of the summer. Do plan to spend the night some place warmer.

15 Kananaskis Country and Peter Lougheed Provincial Park
Walks and Strolls

Upper Kananaskis Lake

Hiking without climbing

MAP 47

Highlight: Mountain lake circuit
Distance: 15.6 km (9.6 miles) circuit
Time: 5 hours
Rating: Strenuous
Elevation gain: Negligible
Footwear: Running shoes
Best season: June through September

Access: In Peter Lougheed Provincial Park, drive the Kananaskis Lakes Trail to the end—the North Interlakes parking lot.

Route: The circuit of Upper Kananaskis Lake, although fairly long, is full of variety and you should never get tired of the views over the water to striking peaks such as Mt. Indefatigible. Hikers only out for a short jaunt might want to turn back at the Upper Lake campground.

Follow the signs for Three Isle Lake-Upper Lake Trail across the barrier at the end of the lake. In 1.1 km, you turn left and descend slightly to stay on the Upper Lakes Trail, a softly-carpeted path near the shoreline. There are good spots for picnics among the driftwood on the shore.

The Trail soon enters a boulder field under the crumbling cliffs at Mt. Indefatigible and climbs gradually to the cutoff at km 3.8 for a well-situated campground on a point.

The main trail crosses Upper Kananaskis River by a mossy fall. Now a narrow, forested path, it ascends out of sight of the lake, then slowly works its way back to the shoreline. From here on, the path stays close to the water and views are stunning.

At Upper Lakes Parking lot, hikers can save time by walking back to North Interlakes on the road. The longer but more scenic option is to continue for another 3.8 km, again close to the lakeshore, for a complete and rewarding circuit.

47. UPPER KANANASKIS LAKE

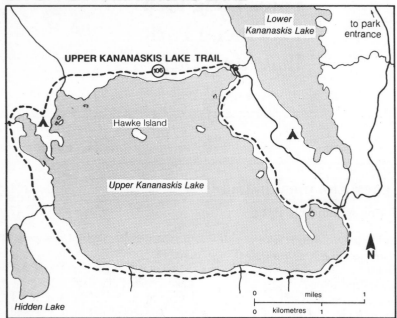

Elk Pass

WALK 107

Hike a ski route

MAP 48

Highlight: Gentle ascent above Kananaskis Valley
Distance: 14 km (8.6 miles) return
Time: 6 hours
Rating: Strenuous
Maximum elevation: 1,920 metres (6,300 feet)
Elevation gain: 220 metres (721 feet)
Footwear: Running shoes

Best season: June through September

The Elk Pass Trail is better known as perhaps the most popular of the designated winter ski routes in Peter Lougheed Provincial Park. In summer, it becomes an ordinary and occasionally tedious fire road. But the route leads on gentle grade through gorgeous country, provides excellent views back over the Kananaskis Lakes to rugged mountains beyond. For the overnight hiker, the trail leads over an easy pass into British Columbia

48. ELK PASS

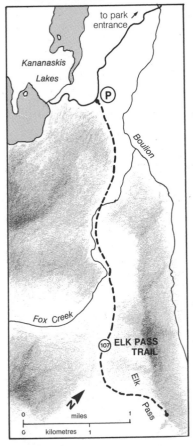

where there is good camping in the relatively-inaccessible Elk Lakes Provincial Park.

Access: In Peter Lougheed Provincial Park, drive the Kananaskis Lakes Trail to the Elk Pass parking lot.

Route: The trail climbs fairly steeply at first. There are good views at the top of the slope down the powder-line cut. The way grows more gentle and the scenery wilder after the route begins to follow Fox Creek through pleasant meadows filled with wildflowers.

(The Hydroline-Lookout Trail which leads left after a bridge is a good option, although steeper. This sidetrail leads in 5.2 km to a fire lookout and outstanding views of the valley. Hikers who want to make a long semi-loop journey can continue on the trail past the lookout, descending to the Pocaterra Trail. Turn left on Pocaterra, then left again onto Whiskey Jack only 0.2 km ahead. Whiskey Jack descends in 4.5 km to Boulton parking area. Total distance 13.3 km.)

Back on the main trail, the Elk Pass route curves through mixed meadows and woodlands, finally climbing above the creek to the gentle pass and the provincial boundary. The trail continues to excellent backcountry campsites near Elk River and just beyond Elk Lakes in about 4 km.

49. BURSTALL LAKES

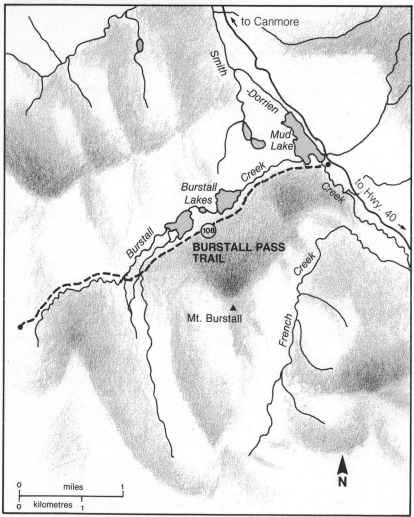

Burstall Pass

WALK 108

Hike a ski route

MAP 49

Highlight: Classic hike to lakes and the alpine
Distance: 15 km (9.3 miles) return
Time: 8 hours
Rating: Strenuous
Maximum elevation: 2,346 metres (7,700 feet)
Elevation gain: 460 metres (1,509 feet)
Footwear: Water-resistant hiking boots
Best season: July through September

Access: From the Kananaskis Lakes Trail (road) in Peter Lougheed Provincial Park, turn north on the Smith-Dorrien Highway and drive 20 km to the Burstall Pass parking area.

Route: Although the first half of the trail is a routine walk on an old logging road, the Burstall Pass Trail does lead in a relatively short distance to splendid alpine terrain. For fishermen and those seeking a shorter hike, the trail passes three pleasant Burstall Lakes in only 3 km.

Be warned that extensive mud flats must be crossed beyond the last lake. Into this big area drains all the water from Robertson Glacier as well as Burstall Pass. Although a few elevated walkways and bridges have been constructed, the hiker can expect wet feet—or even considerable wading in icy water—for part of the summer.

Beyond the flats, the trail climbs steeply up the headwall to the pass which affords splendid views down into the Spray Valley in Banff National Park and back across to craggy Mt. Birdwood.

On a fine day, hikers should plan to leave early enough to give themselves time to explore the alpine terrain.

Short Strolls in Peter Lougheed Provincial Park and Kananaskis Country

1982 Canadian Mount Everest Expedition Trail

Distance: 2.3 km (1.3 miles) loop
Time: 1 hour or more

Access: White Spruce day use area near Upper Kananaskis Lake in Peter Lougheed Provincial Park.

Route: No, it doesn't feel like a Everest expedition to follow this rewarding trail. It was named to commemorate the first Everest ascent by a Canadian team. The trail has signs describing the expedition and leads to a viewing platform on the narrow peninsula between Lower and Upper Kananaskis lakes.

King Creek Trail

Distance: 1.6 km (1 mile) return
Time: 30 minutes

Access: Highway 40 opposite entrance turnoff for Kananaskis Lakes Trail (road).

Route: King Creek has formed a steep-walled canyon in the limestone between the long side ridges of Mt. Wintour to the south and Mt. Hopod to the north. An almost level trail which is well-maintained leads on bridges and walkways for a short distance through the canyon.

Ptarmigan Cirque

Distance: 4.2 km return
Time: 2 hours

Access: Highway 40 in Highwood Pass, about 17 km south of the north winter gates.

Route: Highwood Pass is one of the best places in Alberta for easy, high-level hiking. The pass is the highest reached by a paved road in Canada. Trails begin in extraordinary, delicate sub-alpine terrain.

The short Rock Glacier stroll and the Highwood Meadows walk (across the road from Ptarmigan Cirque Trail) are well-worth a short visit.

Ptarmigan Trail climbs steeply to a trail junction. Keep left as the trail loops up towards treeline. The alpine meadow is glorious with wildflowers among the huge boulders under Mt. Rae. An interpretive booklet is available.

16 Waterton Lakes National Park
Walks and Strolls

Lower Bertha Falls

WALK 109

Tiptoe to tranquility

MAP 50

Highlight: Scenic stroll to waterfall
Distance: 5.8 km (3.6 miles) return
Time: 2 hours
Rating: Moderate
Maximum elevation: 1,479 m (4,825 ft)
Elevation gain: 200 m (656 ft)
Footwear: Running shoes
Best season: June to September

The shady route to Lower Bertha Falls is one of the most popular short hikes in the park—and with good reason. It offers grand views down Waterton Lake and across the townsite to the prairies beyond. In its last stretch, the trail ascends gradually beside a vigorous brook bubbling over rocky cascades. Ambitious hikers can travel beyond the lower falls, ascending the subalpine zone into a steep-walled cirque enclosing Bertha Lake.

Access: In Waterton townsite, head south on Evergreen Avenue to Cameron Falls. Cross Cameron Creek and head south on the dead-end road. The trail begins from a small parking area shortly before the turn-around on this dead-end street.

Route: The trail ascends gradually through an aspen forest which soon opens up to offer views across Waterton Lake. Note the tongue of milky water extending out into the lake from Cameron Creek at the campground. The light color is rock flour or glacial silt, ground up by the glaciers above Cameron Lake. The trees make a gradual transition to the Montane forest of lodgepole pine. Southwards lie deep mountains, to the east beyond the

50. ALDERSON LAKE AREA

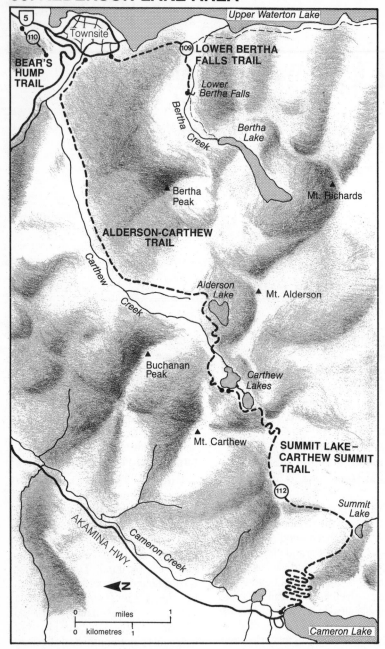

Upper Waterton Lake

5
110
Townsite

109 LOWER BERTHA
FALLS TRAIL

**BEAR'S
HUMP
TRAIL**

Lower
Bertha Falls

Bertha
Lake

Bertha
Creek

Bertha
Peak

Mt. Richards

**ALDERSON-CARTHEW
TRAIL**

Carthew
Creek

Alderson
Lake

Mt. Alderson

Buchanan
Peak

Carthew
Lakes

Mt. Carthew

**SUMMIT LAKE –
CARTHEW SUMMIT
TRAIL**

112

Summit
Lake

AKAMINA HWY.

Cameron Creek

miles
0   1

kilometres
0   1

Cameron Lake

Prince of Wales Hotel is bare, rolling prairie.

A short sidetrail leads to a rocky outcrop with even better views down the lake. Here is the hardy, scrub-like limber pine found only in isolated patches in the park. You can confirm its identity by the needles—clusters of five, which are stiff, slightly curved and from 1 1/2 to 3 1/2 inches long.

Hikers seeking only a short stroll might want to turn back here.

The main trail passes the turnoff for the U.S. border and Boundary Bay, reached in 4.3 km. The main route turns into the steep-walled Bertha Valley and descends towards the creek through groves of Douglas Fir.

The ascent is gradual, past rock ledges and small cascades, and you soon reach Lower Bertha Falls just above a small bridge. While more a long cascade than a waterfall, it is still very pretty. Just below is a picnic table, bench and outhouse.

Hikers with more time and energy can continue 2.8 km further from the falls to Bertha Lake. The trail quickly steepens and climbs to the upper floor of the valley, passing from the montane to the subalpine zone. The switchbacks are relentless through the spruce, fir and low alder as you attain the upper floor of the hanging valley. The creek plunges over the lip, to form Upper Bertha Falls.

Bertha Lake is beautifully set against a glacier-curved cirque. Much of the lakeshore is scoured by avalanches in winter. The trail descends to the lake and the right branch leads to a small but nicely situated backcountry campground in about .6 km. A rough trail circles the lake, ideal for fishermen after rainbow trout . . . or anyone seeking tranquillity.

Bear's Hump

WALK 110

Steep climb, stunning view

MAP 50

Distance: 2 km (1.2 miles) return
Time: 1 1/2 hours
Rating: Strenuous
Maximum elevation: 1,560 m (5,118 ft)
Elevation gain: 210 m (689 ft)
Footwear: Running shoes
Best season: June to September

In less than half an hour up the limestone-dolomite cliffs of Bear's Hump, you can reach one of the most glorious panoramas in a park full of glorious panoramas. The summit makes a breathtaking picnic stop on a sunny day. You could spend an afternoon sketching the view below. The trail is steep—and worth every step.

Access: The trail begins behind the Park Information Centre just east of Waterton townsite.

Route: The trail leads through an aspen grove, then heads steeply up through a forest of lodgepole pine and Douglas fir. You'll catch a few glimpses of Emerald Bay and further on, the Prince of Wales Hotel and the prairies stretching to the east. Views are limited until the top.

The last portion is particularly strenuous. At the top, sweeping views extend across the townsite, lake and prairies. (Note that condi-

tions can be exceedingly windy at the top.)

Do refrain from tossing rocks off the top. Climbers may be using the cliffs below.

Summit Lake-Carthew Summit   WALK 111

Beargrass, mule deer and more   MAP 51

Highlights: Close-up look at lush vegetation in an unusually moist area
Distance: 8 km (5 miles) return
Time: 4 hours return
Rating: Moderate
Maximum elevation: 1,906 m (6,253 ft)
Elevation gain: 250 m (820 ft)
Footwear: Light hiking boots
Best season: Late June to October

You begin at one lovely lake and hike to an equally lovely and more secluded one, climbing steadily most of the way. On the ascent, you pass through a forest which includes 500-year-old spruce. If you tread quietly, you just might see mule deer watering at the lake.

Access: Drive 15.5 km to the end of the Akamina Parkway. The trail begins along the south shore of the lake, just left of the boat rental facilities.

Route: You start at Cameron Lake, which is bisected by the Canada-U.S. border. Grizzlies have been seen—although not often—on the flanks of imposing Mt. Custer at the far end of the lake.

You soon begin to climb steadily. Glimpses open up of the lake and

valley below, although for most of the way, you are enshrouded in a green, damp, ferny forest. The bands of red trees you may see are the result of pine-beetle infestation.

The weather at Cameron Lake is warmed by moist air from nearby mountains, which has made the area a sanctuary for some types of plants and animals usually found further west. Varied thrush and Steller's jay, uncommon in any other parts of the park, are often seen around here.

The trail becomes more level about two-thirds of the way up, and the trees more stunted. Beargrass, which is actually a kind of lily, grows to great heights in this area in summer months. Bears, you'll probably be glad to know, have no particular attraction to it, despite the name.

There's a slight descent to the spruce-fringed lake, a wonderful place to repose. The mountain which dominates across the lake is Chapman Peak in the U.S., at 2,866 metres. Return the same way.

Those who are still energetic might enjoy going on to Carthew Summit. Don't attempt this climb above treeline if the weather is bad. The open ridge can be hazardous.

From Summit Lake, the trail quickly moves out into the open and begins to switchback up above the

51. ROWE LAKES

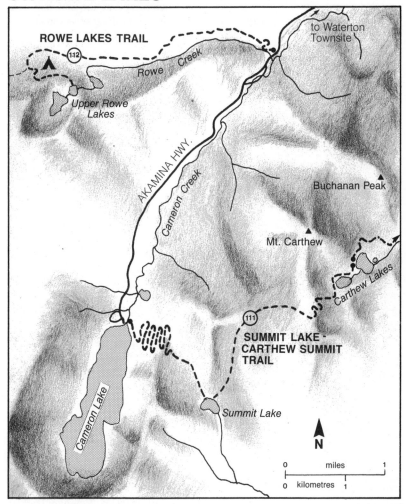

stunted fir trees, providing fine vistas south into the tiny subalpine lakes of northern Glacier National Park and the imposing peaks beyond. The trail crests the windswept ridge and the vistas in the other direction are equally impressive.

Below are the two tear-drops of Carthew Lakes surrounded by red scree. In the far distance, the mountains drop away into open prairie.

You can make out the trail descending steeply to the lakes. This route is for strong hikers willing to put in a long day. It is a total of 19 km from

Cameron Lake to the trail's end at Waterton townsite. The distance to the townsite from Carthew Summit is a hefty 11.1 km.

The upper section of the route by the lakes (including Alderson Lake) is fascinating but the last half is a routine march along a tree-lined path with few views.

Rowe Lakes

WALK 112

Invitation to subalpine wandering

MAP 51

Highlight: Sub-alpine lakes and meadows
Distance: 12.4 km (7.7 miles) return
Time: 6 hours
Rating: Strenuous
Maximum elevation: 2,200 m (7,217 ft)
Elevation gain: 600 m (1,968 ft)
Footwear: Hiking boots
Best season: Late June to September

Set under cliffs amid snow patches that usually linger through the summer, green, larch-rimmed Rowe Lakes seem a magical place. While it takes considerable effort to get there, hikers who make an early start may find the surrounding flower-filled meadows and knolls delightful to explore.

Access: From Waterton townsite, drive west up Cameron Lake Road. At about km 10 (2 km past Oil City historic site) is a parking area for Rowe Lakes trail on the right side of the road.

Route: The trail heads gently up the north side of Rowe Creek through lodgepole pine under the steep gray face of Mt. Lineham, passing outcrops of Waterton's characteristic red rock. The pines soon give way to a denser forest of fir and spruce. The soft-carpeted path continues on a gentle grade as the valley narrows and you begin to cross slide areas bright with fireweed amd astors for much of the summer.

A half-kilometre sidetrail leads across the stream to Lower Rowe Lake, a pleasant though unspectacular green pond set under cliffs. In spring and early summer, a 150-metre waterfall descends from the hanging valley above, draining Upper Rowe lakes.

The main trail ascends again beside the creek and the valley gradually opens up into a grassy basin between Mt. Lineham (right) and Mt. Rowe (left). Above are the scree-covered heights of bare Lineham Ridge and you can make out the Tamarack Trail zig-zagging up to it. At km 5, you reach a beautifully-situated campground in a flower-filled meadow under the red scree slopes. Some hikers will be content to go no further.

On the other side of a meadow,

the Tamarack Trail branches right to begin the ardous switchback up Lineham Ridge.

This is a more demanding, more rewarding option for the energetic hiker because the views from the top, far above treeline, are among the most outstanding in the park. The price is a 3.5-km (one-way) grind up one of the most relentlessly steep trails in Waterton.

The easier and shorter (1.2 km) trail to Upper Rowe Lakes heads off left and begins a steep ascent out of the amphitheatre. Small Engelmann spruce and alpine fir grow sparsely among the rocks. Views are outstanding. Near the top of the ridge, you enter the zone of the light-green alpine larch. Their clusters of needles look like small shaving brushes.

The trail finally levels off, then descends slightly through a fine open forest to meadows and the lake itself. It's a magical place on a fine day. (Don't bother to bring your fishing gear, however. There are usually no fish.) Beaches of flat stones surround the vivid green waters set under cliffs and snow slopes, an invitation to subalpine wandering.

52. CRANDELL LAKE

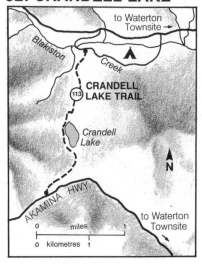

Crandell Campground to Lake Crandell   WALK 113

An undemanding lake   MAP 52

Highlights: Pretty lake set against rocky outcroppings
Distance: 5 km (3.1 km return)
Time: 45 minutes one way
Rating: Moderate
Footwear: Running shoes
Best season: June to September

A gentle trail leads up from Crandell Campground to Crandell Lake, a good family outing, after-dinner leg-stretcher or even a leisurely destination for backpackers. Camping is allowed at Crandell Lake (backcountry permit required).

Some hikers may want to hike right across to the Akamina Parkway if they can get someone to pick them up on the other side.

Access: Start by Crandell Mountain Campground on the Red Rock Parkway.

Red Rock Canyon

Route: The trail begins near the northwest end of the campground. You cross a log bridge and then begin a gentle climb. Views of Mt. Galwey dominate the east horizon. The angle increases before long, and you reach an area of rocky outcroppings and more stunted alpine growth.

Watch for a sign pointing left to Crandell Lake, which you will probably reach before you know it. This is a lovely spot for lingering.

Hikers who have arranged for transportation on the other end can continue past the lake for only .8 km further on a gradual descent to the Akamina Parkway, 7 km west of Waterton townsite. A hiker's shuttle is available through Mountain Sunset Tours in the Tamarack Mall, (403) 859-2612.

Red Rock Canyon Loop

WALK 114

A walk in a rainbow canyon

MAP 53

Highlights: Water-carved canyon
Distance: 0.7 km (0.3 miles)
Time: 20 minutes
Rating: Easy
Footwear: Walking or running shoes
Best season: June to October

The walk is short, the red-hued canyon gorgeous and you're almost guaranteed to come nose to nose with wildlife. You'll also receive an instant geological education. If the day is warm, explore Blakiston Falls as well, then picnic overlooking Blakiston Valley.

Access: Drive 14 km to the end of the Red Rock Canyon road. The surprises can begin right at the Red Rock Canyon parking lot, one of the surest places in Waterton to spot wildlife. Deer and bighorn sheep are frequently seen.

Route: An asphalt path leads past an interpretive display and to the beginning of the trail. The horn of Anderson Peak, at 2,683 metres, dominates the skyline. Downstream is the floodplain of Blakiston Creek,

which has rearranged gravel and glacial silts in the Blakiston Valley for thousands of years.

The canyon ahead is not large, but its rose, red and pink hues make up in beauty what it lacks in size. The canyon began as mud deposited in an

53. BLAKISTON CREEK

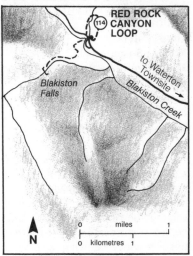

ancient, shallow sea. As parts of the sea dried up, exposure oxidized the iron, forming a red mineral called hematite. Unexposed layers formed green and white bands, causing a layer-cake effect in parts of the canyon. Take a moment to peer at the ancient ripple marks, caused by slow currents and waves in that ancient, shallow sea.

Head uphill to the wooden bridge at the deeper part of the canyon, taking a good look at the varied ribbons of color in the canyon wall. It took 7,000 to 10,000 years for water to carve this small gorge, and the process is continuing. Interpretive signs explain how erosion wears the canyon down by the thickness of a nickel or two a year.

Note that archaeological sites dating back 8,000 years have been found in Red Rock Canyon, which appears to have been used as a seasonal campsite by prehistoric natives. An ancient corridor to South Kootenay Pass existed along the Blakiston Creek.

Continue down on the other side of the canyon.

Hikers with a little more time and energy could continue to walk southwards from the canyon on the wide, easy trail to South Kootenay Pass. It climbs gradually through lodgepole pines and in 15 minutes or so, you reach a good viewpoint overlooking Blakiston Falls.

The falls are especially impressive in spring and early summer. The water is forced through a cleft and down into a clear pool.

Crypt Lake Trail

WALK 115

A walk in a million

MAP 54

Highlight: Extraordinary, variety-filled hike
Distance: 17.2 km (10.6 miles) return
Time: Full day
Rating: Strenuous
Maximum elevation: 1,950 m (6,400 ft)
Elevation gain: 670 m (2,200 ft)
Footwear: Hiking boots
Best season: July to September

The Crypt Lake Trail is simply among the most unusual, interesting and spectacular in Canada. Hikers can visit two countries. The trailhead can only be reached by boat. And, not least, one section of the route is underground—following a natural tunnel through the limestone into steep-walled Crypt Basin. The price for this variety is a very steep, long and often hot ascent and a fair degree of vertical exposure on the high slopes, although there are ladders and cables for help and security.

Access: At the Marina in Waterton townsite, make arrangements for a motorboat charter for the short trip down the lake to Crypt Landing. Get an early start. Pickup and delivery by boat is really the only practical way to get there for day hikers. You'll need to set a time for the boat to pick you up. Allow plenty of extra time.

Route: Crypt Landing is a pleasant place to linger whether you

54. CRYPT LAKE

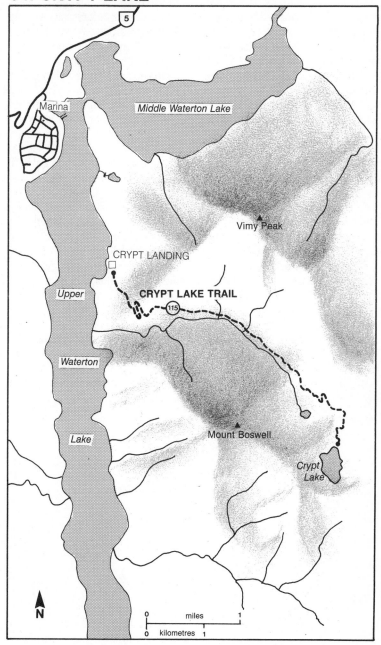

are waiting for your boat ride or camping overnight. The campground is right by the beach in a cove.

The trail initially heads off south along the lake through dense forest of spruce and fir and begins a few switchbacks away from the water. A short side trail leads to Hell Roaring Falls, beautifully set in a canyon of copper-colored rock, although the falls itself really only roars in spring and early summer. The main trail continues up the valley past a good viewpoint for Twin Falls. The trees gradually open after Burnt Rock Falls to provide grand vistas. This protected valley can be very hot when the sun is shining directly into it. Bring lots of water.

The trail leads past a swampy lower lake and heads up on a more strenuous set of switchbacks, finally levelling off in subalpine terrain and reaching the popular campground. Cross the creek by jumping from stone to stone and head up a steep talus slope. At the top, a short ladder takes you up the rock wall to the tunnel entrance. The passageway is about 12 metres long and low enough so that you'll have to crawl along one section. Not for the claustrophobic.

At the end of the tunnel, the route heads up and along a rather exposed rock wall, although a sturdy cable anchored to the rock provides reassurance. The route soon levels off. Just beyond, a creek emerges from the limestone after a subterranean passage from Crypt Lake. The water drops over the edge to create the 175-metre Crypt Falls.

Crypt Lake itself is just over the top of the ridge and is worth all the sweating and steep places you traversed to get here. The deep green lake is set in a spectacular cirque. Snowfields may linger here all summer and icebergs usually dot the lake. The far end of the lake is on the U.S. border. You can walk down to it on a rough trail. The slopes above the lake can be a good place to spot mountain goats. By this time, you probably feel like one yourself.

Travel Information

Province of Alberta

Travel Alberta
Box 2500, Edmonton, Alberta T5J O2Z

Toll-free information available on travel conditions, campgrounds, accommodation, ski reports, attractions and special events. Within Alberta: 1-800-222-6501. In Edmonton only: 427-4321. From British Columbia: 112-800-661-8888; from Saskatchewan; urban: 1-800-661-8888; rural: 112-800-661-8888. From all other provinces, including the Northwest Territories and the Yukon: 1-800-661-8888.

An Alberta Accommodation Guide, Touring Guide and Adventure Guide are available free of charge upon request.

Parks Canada

Information on Canada's Rocky Mountain national parks is available from:

Information Service
Parks Canada
220-4th Ave. S.E.
Calgary, Alberta T2P 3H8

Banff National Park

The Superintendent
Banff National Park
Box 900
Banff, Alberta T0L 0C0
(403) 762-3324

Banff/Lake Louise Chamber of Commerce
Box 1298
Banff, Alberta T0L 0C0
(403) 762-4646/762-3777

Banff Information Centre
224 Banff Ave.
(403) 762-4256

Banff Warden Office: Situated between townsite and highway interchange; open 24 hours. (403) 762-4506.

Lake Louise Information Centre. (403) 522-3833

Lake Louise Warden Office;
Visitor Centre, Lake
Louise; (403) 522-3866.

Jasper National Park

The Superintendent
Jasper National Park
Box 10
Jasper, Alberta T0E 1E0
(403) 582-6161

Jasper Park Chamber of
Comerce
Box 98
Jasper, Alberta T0E 1E0
(403) 852-3858

Jasper Information Centre
Connaught Drive,
Jasper, Alberta
(403) 852-6176

Warden Office: Turn off the
Maligne Road, 8 km east of
Jasper townsite, near
the Sixth Bridge.
(403) 852-6156

Kananaskis Country

Kananaskis Country Office
Suite 412
1011 Glenmore Trail S.W.
Calgary, Alberta T2V 4R6
(403) 297-3362

Kootenay National Park

The Superintendent
Kootenay National Park
Box 220
Radium Hot Springs, B.C.
V0A 1M0
(604) 347-9615

Waterton Lakes National Park

The Superintendent
Waterton Lakes National
Park
Waterton, Alberta
T0K 2M0
(403) 859-2262

Waterton Information
Bureau
Waterton Townsite
(403) 852-2445

Yoho National Park

The Superintendent
Yoho National Park
Box 99
Field, B.C.
(604) 343-6324

Hostels

The Alberta Hostelling Association operates a chain of hostels along the Icefield Parkway between Banff and Jasper. Open to all; reduced overnight fees available through annual membership. Reservations advised in summer and holiday weekends; essential for groups.

Southern Alberta Hostelling
Association
1414 Kensington Road N.W.
Calgary, Alberta T2N 3P9
(403) 283-5551
Administration office, hostel shop, membership, reservations, hostel information, brochure available.

Northern Alberta District
10926 88th Ave.
Edmonton, Alberta T6E 0Z1
(403) 439-3089

Administration office, hostel shop, membership, reservations, hostel information, brochure available.

Ribbon Creek Hostel
(403) 591-7333

24 km south of Hwy 1 along Kananaskis Rd. (Hwy 40). Accommodates 40, family rooms available. Closed Tuesday in winter. For reservations call S.A.H.A. office: (403) 283-5551

Banff International Hostel
(403) 762-4122

3 km from Banff townsite on Tunnel Mountain Rd., new building, accommodates 154 persons, family rooms available, cafeteria, cooking and laundry, accessible to the disabled. For reservations call or write: P.O. Box 1358, Banff, Alberta T0L 0C0.

Spray River Hostel

3.5 km south of Banff Springs Hotel on Spray River Fire Road. Accommodates 47 persons, meals, groceries, outdoor shower, bicycle and cross-country ski rentals. Closed Wednesday in winter.

Castle Mountain Hostel
(403) 762-2367

On Hwy 1A, 1.5 km east of Junction of Hwys 1 and 93, newly renovated. Meals and groceries available. Closed Wednesday in winter.

Corral Creek Hostel

6.6 km east of Lake Louise on Hwy 93. Accommodates 50 persons, closed Monday in winter.

Mosquito Creek Hostel

26 km north of Lake Louise on Hwy 93. Newly renovated. Accommodates 38 people, wood-heated sauna available. Family cabin with self-contained kitchen and common area. Closed Tuesday in winter.

Rampart Creek Hostel

On Hwy 93, 20 km north of Junction with Hwy 11. Accommodates 30 persons, wood-heated sauna available. Closed Wednesday in winter.

Hilda Creek Hostel

8l5 km south of Columbia Icefield Centre on Hwy 93. Accommodates 19 persons, meals and limited groceries. Closed Thursday in winter.

Beauty Creek Hostel

86.5 km south of Jasper townsite on Hwy 93A. Accommodates 20. Closed Thursday and from mid-September to April 30.

Athabasca Falls Hostel

32 km south of Jasper townsite on Hwy 93A. Accommodates 40. Closed Tuesday nights.

Mt. Edith Cavell Hostel

13 km off Hwy 93A along steep Mt. Edith Cavell Rd. Accommodates 30. Winter access by cross-country skiing.

Whistlers Mountain Hostel

7 km south of Jasper townsite on Whistler Mtn. Rd. Accommodates 50.

Maligne Canyon Hostel

15 km east of Jasper townsite on Maligne Lake Rd. Accommodates 24, family rooms available. Closed Wednesday nights.

The Authors

John Dodd and Gail Helgalson have hiked, bicycled, backpacked, canoed, skiied, kayaked, climbed, jogged and sailed in the Canadian Rockies for more than a decade. Both former outdoors columnists for *The Edmonton Journal*, they are also the authors of *Bicycle Alberta* and *The Canadian Rockies Bicycling Guide*. A husband-and-wife team, they have written about the outdoors for a variety of publications, including *Outside*, *Nature Canada* and *Bicycling*. Gail, is also author of *The First Albertans: An Archaeological Search*. Both are full-time freelance writers and editors based in Edmonton, Alberta.

Legend for Maps

Highway	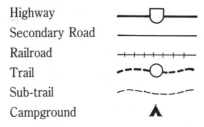
Secondary Road	
Railroad	
Trail	
Sub-trail	
Campground	

Photo Credits

Alberta Photograph Library
British Columbia Ministry of Tourism, Recreation and Culture
Parks Canada
Provincial Archives of Alberta
Travel Alberta
Eric Kuhn
S. Kratochvil
John Dodd
Gail Helgason

List of Maps

Index

Jasper-Pyramid Lake Trail WALK 93

A bench above the valley MAP 39

Highlight: Views over Athabasca Valley
Distance: 7.2 km (4.5 miles) one way
Time: 3 hours
Rating: Moderate
Maximum elevation: 1,320 m (4,330 ft)
Elevation gain: 300 m (984 ft)
Footwear: Sturdy shoes or light hiking boots
Best season: May to October

Among all the tangled networks of trails on the wooded bench behind Jasper townsite, this is a favorite. Some of the bench trails, while handy to Jasper, are little more than secluded woodland routes with few views to speak of, except for a pleasant pond at the end. But the Pyramid trail begins right from the townsite and follows the edge of the

bench providing fine views across the Athabasca Valley and down to the townsite. It leads through semi-open meadows and up a rocky ridge, ending at one of the most beautiful picnic areas in Jasper—on an island.

Hikers planning on walking all the way to Pyramid Lake, could make arrangements for a ride back to Jasper townsite. The return trip otherwise is long and tiring. A bicycle secured in the woods at the end of the Pyramid Lake Road would make for a nearly effortless return. Or get a ride to the end of the road and do the route in reverse.

Access: From the Parks Information Centre in Jasper, drive one block east to Cedar, turn left and keep straight as Cedar turns into Pyramid Ave. At Pyramid Lake Road on the upper edge of town, turn left and park opposite the recreation centre.

The trail leaves where the steep slope begins.

Route: The trail, marked No. 2, edges gradually up the side of the steep hill, climbing above the town. As close as you are to Jasper, this can be an excellent place to see deer, elk and other game. Views across the valley to Mt. Hardisty and east to the Colin range improve as you climb the needle-covered path.

The trail enters the woods, levels off and in 1.8 km reaches the Pyramid Lake Road at a parking area. This is a good alternate place to begin the route. The trail resumes on the other side, crosses Cottonwood Creek on a footbridge and parallels the Pyramid Lake Road for a while. This is a good area to spot such birds as the northern waterthrush, Wilson's warbler and the rufus hummingbird.

The trail, here an old road churned up by horses, gradually veers right. At a junction, take Trail No. 2. It heads slightly downhill and then begins to ascend a ridge, climbing another steep grassy hill. Views open up over the whole valley and townsite. Across is rounded Signal Mountain where the old road to a fire lookout is now being "rehabilitated" back to nature. Behind it is the more craggy Tekarra Mountain, named after an early Indian guide. West is The Whistlers with its aerial tramway.

The route continues along the edge of the bench through beautiful open forest and meadow, offering excellent picnic spots. Ancient Douglas firs guard the path, survivors of fires which devastated lesser trees. Now you can see right down the Athabasca Valley and up to the snowy heights of Mt. Edith Cavell, the Fujiyama of the Jasper area.

Close at hand, the somewhat confusing terrain in the townsite area comes into focus: Lac Beauvert with Jasper Park Lodge at one end. To the left are Lakes Annette and Edith and beyond them the Maligne Valley and the steep Colin Range. The dry, open montane forest below and on the bench constitutes an important winter range for deer, elk and moose. The snow cover is lighter than in the higher subalpine forest. Its easier for grazing animals to dig through the snow for grass and plants. The climate is less severe.

The trail turns left to skirt a ravine that cuts into the bench, then resumes on the other side without loss of elevation. Eventually, it turns left and plunges into the trees again, reaching a junction. Trail No. 2 straight ahead will take you more directly back to the Pyramid Lake Road.

Try 2A, if you have time. It leads right, and into the open again, then begins to climb a rocky ridge to the left. The way ahead is open, providing views over the wooded bench. At the top is a good viewpoint for Pyramid and Patricia lakes, the latter shaped somewhat like a human foot. Behind is the distinctive quartz sandstone peak of Pyramid Mountain with its microwave tower.

If you are turning back to Jasper, this is the place. For those going on to Pyramid Lake, the trail descends steeply, ending at the Pyramid lookout fire road. Turn left on the fire road and in a few metres you come to the parking area at the end of the Pyramid Lake Road. Below the parking area is the bridge to Pyramid Island.

Fishing

Fishermen who hike or mountain walkers who fish may have a considerable advantage. So many fishermen never venture far from the road, never fish lakes or streams that lack vehicle access. Obviously, if you spend an hour or two walking a steep trail to reach a backcountry lake, it's not as likely to be over-fished as one beside the road.

The legend of the almost undiscovered backcountry lake is true—to a point. One backcountry disadvantage is that many high-country lakes and rivers are clouded with glacial silt, not optimum conditions for fish or fishermen. Another problem is that since the water temperature in the high altitude lakes tends to be extremely low, only a few degrees above freezing in many cases, neither the fish nor the aquatic plants grow fast. And few of the remote lakes are stocked while there's a regular stocking program for many of the more accessible lakes.

Some of the high lakes are blanketed most of the year under thick ice covered by heavy snow. This blocks sunlight and kills aquatic plants. Fish may die for lack of oxygen. Because of this winter kill, fishing on any particular lake may vary considerably from year to year. Fishermen should inquire at tackle stores in Banff and Jasper to discover what the best lakes and streams seem to be at that moment and what's bringing them in.

Jasper, by the way, holds the Alberta record for rainbow trout, a trophy of more than 9 kg taken from Maligne Lake.

A national parks fishing permit ($4) is required and is available at the parks information centres and sporting goods stores.

The catch and possession limit is five each for pike, grayling and various trout and two for salmon. It's 10 for whitefish, except in Jasper where the limit is only 5. The overall limit is 10, of which five must be other than trout. No one is allowed to have in their possession more than 10 game fish. The use of live fish eggs, minnows and such is prohibited.

These regulations even caught up with the Duke of Connaught, who early this century was advised by a park warden at Consolation Lake of the 15-fish daily limit, since reduced to 10. "Per angler, per day, perdition," the Duke sputtered. "My good man, I ask you what is the sense of me being governor of this widespread, far-flung, sea-to-sea dominion if I cannot catch all the fish I have a mind to?" The warden was unmoved.

Jasper National Park: Fishing is open year-round on some of the major, lower valley rivers in Jasper: Athabasca, Sunwapta, Maligne (below Maligne Canyon), Snaring and Miette, plus Talbot Lake.

For most of the lakes, plus Ranger Creek and Rocky River, the season is Victoria Day to Labor Day: Annette, Beaver, Buck, Christine, Lower Colefair, Dragon, High Lakes, Long, Lorraine, Marjorie, Mile 9 (Yellowhead East), Mile 16 1/2 (Icefields Parkway), Moab, Mona, No Name, (Icefields Parkway-Km 45), Osprey, Princess, Pyramid, Skyline, First Trefoil, Virl, Maligne and the Fifth (Upper) lake in the Valley of the Five Lakes.

The season doesn't open until Aug. 1 for the beautiful Medicine River between Maligne Lake and Medicine Lake.

The remainder of the lakes and rivers, with the exception of specific closed waters, are open July 1 to Oct. 31.

Closed waters include Cabin Lake and streams emptying into it, all streams flowing into Amethyst Lake, as well as Amethyst Lake close to its outlet, Astoria River between Amethyst lake and a point 400 metres downstream, and the outlet stream from Moab Lake to its junction with the Whirlpool River, including the Moab Lake itself close to the outlet.

Where, among all these lakes and streams, should a fisherman head?

There's not much about fishing in Jasper National Park that the knowledgeable folks at Currie's Tackle, 618 Connaught Dr. (852-5650), Jasper Sports Centre, 622 Connaught Dr. (852-3660) or Online Tackle (852-3630) can't tell you.

They can provide fishing guides, electric motors, rod and reels and most of all, give you advice. Trips are available to Maligne Lake and other spots as well as fly-in trips. They also have boats available at many backcountry lakes: Talbot, Celestine, Marjorie, Hibernia, Dorothy, Yellowhead, Valley of the Five Lakes and others.

Boats and tackle are also available through Maligne Tours, 626 Connaught Drive, (852-3370) or at the boathouse at Maligne Lake. Their Fisherman's Special should appeal to anglers anxious to get away for the day. It leaves the boathouse on Maligne Lake at 8:30 a.m. Fishermen are piloted by small tour boat to Samson Narrows where fishing is often good. They are left for the day with a smaller fishing boat and an electric trolling motor.

Although heavily fished, *Pyramid Lake* on the wooded bench north of Jasper, is regularly stocked and is one of the few in the national parks open to motorboats. Early in the season, you might try casting from shore for rainbow and lake trout. Later, trolling works best. *Patricia Lake* just down the road has rainbow and brook trout up to six pounds and is easily accessible with a (non-motor) boat. Those small, rechargable electric motors may be used wherever boats are permitted.

Medicine Lake on the Maligne Canyon Road is a strange place to fish since the lake drops to a narrow channel by fall because of the underground system that drains water through limestone passages down the valley to below Maligne Canyon. It's known for rainbows and a boat is needed, except in low water.

Maligne Lake, with its extremely cold water, has large brook trout and some rainbows and such scenery as to make fishing only an excuse for being there. *Horseshoe Lake* (Walk 79) is stocked with rainbows and the shore drops off steeply into the water, ideal for casting. *Honeymoon Lake* and *Buck Lake* on the Icefields Parkway are stocked with rainbow and brook trout. *Leach Lake* on Highway 93A is known for its rainbow trout.

Lake Edith (Walk 92) has rainbows and *Annette* has brook trout (Walk 91). *Lac Beauvert* (Walk 87) and the small lakes around Jasper Park Lodge have brook and rainbow trout. Away from the road, try *Wabasso Lakes* (Walk 81) for smaller rainbows and Valley of Five Lakes (Walk 82) for brook and rainbow trout. The first and last lakes are the best and have rental boats.